RELIGION IN PUBLIC SPACES

This book offers more than its title promises. It is not only about Europe or about religion. Insightful, suggestive and as diverse as its contributors, it contains a persuasive reflection on the need to rethink the very notion of public space that Western democracies have used since the nineteenth century.

Javier Martinez-Torron, Complutense University School of Law, Spain

This is a highly important book in a remarkable controversy. Silvio Ferrari and Sabrina Pastorelli present a rich volume full of information, thought, and insight – presenting masterpieces of interdisciplinary research and political guidance. The book is a most valuable contribution to freedom and equality throughout Europe.

Gerhard Robbers, University of Trier, Germany

Cultural Diversity and Law in Association with RELIGARE

Series Editor: Prakash Shah, Queen Mary, University of London, UK

RELIGARE is a project on Religious Diversity and Secular Models in Europe funded by the European Commission under the Seventh Framework Programme. The project brings together an interdisciplinary team of high profile researchers and 13 academic institutions to collaborate on examining how existing policy and practice is suited to the demands of religious diversity within Europe and what legal models can be recommended to accommodate such diversity in future. More details on the project can be seen at its website: http://www.religareproject.eu/. 'Cultural Diversity and Law in Association with RELIGARE' provides an outlet for the results of specific research undertaken within the RELIGARE project.

Other titles in this series:

A Test of Faith?
Religious Diversity and Accommodation in the European Workplace
Edited by Katayoun Alidadi, Marie-Claire Foblets and
Jogchum Vrielink

Religion in Public Spaces
A European Perspective

Edited by

SILVIO FERRARI
The University of Milan, Italy

SABRINA PASTORELLI
The University of Milan, Italy

Routledge
Taylor & Francis Group
LONDON AND NEW YORK

First published 2012 by Ashgate Publishing

Published 2016 by Routledge
2 Park Square, Milton Park, Abingdon, Oxfordshire OX14 4RN
711 Third Avenue, New York, NY 10017, USA

First issued in paperback 2016

Routledge is an imprint of the Taylor & Francis Group, an informa business

British Library Cataloguing in Publication Data
Religion in public spaces : a European perspective. --
(Cultural diversity and law in assocation with RELIGARE)
1. Religious observances on public property--Law and
legislation--Europe. 2. Freedom of religion--Europe.
3. Clothing and dress--Law and legislation--Europe.
4. Clothing and dress--Religious aspects. 5. Public
spaces--Law and legislation--Europe.
I. Series II. Ferrari, Silvio. III. Pastorelli, Sabrina.
342.4'0852-dc23

Library of Congress Cataloging-in-Publication Data
Ferrari, Silvio.
Religion in public spaces : a European perspective / by Silvio Ferrari and Sabrina Pastorelli.
p. cm. -- (Cultural diversity and law in association with RELIGARE)
Includes index.
ISBN 978-1-4094-5058-0 (hardback)
1. Freedom of religion--Europe. 2. Religion in the workplace--Law and legislation--Europe. 3. Religious minorities--Legal status, laws, etc.--Europe. I. Pastorelli, Sabrina. II. Title.
KJC5156.F47

2012012006

ISBN 13: 978-1-138-27937-7 (pbk)
ISBN 13: 978-1-4094-5058-0 (hbk)

Contents

List of Figures and Tables

Figures

Tables

List of Contributors

Katayoun Alidadi is currently a PhD candidate at the Catholic University of Leuven, Belgium, and a researcher in the European project RELIGARE (FP7, 2010–2013). She holds a law degree from the Catholic University of Leuven and an LLM degree from Harvard Law School (2005). Her research focuses on religious freedom, anti-discrimination law and reasonable accommodations, in particular as it relates to the workplace.

Veit Bader is emeritus Professor of Sociology (Department of Political and Socio-cultural Sciences) and of Social and Political Philosophy (Department of Philosophy) at the University of Amsterdam and a member of IMES (Institute of Migration and Ethnic Studies). At present, he is leader of the Dutch teams in two European FP7 projects: RELIGARE (Religious Diversity and Models of Secularism in Europe) where he is also leader of WP7, and ACCEPT (Tolerance, Pluralism and Cohesion) where he is also leader of WP3. He has written on a wide range of issues in critical social theory; social inequalities and collective action; democracy and the rule of law (particularly in the EU); racism, ethnicity and citizenship; ethics of migration and incorporation of minorities; global justice; governance of religious diversity. His most recent book is: *Democracy or Secularism? Associational Governance of Religious Diversity* (Amsterdam University Press, 2007).

Alessandro Ferrari teaches Law and Religion and Comparative Religious Laws at the University of Insubria (Como-Varese). His main interests focus on the present changes of the right of religious freedom in the globalized context. His lastest book is *Diritto e Religione nell'Islam Mediterraneo* (Law and Religion in Mediterranean Islam) (Il Mulino, Bologna, 2012).

Silvio Ferrari is Professor of Canon Law, University of Milan and President of the International Consortium for Law and Religion Studies, Italy. His research interests are in the areas of Church and State in Europe; comparative law of religions, and Vatican–Israel relations. He has published widely on these and related areas.

Marie-Claire Foblets, Lic. Iur., Lic. Phil., Ph.D. Anthrop. (Belgium) is professor of Law at the Universities of Leuven (Louvain in Belgium) and since 2012 also Director of the Department of "Law & Anthropology" at the Max Planck Institute for Social Anthropology in Halle/Saale (Germany). She has held various visiting professorships both within and outside Europe. She has conducted extensive research and published widely on issues of migration law, including the elaboration of European migration law after the Treaty of Amsterdam, citizenship/nationality laws, compulsory integration, anti-racism and non-discrimination, etc. In the field of anthropology of law, her research focuses on cultural diversity and legal practice, with a particular interest in the application of Islamic family laws in Europe, and more recently in the accommodation of cultural and religious diversity under State law.

Anne Fornerod is a researcher at the National Centre for Scientific Research (CNRS-PRISME). After gaining a PhD in public law on religious heritage, she currently works on various issues dealing with law and religion (among others: religious assistance in public institutions, interaction between secularism or *laïcité* and the integration process of foreigners and religious pluralism in cemeteries).

Jean-François Gaudreault-DesBiens is Associate Dean, Research, and Canada Research Chair in North American and Comparative Juridical and Cultural Identities. He has also taught at the faculties of law of the University of Toronto and of McGill University, in addition to having been visiting professor at various universities outside of Canada (Paris-II, Bordeaux-IV, Aix-Marseille, Sciences Po, Case Western). His teaching and research interests are constitutional law (domestic and comparative), civil liberties, legal theory and epistemology, and the sociology of legal cultures. His work currently focuses on the legal treatment of religious claims in multicultural liberal societies, on the relations between the civil law and common law traditions in a globalized economy, and on the legal theory of federalism. He is a member of the Québec and Ontario Bars. He serves as the Canadian correspondent for the British journal *Public Law*. (Publications disponibles sur le site: http://ssrn.com/author=143689)

Noura Karazivan is Professor of Constitutional Law, Faculty of Law, University of Montreal.

Maya Kosseva holds a PhD in History and is project coordinator and researcher at the International Centre for Minority Studies and Intercultural Relations, Sofia, Bulgaria. Her main interests are in the field of Bulgarian history, minority issues and social anthropology.

Iva Kyurkchieva holds a PhD in Ethnology and is a research fellow in the Institute of Ethnology and Folklore Studies with Ethnographic Museum – Bulgarian Academy of Science, Sofia, Bulgaria. Her main interests are in the field of social and cultural anthropology. The main subjects of her research are the Bulgarian Muslim communities as one of the considerable minorities in Bulgaria.

Kjell Å Modéer, dr. jur, dr.h.c. mult., is a former holder of the Torsten and Ragnar Söderberg Foundations' Professorship in Memory of Samuel Pufendorf, and is currently Senior Professor in Legal History at the Law Faculty, Lund University, Sweden.

A. Emre Öktem is an Associate Professor of International Law at the Faculty of Law of Galatasaray University, Istanbul. He is the author of books entitled *Freedom of Religion in International Law* and *Terrorism, Humanitarian Law and Human Rights* and articles on human rights, humanitarian law, minority rights, terrorism, international recognition, continuity and succession, and other fields of international law, as well as historical essays. He a member of the Advisory Council for the Freedom of Religion and Belief at the Organization for Security and Cooperation in Europe, Office of Democratic Institutions and Human Rights.

Javier García Oliva (Manchester University) studied Law at the University of Cadiz, where he obtained his first degree, LLM and PhD (cum laude and European distinction). After finishing his first degree, he became a lecturer at the University of Cadiz (1996–2000) and a Research Fellow at the Centre for Law and Religion, Cardiff University (2001–2004). Javier was appointed as a lecturer at the University of Wales Bangor in 2004, where he stayed until January 2011, when he joined the University of Manchester. He is also a Teaching Fellow at University College London (UCL) and at the University of Oxford. Furthermore, he is a Research Associate at the Centre for Law and Religion (Cardiff University), the Convenor of the SLS Public Law stream and the Book Review Editor of *Law and Justice*.

Vincenzo Pacillo is Associate Professor at the Law Faculty of Modena and Reggio Emilia University, where he teaches Canon law. He is a member of the Executive Committee of the Institute of Canon Law and Comparative Law of Religions (DiReCom) at the Theological Faculty of Lugano, where he teaches and where he carries out regular research activities.

Sabrina Pastorelli is Research Fellow at the Institute of International Law – section of Ecclesiastical and Canon Law – University of Milan, Faculty of Law. She is also a member of the Groupe Sociétés, Religions, Laïcités (GSRL-CNRS/École Pratique des Hautes Études-Sorbonne) and teaching assistant at the Catholic University of Paris – Faculty of Social and Economic Sciences. Her research interests include sociology of religion; new religious movements; law and religion in the Europe; religion and education; regulation of religious pluralism; state public policy and religion. She is a member of the International Society for the Sociology of Religion (ISSR); the Italian Sociological Association (AIS); the Association for the Sociology of Religion (ASR) and the Association International des Sociologues de Langue Française (AISLF).

Hanne Petersen has been Professor of Legal Cultures at the Center for Studies of Legal Culture, University of Copenhagen since 2009. She was Jean Monnet Scholar at the European University Institute in Florence 1993–1994, professor of jurisprudence and sociology of law at University of Greenland, Ilisimatusarfik 1995–1999, professor of Greenlandic sociology of law at University of Copenhagen 2001–2006 and adjunct professor of law at University of Tromsø 2007–2010. Since 2011 she has been Hedda Andersson guest professor at Lund University as part of the university's Gender Equality priority.

She has participated in a number of international research projects, amongst others an EU-project 'Gender Relations at the Turn of the Millennium. Women as Subjects in Marriage and Migration' (2001–2004), and a Nordic project 'Nordic Legal Maps in Transition' (2005–2009).

Adam Seligman is Professor of Religion at Boston University and Research Associate at the Institute on Culture, Religion and World Affairs there. He has lived and taught at universities in the US, in Israel and in Hungary where he was Fulbright Fellow. He lived for almost 20 years in Israel where he was a member of Kibbutz Kerem Shalom in the early 1970s. His books include *The Idea of Civil Society* (Free Press, 1992), *Inner-worldly Individualism* (Transaction Press, 1994), *The Problem of Trust* (Princeton University Press, 1997), *Modernity's Wager: Authority, the Self and Transcendence* (Princeton University Press, 2000) with Mark Lichbach *Market and Community* (Penn State University Press, 2000), *Modest Claims, Dialogues and Essays on Tolerance and Tradition* (Notre Dame University Press, 2004) and with R.P. Weller, M.J. Puet and B. Simon, *Ritual and its Consequences: An Essay on the Limits of Sincerity* (Oxford University Press, 2008). His work has been translated into over a dozen languages. He is director of the International Summer School on Religion and Public Life which leads seminars every year on contested aspects of religion and the public square in different parts of the world. He lives in Newton, Massachusetts.

Sara Silvestri holds a PhD and MPhil from Cambridge University (UK) and a 'laurea' from La Sapienza University (Italy). She is currently Senior Lecturer at City University London, where she teaches courses on Religion and Politics, the EU, and Islamist movements. She is also a Research Associate at Cambridge University and has directed the Muslims in Europe programme for the European Policy Centre in Brussels. Her research and publications focus on Islamic organizations and Muslim–government relations, counter-terrorism, migration, Europe's Muslim women, faith-based lobbies in the EU.

Mehmet C. Uzun (LLM) is a Research Assistant on Public International Law at the University of Bahçeşehir Faculty of Law and a PhD candidate on Public Law at the University of Galatasaray. His published work essentially focuses on human rights law, with specific emphasis on religious freedom issues and international humanitarian law.

Tymen J. van der Ploeg (1947) studied Dutch Law at Leyden University. He has worked at the law faculty of the VU-University in Amsterdam since 1992 as professor in company law (law on partnerships and legal persons). His research includes (comparative) law on not-for-profit organizations and on religious organizations, as well as the relation between the government and these organizations.

Noel G. Villaroman obtained a Master's degree in International Human Rights Law from the University of Notre Dame in the United States and another Master's degree (by research) from Monash University in Australia. As a PhD candidate at Monash, he researches on the impact of local planning regulations on the right of minority religious groups in Australia to build places of worship. He is a member of the Law and Religion Scholars' Network (LARSN).

Chapter 1
Religion and Rethinking the Public–Private Divide: Introduction

Marie-Claire Foblets

The demographic and cultural profile of European societies today is highly dynamic and in constant change. These changes are inextricably linked, at least in part, to the many and complex effects of globalization, including the blending of cultures; they also reflect increasing diversification as well as an individualization of lifestyles and modes of thought.

As a result of these changes, long-standing ways of managing the social fabric are breaking down, and the question inevitably arises as to how to ensure that relations among groups and individuals within a social context that is in constant flux remain fair and equitable and respectful of individual freedoms and civic duties. At the heart of the debate are the controversies between 'liberals' and 'communitarians' regarding the meaning, the scope as well as the limits of the role of public authorities in the face of identity issues, that is, religious diversity, different moral sensibilities and cultures that wish to preserve their particular identity. In Europe today, it is most specifically religious identity and its public expression that appears at the core of the debate.[1] Questions concerning religion are invariably associated either with the challenge of multiculturalism or with the migratory flows of the past few decades, thereby rendering the topic a politically sensitive one.

When, in 2009, the European Commission published a call for proposals for research projects on the theme of religious pluralism under the Seventh Framework Programme (Socio-Economic Sciences & Humanities: SSH-2009. Activity 8.3.3.2), this is the issue to which it referred. The initiative of this volume is linked partly to that call, since it consists of the proceedings of a colloquium held in October 2010 in Como, Italy, within the framework of the research project that had been chosen by the Commission. This research project is known as 'RELIGARE' ('Religious Diversity and Secular Models in Europe. Innovative

1 See especially W. Brugger and M. Karayanni (eds), *Religion in the Public Sphere: A Comparative Analysis of German, Israeli, American and International Law*, Heidelberg; Springer, 2007; M.D. Evans, *Manual on the Wearing of Religious Symbols in Public Areas*, Strasbourg: Council of Europe Editions, 2009; N. Hosen and R. Mohr (eds), *Law and Religion in Public Life: The Contemporary Debate*, London: Routledge, 2010, J.-P. Willaime, *Le retour du religieux dans la sphère publique*, Lyon: Olivétan, 2008.

Approaches to Law and Policy'). The project, entitled RELIGARE, an acronym for 'Religious Diversity and Secular Models in Europe. Innovative Approaches to Law and Policy', is funded by the EU under the Seventh Research Framework Programme (Socio-Economic Sciences & Humanities) under the heading of 'Religious pluralism and secularism' that, as noted above, was one of the themes launched by the Commission in 2009.

This introduction comprises two sections: the first briefly situates the RELIGARE project, explaining its main objectives and the method adopted; the second offers an overview of the chapters that make up the volume.

The RELIGARE Research Project

The project of which this volume forms part is currently still in progress, and hence at this stage it is impossible to anticipate the results of the work. The acronym RELIGARE takes its inspiration from the Latin verb 'religare', which means to connect, form a society by creating bonds among individuals and communities.

The following presentation of the project covers three points: the *first* point explains the reasons why the partners decided to form a consortium. There are 13 teams from 10 different countries involved (nine Member States of the European Union and Turkey). The *second* point has to do with the working method. Finally, the *third* point identifies a few observations – albeit very preliminary ones – that can be helpful in understanding the chapters collected in this volume as well as the topics that have been selected. The documents for the project that are currently available are accessible on the website: www.religareproject.eu.

As regards the *first* point: the RELIGARE project involves the participation of 13 teams of researchers and covers 10 different countries, including nine European Union members (Belgium, Bulgaria, Denmark, Germany, Great Britain, France, Italy, the Netherlands, Spain) and Turkey. The research is focused on the study of the situation in these 10 countries, and hence the RELIGARE project does not cover all Member States of the European Union. The teams are made up largely of jurists and sociologists.

The starting point for the subject of the research – the protection of the freedom of religion in Europe – is practically identical for all the countries involved in the project. The approach is twofold: *on the one hand*, in Europe we are heirs, as regards the management of religious and philosophical diversity, to a range of constitutional models that almost systematically privilege the traditional religions.[2] The power relations between what were once the principal currents of thought within society are reflected in the mechanisms put in place to manage a pluralism of beliefs and opinions. Some of these mechanisms are now outdated, in part because

2 See especially G. Robbers (ed.), *State and Church in the European Union*, Baden-Baden: Nomos, 2005; European Consortium for Church-State Research, *Church and State in Europe. State Financial Support. Religion and the School*, Milano: Giuffré, 1992.

the demographic and sociological profile of European societies has changed, giving rise to new (im)balances among groups and tendencies, secularization, on the one hand, and the fragmentation of belief systems on the other, have rendered some of the existing arrangements anachronistic in the face of the present reality. The result is that legal solutions developed in the past to regulate relations between the State and religions, and the freedom of religion in the broad sense, and that are now outdated, serve to maintain certain privileges for the traditional religions from which the others are excluded. They are, in effect, anachronisms that can no longer be justified. *On the other hand*, case law reveals much hesitation in the face of the religious question and, in particular, its protection in law. Such ambivalence leads to terrible legal uncertainty.

The partners of the RELIGARE project agree that there is an urgent need today to carfully listen to the chemins of the new communities that are made up of minorities in Europe, primarily because their presence in our midst is (still) relatively recent. Most of the persons identifying with these minorities wish to become full citizens. In the face of an outdated approach that is no longer appropriate for the purpose, they may feel excluded. The principle of neutrality which means that public authorities maintain a certain reserve on questions to do with religion and/or metaphysics lacks consistency vis-à-vis these groups. A legislative framework that sometimes still reflects a historical preference for certain religions or currents of thought in this regard is an obstacle. Confronted by this reality it would seem justified, if not urgent, to raise the question of the part that law could play in remedying this injustice: should the law be given a more important role?

The partners associated with the RELIGARE project all agree as well that in the area of religious freedom and its protection, it is essential to invoke the rules of law to achieve precisely that which one might expect of them, namely, to be systematic and fair *to all*.

Moreover, they have taken as their goal the study of the extent of protection *effectively* granted to religious freedom and freedom of conscience in the 10 aforementioned countries, by constituting as comprehensive a collection as possible of the solutions that have been drawn up, whether in legislative and regulatory texts or in case law. The collection covers four fields in particular, each of which addresses a priority area of participation (equitable, if possible) in social life: (1) family law, (2) access to the labour market and protection of freedom of religion in the workplace, (3) access and the use of public space, and, finally, (4) the different forms of support that may (or may not) be offered by the State to religions and philosophical beliefs.

The project is funded for a period of three calendar years (February 2010 to January 2013), which is. The work had therefore to be organized in such a way as to enable data to be collected in the most efficient way possible.

This leads to the *second* point: the working method. The 13 teams involved in the project have split the work up among them in such a way that the data may be collected initially for each country separately and then studied on a comparative basis. The aim, as explained above, is to identify solutions that offer, in each participating country, optimal protection for each person's freedom of belief, without endangering the social cohesion necessary in a plural democratic society. In a second stage the aim is to establish whether certain solutions that appear to ensure a sustainable balance in a given context (national or local) of diversity of religions and beliefs, may in due course serve as an inspiration to other countries, and if so, under what conditions.

This division of labour also applies to the two principal scientific approaches drawn upon for the project: legal enquiry and sociological survey. The task of the teams of jurists is to draw up a repertory of legal responses, whether formulated by the legislators or the courts of the 10 countries involved, to the question of protection for religious freedom and of its scope. The aim is to target the existing protection more closely – be it via legislation or case law, or in exceptional cases via legal doctrine. The period before January 2010 is distinguished from that which coincides with the period of the project. For the earlier period, only the judgments which at the time were considered landmark decisions because of their influence on the debate have been selected. However, for the period starting in January 2010 (start-up of the RELIGARE project), the aim is to be as exhaustive as possible.

The sociologists, in turn, have taken on the task of drawing up, for each country, a questionnaire that, with the aid of the information coming from the case law, can be used as a sort of template for semi-directive interviews. These interviews are being conducted in six of the 10 countries chosen (Turkey, France, the Netherlands, Denmark, Bulgaria and Great Britain). The objective is to collect testimonies, especially from persons of minority background who are likely to have been affected directly by issues of freedom of religion and its legal protection: how did the persons in question experience that protection, in their view does it have any gaps, and if so, in what specific areas? On which questions might they feel inadequately understood?

By supplementing the legal data – which are generally better known or at least more easily identified – with sociological data – often less well known – the 'RELIGARE' project will contribute, it is hoped, an important body of knowledge to the study of growing religious diversity in Europe, that is, the concrete lived experience of the latter and the tensions it can generate for people involved and who are expecting political – and thus legal – solutions appropriate to their situation. The topics selected for the sociological surveys, i.e. the questionnaires, are based on the main tensions and difficulties that emerge from the legal decisions of the past few years in the countries mentioned above as regards the question of legal protection for religious liberty and respect for the principle of non-discrimination.

Through adopting this procedure, the RELIGARE project should ultimately yield three types of research instruments: (1) a database of case law for the 10 countries involved in the research; (2) a series of thematic templates that reproduce, in a synthetic fashion, the arguments made both by the legislative branch and by the courts and tribunals in order to address a number of particular situations;

(3) sociological reports, drawn up for each of the countries on the topics repertoried on the basis of case law and the templates.

The purpose of the first instrument (the case law database) is to make more easily accessible the legal judgments relating to religious freedom handed down in recent years in the 10 countries chosen. The database is maintained in close collaboration with PRISME in Strasbourg, a research unit (CNRS) that has many years of experience in this area and already manages several different case law databases that deal with religious freedom.

A second instrument is the thematic templates. These forms make it possible to sum up in a standardized format, by issue and by country, the arguments made in law, either to ensure protection for freedom of religion or to subject the latter to certain restrictions, and to identify, likewise in schematic form, how the solution adopted is experienced by the target groups. The templates serve as a sort of prism that reveals, via a single format, the legal reasoning used for a specific question *and* the way in which that reasoning is received by those to whom it applies.

One of the thematic templates, for example, relates to places of worship and the conditions either for their construction or for the redeployment of existing buildings to create a space for prayer or devotions.[3] The templates show, for each country, where the existing legislation is now: what is the procedure to be followed? Is there case law that points to the presence of particular problems? And what about potential gaps in the legislation? Is there a demand on the part of certain communities for a problem to be resolved, and if so, what proposed solutions are currently under debate? What do surveys say in this regard? The templates could turn out to be particularly useful to the public authorities as well, when they find themselves having to address questions relating to religious and philosophical pluralism and wishing to know more about the way other countries in Europe deal with these matters. They are of course under no obligation to draw upon them, but at least they will have at hand a richly documented instrument based on an interdisciplinary – legal and sociological – and comparative examination. The idea underlying the decision to create this type of instrument was the controversy in 2009 on the construction of minarets in Switzerland, and the referendum that caused such a stir. A comparative template on the question would have made it possible to find out immediately, without additional research, how the question of the issuance of permits to build and/or open a place of worship is regulated in other European countries, and how the matter is perceived within minority religious communities.

The third and last type of research instrument is the sociological survey. The aim is to make publicly accessible the entire result of the surveys, that is, the lived experience of the communities concerned as regards the legal protection of their freedom of religion and belief. The aim is thus to give a voice to those who are not (yet) or only rarely consulted or listened to. The surveys are conducted on a

3 On this issue, see especially F. Messner (ed.), *Les lieux de culte en France et en Europe*, Leuven: Peeters, 2007.

semi-directive basis, which means that the persons questioned remain free to set their own priorities. This methodology is certain to differ depending on the person whose testimony was collected as well as according to the country and topic at hand, and depending on current events. Certain problems do not come up in all of the countries, and hence the surveys on a given question will remain silent for certain countries; in other countries, if a new problem arises, the interviewers couldgive the interviewees complete freedom to set their own priorities and express their opinions on the question.

A few very tentative conclusions could perhaps already be drawn. This leads to the *third* point. In what follows, three observations are made, ending with a warning.

The *first* observation has to do less with a difficulty in terms of the scientific research, but raises a true problem in practical terms. This has already been mentioned above. It has to do with the sharply divided nature of the case law on the protection of freedom of religion and belief. This division is evident at all levels of jurisdiction and the observation applies to the vast majority of the European countries being studied by the RELIGARE project. The case law sometimes displays relatively improbable about-turns on certain questions that are thus difficult to explain to anyone who is not a specialist in the area. A recent judgment – one that has received extensive commentary – illustrates clearly the hesitation of the judicial authorities in the face of the question of the scope of protection that should be granted to religious freedom: this is the second judgment handed down by the European Court of Human Rights in Strasbourg, sitting as a Grand Chamber on 18 March 2011, in the case of *Lautsi and Others* v. *Italy*.[4] In its judgment, the Court states two things: on the one hand, it raises the awareness of States of the question of the protection of this freedom, while on the other hand, it in a sense places in the hands of the same States the responsibility for determining the balance between the different freedoms at stake, thus taking account of the wide margin of appreciation which they enjoy. In sum, in the opinion of the Court it is up to the States to regulate their relationships with religion. By returning

4 ECtHR, Judgment of 18 March 2011, no. 30814/06, *Lautsi and Others* v. *Italy*. See among others D. McGoldrick, 'Religion in the European public square and in European public life – crucifixes in the classroom?', *Hum. Rts. L. Rev.*, September 2011, 451–502; J. Weiler, 'Lautsi: crucifix in the classroom redux', *EJIL Talk!*, www.ejiltalk.org/lautsi-crucifix-in-the-classroom-redux/; S. Mancini, 'The crucifix rage: supranational constitutionalism and counter-majoritarian difficulty', *EuConst* 6, 2010, 6–27; C. Panara, '*Lautsi v. Italy*: the display of religious symbols by the State', *European Public Law* 17, 2011, 139–168; G. Andreescu and L. Andreescu, 'The European Court of Human Rights' *Lautsi* Decision: context, contents, consequences', *Journal for the Study of Religions and Ideologies* 9, 2010, 47–74; P. Annicchino, 'Winning the battle and losing the war: the Lautsi case and the holy alliance between American conservative evangelicals, the Russian Orthodox Church and the Vatican to reshape European identity', *Religion and Human Rights* special issue, 6/3 2011, 213–219; L. Zucca, 'A comment on Lautsi', *EJIL Talk!*, www.ejiltalk.org/a-comment-on-lautsi/.

the ball to the signatories to the European Convention on Human Rights and Fundamental Freedoms, the Court implicitly reinforces the need and the relevance of the sort of research that RELIGARE seeks to conduct, in view of showing how religious pluralism is regulated, in very concrete terms, within the national and local legal orders.

A *second* observation is in fact more of a question, and has to do with the necessity of legislative intervention. Is such intervention necessary? There are two possible positions in this regard. Either one retains the existing legal frameworks and applies them as best one can, or one argues in favour of a thoroughgoing overhaul. In the latter case, it remains to be determined what amendments are necessary. The observation suggested by the research done by the RELIGARE consortium to date is that the legal frameworks in force are partly outdated, and where amendments are adopted, they are eclectic, haphazard, and often badly received by minority communities, who see themselves as subject to restrictions that they consider unjustified and that, in their view, constitute discrimination against them. In the surveys, they talk about a double standard. The sociological interviews show, in this regard, a need for clearer and more explicit justification on the part of the authorities whenever an amendment is made to the existing legislation. If this is not done, any new restriction is likely to be seen automatically as undue hardship.

The notion of 'undue hardship' is borrowed from the doctrine of reasonable accommodation in labour law, a concept that originates in North America, and refers to the obligation on the part of employers to ensure that they do not discriminate indirectly against persons with physical handicaps. Except in cases where the obligation of accommodation may impose 'undue hardship' on the employer, the latter is required to make sure that a person with physical handicaps does not suffer indirect discrimination, be that in terms of access to a job or the provision of accommodations at the workplace or in the latter's organization.

A position that does not enjoy unanimous support, but that nonetheless deserves to be examined, is one that stipulates that what applies to persons with a physical handicap may, in some cases, be extrapolated to the situation of persons who demand protection for their freedom of religion. The study of the case law shows that, as a rule, such situations are poorly understood. Certain restrictions are not justified in the eyes of persons belonging to religious minorities, who consider that they have not been properly listened to. In the surveys, some members of these communities speak of true suffering, even though they consider that they are entitled to adequate legal protection.

A *third* observation relates to a term that is very much in vogue these days, namely, the concept of 'best practices'. In light of the diversity of the contexts under study, the value of these practices as identified by a project such as RELIGARE is quite limited. Each practice is inevitably linked to a particular context, which explains why it is not automatically transferable to other contexts. As regards reasonable accommodation, a project such as RELIGARE could limit itself to inventorying practices which, notably as regards access to the labour market (a European framework has been put in place on this matter) might help combat indirect discrimination on grounds of a person's beliefs and/or religious adherence. As things stand, it is nevertheless very likely that there is a need to go further than this and look also at the question of whether a more binding commitment on the part of Member States of the European Union than those currently in place might make it easier to combat more effectively – and thus more fairly – indirect discrimination linked to the religious or philosophical identity of persons who are or wish to be active in the labour market. It is quite probable that the RELIGARE project will put forward suggestions aimed at giving the technique of reasonable accommodation a more binding quality.

This first section of the introduction ends with a reflection that should stand as a warning against the temptation to place too much hope in the concrete results that a research project such as the one currently undertaken by the partners of RELIGARE could hope to deliver. As mentioned above, the RELIGARE project consists of research that was commissioned and is entirely funded by the European Commission. However, the subject of the research – the management of religious and philosophical diversity within contemporary European societies – does not fall within the competence of the European Union. On the contrary, it is to this date jealously guarded by the Member States wishing to retain sovereignty over the question of their relationship to religious and other beliefs present on their territory and over the way in which they protect their freedom. Unless the power(s) are transferred to the EU, so far the States have the last word on the way in which they manage religious pluralism in their society, that is, within their territory. They are of course bound by the provisions of the European Convention on Human Rights and Fundamental Freedoms and more recently also by the principles enshrined in the European Charter, but they maintain a considerable margin of appreciation as regards their implementation. National and local traditions are very tenacious, as is evident in each of the countries. As a consequence, the recommendations to be made at the end of the RELIGARE project, and that are addressed primarily to the Commission, will most likely not be taken into account by the Member States, unless a country should wish explicitly to translate into a policy decision and incorporate into its legal order a solution or practice that has been brought to light through the research.

One must therefore be realistic, recognizing that it is not because thematic templates have been filled out that national legislative and/or judicial authorities will make use of them as inspiration for developing concrete solutions to the problems they face. National traditions remain highly diverse, and the way countries manage pluralism is rooted in their history, which explains in part the differences in their perspectives. The option of 'Muslim arbitration tribunals', for example, which Great Britain is experimenting with today, does not (yet) seem easily transferable to other European countries. In time, perhaps, the solution of religious arbitration could find its way into the internal order of other States, but it is too soon to say for sure. Another example is that of the funding of religious bodies – the question is of course meaningful only in countries where religions are entitled to a State subsidy. A final example is that of countries which are heirs to the 'concordat' tradition. The concordat as a tool for managing religious pluralism may inspire countries such as Spain, for instance, but does not make sense in countries that have no experience of this particular form of relationship between the State and certain religions. Other illustrations could undoubtedly be found.

In sum, the difficulty lies in the fact that in the area of management of religious pluralism, countries have developed their own individual policies without an explicit transfer of power(s) to the European level – with the exception of respect for fundamental rights and the prohibition against discrimination based on religion and/or belief. The solutions that a project such as RELIGARE would make possible to repertory could thus be applied only in the specific context from which they emanate. Moreover, the questions relating to religious freedom and its protection are highly sensitive, politically red-hot issues. For some, the status quo is very convenient; it suits the interests of the traditional religions. They do not necessarily feel a need to innovate. For others, one would need to go much further in the practice of State neutrality. An illustration of this latter position, strictly linked to the French context, is the opinion issued in early September 2011 by the 'Haut Conseil à l'Intégration' in France, which calls for a radicalization of the concept of neutrality in the workplace.[5] Still others focus on the existing anachronisms, proposing for instance that one should also revise the calendar of statutory holidays that in most European countries is (still) a Christian calendar, or should rid the public space of religious symbols.

Religion and Public Spaces: Major Conflicts

The Secularist Thesis:
Should we Revise the Separation between the Public and the Private Sphere?

Among the topics the teams participating in the RELIGARE project have taken as their joint aim to investigate is the issue of religion in the public space, or to put it more precisely, religious freedom and the public–private divide.

No doubt, the above-mentioned resurgence of the importance, since some time in 'secularized' Europe, of the relationship between positive State law and religion also defies the private–public distinction (see Chapter 8 by Silvio Ferrari in this volume).

Bhikhu Parekh accurately identified the problem in his book *Rethinking Multiculturalism*:

> Religious persons see life as a whole and seek to live out their deeply held beliefs in their personal and collective lives. This confronts the civil assimilationist with

5 *Expression religieuse et laïcité dans l'entreprise*, Haut Conseil à l'Intégration, www.hci.gouv.fr.

> a dilemma. If he confined religion to the private realm, he would discriminate against religious people, alienate them from public life, provoke their resistance, and endanger the very unity for whose sake he excludes religion from the public realm. If he admitted it into the public realm, he would jettison or at least blur the private-public distinction and face the acute problem of how to deal with what would now be a multicultural public realm.[6]

With a view to ordering these relationships, national legislators in Europe have made the – historic – choice to secularize positive law, that is, the official law enacted by the State:[7] from a secularist point of view, religion and State law (and politics) pertain to different areas of life and should therefore be scrupulously kept separate. This choice can take several forms: in a weaker form, State authorities should in general refrain from identifying with any belief and take a neutral

6 B. Parekh, *Rethinking Multiculturalism: Cultural Diversity and Political Theory*, Hampshire: Palgrave, 2000 (2006), 203.

7 Regarding this choice, one that is quite recent in the history of democratic societies, see especially G. Motzkin and Y. Fischer, *Religion and Democracy in Contemporary Europe*, London: Alliance Publishing Trust, 2008; V. Bader, *Secularism or Democracy? Associational Governance of Religious Diversity*, Amsterdam: Amsterdam University Press, 2007; A. Dierkens and J.-P. Schreiber (eds), *Laïcité et sécularisation dans l'Union européenne*, Bruxelles, Ed. de l'Université de Bruxelles ('Problèmes d'Histoire des religions'), Tome XVI, 2006; M. Grimpret, *Dieu est dans l'isoloir*, Paris: Presses de la Renaissance, 2007; Y. Lambert, 'Le rôle dévolu à la religion par les européens', *Sociétés contemporaines* 37, 2000, 11–33; G.J. Larouche and M. Maesschalck, *La religion dans l'espace public*, Université Laval, Ed. Liber, 2006, n. 8, 60–70; B. Massignon, 'L'Union européenne: Ni Dieu, ni César', *Esprit*, special issue 'Effervescences religieuses dans le monde', March–April 2007, 104–111; M. Milot, *Laïcité dans le nouveau monde, le cas du Québec*, Turnhout: Brepols, 2002; J.-C. Monod, *Sécularisation et laïcité*, Paris: PUF ('Philosophies'), 2007; M. Milot, P. Portier and J.-P. Willaime (eds), *Pluralisme religieux et citoyenneté*, Rennes: P.U. Rennes, 2009; P. Portier, 'Les laïcités dans l'Union européenne: vers une convergence des modèles?', in: G. Saupin, R. Fabre and M. Launay (eds), *La Tolérance* (Colloque international de Nantes, mai 1998, Quatrième centenaire de l'Edict de Nantes), P.U. Rennes, 1999; P. Portier, 'La critique contemporaine du religieux. Essai d'interprétation', in: D. Carsin (ed.), *La liberté de critique*, Paris: Lexis-Nexis, 2007, 67–85; F. Randhaxe and V. Zuber (eds), *Laïcités-démocraties: des relations ambigües*, Turnhout: Brepols ('Bibliothèque de l'Ecole des Hautes Etudes, Sciences religieuses'), 2003, 11–22; E. Tawil, *Norme religieuse et droit français*, Aix-en-Provence: P.U. Aix-Marseille, 2005; R. Torfs, 'Models of freedom of religion in the European Union and in the United States', in: *Between Caesar and the Lord – Relation between Religion and the State in the Countries of Asia and Europe*, Beijing: Kungcki Cultural Group, 2004, 225–252; J.-P. Willaime, 'Religion in ultramodernity', in: J.A. Beckford and J. Wallis (eds), *Theorising Religion: Classical and Contemporary Debates*, Aldershot: Ashgate, 2006, 73–85; J.-P. Willaime, 'Reconfigurations ultramodernes', *Esprit*, special issue 'Effervescences religieuses dans le monde', March–April 2007, 146–155; Willaime, *Le retour du religieux dans la sphère publique*, 2008.

stance toward religions, which means that if any protection or facility is granted to religion, it should apply to all religions on an equal footing. In its stronger version, State policy should be conducted in terms of secular laws – based on secular grounds – alone and therefore kept strictly separate from religious beliefs. In a secularist view, religion is a personal matter and belongs to the private sphere, while State (secular) politics, on the contrary, is a public matter that deals with matters of public interest, which in a democracy require open and public debate. Politics therefore necessitates a public sphere that is considered neutral.

Following upon significant changes within European societies – not least, as a consequence of migratory waves from various geographic regions and cultures of the world – this secularist assumption is now being challenged, in particular on the grounds that the requirement that citizens, as well as newcomers and members of religious minorities, who wish to participate in society and claim the application of the law must set aside (relegate to the private sphere) their religious beliefs, is undemocratic, discriminatory and probably also unwise. To be required to do so is likely to create a crisis of legitimacy by alienating religiously minded citizens from the formal legal system, thereby rendering it ineffective in practice. The convictions most often cited when discussing these risks of alienation are those linked to Islam.[8] Several recent studies, notably in sociology, have warned of the

8 M. Abou Ramadan, 'The misperception of the European Court of Human Rights on the immutability of Sharì'a", *Nordisk tidsskrift for menneskerettigheter* 23, 2005, 375–390; A. An-Na'im, 'Global citizenship and human rights: from Muslims in Europe to European Muslims', in: J.E. Goldschmidt and T. Loenen (eds), *Religious Pluralism and Human Rights in Europe: Where to Draw the Line?*, Antwerp: Intersentia, 2007, 13–55; R. Aluffi and G. Zincone (eds), *The Legal Treatment of Islamic Minorities in Europe*, Leuven: Peeters, 2004; J. Cesari and S. McLoughlin (eds), *European Muslims and the Secular State*, Aldershot: Ashgate, 2005; J. Cesari, *When Islam and Democracy Meet: Muslims in Europe and in the United States*, New York: Palgrave, 2004 (2nd edn 2006); V. Bader (ed.), 'Governing Islam in Western Europe. Essays on governance of religious diversity', Special issue of *Journal of Ethnic and Migration Studies* 33/6, August 2007; S. Ferrari and A. Bradley (eds), *Islam and European Legal Systems*, Aldershot: Ashgate, 2000; F. Fregosi (ed.), *Lectures contemporaines du droit islamique: Europe et monde arabe*, Strasbourg: P.U. Strasbourg, 2004; J. Klausen, *The Islamic Challenge: Politics and Religion in Western Europe*, Oxford: Oxford University Press, 2005; B. Marechal S. Allievi, F. Dassetto and J. Nielsen (eds), *Muslims in the Enlarged Europe: Religion and Society*, Leiden: Brill, 2003; J.S. Nielsen, *Muslims in Western Europe*, Edinburgh: Edinburgh University Press, 1992 (3rd edn 2004); J.S. Nielsen, *Towards a European Islam?*, London: Macmillan, 1999; R. Potz and W. Wiesharder (eds), *Islam and the European Union*, Leuven: Peeters, 2004; M. Rohe, *Islamisches Recht: Geschichte und Gegenwart* [Islamic Law: Past and Present], Munich: C.H. Beck, 2009; M. Rohe, *Muslims and the Law in Europe: Chances and Challenges*, New Delhi: Global Media Publications, 2007; M. Rohe, 'Muslims between Qu'ran and constitution – religious freedom within the German legal order', in: L.A. Tramontini (ed.), *'East is East and West is West'? Talks on Dialogue in Beirut*, Beiruter Texte und Studien 80, Beirut: Orient-Institut Beirut, 2006, 151–176; M. Rohe, 'Islamic norms in Germany and Europe', in: A. Al-Hamarneh and J. Thielmann (eds), *Islam and Muslims*

gap experienced by an increasing number of people – now living in Europe – between the official State law and their religious or philosophical conviction.[9] If the reality of this gap – so difficult to live with – is not taken seriously, it could threaten the social cohesion of Europe.[10]

The debate is now in full swing:[11] which legal framework is best suited to guaranteeing the 'very unity' Bhikhu Parekh is referring to and worries about? If

---

in Germany, Leiden: Brill, 2008, 49–81; W.A.R. Shadid and P.S. Van Koningsveld (eds), *Intercultural Relations and Religious Authorities: Muslims in the European Union*, Leuven: Peeters, 2002; P. Shah, 'Thinking beyond religion: legal pluralism in Britain's South Asian diaspora', *Australian Journal of Asian Law* 8, 2006, 237–260; P. Shah, 'Transforming to accommodate? Reflections on the *shari'a* debate in Britain', in: R. Grillo , R. Ballard, A. Ferrari, A.J. Hoekema, M. Maussen and P. Shah (eds), *Legal Practice and Cultural Diversity*, Aldershot: Ashgate, 2009, 73–92.

9 See especially: N. Alsayyad and M. Castells (eds), *Muslim Europe or Euro-Islam: Politics, Culture, and Citizenship in the Age of Globalization*, Lanham: Lexington Books, 2002; S. Benhabib, I. Shapiro and D. Petranovic (eds), *Identities, Affiliations and Allegiances*, Cambridge: Cambridge University Press, 2007; Cesari and McLoughlin, *European Muslims and the Secular State*; H. Coward, J.R. Hinnells and R.B. Williams (eds), *The South Asian Religious Diaspora in Great Britain, Canada and the United States*, New York: State University of New York Press, 2000; A. Erdemir, H. Rittersberger-Tiliç, A. Ergun and H. Kahveci (eds), *Rethinking Global Migration: Practices, Policies, and Discourses in the European Neighbourhood*, Ankara: KORA, 2008; M. Howard Ross (ed.), *Culture and Belonging in Divided Societies: Contestation and Symbolic Landscapes*, Philadelphia: University of Pennsylvania Press, 2009; G.F. Levey and T. Modood (eds), *Secularism, Religion and Multicultural Citizenship*, Cambridge: Cambridge University Press, 2009; A.F. March, *Islam and Liberal Citizenship: The Search for Overlapping Consensus*, Oxford: Oxford University Press, 2009; J. Nielsen and S. Allievi (eds), *Muslim Networks and Transnational Communities in and Across Europe*, Leiden: Brill, 2002; Y. Yazbeck Haddad (ed.), *Muslims in the West: From Sojourners to Citizens*, Oxford: Oxford University Press, 2002.

10 O. Roy, *La sainte ignorance: Le temps de la religion sans culture*, Paris: Seuil, 2008; F. Dassetto, *Paroles d'Islam: individus, sociétés et discours dans l'Islam européen contemporain*, Paris: Maisonneuve, 2000; A.H. Sinno (ed.), *Muslims in Western Politics*, Bloomington: Indiana University Press, 2009; N. Tietze, *Islamische Identitäten: Formen muslimischer Religiosität junger Männer in Deutschland und Frankreich*, Hamburg: HIS Verlag, 2001.

11 In the application dossier to the Commission the following works are referred to in particular: J.-G. Boeglin, *Etats et religion en Europe*, Paris: L'Harmattan, 2006; P. Cane, C. Evans and Z. Robinson (eds), *Law and Religion in Theoretical and Historical Context*, Cambridge: Cambridge University Press, 2008; H. Goris and M. Heimbach-Steins (eds), *Religion in Recht und politischer Ordnung heute*, Würzburg: Ergon, 2008; H. Lehmann (ed.), *Multireligiosität im vereinten Europa: historische und juristische Aspekte*, Göttingen: Wallstein, 2003; J. Norgren and S. Nanda, *American Cultural Pluralism and Law*, Westport: Praeger Publishers, 2006 (3rd edn); H.S. Richardson and M.S. Williams (eds), *Moral Universalism and Pluralism*, New York: New York University Press, 2009; A. Sarat and T.R. Kearns (eds), *Cultural Pluralism, Identity Politics, and the*

frameworks are to be developed that are respectful of the right of each person to freedom of belief/religion and to non-discrimination on religious grounds, in the context of (European) societies that are increasingly diverse, must the constitutional frameworks that are in place be revised – more or less radically – or is it simply a matter of providing for pragmatic adjustments? Should the relationship between the private and the public sphere be revised, and if so, how thoroughly? Since different European societies have different institutional histories and traditions when it comes to appreciating religious diversity, it is very likely that they will each need to develop their own appropriate framework.

This volume explores some major conflicts revolving around religion and public life that have occurred in contemporary Europe in the past few years and that, as is shown throughout the case studies, are challenging the public–private divide and a number of common assumptions on which this divide is based. The contributions discuss the way(s) in which these conflicts are handled, sometimes by judicial and sometimes by legislative means, or in some cases remain unresolved.

The Public–Private Divide from a Theoretical Angle

The book is divided into three parts. The first contains seven contributions which look at the public/private distinction from a theoretical angle. They provide a rich and stimulating background, which is tested in the following two sections of the book, one devoted to dress codes and the other to places of worship.

Through an historical analysis Kjell Å. Modéer traces the legal 'transnational deep structures', going back to medieval times, which govern the place of religion in the public and private sphere. The author concludes that recent developments in the US Supreme Court case law and transformations of the Church–State systems in the Northern European countries can be considered examples of the search for a new balance between 'progressive private market-oriented theories (new liberalism) and traditional welfare state programs (social democrats)'.

Adam Seligman seeks an explanation for the 'current and reigning confusion in matters pertaining to the public and the private' and focuses on the triumph of a modern culture 'resting on the idea of the individual as moral absolute' and 'enshrining the individual and the private as the arena of virtue and conscience, as the fount of moral obligation'. According to Seligman, 'with the terms of representation defined by the autonomous, rights-bearing individual, the representation of the public sphere (and so of relations between public and private) becomes increasingly problematic'. Once 'the realm of value' is 'relegated to the sphere of the private', it is 'increasingly difficult to represent the collective whole, the realm of the public'.

Law, Ann Arbor: University of Michigan Press, 1999; A. Wagner and V.K. Bhatia (eds), *Diversity and Tolerance in Socio-legal Contexts: Explorations in the Semiotics of Law*, Farnham/Burlington: Ashgate, 2009.

Veit Bader's chapter offers some further 'conceptual, theoretical and empirical clarifications of "private", "public" and its shifting divide from a sociological point of view'. Framed in the context of a political theory based on the principles of liberal-democratic constitutionalism, his contribution aims at providing inputs 'to discuss whether and, if so, what kinds of intervention in religious associations/organizations are compatible with the guarantee of associational religious freedom'. In the second part of his analysis, Bader applies these inputs to the case of non-governmental religiously oriented schools, examining the problems connected to their public funding, regulation and (State) control. He concludes that in this field the public/private divide is not decisive and argues for replacing 'the "shield of privacy" with substantive arguments from minimal morality and from more demanding liberal-democratic morality'.

The two contributions by Alessandro and Silvio Ferrari are more directly focused on the transformations of the relationship between the State and religion that are taking place in Europe. Alessandro Ferrari highlights the dangers of a double-standard secularism: due to the increasing willingness of the European States 'to read secularism in the light of a social cohesion interpreted as a collective good reflecting specific national identities', the right of religious freedom has increasingly taken on the goal of protecting 'a public order unilaterally assessed by the States themselves' rather than autonomies of individual consciences and religious groups. In this situation the right of religious minorities to access the public space is increasingly made dependent on their ability 'to pass a very identitarian and "thick" "reasonable"/"unreasonable" test'. Silvio Ferrari identifies three patterns of relations between States and religions in Europe (connected to the ideal-types provided by France, Italy and the United Kingdom) and maintains that none of them can adequately govern the processes of religious pluralization and publicization that is taking place in Europe. According to Silvio Ferrari it is necessary to deconstruct the notion of public sphere, making a distinction between its personal and spatial dimensions and, in reference to the latter, between common, political and institutional space.

Jean-François Gaudreault-DesBiens and Noura Karazivan's analysis begins with the observation that legal traditions 'constitute "reasoning templates" that may provide deep reasons for adopting one broad regulatory approach over another'. They go on to contrast the common law and civil law traditions 'along three axes: the relative importance of the State in each tradition; the consequence on the treatment of fundamental rights; and the impact on certain legal doctrines such as that of abus de droit'. Their threefold analysis sheds some light on a few important points. According to the authors, 'the civil law tradition seems more prone to accept intrinsic limitations to fundamental rights' (including freedom of religion) and a civil law State may be more likely to 'insist on the religious neutrality of its civil servants' than a common law State, which 'might be more inclined to allow its employees to wear' religious symbols 'because they are deemed not to represent an abstractly defined, sovereign, State but a particular community, with its tapestry of colours, that must be served and represented by the State'.

Finally, Hanne Petersen looks at the public/private divide from a very specific perspective, that of gender. This approach enables her to formulate a few general statements that deserve attention. She writes that 'monotheistic religions are based on distinct gender hierarchies and divisions, which are inherited by secular state organizations and regulations. The "Atlantic-European" inspired secular normative culture introduces a division in public and private spheres, which continues a tradition of gender division and class privilege'. This remark returns to Modéer's 'deep structures' and 'longue durée' processes on the one hand and, on the other, to the impact of different religious conceptions on the legal traditions (including those that are indicated with the expressions 'common law' and 'civil law' mentioned by Gaudreault-DesBiens and Karazivan). How much is the public/private distinction the outcome of a monotheistic or even Christian background, hidden but not deleted? And how far would such a descent, if proved, make this distinction non-exportable outside the West and inadequate even to govern the contemporary religious plurality of the West?

Two Types of Major Conflict: Dress Codes and Places of Worship

It would be presumptuous to claim that the RELIGARE project managed to draw up a comprehensive list of those conflicts which arise in daily life and which revolve around the public–private divide. Two types of conflict have been selected: the *first* broad area relates to the sensitive issue of religious dress codes. Dress codes and the wish of a growing body of believers to accommodate these codes, both in a school context and in the workplace, have been the object of vivid discussions in the past few years in nearly every European country, and have also led to an impressive body of case law. The *second* type of conflict addressed by several contributions in this volume regards places of worship. Various matters may raise serious problems – and therefore need to be settled – in particular in cases where specific requests on the part of the communities involved and/or practices clash with the rules that apply within the jurisdiction of the place where a conflict occurs, or where there are no clear rules on hand.

As the contributions in this book make clear, both types of conflict put into perspective the relations – institutional and other – between a State and the various convictions and/or religious and philosophical communities with which it has to deal. They focus in particular on the constitutional and legal framework set up to govern these relations. The tensions that accompany the conflicts may take different forms and be more or less easily manageable. Much will depend on the willingness of the parties involved – the State and the believers or their spokesmen – to come to an agreement. Rather than set aside or prohibit religion as a fact of social life, the solutions to be preferred by far should be those that take as their starting point two fundamental rights in particular: *the freedom of religion* and *the right to equality of treatment*, as enshrined in the European Convention on

Human Rights and Fundamental Freedoms and more recently also the Charter of Fundamental Rights of the European Union. In principle, applying a classical conception of liberal democracy, equality takes no account of a person's belief(s) and/or philosophical convictions unless, paradoxically, that very indifference were to lead in practice to the opposite result, that is, that the person in question were to be excluded or disadvantaged *because* of his or her belief(s)/convictions. Legal frameworks should offer ways of recognizing, respecting and – within limits – accommodating legitimate differences.

Dress codes Six contributions address the issue of religious dress codes (Katayoun Alidadi, Maya Kosseva and Iva Kyurkchieva, A. Emre Öktem and Mehmet C. Uzun, Sara Silvestri, Javier Garcia Oliva, Sabrina Pastorelli). All eight authors agree that the issue of religious dress codes – directly or indirectly – touches upon a highly symbolic matter. Yet, the question is what makes a religious symbol. M. Evans in his *Manual on the Wearing of Religious Symbols in Public Areas* concludes that there is no universal legal definition of a religious symbol. However, he distinguishes two different approaches: the first approach limits the notion of religious symbols to figures of religious devotion; the other approach includes everything which forms a relevant element in the religious life of a believer.[12] Whether one takes the first or the second approach, in both cases what is to be understood as a religious symbol will to a large extent depend on the concrete context and consequently on factors linked to time and space. Conflicts over the wearing of religious symbols through dress and over the grounds that may be invoked to prohibit it or, on the contrary, to place no restrictions on it – or if at all then only very few – have become increasingly frequent in three contexts: in public schools, in the workplace (see Chapter 9) and more recently also, with regard to the full veil, on the street.

The symbols most vividly discussed these past few years, almost everywhere in Europe, are no doubt the Muslim headscarf – and more recently also the full veil (see Chapter 14) – and the Sikh turban and 'kirpan'. In some EU countries, the issue of dress codes attracted the attention not only of the mass media but also of political authorities. While some countries voted for legislative measures that limit in no insignificant way the wearing of specific religious symbols, as is the case in France, Belgium and Turkey (see for this last country Chapter 10), other countries have not (yet) enacted any specific regulation in this domain, as is the case for example of Bulgaria (see Chapter 13), and there public policies vary from banning to accommodating attitudes.

Here again, three perspectives can be adopted and will lead to different conclusions depending on the angle of approach: a spatial, a personal or a functional approach.

---

12 M. Evans, *Manual on the Wearing of Religious Symbols in Public Areas*, Strasbourg: Council of Europe Editions, 2009, 62–87.

From the point of view that makes reference to the person(s) involved and the service that is (to be) offered, a distinction needs to be made between persons who are offering a public service in the capacity of judge, clerk or teacher, working in and for public institutions, and persons who do not perform but instead use the public service in the capacity of a private person, such as students, patients, litigants, etc. In the case of a judge or a clerk the choice of wearing – and thereby exhibiting – a religious symbol can raise doubts about the neutrality of the institution, while in the case of persons who do not offer any public service, but instead are users of it, wearing religious symbols is a matter of private choice.

Yet, public space can be conceived as *open* – such as a bus, the street, etc. – or as *institutional* – such as a law court, a school, a hospital. While public *institutional* spaces have to comply with rules of access and conduct, public *open* spaces are theoretically equally accessible to all, but in practice, distinctions based on religion or belief can be relevant. One of the first domains on which lawmakers and judges focused, at national as well as at European level, was the school.

In France, a much debated law of 2004[13] bans visible religious signs in schools. In application of this law, Muslim students wearing headscarves as well as Sikh students wearing turbans – all signs revealing a religious belonging – were excluded from public schools. The law aimed at banning mainly Muslim headscarves, in order to preserve the principle of secularity ('laïcité'): in a school context students must be neither distracted nor influenced by religious issues. In the *Kervanci* v. *France* and the *Dogru* v. *France* cases, the ECtHR declared that the law does not infringe upon the principles of the European Convention on Human Rights and Fundamental Liberties.[14]

In the United Kingdom, the debate arose over the *Begum* case in 2002 (see Chapter 11). In the UK wearing the hijab is generally allowed in public schools. The French concern with 'laïcité' is not an issue here. The *Begum* case concerned the 'jilbab', a long, loose tunic that Shabina Begum wished to wear at school.[15] Since the jilbab did not comply with the regulations concerning the school uniform, her claim led to her exclusion from the school. This raised questions concerning the interpretation of article 9 of the ECHR: were the limitations to

13 Assemblée nationale, Loi no. 2004-228 du 15 mars 2004 encadrant, en application du principe de laïcité, le port de signes ou de tenues manifestant une appartenance religieuse dans les écoles, collèges et lycées publics, *Journal Officiel*, no. 65, 17/03/2004, www.legifrance.gouv.fr. See also: Commission présidée par B. Stasi, *Laïcité et République*, Paris: La Documentation Française, 2004; A. Ferrari, 'Velo musulmano e laicità francese: una difficile integrazione', in: S. Ferrari (a cura di), *I simboli religiosi dei diritti del Vecchio continente*, Roma: Carocci, 2006, 93 ss.

14 *Case of Dogru* v. *France*, Application no. 27058/05, Strasbourg, 4 December 2008; *Case of Kervanci* v. *France*, application no. 31645/04, Strasbourg, 4 December 2008, http://cmiskp.echr.coe.int/tkp197/search.asp?skin=hudoc-en. See also: Conseil d'État, décision 5 décembre 2007, requête n. 285394; n. 285395; n. 285396; n. 295671, www.conseil-etat.fr/.

15 For a comment on the case, see among others: M. Mazher Idriss, 'The defeat of Shabina Begum in the House of Lords', *Liverpool Law Review* 3, 2006, 417–436.

her freedom of religion justifiable? At first, the Court of Appeal acknowledged a violation under the Human Rights Act of 1998.[16] However, in March 2006, the House of Lords overturned the Court of Appeal's decision on all counts, assessing that the right to manifest a belief under article 9 of the ECHR had not been violated by the school.[17]

In other countries, the debate focused on the right of *teachers* to wear a religious symbol. In the case of *Dahlab* v. *Switzerland*, concerning the dismissal of a school teacher wearing the Islamic headscarf, the ECtHR considered that the dismissal was legitimate as it was applied in order to grant a religiously neutral teaching to young and easily influenced students.[18] In Germany, a teacher was not hired because she was unwilling to remove her headscarf: the Constitutional Court decided that in doing so the lower court had violated her religious freedom and infringed upon the principles of non-discrimination.[19] In any case, the question is the competence of the Länder, which explains why some of them later adopted legislation that prohibits teachers from wearing Islamic headscarves in public schools.

Religiously oriented private schools are entitled to deal differently with the issues concerning the wearing of religious dress, as they are not obliged to respect the principle of neutrality.

More recently, as mentioned above, some countries have started to express worries about the wearing of religious dress on the street. The argument here is that of public order and security. In Italy so far, no law prohibits dressing in accordance with one's belief and/or wearing religious symbols (see Chapter 12). Yet, in the past few years local authorities have started prohibiting full veils (the 'burqa') in the streets. Some municipalities in the north of the country, where the Northern League Party is particularly strong, began to apply a 1975 law (originally conceived against terrorism) that forbids circulating in public spaces with the face completely covered. Some municipalities enacted council decrees (based on this

---

16 *Human Rights Act 1998*, www.opsi.gov.uk/acts/acts1998/ukpga_19980042_en_1.

17 House of Lords, *Judgments – Begum (FC) (Appellant)* v. *London Borough of Tower Hamlets (Respondents)*, www.publications.parliament.uk/pa/ld200203/ldjudgmt/jd030213/begum-1.htm; House of Lords, *Opinions of the Lords of Appeal for Judgment in the Cause R (on the application of Begum (by her litigation friend, Rahman)) (Respondent)* v. *Headteacher and Governors of Denbigh High School (Appellants)*, www.publications.parliament.uk/pa/ld200506/ldjudgmt/jd060322/begum.pdf. See also: Mohammad Mazher Idriss, 'The defeat of Shabina Begum in the House of Lords', *Liverpool Law Review* 27/3, December, 2006, 417–436.

18 *Dahlab* v. *Switzerland*, Application No. 42393/98, Strasbourg, 15 January 2001, http://cmiskp.echr.coe.int/tkp197/search.asp?sessionid=55553349&skin=hudoc-en.

19 BVerfG, 2 BvR 1436/02 of 09/24/2003, paragraphs No. (1–138), www.bverfg.de/entscheidungen/rs20030924_2bvr143602en.html (accessed 18 June 2010). The Court recognized that 'there is no sufficiently definite statutory basis in the current law of the Land (state) Baden-Württemberg for a prohibition on teachers wearing a headscarf at school and in lessons'.

law) to ban the burqa. The case law, however, disagrees with that view. Several courts in Italy ruled in favour of the religious freedom of women, considering that since the wearing of the burqa can be considered the manifestation of a particular religious tradition, it constitutes a 'justified exception' to the 1975 law. There is one condition, however, under which women are required to accept being identified – if requested by the police.

In Cremona, a city in Northern Italy, another case related to public order and security issues arose in 2007. In a shopping centre an Indian national of Sikh religion was approached by a policeman because he carried a sword: the 'kirpan'. The Criminal Court of Cremona acquitted him of the crime of carrying a weapon or an object, though not conventionally a weapon, which can be employed as one. The Court considered the carrying of a kirpan as an expression of one's religious faith and recognized the religious character of carrying it as a justified reason to exclude the application of the public security law.[20]

In various EU countries, a further issue is that of identity documents. In principle, in most countries, pictures on identity documents show the person without a scarf or any other (religious or non-religious) headgear. That is the case, for example, in France[21] and Portugal. Other countries, such as Italy[22] and the UK,[23] provide dispensation for religious reasons. The case law on this issue, notably in Finland, Belgium,[24] Germany and Ireland, generally shows understanding.

20 Criminal Court, Cremona, 19 February 2009, no.799/08.

21 Conseil d'État, décision n. 289947, 6 mars 2006, www.conseil-etat.fr. On the current debate about the niqab, see: Mission d'information sur la pratique du port du voile intégral sur le territoire national, *Rapport d'information fait au nom de la mission d'information sur la pratique du port du voile intégral sur le territoire national*, no. 2262, le 26 janvier 2010, www.assemblee-nationale.fr/13/rap-info/i2262.asp (accessed 18 June 2010); Sénat de France, *Le port de la burqa dans les lieux publics, Étude de législation comparée*, n. 201, 23 octobre 2009, www.senat.fr/lc/lc201/lc201.pdf (accessed 18 June 2010).

22 Ministero dell'Interno. Direzione generale dell'amministrazione civile, circolare 14 marzo 1995, n. 4: 'Rilascio carta di identità a cittadini professanti culti religiosi diversi da quello cattolico – uso del copricapo'.

23 A case concerned the refusal of the British High Commission in Singapore to renew the passport of a Muslim woman wearing a hijab. Since this case and the consequent public debate, the Home Office has adopted new guidelines allowing Muslim women to cover their heads on their passport photographs. UKBA Photograph Guidance for immigration applications made in the UK, version 04/2009: 'Photographs must also be taken on the full head, without any covering unless worn for religious or medical reasons'. www.ukba.homeoffice.gov.uk/sitecontent/applicationforms/flr/photoguidance0409.pdf (accessed 18 June 2010).

24 See the decision of the Cour de Cassation, 22/12/2000, C990164N, http://jure.juridat.just.fgov.be/pdfapp/download_blob?idpdf=F-20001222-4 (accessed 18 June 2010).

With a view to protecting the religious freedom of the person involved, courts usually accept these kinds of headdresses on identity documents.[25]

Places of worship Four contributions in this volume address the public–private divide in relation to the construction and subsequently the maintenance of places of worship (Anne Fornerod, Tymen J. van der Ploeg, Vincenzo Pacillo and Noel G. Villaroman).

Article 9 of the European Convention on Human Rights as well as article 10 of the Charter of Fundamental Rights of the European Union, guarantee freedom of thought, conscience and religion. This right includes freedom to manifest religion or belief, in worship, teaching, practice and observance. The right to build places of worship is considered part of this right. This represents a major consolidation of the position of religious communities in many European countries. In the past, the question of the places of worship was ruled within the context of the (mainly historical) relations between a State and the religious communities established on its territory. It explains why, in most cases, the right to have a place of worship depended on the quality of these relations and in case of tensions, the right was simply denied or subjected to various limitations. This was unfortunately the case with many minority religions. A new approach came with the introduction of a system of religious liberty. Under this approach, having a place of worship came to be regarded as the manifestation of one's religious freedom.

From this new perspective any religious group, independently from its relations with the State, is entitled to have its own place of worship and this right cannot be made dependent on an authorization by or an agreement with the public administration and cannot be limited to the religious communities that have been registered or recognized at national or local level. As a manifestation of religious liberty, the right to have a place of worship can be limited only by general rules governing land use, planning, construction or intended to protect health and safety in buildings where a large number of persons can gather.

This new approach has been affirmed in a number of international documents, confirmed in several international court decisions (see Chapter 15) and reiterated in various State laws, for example the laws on religious freedom of Spain and Portugal.[26]

Despite this sound foundation, the availability of a place of worship as part of the right of religious freedom is far from being universally recognized. Certain States have simply not accepted it and are therefore not willing to implement the

25 Migration Policy Group, European Group of non-governmental experts in the field of combating discrimination on the grounds of religion or belief, *Rapport de synthèse relatif aux signes d'appartenance religieuse dans quinze pays de l'Union Européenne*, juillet 2004, www.migpolgroup.org/public/docs/42.rapportdesynthesesignesreligieuxUE_FR_09.11.pdf (accessed 18 June 2010).

26 For Spain see article 2.2 of the Organic Law 7/1980 on religious liberty (5 July 1980) and for Portugal art. 23 of Law 16/2001 on religious freedom (22 June 2001).

principle. More recently, the right to have a place of worship is being increasingly questioned even in countries that previously adopted a liberal approach. In the last 10 to 15 years various laws have been enacted that limit the right to establish a new place of worship either by requiring a municipal licence or via the imposition of environmental and architectural prerequisites so strict that a new place of worship cannot be built unless its external appearance follows that which is customary and characteristic of the religious tradition already in place (as is the case in Austria and Switzerland: see Chapter 17). In other countries, like Italy and France (see Chapters 16 and 18), the application of the rules regarding the allocation of land for building places of worship or the transformation of an existing building into a place of worship is very rigid, especially if the requests come from Muslim communities or the Jehovah's Witnesses.

Achieving pluralism that can benefit European societies The issues on which the contributions in this book focus reveal an increasing sensitivity to religious identity claims in the public space. In practice, it is mainly the historical majority religions that are being granted exceptions to the principle of neutrality of the public space; in some cases these exceptions are constitutionally guaranteed. They have for the most part developed over the course of the country's history. But the arrival of new groups and communities across Europe makes it necessary to review certain forms of protection, and to adapt the private–public divide to accommodate these new groups. A gradual familiarization with the reality of an ever-increasing religious and philosophical diversity in European societies will likely mean that, over time, the legal frameworks in place will be modified thus offering more adequate responses, in order to arrive at a sustainable solution and one that takes full cognizance of the plurality of religions and beliefs.

There may not be a fully satisfactory response to all the issues that arise around these matters. Nonetheless, publications like this one are a valuable means for achieving a pluralism that can benefit European societies as a whole. It may do so in two ways: first, by offering a careful collection of basic comparative data drawn from the legislative policies and the relevant case law of the States involved; and second, by providing a selection of significant testimonies on contentious issues of religious pluralism.

PART I
Religions and the Public/Private Divide

Chapter 2
Public and Private, a Moving Border: A Legal-Historical Perspective

Kjell Å Modéer

Introduction

This chapter on the public–private divide in religion from a historical perspective contains many themes also present in contemporary discourses. First of all, they are generally speaking geographically defined. The European discourses are mostly related to differentiation within religion in relation to the concept of modernization and secularization, and to the remaining religious monopoly systems or majority churches within the Church and State model. The judicial jurisprudence from the European Court of Justice related to article 9 in the ECHR is also in an interesting way articulating historical contexts. The American discourses on the other hand do not have their focus on secularization and modernization. As a modern developed country, the discourses in the United States are more related to the concept of an 'open religious market' and religious diversity kept in order with the help of the judicial jurisprudence of the US Supreme Court and its relationship to the First Amendment clauses in the American Constitution.

This chapter will focus on three topics demonstrating this divide. Firstly, the dynamic private–public divide within the relationship between Churches and States from the Papal Revolution of about AD1100 up to current discourses. Secondly, the chapter will focus on three social concepts from medieval times up to today which all demonstrate the deep structures of European law. All three concepts have their legal roots in medieval canon law, namely the *family, education* and *poor relief*. The geopolitical contexts of these concepts have changed throughout history. Even though *family* remained a private concept in early modern times the Enlightenment brought in new perspectives on the religious education of citizens. It became a constitutional issue related to the freedom of religion. From the nineteenth century onwards the legal regulation within the modern social state and its welfare systems contributed to a new dynamic orientation within the public–private divide. So family, education and welfare are topics which divided public and private power from medieval canon law up to current national and European legislation and jurisprudence. Thirdly, before concluding a couple of late modern examples of the divide will be considered. The chapter will also demonstrate that in the current discourses regarding this topic historical argumentation is used to uphold concepts which, in spite of a move, belong to the other (older) divide.

A Few Legal-Historical Reflections

In European legal history the Roman Catholic Church has played a dominant role from the eleventh century onwards. Its cognitive structure from faith to canons has not only been transferred into the legal cultures of European countries, it has also remained more or less as a transnational deep structure throughout the centuries. From this perspective it is the contexts – the political, social and economic circumstances – which are changing and are different from country to country. Therefore, the moving border between the religious public and private to a great extent is due to changing contexts. The changes can be dramatic and result in revolutions; they can also be more continuous and result in reforms. Lawyers administer the law as priests administer the Gospel. Law and Gospel, intertwined in the Bible, are also a common deep structure of the law in relation to the private–public divide right up to the modernity of the twentieth century.

Harold Berman's categorization of European history through topical revolutions can be helpful also in this respect. The medieval Papal Revolution, the Lutheran Protestant Revolution in early modern Europe, the revolution of modernity and secularization as a result of the Enlightenment, and the Socialist Revolution of the twentieth century will also be considered in this chapter (Berman 2000: 739).

From Roman law onwards, private law has been the focus for lawyers. Roman Law of obligation was in focus for European jurists in medieval times as well as in the nineteenth century. The field of public law has historically been related to privileges and fundamental laws, *leges fundamentales*. Constitutional law became fundamental in the nineteenth century as an icon for the creation of the nation state. This dynamic between the internal rules related to conflicts between citizens and the external rules between the individual citizen and the State provides not only the context for this chapter but is also a part of different views on the religious division between the private and public sphere.

From a legal-historical view the religious private–public divide is a question of jurisdiction, the Latin word for power. The struggle for power is continuously creating the moving border. The Justinian rule in the Digest *Suum cuique tribuere*, 'give to each what belongs to him/her', legitimated in medieval times the competition between different privileged jurisdictions, also between the secular courts and the ecclesiastical courts. The public square was the marketplace, but it was also the place where conflicts were resolved. Later on conflict settlement was moved to the town hall, which in medieval towns was situated next to the town church.

The European nation states were divided into countries with State Churches, including the Scandinavian ones, and countries with other forms of contract between the State and different ecclesiastical congregations.

From the Papal Revolution to the Lutheran Reformation

In medieval times the theological argumentation for the divide was found in the Bible. One example of such argumentation is found in the Gospel, John 18:36, where Jesus responded to Pontius Pilate's question as to whether he was the King of Israel. Jesus pleaded for the divide: 'My kingdom is not of this world. If my kingdom were of this world, my servants would have been fighting, that I might not be delivered over to the Jews. But my kingdom is not from the world'. His religious teachings were separate from earthly political activity. This quotation legitimated the traditional division in Christian thought by which State and Church have separate spheres of influence.

Another classic quotation from Matthew 22:21 stated the relationship between Christianity and the secular authorities: 'Render unto Caesar the things which are Caesar's, and unto God the things that are God's'.

The Papal Revolution (1075–1122) created for the first time a state model of the Pan-European Church with canon law as its authoritative legal regulation (Berman 1983). Gratian's Treatise of 1140 and other ecclesiastical statutes became a norm-system differentiated from secular law. Secular law covered matters of royal, feudal or local jurisdictions related to sovereignty, property and crime. Canon law on the other hand had a much wider scope of rules – a wider jurisdiction. The Roman Catholic jurisdiction administered the crimes and actions related to God, *crimen laesae majestatis divinae* (heresy), and the king administered those crimes which insulted his sovereignty or person, *crimen laesae majestatis humanae*.

Penal law was regarded as a part of public law. Only the king and later the State has the right to punish; up to the increasing secularization in modern times with the mandate from God.

More interestingly, family law belonged to the canon law jurisdiction; the huge records of the *Penitentiaria Apostolica* in the Vatican demonstrate the breadth of this medieval European jurisdiction (Risberg and Salonen 2008).

The relationship between the Catholic Church and sovereign territorial kings was regulated in agreements, *concordats*. Such agreements regulated the jurisdiction of the Church, including both recognition and privileges. What Harold Berman (2003) defined as the Papal Revolution was confirmed with the Concordat of Worms in 1122 (sometimes called the *Pactum Calixtinum*), which was an agreement between Pope Calixtus II and the Holy Roman Emperor Henry V that ended the 50-year *Investiture contest* between the Church and the territorial sovereigns. This concordat has been regarded as the embryo of the nation-based relationship and sovereignty, later confirmed in the Treaty of Westphalia in 1648. The relationship between the public authorities and the Holy See was identified through such concordats with many European territories.

A new relationship between Church and State came with the reformations within the Roman Catholic Church, especially the Lutheran Reformation in the early sixteenth century – which Berman (2003) called the Lutheran Revolution. It is also the starting point of a new period within European history, the *early modern period.* From this point on the jurisdiction of the Catholic Church was diminished, and Christian Europe was divided between the Roman Catholic south and the Protestant north. In the countries involved in this spiritual revolution a new (it can already be called modern) relationship between Church and State evolved. It was based on the Lutheran 'two kingdoms' theory: the heavenly kingdom of grace and faith, governed by the Gospel; and the earthly kingdom including the visible institutional Church, governed by law.

Philipp Melanchthon's topical method emphasized the unity of the entire body of law and its division into branches: first of all public and private law. This division between the spiritual and the earthly regimes started a new competition between the private and the public.

The Decalogue in the Old Testament became a natural-law statute which demonstrated Melanchthon's topic of public jurisdiction. The commandment 'Thou shalt not kill' founded criminal law, 'Thou shalt not steal' founded property law, and 'Thou shalt not commit adultery' founded family law in the Lutheran legal topics. This Lutheran Protestant categorization of the law resulted in a transition of the ecclesiastical canon law jurisdictions into secular state jurisdictions in the Protestant nation states in northern Europe in early modern times. The public–private border was on the move. In Scandinavian countries the State Church model was founded and for centuries cemented during the reigns of autocratic monarchies. Lutheran orthodoxy not only resulted in State-regulated Church laws but also the Bible as a State-ratified code. In courtrooms, both the Bible and the secular code were placed on the bench.

A result of declining Papal power was that in many Lutheran territories Catholics as well as Jews were prohibited. Religion was a State matter. But in other nations, such as in the Holy Roman Empire of the German Nation, tolerance was introduced as a model for reconciliation between religious congregations. In the German Empire, Charles V agreed to tolerate Lutheranism in 1555 at the Peace of Augsburg. Within the Empire each State was to take the religion of its prince, but within those states there was not necessarily religious tolerance. Citizens of other faiths had to relocate to a more hospitable environment. The concept of tolerance of the State was ratified in the Treaty of Westphalia 1648 in which the German dual religious system was established between the evangelical Lutheran Church and the Roman Catholic Church.

The early modern era introduced State Churches into northern Europe where the absolute king also became the head of the Church. Even though rational natural law and its legal principles were introduced, the State and its citizens were still founded on Christian belief. Family law is a good example of the intertwining of private law and public Church law. Catholic canon law doctrine did not admit divorce, nor did Lutheran Church law. In family law adultery was still regarded as a public crime. However, divorce cases were transferred from ecclesiastical to secular courts.

The Post-Enlightenment Developments

The Enlightenment introduced flexibility into the relationship between Church and State. As a reaction to absolute and orthodox Lutheranism, the Pietism movement arose in about 1700 in Germany, where Halle became a centre for this State control related to religion. Members of the Pietism movement met in *Collegia Pietatis*, and they held private worship and met for biblical studies in their homes, *conventicles*.

In the early eighteenth century such pietistic meetings were regarded as a threat to the State religion. In Sweden they were explicitly prohibited in the 1720s. This State prohibition of the free exercise of religion endured up to the late 1850s (Dahlman 2009).

However, respect for the freedom of religion of the citizen became one of the important claims within constitutional law in the Enlightenment. This freedom was included in the French Declaration of the Rights of Man in 1789, although with a reservation: as long as religious activities did not infringe on public order in ways detrimental to society.

Patriotism became a keyword in the construct of the modern nation state. The patriotic rhetoric of the late eighteenth century identified the borderline between private virtue and public interest (Horwitz 1982: 1424). The Enlightenment introduced the modern view that religion is a private matter which has to be guaranteed publicly by the State in a constitution.

A bill of individual rights including freedom of religion was included in Western constitutions – also in that of the United States in the First Amendment. The modern legal concept of religious freedom as the union of *freedom of belief* and *freedom of worship* with the absence of any State-sponsored religion originated in the United States of America and became an archetype for the modern secularized State.

Thomas Jefferson's famous statement in 1803 that 'There is a wall of separation between Church and State' has for centuries been of great importance for the US interpretation of the limits of the religious in relation to the State's public law.

The modern way of interpreting freedom of religion also included negative freedom, i.e. the freedom and right not to have a religion. The modernization of the society of the *ancien régime* into a modern developed society was also identified with the help of its secularity.

One of the central goals of nineteenth-century legal thought was to create a clear separation between constitutional, criminal and regulatory (administrative) law – public law – on one side, and the law of private transactions, such as torts, contracts, property and commercial law on the other (Horwitz 1982: 1423ff.). In State–Church countries *Church law* was regarded as public law. At European universities the field of Church law was a part of the curriculum at law faculties. Secularization brought this discipline over to the Divinity schools, at least in the secularized Scandinavian countries.

The majority of State Churches were challenged by the Free Church movement in the nineteenth century. Religion became liberal and private. The result was again a diminishing power (jurisdiction) of the majority churches.

Modernization of society meant a critical rational attitude to religion especially in relation to the public square. In France there was a blunt divide between Church and State in 1905 with a law on the separation of the Churches and the State. Symbolically, crucifixes were taken away from French courtrooms (Taylor 1993).

To sum up: in the modern State, religion was regarded as a private matter. The separation of religion from government power is legally referred to as *laïcité*.

Modernity and the Public/Private Divide

Modernity within European legal cultures had important consequences for the religious divide between private and public. The critique against the public State Church construct became increasingly strong in the twentieth century. The private–public positions shifted again, in this case in the direction of a strong secular social state. The laissez-faire liberalism of the nineteenth century with its strong freedom of contract principles within private law changed direction towards socially orientated private law. Modern concepts of the crime of usury were in earlier periods regarded as a religious crime. Instead from this time onwards the attitude was to protect the weaker party in the freedom of a contract situation. The German statute on usury from the 1880s not only decreased the freedom of contract principle (private law) but it also criminalized such an act (public law) (Modéer 1983: 519ff.).

Modern family law also became more secularized. The beginning of the twentieth century brought new options for civil marriage. The parties not only had the possibility to marry without a religious act, but divorce options also increased. The civil marriage became the public act, the Church could only offer a marital blessing. In Protestant countries civil marriage became an alternative to the Church wedding. In Sweden, the Church of Sweden decided to agree to marry the parties in same-sex relations.

Religious education became a politically vulnerable topic when the question of the difference between confessional education in religion and more encyclopaedically orientated education about religion was raised. In France in 1882 the so-called Jules Ferry laws prohibited the spiritual Jesuit schools and religious education in French schools. This debate was also transferred to Scandinavia. In Sweden the claims for secularization of the school system started in 1895 and the statute was adopted in 1905. Religious education has been a topic in Scandinavia throughout the twentieth century (Selander 1993).

The introduction of the welfare state did not only mean State-regulated social security systems, it also meant a move from philanthropic and voluntarily organized welfare and local constructs regarding the poor to much greater State responsibility.

In Harold Berman's (2003) categorization, this period is characterized as the socialist revolution which started out in Russia in 1917. It was characterized by atheist totalitarian socialism and gave priority to the public. This development was important also for the crisis of the traditional legal cultures in the West. The emergence of the bureaucratic state meant direct public control regarding the economy, communication, education, healthcare and other aspects of social life. In Europe it meant the creation of the strong welfare state with a substantive increase of administrative regulations. With the help of the content of the law the State shaped and identified the beliefs and attitudes of the citizens. Moreover, after the Second World War in the preambles and so on of the revised European constitutions was embedded, for example, a State-defined secular religion, a *civil religion*, for concepts like democracy, solidarity, human dignity, rule of law and human rights (Bellah 1967: 1ff.).

The period after the Second World War can be characterized as a period of more outspoken secularization and as the peak of modernization. The US rhetoric of a *living constitution* meant that Mr Jefferson's metaphor of 'the wall of separation' was upheld in all cases regarding separating Church and State (especially by the Earl Warren court).

To sum up so far: the *longue durée* in the private–public divide regarding religion demonstrates transnational *deep structures* which can be traced back at least to medieval times. Since the twelfth century as a public entity with a substantial jurisdiction the Roman Catholic Church has signed concordats with its secular territorial counterparts. The Lutheran Reformation not only divided Europe, in northern Europe it also introduced a new Church–State relationship in which the sovereign mastered the spiritual as well as the secular kingdom. The Lutheran Church went public. In the eighteenth and nineteenth centuries the liberal movements within the Church urged for a more liberal attitude in Church rituals towards privacy and religion as a private matter. The main document in the modern nation state became the constitution. The modern constitutions regulated the individual's rights including the freedom of religion – at first in a positive sense, but later on also the consequent negative freedom of religion. Religion was turned over to the private sphere. Religion was prohibited in the public sphere.

Modernization and secularization dominate the role of religion in society as a *progressive tradition*. In the modernity of the twentieth century the public Church–State construct was to a large extent abolished. The jurisdictions of the Church have been transformed from being dominant to being marginalized. Even Pope Benedictus XVI has defined the Roman Catholic Church as a dynamic minority Church in the current European secularized landscape (Ratzinger 1991).

Conclusion

This survey will conclude with a brief comment on the latest period in European legal history, *late modernity*. From our point of view this period started in 1989. The construct of this period can be regarded as a synthesis to earlier periods here described. This new paradigm has not yet been concluded, but from our perspective as it is related to a moving border between private and public it is an interesting period, due to the desecularization and retraditionalization of our post-secular time (Modéer 2009: 340).

This late modern synthesis can be identified as a struggle between progressive private market orientated theories (new liberalism) and traditional welfare state programmes (social democrats).

In the United States the judicial jurisprudence has changed dramatically from the Earl Warren court in the 1950s–1960s to the current Rehnquist/Roberts court. Since the 1980s the conservative majority of the Court has implemented a historically based interpretation of the Constitution called the original intent or original meaning theory (Scalia and Gutmann 1997). In the last decade this majority of the court has eroded the 'wall of separation' principle in several cases and has agreed to economic State support for various religious organizations. Religion is in that respect back in the public square. Within the comparative legal culture discourse the term *Scandinavian exceptionalism* has been introduced as an 'in-between' system, between civil law and common law (Modéer 2004: 193ff.).

The last traditional State Churches – the Scandinavian Churches – are involved in what can be regarded as a delayed break-up of their state relationship and they are following a long European trend of the twentieth century. After a long and intense political discourse in 1999 the Swedish parliament decided to separate the Church from the State beginning from the new millennium. However, this separation was accompanied by a parliamentary law on the Swedish Church which regulated some requisites for the majority Church: it should be democratic and should cover all parts of the country. Consequently the relationship between State and Church has not been totally abolished. The Church of Sweden is privileged in relation to other religious communities. The jurisdiction of the Church, however, is very limited. Labour conflicts are for example solved in ordinary courts, even though the Church has the ultimate right to give notice to employees of the Church (Modéer 2010: 81ff.).

In Norway in 2008 a parliamentary committee delivered a draft regarding a similar constitutional reform. The Norwegian parliament, however, made a compromise which resulted in what – in a family law metaphor – can be called not a separation but a 'division of joint property' between the State and Church. The revised Norwegian Church will still be a State Church in an increasingly multi-religious society (Petersen and Modéer 2009). Also in Denmark, the State Church is regulated in the Constitution (1849). Until today Denmark has not taken any steps to make a revision of the traditional Church–State relationship. And in

Sweden and Norway, even though there has been a move from public to semi-public churches, this process is far from concluded.

With their transparent boundaries the multicultural European countries of today are creating increasingly multi-religious societies which from a legal historical perspective are once more bringing into focus the various concepts discussed. Jurisdiction, the *Suum cuique* principle, the concepts of family, religious education, and privatization of welfare institutions are some examples of this movement of the border regarding religion in the private–public divide.

Historical argumentation and *longue durée* perspectives are today competing with an ongoing secularization of the European nation states. Medieval principles are competing with modernization theories in a way which at least can be described as interesting. From a religious perspective it is both challenging and fascinating.

References

Bellah, R.N. (1967), 'Civil Religion in America', *Daedalus*, 96:1, 1–21.

Berman, H. (1983), *Law and Revolution: The Formation of the Western Legal Tradition* (Cambridge: Harvard University Press).

Berman, H.J. (2000), 'The Western Legal Tradition in a Millennium Perspective. Past and Future', *Louisiana Law Review*, vol. 60. (2000): 739–763.

Berman, H.J. (2003), *Law and Revolution: The Impact of the Protestant Reformations on the Western Legal Tradition*, vol. 2 (Cambridge, MA: Belknap Press of Harvard University Press).

Christoffersen, L., Modéer, K.Å. and Andersen, S. (eds) (2010), *Law & Religion in the 21st Century – Nordic Perspectives* (Copenhagen: DJØF Publishing).

Dahlman, P. (2009), *Kyrka och stat i 1860 års svenska religionslagstiftning* (Church and State in the 1860 Swedish Legislation on Religion) (Skellefteå: Artos).

Horwitz, M.J. (1982), 'The History of the Public/Private Distinction', *University of Pennsylvania Law Review*, vol. 130, 1423–1428.

Kekkonen, J. (ed.), *Norden, rätten, historia: Festskrift till Lars Björne* (Helsinko: Suomen lakimiesyhdistyd).

Modéer, K.Å. (1983), *God affär' eller 'Brottslig gärning': Om tillkomsten av 1901 års lag om ocker* (Norstedt Stockholm: Festskrift till Hans Thornstedt), 519–555.

Modéer, K.Å (2004), 'Östersjöområdets rättsliga kartor – rättskulturella konstruktioner i förändring', in Kekkonen (ed.), 193–205.

Modéer, K.Å. (2009), 'Det historiska argumentet i senmodern rättslig diskurs', *Svensk Juristtidning*, vol. 94, 340–352.

Modéer, K.Å. (2010), 'The Long Way towards Traditional Autonomy. The Swedish Church and the Law 1968–2008', in Christoffersen, L., Modéer, K.Å. and Andersen, S. (eds), 81–88.

Petersen, H. and Modéer, K.Å. (2009), *Believing in Norway, Beliefs in Norway: A 'Humanitarian Great Power' under Globalization* (Norwegian Centre for Human Rights), Report 3.
Ratzinger, J. Cardinal (1991), *Wendezeit für Europa? Diagnosen und Prognosen zur Lage von Kirche und Welt* (Freiburg: Johannes Verlag).
Risberg, S. and Salonen, K. (2008), *Auctoritate papae: The Church Province of Uppsala in the Apostolic Penitentiary 1410–1526* (Stockholm: National Archives of Sweden).
Scalia, A. and Gutmann, A. (eds) (1997), *A Matter of Interpretation: Federal Courts and the Law* (Princeton: Princeton University Press).
Selander, S.Å. (1993), *Undervisa i religionskunskap* (Lund: Studentlitteratur).
Taylor, K.F. (1993), *In the Theatre of Criminal Justice: The Palais de Justice in Second Empire Paris* (Princeton: Princeton University Press).

Chapter 3

Socio-Historical Perspectives on the Public and the Private Spheres[1]

Adam Seligman

Introduction

This chapter aims to broaden the perspectives used to analyse the public and private spheres with the help of sociological and historical perspectives on the meaning of privateness and publicness and the relations between them. It begins with the very diverse and sometimes opposing meanings and definitions attributed to these concepts. One example of this type of divergence can be found by comparing Hannah Arendt's conception of public and private with that of other philosophers and social theorists. For Arendt, the very distinction between public and private began to disappear in modernity with the 'rise of the social', a concept which in her usage subsumes the very distinction that had previously existed (in Antiquity for example) between public and private realms. This very compelling account stands however in contradiction to that of most other theorists, from Karl Marx and Benjamin Constant, down to Jurgen Habermas, all of whom see in the eighteenth century and the beginnings of modern capitalist culture the very origins or emergence of that distinction between public and private realms whose demise Arendt posits in the selfsame period (Arendt 1958: 22–78).

Similarly, Norberto Bobbio's now classic essay on "Public and Private: the Great Dichotomy" can be looked at, in which he classifies these concepts in relational terms of inequality vs. equality and of relations between the parts and the whole and relations among parts (Bobbio 1989: 1–21). His scheme would appear something like this:

Public	***Private***
unequal	equal
relations between parts and whole	relation between parts
God	brothers
state	kin
family	friends
citizens	enemies

1 A much shorter and schematic version of this chapter appeared in Seligman (1998).

Here of course are the beginnings of a fascinating cross-cutting categorization, but one laden with problems as soon as the field of political philosophy is left behind and the minutiae of daily life considered. Thus, relations between God and man, while certainly unequal and pertaining to the relations of the part to the whole, are also, often, defined within the privacy of conscience and in many circumstances the privacy of a home or other secluded space (at least since the Protestant Reformation). So too the family has, in modernity, entered into the private realm as, for that matter, has the state penetrated into the regulation of private lives and agendas. On the other side of the ledger, the relations between brothers are characterized by equality only in some cultures and not in others (primogeniture being a good example of the inequality reigning between brothers). In tribal societies kin systems may be ordered according to principles of equality or hierarchy and one does not take analytic preference over the other. Friendship, too, as an informal relation between equals is a most modern phenomenon with vast variations across cultures and historical periods. What does remain of Bobbio's definitions is the crucial and thought-provoking identification of the public with the relation between parts and whole, and the private with the relations between the parts. It is a distinction that should be kept in mind as we view the conflicts in Europe today over religious issues pertaining to minority religions especially Islam and the claims put forward by European Muslim citizens for a public presence, symbolic and otherwise, to various forms of observance. Such conflict would seem to substantiate Bobbio's claim and his essay should, in turn, help to focus thinking on the nature of the public, its parts and the relation between them in contemporary Europe – a task which is no doubt a challenge to many and to which this chapter shall return.

This chapter will claim that, since the seventeenth century, our very ideas of the private realm have been defined by our moral valuation of the individual. In fact, the moral or ethical elevation of the private over the public (as that arena where virtue, morality and conscience are realized) emerged concomitantly with the growing, Western realization of individual agency and autonomy. Needless to add, these conceptions stand at the core of Western liberalism as it developed from the writings of Hobbes and Locke in the seventeenth century.

Thus it can be noted at the outset that the very construction of that eighteenth-century 'publicness' that was theoretically articulated by Habermas and admirably charted by numerous historians had its complement in the very definition and isolation of the private as a realm of value (Aries 1962; Aries and Duby 1987–1991; Chartier 1991; Maza 1993). Not surprisingly both realms can be seen as defining themselves concomitantly and in mutual recognition. Ultimately, this chapter argues, both rested on the newly emergent *idea* of the individual and of individual agency as coming to exist beyond the normative expectations of, what is termed, social status and role.

Necessary for this development was a reformulation of the reigning terms of sociability (and of the laws governing such sociability). Indeed, and as Aries himself has noted, 'the entire history of private life comes down to a change in the forms of sociability' (Aries and Duby 1987 1991: 9). Inherent to this eighteenth-century change in the terms of sociability was the gradual transformation of the meaning of the private from that which was hidden and withdrawn (either on the cause of shame or the *imperia arcana* of royal justice for example) to what pertains only to the individual. To be sure both meanings continue to be used today, often contributing too much confusion in our understanding of the phenomena.

The Private, the Individual and the Role of Complexity

The emergence of a private sphere as identified with the morally autonomous individual arose, this author would argue, very much as a 'Durkheimian' social fact out of the growth and proliferation of social roles that came to characterize polities and societies in Western Europe. Analytically, this process involved the multiplicity of roles and so the unique configuration of role sets that becomes every 'individual identity'. Connected to this was the developing propensity to negotiate the contents and expectations involved in each role. These developments allowed the crucial possibility to judge one role (or role set) from the perspective of another (or others). As the person became a vector of more and more roles the very idea of the individual became a means to specify the unique aggregation of roles that each social actor bears. This very multiplicity of roles carries with it the potential for mediating and blurring the boundaries between roles in a singular manner and for the progress of an almost infinite self-reflexivity as each role can become the Archimedean point from which others can be judged, negated, modified, and so on. Facilitating this process is the fact that as roles and role sets proliferate within social formations the boundaries between the roles become more permeable and the moves from one to the other less structured by formal (ritualized) criteria. There is then not only more negotiability in the definition of each role but, crucially, in the moves from one to the other. This too became a process that each social actor negotiates alone, in private, rather than within the confines of normative group-held injunctions.

While some notion of the individual and of the private sphere as separate from the group exists in all societies known, there is little doubt that the type of individualism (which sees in the individual the locus of the moral and political orders, the fount of agency and intentionality, a transcendental subject invested with transcendent rights) associated with Western Europe is a relatively unique phenomenon. It is moreover one which came to invest the private sphere with a unique and moral priority.

While the uniqueness of this phenomenon has been studied by scholars ranging from Max Weber and Marcel Mauss down to contemporaries such as Charles Taylor and, in a very different mode, Louis Dumont, the above-noted perspectives on role open some imposing questions for existing traditions and understanding of Western individualism and its concomitant ideas of the private sphere as realm of value (Weber 1958, 1975: 1204; Mauss 1985: 1–25; Taylor 1989; Dumont 1986).

For, and to a great extent, these traditions see Western individualism as rooted, in one form or another, in the soteriological assumptions of Christian belief. That is to say, the very positing of a monotheistic creator God and – especially with Christendom – the personal relation of the 'individual' to the Godhead are, to a large extent, the foundation of our notions of individualism and of the transcendent subject. This chapter will explore the notion that it is not in Christianity per se, that is in its soteriological doctrines, that the origin of modern individualism is to be found, but rather in the specific differentiation, division and definition of roles that it brought to the cultural, political, social and economic arenas that is perhaps at the core of our own understanding of the individual (on this connection see Laub Coser 1991).

For arguments sake this chapter will consider only three historical periods that have, in the past, been seen as critical points in the development of Western ideas of the individual: Late Antiquity, the Renaissance, the Protestant Reformation. All have been identified with the development of Christian individualism through the refinement of Christian salvational doctrines, but also, as claimed here, of changing forms of group affiliation (Troeltsch 1960: 39–89).

Late Antiquity

Late Antiquity was the period of the emergence of Christianity as a world-historical religion with its own salvational dogma of grace – it was also the period of the emergence of a whole new set of roles and role definitions identified with Christianity (as for example in the transformation of sexual relations from a public matter to the private concern of the individuals) (Brown 1988). This is, after all, the central dynamic behind the replacement of kinship identities with membership in a sacramental community (on these perspectives see Brown 1978; Wolin 1960). Similarly, the positing of the City of God provided a most central counterfactual from which the City of Man could be judged, negated or affirmed. It injected a dimension between social reality and ontological reality (through of course the redefinition of the later in terms of transcendence) that gave to the former a lability and negotiability not hitherto existent (Dumont 1986).

The development of early Christianity saw, after all, the construction of a new 'moral community' of believers differentiated from the societies in which they lived and united by bonds of exclusive communal fellowship (Wolin 1960: 95–140; Cochrane 1957; Brown 1978: 56–77). These groups of early Christians, scattered across the Roman Empire, were united by social ties of a charismatic nature. Cutting across existing solidarities of kith and kin, the message of the early Church was one of a social solidarity rooted only in a shared experience of the sacred. In the words of St Paul: 'There is neither Jew nor Greek, there is neither bond nor free, there is neither male nor female: for ye are all one in Christ Jesus'.

Early Christianity thus presented an alternative locus of social identity and of community that was rooted in the experience of grace. The bond established between communal members was one rooted not in primordial givens, but in an immediate connection to the fount of transcendental order. The new locus of communal solidarity and of the moral order was epitomized in St Paul's rejection of the 'ascriptive confines of Jewish ethical monotheism' (Schluchter 1985: 152). This redefinition of the terms of community in the experience of grace and a direct relation to the source of cosmic order and salvation (and not in legal prescriptions or primordial networks) allows to speak of the early Christian ties of community as essentially a reformulation of existing roles and role definitions within the social world of Late Antiquity.

These new roles were those of members of a new corporate body (the Church) which subjected the *nova creatura* to the new laws of regenerate man. What this new *congregatio fidelium* implied however was precisely a transformation of the terms of the *fidelis* 'now subjected as far as his social and public life went, to the law as it was given to him, not the law as it was made by him. The consequences of the incorporation was that his *fidelitas*, his faithfulness, consisted precisely in his obeying the law of those who were instituted over him by divinity' (Ullmann 1966: 9). The very absorption of the individual in and by the new corporation of the Church was thus a transformation of those social bonds, roles and role expectations that had hitherto defined the social world.

The Renaissance of the Twelfth Century

A similar emergence of role differentiation and the development of individual identities, especially in the refinement of ideas of conscience and agency characterized the Renaissance of the twelfth century (Bynum 1980; Southern 1953: 1–17). The very differentiation of corporate bodies engendered by the papal revolution together with the development of myriad new roles as group identities proliferated in this era were all central to the development of ideas of an inner life and of intentionality (as opposed to just action) as an aspect of the individual agency and morality. In fact, this period was characterized not solely by the growth of different group identities (of which the new corporate identity of the clergy was by far the most important) and by the increase in horizontal mobility as the immediate family differentiated itself from wider kin groups – but by the very recognition of different orders of knights, clerics, priests, married men and women, widows, virgins, soldiers, merchants, peasants, and craftsmen – each with their different talents, institutions and roles in society (central here was the growth of different religious orders). All these developed concomitantly with the growth of individual and private modes of self-expression through the revival of the religious tradition of autobiography, confessional literature, courtly love poetry as well as the emergence of legal differentiation, of a legal corpus no longer bounded by custom or Germanic tribal ideas of honour and fate (Brown 1982: 302–303). This later development stressed the legitimacy of enacted, objective law over the consensual mould of tradition and custom. In so doing the new legal system of the twelfth century set up a generalized conceptual legal system that broke with existing group (clan and household) loyalties and posited new corporate definitions of what were, essentially, new social roles and role expectations (Berman 1983: 103, 145, 149–151).

Of crucial sociological importance is the fact that these developments took place against a backdrop of increasing structural differentiation. Central to this increasing complexity of the system were:

1. the separation of the nobility from the rest of society through its increasing tendency to be defined in hereditary terms;
2. the growth of commerce and of cities with the vast degree of internal differentiation among the different urban orders that characterized their growth;
3. the post-Gregorian Church which not only freed Episcopal elections (and elites) from political impingement but 'created a clergy that was set apart much more radically than before from ordinary Christians' (Bynum 1982: 11).

In fact, and as Caroline Bynum has noted, the Gregorian Reform not only separated the clergy from the laity (most especially through the campaign for clerical celibacy) but led to a vast proliferation of new institutional (and sometimes only semi-institutional) religious orders or roles – most formidably in the development of the friars (for men) and in the creation of new roles for women, such as the Beguine (Bynum 1982: 15).

Note then the very structural correlation between the development of individual identities together with the ever-growing complexity of social organization and its roles and role expectations. The same period which sees the 'fundamental religious drama' relocated into the self is the period that sees a proliferation of religious orders, vocations, 'callings' and 'lives'. The same period that saw a growing literature of private passion and theories of love, of 'the enlargement of the opportunities of privacy, in the renewed study of the theory of friendship, of conscience and of ethics' is also a period marked by a greater social differentiation, complexity and distinction in the forms of social life (Southern 1953: 221).

Transformations of the Protestant Reformation

The importance of the Protestant Reformation, especially of its sectarian variants, in the developing idea of conscience is so well studied as to need almost no explication. But the Reformation also saw the radical, painful, often violent breaking of established group identities and the re-establishment of new group solidarities and new role definitions (through, among Puritans for example, the whole covenantal theology) (Hunt 1985; Little 1984; Collinson 1989; Haller 1972; Zakai 1992).

The new bonds forged under sectarian Protestantism were, in essence, a recasting of the bonds of 'community' as a shared tradition, into new bonds of 'communality'. These bonds of a new 'communion', in Herman Schmalenbach's sense, were to be the basis of the new communities forged by religious virtuosi throughout European societies (Schmalenbach 1961: 331–347). The social restructuring of the bonds of communality was, in essence, part of the restructuring effected by the Reformation in general, but specifically in ascetic Protestantism, of the relation between the Church and the world. Within medieval Catholic Europe, the only 'life-calling' legitimized in sacred terms was that of the monastic orders. As noted by Weber and others, the importance of the Reformation lay precisely in its 'endowment of secular life with a new order of religious life as a sphere of "Christian opportunity"' (Parsons 1967: 51). It was thus only with the Reformation that secular callings were given a religious legitimation and were perceived as possible paths to salvation.

Famously, within the Puritan context, these religious orientations took a particularly intense expression.[2] On the level of social organization, the covenanting of communicants implied primarily a break with existing solidarities of both Church and neighbourhood. Covenanting together, the Puritans also covenanted themselves off from the major existing institutional loci of solidarity – the Church, village or parish – and so of those social identities which prevailed in English society. The withdrawal from existing loyalties both national and ecclesiastical to the Church of England and the growth of a new set of commitments, loyalties and identities to the individuals covenanted together in pursuit of a new spiritual and moral life was a fundamental element in the construction of new loci of social life and individual identity.[3]

As Puritan communities underwent a process of institutionalization in the late seventeenth and early eighteenth centuries the privileging of conscience and individual agency in the definition of the moral life (i.e. as an attribute of virtue) became a constitutive component of many such communities. Perhaps more than anyone else, Margaret Jacob has developed this argument in respect to English Unitarians, Dutch Collegians and the increasingly secular French Freemasonry. The central tenet of these groups' religiosity was, as Andrew Fix has described it, that they 'rejected the authority of ecclesiastical institutions and based religious life on the individual believer and his inner ability to know religious truth' (Fix 1991: 118). By the second half of the seventeenth century this conception, wedded

2 Much has been written on the institutional implications of Puritan religiosity. For some of the more relevant analyses see Waltzer (1963: 59–90); Mosse (1952: 67–80); Mosse (1954: 109–125); Mosse (1957); George, C. and George, K. (1968: 77–104); George, C.H. (1958: 351–366); Lamont (1969: 133–146); Brauer (1954: 99–108); Marshall (1980).

3 Zakai (1986: 14). Impressive discussions of this process whereby new loci of community were formed within the overall Puritan movement and its separatist tradition can be found in Collinson (1975); Watts (1978: 14–26); Tolmie (1977); Haller (1972). The tension formed within society by the growth of Puritanism is amply attested to in such satires as 'Zeal-of-the-land-Busy' in Ben Jonson's *Bartlwlomew Fayre* (1964). Other aspects of the Puritan break with established authority can be found in New (1964).

to a belief in the workings of natural reason in the apprehension of truth, led to an emergent belief in the 'principle of individual conscience' (Fix 1991: 119).

This new ethical being emerged as the universal subject who, qua individual, became the new locus of solidarity, orientated around new definitions of moral autonomy and economic agency.

Finally, and beyond Christian civilization proper, eighteenth-century bourgeois society can be looked at, with its doctrines of civility and moral individualism – those beliefs given philosophical form by Kant and embedded within sociological understanding by Durkheim. Here, the idea of the individual sheds its religious garb and is no longer constituted by relations with the transcendent but achieves its meaning in the autonomy of the individual conscience. Here too, contemporary social thinkers, from Adam Ferguson in the eighteenth century to Benjamin Constant and Alexis de Tocqueville in the nineteenth, all noted the importance of what is termed role differentiation to the making of bourgeois culture.

In all periods a number of similar, related and central developments can be witnessed:

1. the breaking of existing group bonds and their replacement with new ones – including new roles and new definitions of existing roles;
2. the move from fewer roles to more roles and more complex and multitudinous role sets and status sets;
3. the move from more rigid, publicly sanctioned modes of role transition (and definitions) to ones less anchored in public constraints (tribal, civic, fraternal and, later, confessional boundaries between roles are replaced by actor orientated ones) (Becker 1994). In all the idea of the individual emerged slowly as did the idea of a private sphere. Both would of course only begin to be fully articulated in the eighteenth century when, not surprisingly, the tension between them and more public, legally sanctioned modes of interaction and expression became apparent.
4. It was to a great extent some awareness of the above developments (if phrased in different terms) that led the eighteenth-century moral philosophers to posit a personal or private sphere of friendship and trust (as opposed to interest) as one of the unalterable benefits of 'commercial' (what can be termed 'modern') society (Silver 1997). In so doing they were in effect noting those changing terms of sociability remarked upon above. For in pre-modern and feudal society bonds of personal affinity were rooted in codes of status and honour while in court societies they were tied to a personalized politics of court status. Freed from the constraints of calculation and interest the private sphere became, in the eighteenth century, a realm where the personal nature of individual relations (i.e. friendship) was freed from concerns of social station. Just as the idea of the morally autonomous individual emerged through the myriad of new and impersonal role relations in the public sphere so did the very idea of the private, which

came to be conceived as a realm of trust and mutuality existent apart from the legally defined relations of the public sphere.

Conclusion

Cultural values, this chapter has attempted to claim, result from structural conditions, no less than from religious or ideological orientations and it is well to remember this when reflecting on such issues as the place of European Islam or religion in the public sphere of European cities in the twenty-first century. The 'truths' of our civilizational endeavour, enshrining the individual and the private as the arena of virtue and conscience as the fount of moral obligation, are the product of a long process of structural differentiation and not simply of any essential Christian or European consciousness or civilizational message. This should be born in mind when contemplating the compatibility (or lack thereof) of different values, cultures and orientations with those of contemporary Europe.

It is also of extreme relevance to the distinction made by Norberto Bobbio between relations between parts (private) and between the parts and the whole (public). For while Bobbio's distinction holds for pre-modern and classical modern culture where the public realm was one which included the relation between different individual identities (and structures or institutions) and the representative social whole – the very logic of modernity, resting on the idea of the individual as moral absolute, fundamentally transforms this set of relations. With the terms of representation defined by the autonomous, rights-bearing individual, the representation of the public sphere (and so of relations between public and private) becomes increasingly problematic. This problem is essentially that noted by Luhmann of the part (the private/individual) supporting the whole (the public/collective) (Luhmann 1987: 102). With the realm of value relegated to the sphere of the private it becomes increasingly difficult to represent the collective whole, the realm of the public. However, and contrariwise, such a radically constituted private cannot support itself either, cannot, in fact, represent itself.

The sociological consequences of this situation are of great importance to understanding the current and reigning confusion in matters pertaining to the public and the private. One such confusion is the phenomenon of projecting the private into the public realm as an attribute of representation. The other is the re-imposition of public definitions onto the private realm. This can be seen continually enacted in Europe today over issues of religion: whether in the use of private behaviour to adjudicate rights to citizenship (one's public role) or in the circumscription of private religious behaviour in the name of a public good.[4] This

4 On private behaviour, such as shopping, as indice of citizenship see the [French] Council of State Decisions of the Council of State Litigation Section, united 2nd and 7th sub-sections Hearing of May 26, 2008 Read June 27, 2008 No. 286798. See also, Emon (forthcoming).

dual moment being in a sense the core dynamic of what Arendt referred to as the 'rise of the social' and the loss of all distinction between public and private realms (Arendt 1958: 38–49). Our challenge is to reconceptualize the problem in such a manner as will allow for both representation and inclusion of all in a shared space of public difference.

References

Arendt, H. (1958), *The Human Condition* (Chicago: University of Chicago Press).
Aries, P. (1962), *Centuries of Childhood* (New York: Random House).
Aries, P. and Duby, G. (eds) (1987–1991), *A History of Private Life*, vols 1–5 (Cambridge, MA: Harvard University Press).
Becker, M. (1994), *The Emergence of Civil Society in the Eighteenth Century* (Bloomington: Indiana University Press).
Berman, H. (1983), *Law and Revolution* (Cambridge, MA: Harvard University Press).
Bobbio, N. (1989), *Democracy and Dictatorship* (Minneapolis: University of Minnesota Press).
Brauer, J. (1954), 'The Nature of English Puritanism: Three Interpretations', *Church History*, 23, 99–108.
Brown, P. (1978), *The Making of Late Antiquity* (Cambridge, MA: Belknap Press).
Brown, P. (1982), *Society and the Holy in Late Antiquity* (Berkeley: University of California Press).
Brown, P. (1988), *The Body and Society: Men, Women and Sexual Renunciation in Early Christianity* (New York: Columbia University Press).
Bynum, C. (1980), 'Did the Twelfth Century Discover the Individual?', *Journal of Ecclesiastical History*, 3:31, 1–17.
Bynum, C. (1982), *Jesus as Mother: Studies in the Spirituality of the High Middle Ages* (Berkeley: University of California Press).
Carrithers, M., Lukes, S. et al. (eds) (1985), *The Category of the Person* (Cambridge: Cambridge University Press).
Chartier, R. (1991), *The Cultural Origins of the French Revolution* (Durham, NC: Duke University Press).
Cochrane, C. (1957), *Christianity and Classical Culture* (New York: Oxford University Press).
Cole, C. and Moody, M. (eds) (1975), *The Dissenting Tradition* (Athens: Ohio University Press).
Collinson, P. (1975) 'Towards a Broader Understanding of the Early Dissenting Tradition', in Cole, C. and Moody, M. (eds), 3–38.
Collinson, P. (1989), *The Puritan Character: Polemics and Polarities in Early Seventeenth Century Culture* (Los Angeles: William Andrews Clark Memorial Library).

Dumont, L. (1986), *Essays on Individualism: Modern Ideology in Anthropological Perspective* (Chicago: University of Chicago Press).
Emon, A. (2012), *Religious Pluralism & Islamic Law: Dhimmis and Others in the Empire of Law* (Oxford: Oxford University Press).
Fix, A. (1991), *Prophecy and Reason: The Dutch Collegians in the Early Enlightenment* (Princeton: Princeton University Press).
George, C.H. (1958), 'Protestantism and Capitalism in pre-Revolutionary England', *Church History*, 27, 351–366.
George, C. and George, K. (1968), 'Puritanism as History and Historiography', *Past and Present*, 41, 77–104.
Haller, W. (1972), *The Rise of Puritanism* (Philadelphia: University of Pennsylvania Press).
Hunt, W. (1985), *The Puritan Movement: The Coming of Revolution in an English Country* (Cambridge, MA: Harvard University Press).
Jonson, B. (1964), *Bartlwlomew Fayre* (London: Cass).
Lamont, W. (1969), 'Puritanism, History and Historiography', *Past and Present*, 44, 133–146.
Laub Coser, R. (1991), *In Defense of Modernity: Role Complexity and Individual Autonomy* (Stanford: Stanford University Press).
Little, D. (1984), *Religion, Order and Law: A Study of Pre-Revolutionary England* (Chicago: University of Chicago Press).
Luhmann, N. (1987), 'The Representation of Society Within Society', *Current Sociology*, 35, 101–106.
Marshall, G. (1980), *Presbyters and Profits: Calvinism and the Development of Capitalism in Scotland 1560–1707* (Oxford: Clarendon Press).
Mauss, M. (1985), 'A Category of the Human Mind: The Notion of the Person, the Notion of Self', in Carrithers, M. et al. (eds), 1–25.
Maza, S. (1993), *Private Lives and Public Affairs: the Causes Célèbres of Pre-revolutionary France* (Berkeley: University of California Press).
Mosse, G. (1952), 'Puritanism and Reasons of State in Old and New England', *William and Mary Quarterly*, 9, 67–80.
Mosse, G. (1954), 'Puritan Political Thought and the 'Cases of Conscience', *Church History*, 23, 109–125.
Mosse, G. (1957), *The Holy Pretense: Christianity and Reasons of State from William Perkins to John Winthrop* (Oxford: Basil Blackwell).
New, J.P. (1964), *Anglican and Puritan: The Basis of their Opposition 1558–1648* (Stanford: Stanford University Press).
Parsons, T., Shils, E., Naegele, K. and Pitts, J. (eds) (1961), *Theories of Society* (New York: The Free Press).
Parsons, T. (1967), 'Christianity and Modem Industrial Society', in Tiryakian, E. (ed.), 33–70.
Schluchter, W. (1985), *The Rise of Western Rationalism* (Berkeley: University of California Press).

Schmalenbach, H.S. (1961), 'The Sociological Category of Communion', in Parsons, T. et al. (eds).

Seligman, A. (1998), 'Between Public and Private: Towards a Sociology of Civil Society', *Society*, 35:3, 28–36.

Silver, A. (1997), 'Two Different Sorts of Commerce – Friendship and Strangership in Civil Society', in Weintraub, J. and Kumar, K. (eds), 43–74.

Southern, R.W. (1953), *The Making of the Middle Ages* (London: Hutchinson).

Taylor, C. (1989), *Sources of the Self* (Cambridge, MA: Harvard University Press).

Tiryakian, E. (ed.), *Sociological Theory, Values and Sociocultural Change* (New York: Harper & Row).

Tolmie, M. (1977), *Triumph of the Saints* (Cambridge: Cambridge University Press).

Troeltsch, E. (1960), *The Social Teachings of the Christian Churches*, vol. 1 (New York: Harper & Row).

Ullmann, W. (1966), *The Individual and Society in the Middle Ages* (Baltimore: Johns Hopkins University Press).

Waltzer, M. (1963), 'Puritanism as a Revolutionary Ideology', *History and Theory*, 3, 59–90.

Watts, M. (1978), *The Dissenters* (Oxford: Oxford University Press).

Weber, M. (1958), *The Protestant Ethic and the Spirit of Capitalism* (New York: Scribners).

Weber, M. (1975), *Economy and Society* (Berkeley: University of California Press).

Weintraub, J. and Kumar, K. (eds), *Public and Private in Thought and Practice* (Chicago: Chicago University Press).

Wolin, S. (1960), *Politics and Vision* (Boston: Little Brown and Company).

Zakai, A. (1986), 'The Gospel of Reformation, the Origins of the Great Puritan Migration', *Journal of Ecclesiastical History*, 37, 14.

Zakai, A. (1992), *Exile and Kingdom* (Cambridge: Cambridge University Press).

Chapter 4
The 'Public–Private' Divide on Drift: What, if Any, is its Importance for Analysing Limits of Associational Religious Freedoms?

Veit Bader

Introduction

Both the appropriate 'division of private and public spheres' and the legitimate or illegitimate intervention by the state in 'private' religious associations and organizations belong to the most hotly contested issues in recent theory and legal and political practice, particularly in Europe (Foner and Alba 2008). The aim of this chapter is twofold: first, to provide some conceptual, theoretical and empirical clarifications of 'private', 'public' and its shifting divide from a sociological point of view, including some working definitions. Secondly, to provide some minimalist moral and legal principles and recommendations in order to discuss whether and, if so, what kinds of intervention in religious associations/organizations are compatible with the guarantee of associational religious freedoms from the perspective of the political theory of liberal-democratic constitutionalism. The special claim of this chapter is that, in discussing and deciding these issues, the varying and shifting *legal status* of these associations and organizations *as either 'private' or 'public'* or something in-between is not irrelevant but clearly *not* exclusively *decisive*.

Public Spheres or Spaces and the 'Public–Private Divide': Some Critical Reflections and Conceptual Clarifications

Not surprisingly, even the basic concepts of public-sphere research are not only contested, as all basic concepts are, but highly metaphorical and fuzzy. The chapter begins with some comments and suggestions on *spheres/spaces* (or comparable notions meant to supplement or replace them) in which different kinds of *publics* then do different things.

Networks of Public Communication: Public Networks, Spheres, Fields, Public Spaces, Arenas, Fora, Agoras, Places or Localities?

The title of this section indicates a broad variety of terms, concepts or metaphors used in theory and public talk, and there is not even a minimal consensus with regard to their meanings and connotations. In the diverging distinctions and definitions a broad range of *criteria* are used. Here, a preliminary list is followed by an attempt to give plausible working definitions. Some fairly general distinction between *publics* as specific actors and *public spheres* is needed. Starting with the latter, 'public spheres' can be used as a catch-all phrase for 'fields, networks, public spaces, public arenas, fora, agoras, places', to be distinguished in later.

Public spheres are *constituted*, most generally, by *communications* of a certain kind. The term communication is more appropriate than the often-used concept of 'interaction' because interactions require the physical presence of communicators. Most generally, public spheres are *networks of communication*. Communications can be understood very broadly as including *non-verbal* communications, or narrowly as *verbal* communications, more narrowly as *opinions* or even as a very specific and demanding type of communication: as *deliberations* or *discourses*. The following questions: *which types of communication, and on what?* shall be addressed in the following seven steps.[1]

First, these communications are *not specified by media and code*. Hence the 'public sphere' cannot be understood as a differentiated social system in Luhmann's sense, either related to the political system (as earlier by Luhmann 1971: 9, 27ff.) or as a 'medium' (1990: 174, 181ff.).

Second, *public* communications are distinct from *intimate*, from *secret*, and from *private* communications – all three in the sense of communications that are made/*declared to be* intimate, secret or private, because none of these properties is inherent in the 'nature' of the communication or its content. Normatively speaking, from the position of liberal-democratic constitutionalism (Bader 2010) the more *proper opposites* are not 'private' but 'intimate' and 'secret' (see also Peters 2007: 57; Luhmann 1990: 170): *secret* communications are not, or are not

1 The first section of this chapter is a brief summary of the detailed treatment in Bader (2008b).

meant to be or should not become public. The existence of 'publics' and claims to 'publicity' within 'private organizations' (such as capitalist corporations or Churches) already indicates that the classic liberal public/private dichotomy hides lots of publics and tries to keep lots of political or public issues (e.g. structural power-asymmetries) 'private', i.e. off the public/political agenda.[2] Yet the feminist slogan of the 1960s 'to politicize the private', while rightly criticizing that the private/public divide keeps patriarchal power-asymmetries within the family off the public and political agenda, ignores the important *distinction between 'private' and 'intimate'*.[3] More in general, the boundaries between the 'private' and the 'public' are socially defined or constructed, the boundary-drawing and -shifting is embedded in structural power-asymmetries and the actual use of all, not only symbolic, power resources. Traditionally speaking, boundary-drawing is an important part of the conflicting interests of relevant actors. The analysis of this boundary drawing and shifting is the task of social and historical sciences (including comparative history of law).[4] Yet any critical normative debate of the 'appropriate' boundaries between private and public has to also be aware of and sensitive to this fact, otherwise the definitions (e.g. the narrow 'liberal' ones) of the entrenched privileged classes, elites, and ascriptive or cultural majorities tend to be 'normalized' or 'naturalized'.

Third, *traditional concepts of 'public'* presuppose a very *narrow 'liberal' concept of public as 'not private'* but still are ambiguous with regard to the *scope* of the public: it may be conceived of (1) broadly as '*social but not political*': 'civil society' and civil society organizations, such as NGOs and Churches, can then be seen as 'public' instead of 'private spheres' and 'private institutions/ organizations'; or (2) more narrowly as *'political' but not reduced to 'the state'*: political parties then can be seen as public bodies and be subsumed to public law, as in many European Constitutions, and not as 'private organizations', as in the United States; or (3) it may coincide with the '*state*' or with *territorial polities*.[5]

2 See the traditional Marxist criticism of the private/public divide. See for the legal history of the shifting private/public divide: Modéer (Chapter 2, this volume), Gaudreault-DesBiens and Karazivan (Chapter 6, this volume), and Petersen (Chapter 7, this volume).

3 See Fraser (2007); Salvatore (2007); Pateman, Young, Cohen and many others for the feminist criticism of the private/public divide (see Kymlicka 2002: 102–165).

4 See Gaudreault-DesBiens and Karazivan (Chapter 6, this volume) for the role of Churches, early-modern states, radical secularist states and organizations, political parties, etc. in the shifting boundaries between 'private law' and 'public' or 'state law' in family law, labour law, social law in the common law and civil law traditions.

5 For these distinctions see Rawls (1993) (and criticism in Bader 2008a), Casanova (1994) and others. Silvio Ferrari started his 'deconstruction' of the public sphere with a fairly traditional twofold, private/public divide (see WP5 State of the Art Report). Then 'public institutions' are state institutions and one is unable to conceptualize and analyse the specific status of 'in-between' institutions such as non-governmental schools, hospitals (and organized religions or political parties): they have to be 'private' (private religious schools, private religious hospitals). The preferred term here, 'non-governmental', does not

These distinctions are traditionally indicated in terms of 'spheres' – of 'civil society', of 'political society', of the 'state' – but this does not elucidate much because it only reproduces the ambiguities of 'civil society'.

Fourth, the appropriate *core of public communications* are *problems of coordination and collective decision* (including non-decisions) in societies, in societal fields/systems, institutions, organizations, associations and communities, whether these are declared or treated by existing law as 'private' or 'public'. Public communications in this sense refer to:

1. *all stages of the policy cycle*: what is at stake? problems/issues (including issue-cycles); alternative problem-solutions; decision; implementation; and control;
2. *wherever these problems occur*: on all levels of polities, in all societal fields, specialized sub-systems; in organizations, institutions, encounters;
3. the *aim* of the relevant public communications (contested opinions, discourses) is to *reach common definitions of what is at stake (what is the problem) and how this problem should be solved or*, traditionally, the 'common good', the 'common interest' or 'common affairs' (Luhmann 1990: 179; Peters 2007; Fraser 2007: 20; Dewey 1927).[6] Wanting to participate or actually participating in public communication presupposes this orientation. Otherwise 'one does not care' (and hence does not participate) or 'one imposes' one's own preferences straightaway if one has the power to do so (one is not in need of participating in public talk). This *minimalist aim* should be clearly distinguished from the fashionable, very *demanding* and highly implausible aims of 'reaching consensus' under more or less idealized conditions.

take an implicit decision and allows to analyse when, where and why 'religious schools' are legally 'public' (as in England) or 'semi-public' (as in the Netherlands, '*bijzonder*') or 'private' (as in the United States, France, Italy, Germany) and what this actually does mean (see below). In Chapter 8 of this volume, the multi-spatial deconstruction is taken one step further by distinguishing between 'common space, political space and institutional space' (pp. 139–156). In this author's view, the 'common space' is not by definition a 'public space' but becomes so only if people do not just go to work or shopping but communicate on common concerns. The distinction between 'political space' and 'institutional space' does not cover the issue of non-state public institutions because the latter is still defined by coercive decision-making by state-institutions (pp. 149ff.). The public status of non-state institutions is eventually covered by the criterion of 'public service' (pp. 153ff.), which is part of an enlarged 'personal dimension' (functions of organizations or institutions, see pp. 152ff. for schools).

6 See Silvio Ferrari's working definition: 'Space where citizens exchange information and take decisions about affairs of *collective interest* in order to influence the policies that affect their lives' (my italics; WP5 RELIGARE, Brussels, 14 January 2011. 'Policies', however, are narrowed down – in his definition – to state-policies and participants to citizens (but see pp. 149ff. for a revised version).

Fifth, the *norms* that should govern public communication, from the perspective of liberal-democratic constitutionalism, are the general but minimalist *freedoms of political communication*: freedoms of speech and expression, of assembly, of demonstration, of association and organization.[7] Public communications are also served and constrained by minimalist *civic-democratic virtues* such as self-discipline, civility, moderation, toleration, mutuality, reciprocity, a minimalist sense of justice and, maybe, more demanding 'deliberative virtues' (see Bader 2007: 180ff.). 'Public institutions', 'public organizations' and 'public roles' in a more narrow sense are governed by more specific norms, belonging to the 'political' or 'legal' systems with specified media and codes or, in another language, constituting a specific 'sphere' (Bauböck 2007). Public spheres are *not coordinated by 'hierarchy'*. 'Publicity' is in a very specific sense *anarchic* or *informal*.[8] It is not 'herrschaftlich organisiert', it is in 'no one's hand', or it is 'out of control' (Habermas 1992a), but certainly not 'beyond power asymmetries'.[9]

Sixth, public communications/spheres are not only anarchic but also *not closed. They are more or less open*, characterized by different degrees of openness of access, containing more than one (individual or collective) actor. A certain minimal degree of empirical *inclusiveness* is a precondition of the existence of public spheres. From a democratic normative perspective, public spheres should 'be open to all with a stake in the outcome' (Fraser 2007: 20) or 'generally accessible' (WP5 State of the Art paper: 2) or, more modestly, to all relevant stakeholders because some public spheres (e.g. '*organisationsinterne Öffentlichkeit*' but also social/functional public spheres) require minimal thresholds for participation and, hence, a certain degree of closure.

Seventh, publicity and actual *publics* are composed of *active participants* (broadly understood as 'speakers') and of *passive participants* ('listeners', addressees', '*Publikum*') but also should allow and empirically allow for a more or less swift role change in this regard.

Finally, two more general remarks on the *ways and kinds of public communication* may be in order. *First, bottom up and/or top down communication?* Whether we like it or not, democratic communication is a two-way process in which *organizations and elites* (in all public arenas) play a vital role. There are good theoretical reasons why this is so and why it should be the case even under the 'ideal conditions' of *herrschaftsfreien Diskursen*: information, qualification,

7 See for a brief defence of these freedoms against a whole bunch of traditional limitations: Bader (2010).

8 See Silvio Ferrari's distinction between an 'informal public sphere' (street, Internet: debate) and an 'institutional public sphere' (court, parliament: decision) 2011 WP5 paper.

9 Bader (1993). In opposition to more emphatic 'deliberative democrats' such as Eriksen and Fossum a *minimalist and agonistic concept of democracy* is put forward (see Bader 2007: chapter 6). See for the role of contestation about issues in the formation of European public spheres: Vreese and Schmitt (2007: 5), Kohler-Koch and Larat (2007: 2).

practical knowledge and expertise.[10] Actually, '*individual voice is noise*' and individuals are grouped around issues and have to cooperate and organize around issues in order to surpass inevitable thresholds of selectivity.

Second, regarding *types of communication*, five explications are important.

1. Public communication is, as already said, clearly not restricted to speaking/listening and writing/reading or to verbal communication. It includes a variety of forms of non-violent collective action such as demonstrations and strikes, as well as violent collective action (against 'property' or 'captive audience', see Frankenberg and Rödel 1981: 333–335).
2. Communication does not require direct interaction but includes all forms and kinds of indirect or 'mediated' interaction.
3. Public spheres and 'communication' does not require 'actual' spaces but can – and increasingly does – take place in 'virtual spaces'.[11]
4. Communication is not restricted to 'rational' or 'reasonable' communication but includes (and normatively speaking should include) sentiments, emotions, symbolic communications (pictures, cartoons, songs, prayers).[12]
5. A more tricky and contested question is whether communication in public spheres empirically is, or normatively speaking has to be, 'integrated' or 'centred' or whether it is more or less de-centred and dis-integrated even from a democratic point of view (see Bader 2008b: 21–24).

Distinguishing and Defining Concepts

The terms *networks*[13] *and systems* have the considerable advantage of not implying spatial metaphors. The neutral and open concept of *networks of public communication* is preferred as a general term because 'systems' may uncritically presuppose too much 'systematicity'. Some spatial metaphors may, however, be unavoidable if space is used in the literal sense of 'locality': *public places* such as streets, meeting halls or buildings, arenas or meeting places (the original sense of forum, agora) where real people meet in real time in direct interactions (*direct public communications*). *Territorial* (political, legal, administrative) *borders* are also spatial in this sense. Yet they do not denote actual meeting localities but delimit boundaries of (legal or more contested: legitimate) public communications in terms of '*membership*' (non-members, e.g. non-citizens or non-residents, are

10 In addition, political communication is also a 'two level process' (Schmitt 2007: 12) with citizens/residents–elite communication 'at level one (in one's first language) and elite–elite communication at level two (in whatever language works best)' for the EU.

11 As is recently vividly demonstrated in protests and revolutions in the Arab world. See for the EU: Os and Jakowski (2007); Koopmans and Zimmermann (2007).

12 See Ferrari (Chapter 8, this volume, p. 150) referring to Calhoun and Cover.

13 See also Habermas (1992b: 360); 'a network', not an institution, an organization, a system; Esmark (2007: 333ff.).

partially or fully excluded as actors from participation in public communications). '*Public space(s)*' (as well as arena, fora, agora), however, are used both in the literal sense and in the metaphorical meaning indicating non-spatially limited 'social spaces' or 'fields' or 'public spheres' (or 'realms', 'areas') bound by other, non-spatial criteria. As such, they carry more or less welcome connotations resulting from their original meanings that have to be reflected upon: *'agora' and 'forum'* carry the image of talking/deliberating individual (originally: male) citizens; *'arena' and '(battle) fields'* go with *contest, agon, conflict, struggle*, and '*spheres*' is commonly associated with *harmony and consensus* that make disagreement, negotiation-cum-deliberation, contest, agon, conflict or struggle invisible. My proposal is to use *public places* only in the literal sense: public communication by way of *direct interaction* requires and takes place in public spaces. *Indirect public communication* requires media of communication allowing communication in the physical absence of speakers/listeners, even if speaking/listening are nearly synchronous (as in chat-rooms). The *boundaries* of direct interaction are more or less clearly visible: those present in localities where communication takes place. The boundaries of indirect or mediated public communication are fuzzier but can be clarified by network-terminology and network-analysis: *actual (and potential) networks* of public communications – whether synchronic or diachronic, whether in 'real' or in 'virtual space' – are constituted by *linkages amongst all actual (or potential) participants*.

I propose to use *societal fields instead of subsystems* because the latter language often overestimates the functional differentiation, particularly when it comes to institutions, organizations, roles and actions, and underestimates structural inequalities and conflicts.[14] The terms *'Public sphere' or public spheres* should rather be avoided because of the unwelcome connotations of harmony and consensus. They could better be called '*public arenas*' if one wants to highlight the contestational character of communications among all kinds of actors but particularly of collective actors, or '*fora*' if one wants to indicate the more deliberative (and often highly individualistic) character of communications.

Structural and Institutional Differentiation of Public Spheres in Europe

Public communications are *delineated by boundaries* that can be/are constructed by making use of *criteria* such as: *territorial-political* borders (public communications in polities on all levels), *functionally differentiated fields, institutions, organizations and associations* (membership), *belonging* to communities of practitioners, and *actual presence* in physical spaces/localities. Networks of public communication can be differentiated along these structural and institutional lines.

14 See, for criticism, Bader (2001: 141–148; 2007: 47ff.).

1. 'Internal public spheres' or 'internal publicity' (in a specific sense): '*organisations-interne Öffentlichkeit*' versus more '*general publicity*'. The boundaries of access and participation are defined by membership. In bigger organizations internal public communications are usually mediated by organization-specific media of communication.
2. *Group- or community-internal publicity* is constituted by public communications within 'communities' ('groups of practitioners' of all sorts, e.g. linguistic, ethno-cultural, religious, gender but also socio-cultural, occupational, professional, recreational, sports). The boundaries of access and participation are *informally* defined by 'belonging' (self-definition/identification and by being recognized by other practitioners as belonging). Stronger *communities* create their own organizations, their *arenas* (Haug 2008) and *media* of communication.
3. *Territorial-political public communication networks* are typically based on a specific combination of communal *belonging* (in the case of 'national public spheres': to an *ethno-religious nation*) and of formally defined *membership* (in this case: nationality as 'state-membership': *citizenship and residency/denizenship*). Similar combinations of *local*, more or less aggressively 'parochial' and 'anti-national' *communities* and *city-zenship* are characteristic for *local/municipal public 'spheres'*, for *regional ones* and for *national-minorities*. *Supra-state public communications*, on the other hand, presuppose much thinner and more 'cosmopolitan' belongings, and membership in supra-state polities (e.g. EU-citizenship and Third Country Nationals (TCNs)). 'Public spheres' in this territorial-political sense are, compared with '*organisationsinterner*' and with community-internal publicity, more open, less closed for non-members and 'outsiders' that do not feel they belong and are not perceived to belong but they are certainly not simply open (as is assumed when 'public' is defined by 'accessibility' (see Chapter 8, this volume, pp. 148–150; Bulgarian Religious Denomination Act 2006).
4. *Field-specific publicity* or 'functional'/sectoral public arenas are distinguished from each other by differentiated practices, e.g. of (sectorally highly differentiated) *material production* and of highly differentiated *service-provision* (such as education, care, sports, arts, science, religion). They usually contain many organizations and internal publicity (e.g. Churches, Faithbased Organisations (FBOs), religious political party) and media of communication but are much more encompassing. Access is not defined in terms of membership in field-specific organizations but broadly in terms of all those *stakeholders* that are directly involved in the respective practices: as producer/providers (both employers and workers) and as consumers/clients and their respective organizations, or more indirectly as relevantly affected stakeholders. Inside *institutions* that provide public services it is also clearly relevant to distinguish rules and practices for the different roles or functions which may require different

kinds of regulations: teachers/students; doctors/patients; care personnel/ clients (see Chapter 8, this volume, p. 152).

In addition to – and in combination with – these already institutionalized public arenas, we find *issue-specific networks of public communication*: old and, particularly, new issues in search of more appropriate public arenas and/or forcing existing arenas and institutions to cooperate in a new and more productive way. New issues – including the issue of urgent institutional reform – are raised by new collective actors (most prominently social movements and Social Movement Organisations (SMOs)) or by coalitions of old and new ones.[15]

Different Kinds of Publics

As already indicated, actual publics are composed of *active participants* ('speakers' broadly understood) and of *passive participants* ('listeners', addressees', 'audiences', '*Publikum*') but publics should allow at least some role change sometimes. Publics 'inhabit' or 'occupy' public arenas, and public arenas are, vice versa, created by publics. A public is, in a strict sense, not an actor. It lacks the capability to act that requires some minimal 'group-ness' and 'netness' (*soziale Organisiertheit*, Bader 1989: chapter 7) as well as spontaneous or informal leaders and, for continuous collective action also a certain degree of organization and leadership (from crowds to social movements, SMOs, movement entrepreneurs and media; and the respective group- or movement-internal publicity). Still, public opinion *empirically* has some influence or 'political efficacy', particularly as 'published' opinion, but this impact is massively reinforced if backed by powerful actors. *Normatively*, a certain minimal degree of political efficacy of the public is a conditio sine qua non of modern democracy (Fraser 2007).

Most distinctions of different kinds of publics refer to this power-dimension or the influence of publics in the political process in all its stages, either directly or indirectly:

- *general* versus *specific* publics;
- *unorganized* versus *organized* publics;
- *weak* or *strong* publics (Young, Eriksen et al.) or, related but not identical, *new* versus *institutionalized* publics.[16]

---

15 Clearly, these are analytical distinctions. Public arenas do not have quasi-natural borders. Actual public arenas are intersecting or overlapping, their borders can be crossed and formerly separated ones can be linked or aligned.

16 The degree of political efficacy of different kinds of publics can best be explained by a detailed discussion of the respective *mix of power- and mobilization-resources* possessed by the different actors (see Bader 2008b: section II.2).

Many Public Arenas, Many Publics and Actors, Many Levels

Table 4.1 Many, internally diverse, public arenas and publics in compound polities. Many, internally highly diverse European Public Arenas

Levels / Arenas	Local public spheres	Regional/ provincial public spheres	Member-state ('national') public spheres	European public spheres (EU + CoE + OSCE)
Political/ territorial pluralism	Neighbourhood, city councils, administrations, political parties, NGOs, media, etc.	Regional parliaments, administrations and jurisdictions; 'political' actors, media, etc.	Federal parliaments, administrations, jurisdictions; 'national' political actors	EUP, Council, Commission, ECJ, Committee of the Regions; CoE; ECtHR; OSCE; European 'political' actors and media
Social/ functional or sectoral pluralism	Firm, hospital, school, university; corporate governance; orga-nized 'stakeholders' (labour, capital, pro-fessional organiza-tions; others); media; (organized) religions	Regional chambers of industry, sectoral (neo-) corporatist councils; organized 'stakeholders' and their media	Federal neo-corporatist councils and the relevant stakeholders, media; 'selective cooperation between state and organized religions'	Economic and Social Council; EU Committees; relevant stakeholders and their media, etc. 'A Soul for Europe', Dialogue with EU President, etc.
Ascriptive minority pluralism	Local ethno/ religious communities, councils, organiza-tions, media, etc.	Regional minority institutions, councils, etc.	Federal institutions of ethno/religious or national minorities	EU ethno/ religious institutions; OSCE declarations, etc.
	Representation of territorially dispersed ascriptive minorities (such as immigrants, women, homosexuals, elderly) in different societal fields and at different levels; their organizations, leaders, communal media, etc.			

Table 4.1 is a simplified figure of political, social and minority *(institutional) pluralism* in the European multi-level polity, indicating the most relevant institutional arenas and relevant actors. It is the result of an attempt at the 'institutional anchoring' of public spheres on the basis of 'institutional polycentrism' (see Esmark 2007: 346ff.). In this logic, first and foremost, the *existing institutions create their own public arenas and publics*:

1. Multi-level Polity (MLP) and *territorially bounded institutions*, 'representation' and publics: from neighbourhoods to Europe, particularly to the EU; and the related *territorial-political public arenas* which are crowded by general but weak publics but also by more specific and stronger, highly diverse publics.
2. Multi-layered Governance (MLG): *social/functional or sectoral 'neo-corporatist' institutions ('societal structures' or governance structures)* and the related, segmented public arenas that are crowded by fairly strong but stratified publics.
3. *Minority* representation, institutions and publics (if any) in the cases of territorially concentrated, particularly '*national*' minorities (different degrees of institutional and political autonomy) and group-internal publicities, or in the cases of territorially non-concentrated minorities (e.g. women, homosexuals, elderly, ethno-religious immigrant and non-recognized linguistic minorities), their institutions and group-internal publicities.

On the basis of such a frame one could comparatively analyse the different degrees of openness and closure, of boundary-drawing, crossing and linking and discuss questions such as: which types of individual or collective actors are characteristic for the different kinds of publics and public arenas? What are their chances to influence public opinion and decision-making, to put new issues on the agendas, create new public spaces or to link existing ones? All this obviously depends on serious societal inequalities, their objective power- and their mobilization-resources, another complex story (Bader 2008b: sections II.2 and II.2). Here, the frame will be used to address only one issue: what, if anything, is the importance of the 'Private–Public Divide' for analysing and evaluating the tensions between individual and associational religious freedoms and with other rights and freedoms, particularly in the case of non-governmental religious schools.

The 'Shield of Privacy' and Religious Communities, Associations and Organizations. Contested Autonomy of Religious Schools

The '*private*', in opposition to the 'public', has traditionally been understood as relations, institutions, organizations or – spatially – places, spaces or spheres that are *protected from involuntary interventions by outsiders*, be they other individuals or a whole variety of collective actors (other 'private' organizations, all kinds of 'public organizations' including the state). In analogy to the twin development of 'absolute private property' and 'absolute state-sovereignty' (against involuntary interventions by other states), this non-intervention has been seen as an *absolute* and *completely unconditional stop-rule*: it is none of other people's business and others should not be legally or actually allowed to interfere in 'private affairs': in intimate relationships, sex relationships, friendships, families, in all kinds of private communications (from letters to all varieties of ICT-communications guaranteed by privacy), whatever people do or communicate under the condition that they do not harm others or neglect their same rights and freedoms. Nor should outside intervention be allowed in all kinds of institutionalized, organized, 'collective' private actors such as SMEs, big private corporations, all kinds of educational, care, cultural, artistic, social, political and religious associations, organizations and institutions, religious congregations, churches, temples, sanghas amongst them, whatever they do under the condition that they do not harm others or neglect the same rights and freedoms of others.

As with its twin, 'absolute' state-sovereignty,[17] the absoluteness of non-interference in 'private affairs' has always been a more or less effective myth from which reality departed more or less widely, for more or less morally and legally legitimate reasons. From a perspective of liberal-democratic constitutionalism the most important legitimate reasons are: conflicts with 'security, safety and *ordre publique*'; concerns with degrees of 'voluntariness' (free entry, free exit) and 'consent' in 'private affairs' and, particularly, with serious violations of basic rights; with serious internal inequalities and with serious structural domination (democratically absolutely illegitimate structures of authority, undemocratic decision-making procedures, etc.), especially inside organized 'collective private actors'. For a long time now, the 'shield of privacy', upheld by important associational or collective freedoms – not only 'religious freedoms' but also freedoms of 'businesses', of 'education', of 'political parties' – has become ever more conditional and does not and cannot any longer protect 'whatever they do'. A more or less dense web of detailed legal or conventional regulation of what they are not allowed to do can be seen (in family law, in labour law, in corporate law, in environmental law, in educational law, in criminal law, etc.). Hence, people are confronted both with legitimate concerns to safeguard privacy and with legitimate restrictions and interventions into 'private affairs'.

These conflicting concerns and principles have to be weighed and balanced and cannot be brought into a context-independent lexical hierarchy – such as 'privacy' is the ultimate value that trumps all others or 'autonomy' (see critically Bader 2011), 'democracy', 'human rights' are the ultimate values always overriding privacy. Instead, a reasonable balance depends on a whole variety of 'factors' such as: the types of minorities/groups (Bader 2007: 136ff.), the power-relations between groups, the relevant conflicting issues such as conflicts with minimal morality, with the core of modern criminal law, with more demanding liberal-democratic morality and non-discrimination and equal opportunity, with the core of modern state-enforced private personal law, as well as with issues of the practical and symbolic accommodation of private and public institutions and practices formed and impregnated by majority cultures and traditions. Here

17 See Hallebeek (2005: 175–180) for an excellent discussion of Church Asylum which, in early modernity, was increasingly constructed as a 'concession by the Emperor' and not as an autonomous 'competence of the Church'.

I have to bracket conflicts with minimal morality (where the 'shield of privacy' and religious legitimations of violations of basic needs and rights should be powerless, see Bader 2007: 148ff.), with modern private personal law (where there should be a wide range of legitimate accommodations (see Bader 2007: 190ff. and Bader 2009) and most of the softer cases and symbolic issues (Bader 2007: chapter 5). Instead, this chapter shall focus on the tensions between the protection of associational freedoms of non-governmental religious schools and legitimate concerns of public regulation and control.

Racist, sexist, genderist and all other ascriptive discriminations are now widely perceived as morally wrong and proscribed by international, constitutional and criminal law (*non-discrimination*). Yet it is also widely accepted that ascriptive exclusion and discrimination – however morally wrong – have to be legally tolerated in some cases, depending on the goals of associations (broadly understood) and the degree of voluntariness of membership (Bader 2007: 142ff., *associational autonomy*). This is not the place to discuss the tension between non-discrimination and associational autonomy in depth or to go into the exploding legal and philosophical literature. The following claims can be plausibly defended. With regard to the *kinds and goals of relations and associations* it is broadly accepted that intimate relationships should be treated differently to strictly private clubs, Churches and FBOs, profit organizations and political parties. Ascriptive discrimination and exclusion from *close interpersonal relations* (Warren 2001: 129) cannot be effectively prevented by law and seem also morally more legitimate. An inherent side effect of the shield of intimacy and privacy in this regard is the protection or toleration of ascriptive discrimination (but certainly not of violence or marital rape). Yet the shield of privacy loses its prima facie legitimacy the farther the goals and practices are removed from intimacy, as in *religious core-organizations*, *faith-based organizations* in education, healthcare and care for children, youngsters, elderly, handicapped, etc. In all these cases defining the organizations' goals and activities as 'private' does not close but instead opens the debate and the following general arguments are relevant:

1. Are the organizations religious, non-profit or profit organizations?
2. Are the ascriptive discriminations/exclusions explicitly connected to the core of beliefs and practices?
3. Are the activities/functions central or peripheral to faith?
4. Do they unduly disadvantage outsiders?
5. Do they protect minorities or majorities?[18]

In any case the burden of proof for exemptions from anti-discrimination laws and regulations and collective labour agreements should rest on the claimants and is

18 See Bader (2007: chapter 4). See RELIGARE WP4 (www.religareproject.eu/content/work-place) for research on law and jurisprudence in relevant European Countries and the ECJ, ECtHR.

fully open to public criticism and scrutiny. 'The farther one moves from religious core organisations and core activities, the weaker the shield of "Free Exercise" should be and the more legitimate the legal imposition of non-discrimination and equal opportunity legislation becomes. In addition, it is more legitimate that the standards and procedures of public scrutiny become more demanding' (Bader 2007: 148).

Public Funding? Does the 'Public Trust Theory' or the 'Private–Public Divide' Matter Empirically, Legally, Morally?

As we all know, educational systems vary widely with regard to the recognition and financing of religious schools, the mix of governmental and non-governmental schools and their relative 'market share', the freedom to shape the curriculum and to select teaching materials, to govern diversity in the school context, to recruit teachers and staff, and to select/admit pupils. This is not the place to map these differences. Instead, two issues are significant: first, in what minimal morality and liberal-democratic morality, minimally understood, requires from all different arrangements, and, second, whether the divergent and shifting 'private–public' distinctions help or hinder such a discussion.

The background assumptions are that all institutional arrangements and policies do have to deal with *tensions and trade-offs* between principles/rights: educational freedoms of parents and emerging freedoms of children; educational freedoms of schools and non-discrimination (of teachers, of pupils); educational freedoms and equal/adequate educational opportunities for all; educational freedoms and demanding liberal-democratic citizenship and virtues. These tensions have to be acknowledged in order to find reasonable, context-specific solutions but from the outset it should be clear that no one institutional and policy-model fits all countries or contexts. Instead of looking for 'the optimal' arrangement or 'best practices' we have to look for 'satisficing' solutions, i.e. minimally morally permissible versus impermissible solutions or, more demanding, better or worse solutions given these contextual constraints (Bader 2007: 263, 288ff.; see also Vogt 1997: 213ff.).

International human rights law, the ECHR and the ECtHR as well as most liberal-democratic constitutions and courts oblige states to permit *freedoms of education* in all their consequences for religious schools (Vermeulen 2004: 38; Glenn and Groof 2002a: 245ff.).

Yet it is an open, hotly debated issue whether they also oblige states to *fairly equal public funding. Minimal morality* may not require public funding of non-governmental religious schools but in all cases in which majority religious schools are recognized and publicly financed *equality before the law* requires a fair and even-handed treatment of all religious schools (Bader 2007: 160).

As a matter of fact, however, the overwhelming majority of states with liberal-democratic constitutions, one way or the other, *empirically* do publicly finance non-governmental religious schools. Only Greece, Bulgaria and most Swiss cantons still reject any and all public financing but even the United States and Italy, which did so until fairly recently, have now allowed some indirect financing. Bracketing the stunning complexity of existing systems of direct and indirect public financing as well as the lack of transparency, we can sketch a rough picture of the comparative overall amount of public money for non-governmental religious schools compared to governmental schools: some states (Austria, Belgium, the Netherlands, England and Wales, Ireland) cover virtually all costs (*full funding*); the Scandinavian countries (Denmark, Finland, Sweden) are characterized by large subsidization, and *partial funding* is known in many other countries as well (Australia, Germany, Hungary and France, Portugal, Spain, New Zealand (partly), and Iceland (contract funding); see briefly: Bader 2007: 58ff.).

As a consequence of this, one could conclude that public financing of religious schools is an '*emerging international legal norm*' (Glenn and Groof 2002: 578), expressed in most detail in the *Lüster Resolution* of March 1984 of the European Parliament representing 'the high-water mark, to date, in the international recognition of an *effective* right to education freedom, supported by its appropriate share of public resources'. 'Appropriate share' clearly does not require fully equal funding but is compatible with 'adequacy' standards.[19]

Only strict 'separationist secularists' condemn public financing as incompatible with *liberal morality* yet they should be honest enough to emphasize that their ideal differs widely from the actual and legal situation in the real world of 'liberal democracies' and, hence, raise the red flag of revolution. What follows is a brief summary of the arguments why *liberal democratic morality, in the real world*, includes a moral obligation to fairly equal public financing of religious schools which should be acknowledged also by egalitarian civic republicans who are usually so fiercely opposed to it, particularly in the United States. The argument is based on the conception of *differentiated morality* – minimalism, more demanding liberal and democratic moral standards wherever this is possible, non-infringement proviso (see Bader 2007: chapter 2.2)– and proceeds in seven consecutive steps.

1. Freedoms of education include *free establishment and running of religious schools* and does not allow enforcing or imposing a monopoly for governmental schools. This is why we all, and not only libertarians and pluralists, should be in favour of mixed or pluralist educational systems: neither a monopoly for governmental schools nor no governmental schools and no public financing as some libertarians propose.
2. If governments fund some non-governmental – including some religious – schools they have to treat all equally that live up to minimal standards.

19 The legal situation in the United States after Zelman is open: Galston (2004: 321ff.), Garnett (2004. 324); McConnell (2002: 120). This understanding of 'fairly equal funding' is compatible with new 'adequacy' standards increasingly used by US courts and does not require to fully equalize per-pupil expenditures across states and districts in governmental and non-governmental schools (see Liebman and Sabel 2003: 24ff.).

This is why all libertarians and liberals for reasons of *equal treatment and non-discrimination* are morally and legally obliged to defend fairly equal funding.

3. Private, including religious, schools *under ideal conditions of equal distribution of socio-economic resources and opportunities* may not require public funding, but structural economic, educational, residential inequalities require changes in the residential assignment-regimes of students in governmental schools and fairly equal funding of non-governmental schools in order to achieve more fair and equal educational chances for all *pupils*, independent of socio-economic 'status', parental education (economic, social, and cultural status [ESCS] Index in Pisa studies) and of all ascriptive categorizations instead of reproducing societal inequalities in the educational system. Only defenders of 'libertarian archipelagos' in education may be more or less immune to such arguments. This is the major reason why civic republicans, if they are seriously committed to *more substantive notions of equality*, should be in favour of fairly equal funding in the real world. In addition, a more substantive notion of equality morally requires more than equal funding and gives *preferential treatment* either to all schools directly (e.g. additional funds, teacher training) 'which make special effort to include pupils from minority, immigrant [insofar as they are structurally disadvantaged – author's explication], or low-income families, in the name of a "preferential option for the poor"' (Glenn and Groof 2002a: 246), or to enrolled students by way of a weighted voucher system, or through income dependent tax-grants for parents.[20]
4. Free choice for *parents* is a 'formal, empty, illusory', not an 'effective', right (Glenn and Groof 2002a: 247; 2002: 578), it is a 'dead' term without adequate public subsidies. If tuition fees are allowed and have to be paid, then there should be either income-corrections or grants.
5. If, and to the degree in which governmental schools cannot and do not live up to the principle of 'neutrality', at least in the considered opinion of parents/students who fear that governmental schools unduly promote – in content and practice of teaching – a specific secularist way of life, even defenders of *'strict neutrality' in the real world*, and obviously all proponents of *relational neutrality and fairness as evenhandedness* (or 'inclusive neutrality'; Chapter 8, this volume, p. 152) should be in favour of fairly equal funding.

20 Only Bulgaria, Greece, Iceland, Italy, Luxemburg, Portugal, Russia, Scotland and Switzerland do not (Glenn and Groof 2002a: chart 2 row 5). Since 1967 Ireland has had a system of preferential public funding (as a 'block grant') for the geographically dispersed Protestant population to maintain affordable education provisions paid to a committee representing Protestant fee-paying schools which has been declared 'unconstitutional' and cut off by the Minister for Education Batt O'Keeffe in 2008/2009 (see Honohan and Rougier 2011 for the story and the debates).

6. If, and to the degree in which governmental schools cannot or do not live up to the requirements of legitimate or reasonable *pluralism or cultural diversity* of all sorts in content and practice of teaching (see Bader 2007: 155–160), defenders of a more demanding 'ethos of pluralism' also should favour pluralist school regimes and fairly equal funding in order to realize more overall pluralism in education.
7. Lastly, if states depend considerably, as so many actually do, on religious schools to live up to their obligations to provide education for all (for whatever historical or recent reasons), i.e. if religious schools meaningfully *help to realize mandatory public services*, fairness requires that they should be equally publicly funded.

Public funding is and, obviously, should be conditional on living up to minimal standards. This is why all reasonable defenders of non-governmental schools should be in favour of *public regulation and control of all schools, including governmental and religious schools.*

Public Regulation and Control

Obviously, the *empirical variety of public regulation and control* of non-governmental religious schools is considerable with regard to the selection of staff and of students, the forms of organization, the content of the curriculum and even classes and lessons, the selection of teaching material, didactics, examination, recognition of diplomas, and public inspection, ranging from strongly centralized and specified *nearly full control* with little or no autonomy to *minimal* regulation and control (Bader 2007: chapter 10.6). If all schools, including 'private' or 'independent' religious schools, which do not ask for or accept public money, have to be minimally controlled, *does public financing make a difference at all* empirically?[21] Should it make a difference morally speaking? In other words, what is the normative worth of the 'public trust theory' in education?

Its main impact, in this author's view, lies in legitimate rules requiring schools to be *non-profit* organizations (actually imposed in all countries) and in legitimate control of *financial* affairs: private schools may squander their own money if they so wish but publicly financed schools are *accountable (standards of efficiency and effectiveness)*. Its impact is much weaker and more dubious with regard to the *selection of teachers and students*: private religious schools, which are not publicly funded, are still subject to non-discrimination in employment and student selection, though all religious schools may argue for mission-based and circumscribed exemptions. It is even weaker regarding matters of *content* and pedagogy: they have to teach 'non-discrimination and non-oppression' and,

21 Some are not: *independent schools* in England/Wales, in Belgium only if a school asks for community support and for 'recognition of certificates' (Groof 2004: 166); *Vrije scholen* until fairly recently in the Netherlands.

obviously, if they want their exams to be recognized, the minimal cognitive content of the curriculum. In the end, the moral intuition that public funding of schools also makes a huge difference in terms of content-control seems correct only prima facie. The *moral* trade-off between autonomy and control seems smaller than the empirical trade-off, which also may be exaggerated in phrases like 'the more choice, the more regulation/control' (Wolf et al. 2004: X).

Finding reasonable balances, then, crucially depends on finding the *least invasive or obtrusive but still effective ways and means of public regulation and control.* Regulation and control of *accreditation* ranges from the pole of detailed specification in advance of maximum conditions in terms of numbers of expected/enrolled students, facilities, geographical spread, qualification of teaching staff, trustworthiness of provider, mission, curriculum guide, etc. (approached by Russia and, to a lesser degree by France and Germany) to more lenient rules and practices and shorter periods between recognition and public financing. In some countries accredited schools are controlled *regularly* (e.g. England/Wales once every six years), in others only *after a 'notice of complaint'*, and *withdrawal* of financing or accreditation is more or less imminent and open to judicial appeal. Fairness, in this author's view, requires low thresholds in terms of numbers of students and short waiting periods before financing is granted because high numbers and long periods tend to exclude or discriminate against smaller and new religious minorities or alternative candidates and directly or indirectly privileges established providers.

Input regulation and control can be detailed and specified in all possible regards. In addition to general curriculum-guides or frameworks, accepted in most countries, some require curriculum plans specifying in detail not only subjects[22] but also courses, minimum number of lessons or hours, schedules or even prescribe textbooks and teacher guides. The more detailed these regulations and controls are, the less autonomy for teachers and schools generally, for religious schools in particular. Opposition against this tendency is mounting even inside governmental schools.

Morally more apt alternatives are 'outcome driven approaches' or *output regulation and control* favoured by 'pro-choice' authors as 'smart regulation' (Glenn 2011). They require *final attainment targets* following from general curriculum guides or frameworks but leave schools and teachers – also in governmental but particularly in non-governmental schools – 'free to express its distinctive character and its method of teaching and to a considerable extent in the content of teaching, as well as in other aspects of school life' (Groof 2004: 172). In order to make outcomes comparable and to test whether cognitive and non-cognitive achievements live up to minimum standards, they also require

22 Hotly contested cases are *music and drama* (*Talmud Torah School* case in the Netherlands), *sex education* (Kjeldsen case, ECtHR) and, obviously, *evolution theory vs. creationism* or *intelligent design.*

common, state or nation-wide *examinations*[23] at least at the end of primary, secondary and high-school education. The kinds of exams differ widely (oral, written, from Multiple Choice to open essays, coursework) and legitimately so regarding different subjects. Yet, one should be aware of two combined dangers. First, one can use common exams as a backdoor strategy to impose statism and professionalist secularism on all schools. This danger can effectively be prevented only by integration of the different educational providers in standard settings and preparing common exams. Second, one should also be aware of the combined pressure from the side of 'free-choice-parents' and governmental authorities to introduce testing in all schools and classes all the time starting from pre-schooling: teaching to the test from the cradle to the grave.[24]

Particularly in *examinations in civic education*, essays – e.g. in the 'curriculum-based external exit examination system' (CBEES) in Alberta – are preferable because they avoid the 'negative outcome of standardized testing' (Campbell 2004: 209) but they also can only test cognitive outcomes. The 'pedagogical climate' of a school, its 'atmosphere, ethos or culture', the character of interactions in classes, school, and school environment as well as the actual learning of civic/democratic virtues could be controlled, if at all, only by *throughput control* or *external inspection in classes or schools* (Eisgruber 2002: 70, 82). Some countries, e.g. France, go very far in this regard at least in theory, others are much more reluctant.[25] Throughput control, particularly unannounced state-inspection, is clearly the most effective control if 'we' really want to know what is actually going on in classrooms and schools but it is also the most invasive one. The desire to know and to control (the ceaseless 'quest for control') generally stimulates the tendency towards massive overregulation but particularly if it is driven by dramatized 'fringe' cases and by the logic of moral and political panic, of distrust and its escalating dynamics. If at all, it should be confined to cases of 'clear and present danger'.[26]

In a comparative perspective, in sum, there are many, combined moral and pedagogic reasons to prefer regimes of regulation and control, which are mainly

23 Hotly contested in federal education regimes like Germany or the United States. The Dutch regime is fully centralized in this, as in all other regards.

24 Yet schools have to provide information on (1) admission of students; (2) curriculum and pedagogy; (3) student achievements; (4) expenditure and financial information (Witte 2004: 363ff.). Both in Denmark and in Sweden, the public ranking of schools is proscribed.

25 See for the excessively comprehensive and centralized rules: Meuret (2004: 247ff.). Norway seems still to be free of any inspection (Glenn and Groof 2002: 593) and also of standard testing until the end of compulsory education (401ff.). In Sweden and Denmark there is also no national inspectorate, quality control is left up to parents 'who can select the person who will supervise their compliance' and either may appoint an external evaluator or ask the municipal council to assume this role, based on self-assessments (Glenn and Groof 2002: 197, 200, 579).

26 In Denmark, for example, only in 'extraordinary circumstance' or 'extreme cases' do direct inspection and supervision take place (Glenn and Groof 2002: 198).

output-oriented and 'humble' but maybe not so 'devolved' (Witte 2004: 362). In all regards, it is crucial that all standards and procedures of regulation and control, even if minimal, are as '*objective*' (Glenn and Groof 2002) – or in the language of this author: as *relationally neutral and even-handed* – as possible. Instead of counterfactually assuming that government educational authorities and teaching professions are 'neutral' by definition, institutions and processes of defining general curriculum frameworks, final achievement targets and also exams should try to guarantee that the divergent perspectives be *included.* This is particularly relevant if one realizes that worldviews or perspectives are not only important when it comes to religious instruction. It is remarkable that only very few countries have tried to set up fair and even-handed institutions and procedures for standard-setting and control. Most trust that fairly intransparent institutions and *committees* composed of state-officials and co-opted teachers and scientists (as the *Onderwijsinspectie* and *Onderwijsraad* in the Netherlands) would be best in realizing 'independence and objectivity'. Belgium and Denmark are the exception. Belgium knows a 'longstanding tradition of consultation with educational networks and stakeholders' (Groof 2004: 171). The Flemish Education-Council (*Onderwijsraad*) is composed of 'representatives of networks (i.e. recognized umbrella-organizations of religious or philosophical and communal providers), trade-unions, parents, students, economic and social experts, ministry officials'. Government supports parent and student-associations. The Educational Inspectorate (*Onderwijsinspectie*) is composed of 50% from the official governmental networks and 50% from the subsidized private educational networks, and this 'equal representation in the inspectorate corps is intended to guarantee objectivity' (Groof 2004: 177). In Denmark also, non-governmental schools participate in selecting inspectors (Glenn and Groof 2002: 593, see Olsen and Ahlgren 2011). Both are working examples of *associational standard setting and control* as proposed by associative democracy (Bader 2007: 283ff.; see Kaspersen and Ottesen 2001).

In conclusion: not only does the legal status of (organized) religions differ widely, the same is true for the legal status of non-governmental religious schools. In some countries such as Britain, VA and VC schools (most of them Anglican, some Roman Catholic, only very few others) are treated as 'public schools', in many countries they are classified as 'private schools' (such as in the United States) and in the majority of countries their legal status is a '*status a parte*', neither fully public nor private but something 'in-between' (such as 'special' or '*bijzonder*'). This can be seen as the reason to choose a term as neutral and precise as possible. In the above, '*governmental schools*' are understood to be owned, run and financed by (a flexible combination of) governmental (federal, state, municipal) authorities. '*Non-governmental religious schools*' are owned and run by (central or local) religious organizations or associations whether (partly or fully) publicly financed or not. It would therefore be preferable also for RELIGARE WP5 to use such neutral and precise terminology. The most important reasons for this are, first, that their 'legal status' should be kept open and not closed by 'definition' and, second, that their specific legal status seems to be much less decisive in answering the tricky legal and moral questions of public financing and public regulation and control, as this chapter has tried to show. If we argue *de lege ferenda* – whether the constitutional and legal status of religious schools and their practical administration should be changed and if so, how and why – the 'public-private divide' cannot be informative, let alone decisive: it allows a huge variety of diverging and partly incompatible regulations and practices in different countries as well as within the same country. The 'shield of privacy' should be replaced with substantive arguments from minimal morality and from more demanding liberal-democratic morality. As in the case of normative 'secularism' (see Bader 2010) 'privacy' rather troubles the waters instead of getting into clear focus which tensions between which principles and rights and which dilemmas of balancing are at stake and how they can be resolved in the context in which they emerge.

References

Bader, V. (1989), *Kollektives Handeln* (Opladen: Leske – Budrich).

Bader, V. (1993), 'Viel Geltung und immer weniger Faktizität. Zur Kritik von Jürgen Habermas' diskurstheoretischer Rechts- und Demokratietheorie', in Ganßmann, H. and Krüger, S. (eds), 50–78.

Bader, V. (2001), 'Cohesion, Unity, and Stability in Modern Societies', in Harskamp, A. and Musschenga, A. (eds), 129–154.

Bader, V. (2007), *Secularism or Democracy? Associational Governance of Religious Diversity* (Amsterdam: Amsterdam University Press).

Bader, V. (2008a), 'Secularism, Public Reason or Moderately Agonistic Democracy?', in Levey and Modood (eds), *Secularism, Religion, and Multicultural Citizenship.* Cambridge: Cambridge University Press, chapter 5; 110–135.

Bader, V. (2008b), 'Eurosphere(s)? Fragmented and Stratified or Integrated and Fair?' A Conceptual and Pre-Theoretical Mapping Exercise'. *Working Paper* no. 6, available at http://eurospheres.org/publications/working-papers-2/2008-2 (accessed 1 June 2012).

Bader, V. (2009), 'Legal Pluralism and Differentiated Morality: Shari'a in Ontario?', in Grillo, R. et al. (eds), 49–72.

Bader, V. (2010), 'Constitutionalizing Secularism, Alternative Secularisms or Liberal Democracy? A Critical Reading of Some Turkish ECtHR and Indian Supreme Court Cases on "Secularism"', *Utrecht Law Review*, 3, available at www.utrechtlawreview.org (accessed 1 June 2012).

Bader, V. (2011), 'Individual or Collective Autonomy and/or Cultural Authenticity? Some Polemical Reflections in Defense of Minimalism', in Levey, G. (ed.).

Bauböck, R. (2007), 'Why European Citizenship? Normative Approaches to Supranational Union', *Theoretical Inquiries in Law*, 8:2, 452–488.

Campbell, D. (2004), 'The Civic Implications of Canada's Education System', in Wolf, P. et al. (eds), 187–212.

Casanova, J. (1994), *Public Religions in the Modern World* (Chicago and London: University of Chicago Press).

Coppens, E.C. (ed.) (2005), *Secundum Jus: Opstellen aangeboden aan prof. mr. P.L. Nève* (Nijmegen: Gerard Noodt Instituut).

Dewey, J. (1927), *The Public and its Problems* (Chicago: The Swallow Press).

Eisgruber, C. (2002), 'How Do Liberal Democracies Teach Values?', in Macedo, S. and Tamir, Y. (eds), 58–86.

Esmark, A. (2007), 'The Europeanization of Public Spheres – Modes of Resonance and Institutional Anchorage', in Vreese, C. and Schmitt, H. (eds), 329–361.

Ferrari, S. and Pastorelli, S. (2011), WP5 State of the Art Report: The Public Space. The Formal and Substantive Neutrality of the Public Sphere, available at http://www.religareproject.eu/system/files/WP5__State_of_the_art_paper_e-version.pdf (accessed 1 June 2012).

Foner, N. and Alba, R. (2008), 'Immigrant Religion in the U.S. and Western Europe: Bridge or Barrier to Inclusion?', *IMR*, 42:2, 360–392.

Frankenberg, G. and Rödel, U. (1981), *Von der Volkssouveränität zum Minderheitenschutz* (Frankfurt: EVA).

Fraser, N. (2007), 'Transnationalizing the Public Sphere', *Theory, Culture & Society*, 24:4, 7–30.

Galston, W. (2004), 'Civic Republicanism, Political Pluralism, and the Regulation of Private Schools' in Wolf, P. et al. (eds), 315–323.

Ganßmann, H. and Krüger, S. (eds) (1993), *Produktion, Klassentheorie* (Hamburg: Festschrift für Sebastian Herkommer).

Garnett, R. (2004), 'Regulatory Strings and Religious Freedom', in Wolf et al. (eds), 324–338.

Glenn, C. and Groof, J. de (2002), *Finding the Right Balance. Freedom, Autonomy and Accountability in Education*, vol. I (Utrecht: Lemma Publishers).

Glenn, C. and Groof, J. de (2002a), *Finding the Right Balance*, vol. II (Utrecht: Lemma Publishers).

Glenn, R. (2011) *Contrasting Models of State and School: A Comparative Historical Study of Parental Choice and State Control* (New York: Continuum).

Grillo, R. et al. (eds) (2009), *Legal Practice and Cultural Diversity* (Aldershot: Ashgate).

Groof, J. de (2004), 'Regulating School Choice in Belgium's Flemish Community', in Wolf, P. et al. (eds), 157–186.

Habermas, J. (1992a), *Faktizität und Geltung* (Frankfurt/Main: Suhrkamp).

Habermas, J. (1992b), *The Structural Transformation of the Public Sphere* (Hoboken: Wiley).

Hallebeek, J. (2005), 'Church Asylum in Late Antiquity. Concession by the Emperor or Competence of the Church?', in Coppens, E.C. (ed.), 163–182.

Harskamp, A. and Musschenga, A. (eds) (2001), *The Many Faces of Individualism* (Leuven: Peters).

Haug, C. (2008), 'Public Spheres within Movements. Challenging the (Re)search for a European Public Sphere', *RECON Online Working Paper*, 2008:02.

Hirst, P.Q. and Bader, V. (eds) (2001), *Associative Democracy: The Real Third Way* (London: Frank Cass).

Honohan, I. and Rougier, N. (2011), 'ACCEPT Pluralism', WP3 country report on Ireland.

Kaspersen, L. and Ottesen L. (2001), 'Associationalism for 150 Years and Still Alive and Kicking: Some Reflections on Danish Civil Society' in Hirst, P.Q. and Bader, V. (eds), 105–130.

Kohler-Koch. B and Larat, F. (2007), 'Foreword', in Vreese, C. and Schmitt, H. (eds), 1–2.

Koopmans, R. and Zimmermann, A. (2007), 'Visibility and Communication Networks on the Internet', in Vreese, C. and Schmitt, H. (eds), 213–264.

Kymlicka, W. (2002), *Contemporary Political Philosophy* (Oxford: Oxford University Press).

Levey, G. (ed.) (2011), *Autonomy, Authenticity, Culture* (Cambridge: Cambridge University Press).

Liebman, J. and Sabel, C. (2003), *A Public Laboratory Dewey Barely Imagined: The Emerging Model of School Governance and Legal Reform*, on Charles Sabel's website, available at www2.law.columbia.edu/sabel/papers/deweySAE3NYUEDITjslcfsedi.doc (accessed 1 June 2012).

Luhmann, N. (1971), 'Öffentliche Meinung', in: Luhmann, *Politische Planung.* Opladen: Westdeutscher Verlag, 9:34.

Luhmann, N. (1990) 'Gesellschaftliche Komplexität und öffentliche Meinung', *Soziologische Aufklärung*, 5 (Opladen: Westdeutscher Verlag), 170–182.

Macedo, S. and Tamir, Y. (eds) (2002), *Moral and Political Education* (New York: New York University Press).

McConnell, M. (2002), 'Educational Disestablishment', in Macedo, S. and Tamir, Y. (eds), 87–146.

Meuret, D. (2004), 'School Choice and its Regulation in France', in Wolf, P. et al. (eds), 238–267.

Olsen, T.V. and Ahlgren, S.M. (2011), 'The Embodiment of Tolerance in Discourses and Practices Addressing Cultural Diversity in Danish Schools', ACCEPT Pluralism, WP3 country report.

Os, R. van and Jakowski, W. (2007), 'An Online European Public Sphere?' in Vreese, C. and Schmitt, H. (eds), 53–78.

Peters, B. (2007), *Der Sinn von Öffentlichkeit* (Frankfurt/Main: Suhrkamp).

Rawls, J. (1993), *Political Liberalism* (New York: Columbia University Press), Preface 2nd edition, 1996.

Salvatore, A. (2007), *The Public Sphere* (Houndsmill: Palgrave Macmillan).

Schmitt, H. (2007) 'The Nature of European Issues: Conceptual Clarifications and Some Empirical Evidence', in Vreese, C. and Schmitt, H. (eds), 11–22.

Vermeulen, B. (2004), 'Regulating School Choice to Promote Civic Values: Constitutional and Political Issues in the Netherlands', in Wolf, P. et al. (eds), 31–66.

Vogt, W.P. (1997), *Tolerance and Education: Learning to Live with Diversity and Difference* (Thousand Oaks: Sage).

Vreese, C. and Schmitt, H. (eds) (2007), *A European Public Sphere: How Much of it Do We Have and How Much Do We Need?* (Mannheim: CONNEX), vol. 2.

Warren, M. (2001), *Democracy and Association* (Princeton and Oxford: Princeton University Press).

Witte, J. (2004), 'Regulation in Public and Private Schools in the United States', in Wolf, P et al. (eds), 355–367.

Wolf, P. et al. (eds) (2004), *Educating Citizens* (Washington, DC: Brookings Institution Press).

Chapter 5
Religious Freedom and the Public–Private Divide: A Broken Promise in Europe?

Alessandro Ferrari

Introduction: Fluctuating Paradigms

The distinction between private and public spaces has always been, simultaneously, very porous, dynamic and ideological, and strongly influenced by political contingencies. This has been so in particular since the appearance in Europe of the modern Nation State that claims the monopolistic competence of ruling the public arena and drawing the boundaries between the public and private domains. Consequently, the changes of this peculiar European institution during history represent a central place from which to observe the shift in the private–public divide. Indeed it is the modern State that has defined, in different ways according to the times, the space and role of its 'counterpart', the private sphere. The latter can be free – and distinct – from the State only when the State agrees and restrains itself, in this way giving spaces of freedom to individuals and groups. Thus, if it is not possible to conceive of a State without a previous private space, it is also not possible, in Europe, to conceive of a private space without a State disposed to guarantee it. This situation is evident in the classical definition of the right to religious freedom, intended as the right that 'grants individuals a legal space free of state interference in which they can follow a way of life corresponding to their belief'.[1]

Post-Second World War constitutions have deeply transformed the relationships between State and 'private sphere', turning the role of the State from an 'end' into a 'means' for the effective implementation of fundamental rights. In this way the State has lost its previous monopoly and constitutional rights have become the borderlands between the State and society. Constitutional rights are therefore the 'symbol' that requires both halves – the public and the private – in order to function. This 'symbolic role' played by constitutional rights gives rise to a sort of Trinitarian model consisting of three distinct, autonomous but interconnected spheres: private, public institutional (the State) and public informal (civil society).

1 In this way the German Constitutional Court quoted by (Doe 2011: 43).

Pluralism, at the same time a social reality and a legal principle, summarizes this relationship of separation and connectedness between all societal actors.

These transformations have been accompanied by the changeover from formal to substantial rights which requires continuous exchanges between the State and civil society, and this has made the private–public divide much more complicated than in the past. The State has entered deeply into the private domain and it has itself been strongly influenced by private attitudes and forces. In its turn, the stable presence of non-Western immigrants, with their own cultures and religions, has made real the pluralism promised by Constitutions. It is well known that this pluralism has also been particularly characterized by the post-modern deconstruction of human representations and living spaces, triggering a widespread feeling of general atomization that has been perceived by Nation States and a large part of their 'autochthonous' inhabitants as a concrete threat to civil cohesion.

The equivalence between pluralism, atomization, the presence of 'foreigners' and societal fragmentation has activated an opposite reaction where Nation States are, once again, in the front line. This reaction is not founded so much on an attempt to strengthen societal cohesion through the pluralist and tendentially universalistic framework of contemporary constitutions, emphasizing 'thin' but substantial overlapping common links. On the contrary, the reaction is often founded on essentialist and imaginary identities, characterized by a reassessment of the more substantive, institutionalized and specific national features.

In this framework, it is not surprising that religion has started once more to play a central role. Indeed, historically speaking, religions are not only a perfect tool for Nation States to build social cohesion but also an ideal lightning conductor for reactions against social fragmentation. As the first subjects to be 'privatized' by modern States, religions have been the classic State-counterpart as they are realities able to catalyze all the symbolic elements that compose 'identity' in both its private and public dimensions. Between the end of the nineteenth and the early twentieth century, the time of the States' monopoly coincided with a 'separation age' and privatized religions: the State was strong enough to ensure social cohesion without or even against these latter. However, since the end of the Second World War the trend has been in the opposite direction, towards the end of the State monopoly and the past separation and towards a fully legitimated repositioning of religions in the public space. In this new situation, religions regain their role of factors of social cohesion or of fragmentation and States cannot be indifferent towards them.

In today's European scenario two religions play a very peculiar role: Christianity and Islam. In particular, while Christianity is experiencing a vaporization of its cohesive role in the private sphere, it now plays the role of cohesive factor of the public – especially institutional – sphere. On the contrary, Islam appears as the religion of a private-communitarian cohesion and is perceived as playing a strong fragmenting role in the European public sphere. Consequently, Islam has become the natural adversary of European Nation States. Faced with the Islamic threat, Nation States are tempted to cross the borders between spheres, reducing pluralism and making the mediation of constitutional rights very difficult.

This dynamic affects the right to religious freedom in particular, due to the peculiar characteristic of the latter to be one of the most delicate points of convergence between Nation States' 'public' traditions and individual and groups' 'private' identities.[2] More precisely, the weakening of the public–private divide, and the will of Nation States to carefully select the actors qualified to enter the public sphere produces a major change in this right in Europe. The result is a reduced space for religious diversities due to the growing indisposition of State legal systems to 'see' and accept them.

This chapter will stress the main feature of post-Second World War European constitutional secularism. It will emphasize the tensions experienced by this principle in its effective implementation and highlight the present attempt of the European Nation States to translate its pluralistic feature into a selective 'double-standard' approach, which is at the same time fiercely separatist and totally inclusive, depending on the degree of the presumed assimilation of religious actors into Nation States' mainstream orientations. The chapter will also focus on some changes in the right to religious freedom due to this double-standard secularism, pointing out the need for the European Union to play a more decisive role to overcome two opposite weaknesses emerging in the European legal space: too abstract a consideration of constitutional rights and religious identities, on the one hand, and too large a space left to national margins of appreciation, on the other. Indeed European Union law could make the universalistic approach of the Council of Europe more effective and concrete. In so doing it would be able to revitalize the European right to religious freedom accompanying the multiculturalization of the liberal heritage, especially through rediscovering the role played by civil and religious communities, by municipalities and religious associations in shaping dynamic and always changing relational models.

From Pluralism to 'Double-Standard Secularism'

As noted earlier, the recognition of pluralism as a space where public and private actors could cooperate while legitimately keeping their specific identities emerged in Europe with the end of the Second World War. This recognition of pluralism also coincided with a new and fundamental stage in the recognition of constitutional rights. It was one of those *moments* in history when, under a veil of ignorance, men do their best.[3] In fact, as soon as it was realised that to the

2 Cf. European Court of Human Rights (ECtHR), *Kokkinakis* v. *Greece*, Application No 14307/88, Judgment of 25 May 1993, paragraph 31.

3 'In 1948, in the aftermath of World War II, a Universal Declaration of Human Rights was proclaimed. But it was less the annunciation of a new age than a funeral wreath laid on the grave of wartime hopes. The world looked up for a moment' (Moyn 2010: 2).

pluralism in the books in effect there was a corresponding pluralism in action, European Nation States started being very reluctant to attenuate their monopolistic customs. In particular, the discovery of plural and potentially fragmenting cultural and religious diversities has been the avalanche that has swept through any illusion about a possible Western-oriented 'end of history' and this has provoked the shift from a 'multiculturalism of hope' to a 'multiculturalism of fear'.[4]

This discovery is due to many causes which could be summarized in two phrases: globalization and non-Western immigration. Both are maximally plural, hostile to any kind of borders and productive of different changes destined to profoundly affect both the public–private divide and the right to religious freedom. This 'Pluralism Spring' involves the societal structuring legal basis of the 'Old Continent' and influences the following in particular.

1. The subconscious: if the United States were born from pluralism, European Nation States have traditionally interpreted pluralism more as a threat than as an opportunity and hardly consider it as a constitutional duty: contemporary 'ostentatious' pluralism awakens ancient ghosts.
2. The mainstream culture: European Nation States, even those which formally seemed to have privatized religion in the past, never brought into question the cultural homogeneity which linked political elites and popular masses. On the contrary, contemporary pluralism does this, highlighting the attempts of political leaderships to exploit, if not encourage, identitarian reactions to avoid policies aimed at legitimately including non-traditional identities in the public sphere.
3. The institutions: historically, relationships between private and public spheres in Europe regarded stable, clear and centralistic institutions – Nation States and (usually monopolistic) National Churches. Today, both these actors are much more 'liquid'. Local State powers in particular often consider central authorities to be absent and so they counter pluralism on the local level, thus strengthening communitarian links and forcing central institutions to follow them down the same path. Moreover, the difficulty in finding efficient and constitutionally legitimate political responses gives a new role to the judiciary, giving rise to considerable tension between the latter and the legislature, between 'formal technique' and 'substantial politics'. The political powers are more sensitive to 'national identities' and far less willing to accept the accommodations towards the needs of new religions which are sometimes made possible in the public sphere by judges.
4. The economy: at the level of Nation States the difficulty of making 'substantive rights' effective because of their cost questions the States'

4 Tariq Modood, 'We Need a Multiculturalism of Hope', *Guardian*, 24 September 2010, in www.guardian.co.uk/commentisfree/belief/2010/sep/24/multiculturism-hope-secularism-religion (accessed 1 September 2011).

ability to share justice and tackle conflicts between the 'native' population and the new 'immigrants' from outside the European Union. States therefore have a tendency to delegate these powers to (traditional) private actors, religions included. At the European Union level too sharp a dissociation between economy and policy jeopardizes the legitimacy of supra-national interventions, weakening the management of pluralism.

These upheavals converge in secularization, which also plays an important role in producing and revealing pluralism with its individually-oriented side and openness to religious diversities. In particular, secularization seems to have weakened the cohesive force of European Christianity and to have, on the contrary, amplified the fragmenting action of Islam, the traditional 'Other', whose 'pluralizing' action is perceived as directly proportional to the monolithic (i.e. not secularized) nature attributed to this religion. From here it is just a short step to lay the responsibility for weakening not only the institutions of Christianity (i.e. Churches) but also the European Nation States' institutions at the door of secularization. In this way State reactions to the dangerous threat to social cohesion brought about by secularization reverberates in a reinterpretation of secularism as a constitutional principle. Indeed Nation States may well somewhat regret the old style State–Church jurisdictionalist separation able to draw an (apparently) clear line between public and private spheres and above all ensure State control of the intermediate space. That said, the outcome of this State reaction to secularization is a little paradoxical. States, in fact, end up by simply applying a sort of 'more secularized religions clause', reserving the best treatment precisely to those religious groups that are perceived as most affected by secularization. And the instrument for this policy is an explicit double-standard secularism, i.e. a very discretional – and sometimes discriminatory – use of constitutional secularism. Indeed the latter becomes very supportive and inclusive towards traditional religions, which have already crossed the 'Secularization Sea', spreading their influence in civil society and absorbing its values. At the same time, it is very harsh and exclusionary towards non-traditional religions and, above all, towards Islam, which is perceived as against the Western public–private divide and impermeable to all influences even when this religion does cross the borders between the private and public spheres.[5] European Nation States, which are so compliant and reluctant to intervene in the private sphere of economic forces, do not show the same concern towards private cultural and religious players, trying to assimilate and transform the ones they feel closer to into comrades in arms and to drive back into a hermetic private sphere – behind a new 'Hadrian's Wall', out of the intermediate space of civil society – the

5 Cf. for an Italian example, Sartori (2000) and, as an eloquent example of the same thinking, the interview with Karl Albrecht Schachtschneider, Professor of Law at Erlangen-Nurnberg University in http://vladtepesblog.com/?p=37626 (accessed 4 October 2011).

players that seem to jeopardize State monopoly over the whole public sphere.[6] The main consequences of this double-standard secularism are as follows. The first is the automatic recognition of traditional religions' needs as public needs. Moreover, despite their (often legitimate) discriminatory attitudes, the activities of these religions are recognized as subsidiary to those of the State. The traditional religions are consequently included in a homogeneous public sphere from which the 'Others', whose discriminations are not acceptable, are excluded.

This change in the implementation of constitutional secularism highlights the increasing influence of the political and ideological sides of this principle on its legal feature. The situation is not totally new, indeed 'legal secularism' and 'narrative secularism' have often clashed with alternating outcomes.[7] Interpreted more as an ideological weapon throughout the nineteenth century, secularism-*laïcité* entered the European legal world as a constitutional principle only with the Constitution of the Fourth French Republic in 1946, approved by referendum with the support of the Catholic Church. It embodied the pluralistic approach and the universal openness typical of the 'Constituent moment' following the Second World War.[8]

Two National Constitutional Court decisions, from two opposite sides of the Atlantic, seem to represent this post-Second World War and global constitutional secularism well. The first is a 1989 decision by the Italian Constitutional Court which defined *laicità* as a 'supreme constitutional principle' and described it 'not (as) the State's indifference towards religions, but (as) the State's guarantee for the safeguard of religious freedom in a regime of confessional and cultural pluralism'.[9] The second is a decision by the Canadian Supreme Court in 2002 for which 'the religious origin of the parents' objections is not in itself fatal to the Board's decision'. For the Court '(T)he requirement of secularism in s. 76 does

6 This State support to traditional institutions is perfectly symmetric to the attempts of the latter in 'trying to gain more influence over the public sphere in order to compensate for the decline in religious practice and consequent loss of influence which (they) incurred in private': in this way (with reference to only the Catholic Church) Neuwahl (2009: 363). Interestingly, European Nations States, in selecting their interlocutors among 'moderate Muslims', are trying to create an Islamic Church in the image of traditional religious institutions and, consequently, in some ways, in the image of the central secular government itself. It would be perhaps a first divide between two institutional spheres before a future spread of Islam in the intermediate sphere.

7 This question is analysed in Ferrari (2009).

8 The same 'legal side' had therefore already triumphed at the time of the approval of a moderate separation law in 1905. Nevertheless, this law does not refer to *laïcité* but to 'separation', in an explicit connection with the First Republic of 1795. The reference for the Turkish and Mexican Constitutions that consecrated 'secularism' in their pre-Second World War Constitutions is consequently 'separation' and not constitutional *laïcité*.

9 Decision no. 203 of 11 April 1989, no. 4, in www.giurcost.org/decisioni/1989/0203s-89.html (accessed 4 October 2011).

not preclude decisions motivated in whole or in part by religious considerations'.[10] Nevertheless, the Court continues, 'religious views that deny equal recognition and respect to the members of a minority group cannot be used to exclude the concerns of the minority group' because 'a secular school system cannot exclude certain lawful family models simply on the ground that one group of parents finds them morally questionable'.[11] The school Board's decision to decline to approve three books depicting same-sex parented families was, consequently, 'unreasonable' in view of 'the context of the educational scheme mandated by the legislature'.[12] These two decisions seem to well summarize the features of contemporary Western secularism, indicating that it allows religions full citizenship in the public sphere and even admitting explicitly religiously-founded binding decisions. This stance is the result of an integrated, rather than a separatist, pluralism which derives from the concept that religions are able to stay in a public space inhabited by different Weltanschauungen that agree about a common, albeit 'thin', morality. In other words European constitutional secularism presents, at least 'in the books' many of the features that Rajeev Bhargava associates with contemporary Indian secularism, taken as a model for Europe.[13] Post-Second World War constitutional secularism, in fact, (1) 'does not erect a wall of separation between state and religion', but it is aimed at managing pluralism; (2) it shows the non-indifference of the State towards religious freedom, non-indifference which 'allows the state to intervene in religions, to help or hinder them without the impulse to control or destroy them'; (3) 'it interprets separation not as a strict exclusion or strict neutrality but rather' as what Bhargava calls 'principled distance', which could also perhaps be presented as a 'principled pluralism'.[14] For this reason, this legal secularism is not 'averse to the public character of religions' but through this principle States try 'to balance different, but equally important values. This makes this secularism a politically

10 *Chamberlain* v. *Surrey School District* no. 36, [2002] 4 S.C.R. 710, 2002 SCC 86, no. 59. For no. 19 '(T)he Act's insistence on strict secularism does not mean that religious concerns have no place in the deliberations and decisions of the Board. Board members are entitled, and indeed required, to bring the views of the parents and communities they represent to the deliberation process. Because religion plays an important role in the life of many communities, these views will often be motivated by religious concerns. Religion is an integral aspect of people's lives, and cannot be left at the boardroom door. What secularism does rule out, however, is any attempt to use the religious views of one part of the community to exclude from consideration the values of other members of the community'.

11 Ibid., nos 19–20.

12 Ibid., no. 59.

13 R. Barghava (2011), 'Should Europe learn from Indian Secularism?', paper presented at the RELIGARE workshop: *Accommodating Religion in the Public Space. Looking beyond Europe*, Sofia, on 20 October 2011.

14 Even if not completely in the sense used by Ahdar and Leigh (2005: 84–87), but rather as a cooperationist-separatist pluralism.

negotiated arrangement … rather than a scientific doctrine'[15] as nineteenth-century secularism was.

This constitutional secularism curbed its 'narrative' State-centred side until the beginning of the twenty-first century, covering many accommodations between European Nation States and religions, officially including the latter in the public sphere. However, little by little as the twenty-first century has proceeded, constitutional secularism has started to become shakier and its concrete implementation has revealed its permanent character, which is now hidden but persistent.[16] Perhaps in contrast to the Indian experience, it is very difficult for European Nation States to accept their transformation into guarantors of plural and multi-level societal systems. Contemporary multicultural changes would have needed to be explicitly integrated at a 'Constituent moment', but European Nation States and their societies have not been aware or ready for it. The result has been continuous pressures on the constitutional concepts – secularism included. On the one hand there are judges who are more oriented towards a homeostatic approach and who prevalently try to play an accommodationist role. On the other are politicians who are more sensitive towards the call for narrative secularism; an intransigent part of their number are against extending the benefits of this inclusive secularism to newcomers, and to Islam in particular. In this way, with the affirmation of a double-standard, secularism and its policies cease to be pluralism-oriented, instead becoming an instrument for repackaging public spaces by coercively reducing differences. At the same time, secularism ceases to be a rallying cry of the left and becomes an instrument for the right against Islam and, more generally, against what are perceived as dangerous differences.[17]

---

15 Bhargava (2011) for all quotations.

16 2004 was a crucial year, both because of the French law 'on headscarves' (the first law where the word *laïcité* textually appears) and of the French Constitutional Council decision no 2004-505 of 19 November which subordinated the ratification of the European Constitutional Treaty signed in Rome to the consideration that the European Court of Strasbourg '(avait) ainsi pris acte de la valeur du principe de laïcité reconnu par plusieurs traditions constitutionnelles nationales et qu'elle (laissait) aux Etats une large marge d'appréciation pour définir les mesures les plus appropriées, compte tenu de leurs traditions nationales, afin de concilier la liberté de culte avec le principe de laïcité; que, dans ces conditions, (étaient) respectées les dispositions de l'article 1er de la Constitution aux termes desquelles "la France est une République laïque", qui interdisent à quiconque de se prévaloir de ses croyances religieuses pour s'affranchir des règles communes régissant les relations entre collectivités publiques et particuliers', no. 18, in www.conseil-constitutionnel.fr/conseil-constitutionnel/francais/les-decisions/depuis-1958/decisions-par-date/2004/2004-505-dc/decision-n-2004-505-dc-du-19-novembre-2004.888.html (accessed 23 October 2011).

17 This right-wing *laïcité*, which has to defend itself against 'le multiculturalisme et le communautarisme', has been officially consecrated by the 'Rapport Baroin', titled *Pour une nouvelle laïcité*, presented to the Prime Minister Raffarin in May 2003: cf. the text in www.aidh.org/laic/bar-present.htm (accessed 20 September 2011).

In this light, the constitutional decisions previously quoted assume a different meaning. The decision of the Italian Constitutional Court, for example, certainly recognized a clearly pluralistic principle but used it to sustain the monopolistic presence of Catholic religious teaching in Italian State schools. This highlights the attention of European States not to endanger established religious institutions. At the same time, the Canadian decision certainly emphasized the need for religions to become able to overlap other ideal approaches,[18] but this can easily be turned into a secularism which is used as a tool by the majoritarian secularized mainstream to force minorities to pass a very identitarian and 'thick' 'reasonable'/'unreasonable' test before entering the public sphere. In other words, the multicultural changes of European societies have pushed European Nation States to de-universalize constitutional secularism and to encourage local and majoritarian religions that are better equipped to pass a 'reason-test' which is far from being simply based on the respect of constitutional rights.

This shift towards a double-standard highlights the difficulty to simultaneously harmonize the classical liberal contents – the formal rights of the nineteenth century – and its post-modern pluralistic developments in the same constitutional secularism. If a traditional liberal approach can guarantee 'departure'-equality and spaces for 'unreasonable' minorities, a pluralism interpreted as the total overcoming of the public–private divide and, consequently, of the distinction between secular and religious spheres will tend to openly recognize religion as a source of public binding decisions; to open (all) public sphere(s) only to selected religions and to irremediably reduce the intermediate free public space between private and institutional spheres.

At the supra-national level this defensive and selective attitude of European Nation States seems to be justified by the Council of Europe. Despite having repeatedly stressed that religion and democracy are not incompatible and that member States should encourage the role of religions in the public sphere extending, even very prudently, this opportunity also to Islam,[19] the ECtHR decisions do not always go in this direction. Indeed its jurisprudence connects secularism with pluralism[20] but uses the former principle more as a limit than as an opportunity for non-traditional religions, especially Islam. In particular, this jurisprudence seems

18 Cf. for a general overview, McRea (2010).

19 Cf. especially the Resolution 1743 (2010) *Islam, Islamism and Islamophobia in Europe* and the Recommendation 1927 (2010).

20 Nevertheless, differently, for example from Italian jurisprudence, the stronger influence of the French secular 'narrative' (more than the traditional French legal approach) has contributed to giving ECtHR secularism more a State-centred than a pluralist image, pluralism being more connected to neutrality than to secularism itself: cf. the concurring opinion Judge Power in *Lautsi & Others* v. *Italy*, Application no. 30814/06, Grand Chamber Judgment of 18 March 2011. However, the connection between secularism and pluralism and its exclusionary effect on Islamic difference is very clear in no. 116 of *Leyla Şahin* v. *Turkey*, Application no. 44774/98, Grand Chamber Judgment of the 10 November 2005.

to make the double-standard an 'a priori' of its decisions.[21] Such decisions very often appear to be the execution of principles expressed in a general way by the *Refah partisi* decision, a clear theological *summa* about the absolute impossibility for Islam to experience 'inclusive secularism' and, in general, the public reason and public language that this secularism would require.[22] Consequently, for example, if a crucifix is a 'modest' and 'passive' symbol, neutralized by secularization and, for this reason, legitimated to stay in the public arena, on the contrary, the Muslim headscarves are, without exceptions, too 'conspicuous' and 'active'. By so doing ECtHR seems to willingly support the conservative and securitarian use of secularism made by Nation States and, finally, the shift of the pendulum from a legal liberal-constitutional tradition to a simple post- or a-constitutional narrative approach to this principle.

Nevertheless, if in the nineteenth century narrative secularism had the hard face of separatist anticlericalism, in today's Europe it tends to show a totally different mellow, inclusive and 'unionist' face. Now if 'inclusive' secularism is currently a consolidated mantra, the contradictions and dangers of this category are far less stressed. For this reason, it is important to distinguish between constitutional and simply 'inclusive' secularism because the pervasive 'reasonable' public space that this latter is creating is fiercely concealing two assimilationist and separatist sides that endanger not only the excluded religions, but also those that are included. In fact, no religion may benefit from others' *deminutio* in the long run and the movement of the 'secularism pendulum' is not without effect on the shape of the right to religious freedom as a whole.

'Double-Standard' Secularism: A Double Danger for Religious Freedom ...

The present inclination of States to prevalently read secularism in the light of the protection of a social cohesion interpreted as a collective good reflecting specific national identities causes an abrupt passage of the right of religious freedom from the goal of protection of individual consciences and religious groups' autonomies to the protection of a public order unilaterally assessed by States themselves. The same passage is experienced by pluralism: cooperationist-separatist pluralism, typical of constitutional secularism, seems to be substituted for consociational pluralism, based on fully-assimilated goals between Nation States and National Churches.

These shifts are very seminal. First of all, to enhance the interpretation of religious freedom on the basis of social cohesion risks (re-)introducing a

21 Cf. also Mégret (2009) but, more in general, pp. 292–296 referring, in particular, to the Grand Chamber decision on the Şahin case, no. 114.

22 The Moloch Islam is well summarized by paragraph 123 of the Grand Chamber decision, Applications nos. 41340/98, 41342/98, 41343/98 and 41344/98, Judgment of 22 January 2003. Cf. on the matter, Danchin (2011) and Augenstein (2009a).

majority/minority polarity that is fatal in relation to fundamental rights. At the same time, moreover, this interpretation strengthens the positions of traditional institutionalized religions and Nation States.[23] It melds the margin of appreciation of Nation States with the needs for visibility in the public arena of traditional institutionalized religions while overtly questioning one of the historical Western paradigms such as, first of all, the distinction between the secular and the religious spheres. One consequence of this confusion is the skilful juggling of classical 'religious exemptions' with 'cultural exemptions' to ensure the (religious) identity of Nation States and to limit genuine personal and communitarian claims of religious freedom. The parallel history of the Muslim headscarf and the Christian crucifix on State school walls is, once again, eloquent. Indeed the difficulty of European institutions to accept the 'religious' interpretation given by Muslim women to this garment shows how complicated it is to distinguish between culture, politics and religion even in the *dar al-tamiyz* – in the … 'distinction house'. But when a State interpretation precedes the individual or the religious community, the right to religious freedom tends to become a rigid status that is paradoxically not so far from the 'millet system' condemned by *Refah Partisi* jurisprudence.

This discourse is evidently connected with changes affecting a cornerstone of the right to religious freedom: religious autonomy. In the 'separation age' religious autonomy served to safeguard a 'private sphere' – which was indispensable for individual (personal autonomy) and for communities (institutional autonomy) – from State interventions.[24] Today, when private sphere boundaries are narrowing, also spaces for religious autonomy share the same fate. European States only seem to accept self-qualifications on matters of religion corresponding to a mainstream-majority approach. Too differentiated choices are often downgraded as 'merely' cultural and/or political, disappearing from the screening of religious freedom. Nevertheless, this selection and the States' 'authentic' separation between sacred and profane, particularly highlighted by the '*burqa* affairs', exceeds by far the classical Western distinction between religious activities and those that are not. Indeed globalization is replacing this latter distinction, functional to a specific regulation of religious freedom as a peculiar expression of human conscience, with a much more internal and pervasive separation by which States arrogate the right to separate 'true religion' from simple 'traditions'. In this way, on the one hand the distinction between religious and secular activities, between religion and culture, leans towards traditional religions, able to choose the table – and the rights – on which to play; on the other, an excluding separation only works as a limit for non-traditional religious groups (read Islam). In effect, if the link between mosques and headscarves with a mixture of sacred and profane reasons justifies restrictions on religious freedom, paradoxically the same mixture which

23 The Muslim presence, in fact, seems to radicalize the European national models of State–Church relations.

24 This has been particularly evident in Catholic Europe whereas in Orthodox and Protestant Europe the issue of autonomy has become openly crucial in more recent times.

characterizes the State-school crucifix or other Christian religious traditions is a precondition for their presence in the public space. Thus, towards non-traditional religions this new 'separation' is used to deny and neutralize many references to 'religious' identity, making them generic cultural expressions. In this way, State neutrality and public order will have a free hand – considering themselves released from any compulsory balance – to more easily expel minorities and their fragmenting identities from the public arena. Consequently, while the religious side of a practice would make its expulsion from the public sphere more difficult, 'public theologians' will emphasize its cultural, social and/or indifferent religious character, but when it is the religious side that expels the practice, no aesthetic or cultural reference will be able to save it.[25]

In this approach, which emphasizes the possibility to distil pure religion from its cultural backgrounds and that ignores the fact that 'social worries' must be balanced not only with the right to religious freedom but also with other, 'generic', constitutional rights, the majority ignores individual interpretations in the name of a public order conceived more in its ideal than in its material aspects.[26] The spread of 'crimes of danger' in religious and cultural matters like the interdiction of the *burqa* and, outside the penal code, the interdiction of the headscarf in State schools, seems to indicate the victory of the virtual and ideal over concrete and more pragmatic approaches.[27] Finally, in limiting personal religious autonomy States add a further device to the 'true religion argument', which is aimed at excluding the religious character of an action. This device is the 'indifferent practice argument', which aims to demonstrate that interdictions do not constitute

25 Cf. for example, the ridiculous (or tragic) story of the French employee suspended for three months for his beard in www.leparisien.fr/seine-saint-denis-93/tremblay-ne-renvoie-plus-son-employe-barbu-08-09-2011-1597310.php (accessed 8 September 2011). As we will see later, both this mainstream cultural filter through which religious choices have to pass and the same (apparent) separation between 'true' and 'fake' religions disclose a progressive difficulty to 'see' religion and, consequently, to protect it as a right.

26 Although '(C)laims to justify interference based on the protection of public morals have been rather less successful' (Doe 2011: 61), it would seem that a progressive overlap between this notion and public order is in progress.

27 Also with relation to this question it is possible to note a strong difference in the treatment of religious symbols: if, in the Lautsi case, Judge Power could argue 'that the Grand Chamber has correctly noted that there was no evidence opened to the Court to indicate any influence which the presence of a religious symbol may have on school pupils' (paragraph 66), 'that … subjective perception is not sufficient to establish a breach of Article 2 of Protocol no. 1' and that 'a body of settled jurisprudence … recognises that mere "offence" is not something against which an individual may be immunized by law', in Şahin Judge Tulkens was left alone in affirming the same principle, that '(O)nly indisputable facts and reasons whose legitimacy is beyond doubt – not mere worries or fears – are capable of satisfying that requirement and justifying interference with a right guaranteed by the Convention' (no. 5 of her dissenting opinion to the Grand Chamber judgment already quoted).

any serious limit to the right of religious freedom. On closer inspection this logic, which tends to avoid any reference even to paragraph 1 of article 9 of ECHR, is the complete reversal of the Lockean argument that the State has to implement a regime of tolerance and freedom exactly towards issues relating to 'indifferent things'.

But, as we said earlier, 'inclusive' double-standard secularism influences the right of religious freedom also in another way, through its assimilationist side. The importance assumed by the relationship between social cohesion and religious freedom, the extension of the public sphere and the confinement of the private to the home, where real religious differences are restrained, reduce the room for 'public tolerance' and narrows the influence of the right of religious freedom. Consider, for example, religious education in State schools. Born as an answer to religious needs, this teaching has become functional to civic cohesion and, consequently, more connected to a generic right to education than to specific religious freedom, with a change that is a source of tensions between States and (traditional) Churches. Secondly, European States have not only set out in many ways to organize, i.e. verticalize in their own image, 'non-organized' religions but, more generally, they also do not hesitate to impact religious autonomy when a post-religious interpretation of human rights is at stake. Many examples prove that the 'reasonableness' governing the contemporary public sphere is not necessarily the expression of a translation into a secular language of religious voices nor a simple overlap between different reasonable discourses. This 'reasonableness' often seems more the quintessence, the distillate, of a process of an increasingly uncontrollable liquefaction of institutional belongings that concerns both traditional – and non – religious groups (Islam included) and State legal orders. This explains not only the present defensive entrenchment between these latter and their historical religious counterparts but, above all, the subordination of religious discourses in the public sphere to an ephemeral 'reasonableness' that does not always well calibrate the slippery-slope effect towards the (presumed) 'reasonable religions' of its jurisdictionalist 'pitch invasions' with 'unreasonable' and dangerous religions. In a nutshell, State provisions against the 'unreasonable' religions end up by also penalizing the 'reasonable' ones: the 'reasonableness' demanded by the State can only accommodate the real areas of the religious difference with great difficulty. Two examples of this come from Norway, a State with a broad public-institutional sphere where religion, and particularly the National Church, plays a fundamental role. The first example is the decision to oblige religious communities that celebrate marriages with civil effects to ask couples to sign a declaration whereby each partner pre-emptively allows an eventual choice for divorce by the other. The 'reason' is to avoid 'limping marriages' (above all among Muslims), but the effect has been to cause the Catholic Church to celebrate canonically void marriages.[28]

28 Cf. J.Y. Cramer (2005), *Stumbling Legislation and Limping Marriages. A Case Study from Norway*, in www.kim.no/upload/2325/Balancing%20Gender%20Equality%20and%20Religious%20Diversity%2012.10.05.pdf (accessed 26 September 2011).

The second example is the proposal of the Children's Ombudsman for a minimum age for male circumcisions. The targets here are Middle Eastern and African groups, but the most sensitive reactions come from the Jewish community.[29]

All these changes bring out two comparative paradoxes, one 'domestic' and one 'external', which affect Europe and the Muslim world.

The domestic paradox is that the more emblematic separatist country, France, the land of individual rights, seems to protect more institutional than personal religious freedom, concentrating its efforts on cleaning up the public sphere of individuals who are judged too shocking and on doing its best to build religious institutions able to frame individuals. In this way, France appears more 'communitaristic' than national Church countries. Indeed in the latter it is the protection of the individual that narrows institutional religious autonomy in the public sphere.[30] The 'external' paradox is that, after September 2001, 10 years of the overt 'clash of civilizations' have highlighted not an incommensurable distance between Western 'separatist' and Islamic 'unionist' models but, rather, a sort of commensurable approach. This latter is not only visible in the 'democratic' aspirations of the 'Arab Spring', in a State jurisdictionalism that very often too largely interprets the 'principled distance' towards religious affairs or in some accidental convergence between (some) Islamic and (some) European trends.[31] The most important and profound commonality between these models lies in an inextricable and dynamic connection between secular and religious laws (see Ahdar and Leigh 2005: 42–46). This connection makes the bets on 'Mediterranean democratization' depend not so much on an absolute enfranchisement of State law from *shari'a*, as on an exchange between secular and religious views able to guarantee the formal and the substantial sides of constitutional rights, like in Europe. It is also for this reason that a 'European wall' against a differentiated pluralism seems destined to suffer the common fate of this kind of defence. This is not only because this European strategy would not be the best presentation for exporting 'universal rights' including religious freedom. It is because, more pragmatically speaking, it is not possible to fight pluralism when the latter is both an inescapable reality and a constitutional principle and when this wall stands against enemies who have already – physically, but also spiritually and mentally – crossed it thanks to the multiple intersections between 'Western universal rights' and other cultures and legal traditions.

---

29 Cf. http://islamineurope.blogspot.com/2011/09/norway-childrens-ombudsman-proposes.html (accessed 26 September 2011).

30 One hypothesis to explain this first paradox could be a sort of hypertrophy of separation which is no longer concerned about the activities of institutional churches in the public sphere, and that now wants to separate from the latter those individuals who have not been completely filtered by the homogenizing and neutralizing post-secular approach.

31 It is the case, for example, of *burqa/niqab* interdictions where the privatization of women, which leads to prohibition to accede to public spaces, ends up with coinciding with some Muslim representations.

… and the Risk of Invisibility

Nevertheless, it is possible to individuate one essential similarity and one important difference between the two sides of the Mediterranean, both of which are connected to the difficulty in managing the public–private divide. If both Europe and Mediterranean Islam experience difficulties in managing such a divide, the causes seem opposite. In the 'Islamic system' the difficulty is in an undue emphasis on religion, which would like to explicitly pervade the entire public sphere, leaving the State legal system with a totally subordinate role. In the post-secular Western model, on the contrary, it is the State that pervades the public sphere and tends not to differentiate religion from other social phenomena. In other words, within the European context, religion seems to lose its specialty. This last situation appears as a sort of extreme consequence of the difficulty in justifying religious freedom merely by using a liberal approach. In particular, this loss of specialty of religion in the Western context indicates a sort of short-circuit of 'macro' and 'micro' liberal justifications of the right of religious freedom, with a final convergence in their outcome.[32] On the one hand, 'macro' justifications and the consequent commingling between State identities and national religions tends to attract the latter into the political field; on the other, 'micro' justifications and the extreme individualization of religious freedom tends to transform the latter from a specific 'claim of conscience' into a simple 'preference', achieving the same neutralization and 'generalization' produced by the first dynamic.[33] The result of this 'invisibility' of religion is a progressive reduction of the right of religious freedom both for communities and individuals, a reduction that means less space for diversities. More precisely, we could say that there seems to be a relationship of inverse proportionality between social (perception of) visibility of a religion as a religion in the public space and its legal recognition: from (at the moment) their different sides, Christianity and Islam know this well.

This difficulty in ensuring full recognition and protection of the right of religious freedom in a multicultural age by only using liberal rationales seems to depend on the double hypertrophy of States and individuals, which underestimates the role played by religious communities in interpreting religious freedom not just through following a functional approach but in the light of a an established living experience whose legitimacy is generally placed beyond mere human will acquiring a sort of per se value.

If this hypertrophy concerns both States and individuals, and if their own hypertrophies are strictly connected to each other, even in their final results,[34] it is

32 Ahdar and Leigh (2005: 52–64), include among 'macro' justifications civil peace, the intermediate role of religions and their attitude to fostering civic virtue; in the 'micro' category the concern for personal autonomy.

33 Ibid., with the quotation of Michael Sandel, p. 61.

34 Cf. for example, with reference to the 'Amselem case' discussed at the Canadian Supreme Court, Lefebvre (2009: 195–212).

especially important to sketch here the impact of State hypertrophy on religious freedom and on the public–private divide. The overcoming of modern State separation towards traditional religions and the opening of the public sphere to religion subordinated to the desire for homogeneity are at the basis of the States' difficulty in managing religious differences. This difficulty is strictly associated with the States' attempt to control the entire public sphere by absorbing the 'informal', especially by dictating unilateral and uniform rules and goals to all social actors. Religious actors that accept these generic rules take full advantage of this 'Hegelian-Schelling's night' but also run the risk of losing their specific identity: even traditional Churches, when they are transformed into civil religion, risk losing control of their discourses. The 'inclusive' approach of contemporary secularism has engendered a process of assimilation, of 'public-sharing' where institutional public and institutional (traditional) religious actors share important public roles and even functions classically connected with State sovereignty. This public-sharing produces a sort of Benetton-system, a franchising organization where the colours are many but the brand only one, the one drawn by the State. If it is true that publicization of the private (and religious) sphere is also accompanied by the privatization of the public, in a process that, like all 'integration', is bi-directional, it is also true that 'subsidiarity' can easily slip into conformism and religions will rapidly realize how much they have to accept to stand, on a par with the State, within the public arena.[35]

It would be possible to argue that uniform and (religious) differences-blind State laws could confirm a strictly neutral approach, allowing de facto differences and reducing State intervention towards civil society; such laws could also recall the limits of policies and highlight that social questions are not entirely political or juridical. Following this scheme, differences would find space in 'facultative laws' that would foresee spaces for objections of conscience when sensitive issues were concerned. More in general, protection of religious freedom would move from specific laws, especially tailored to religious needs, to generic laws which might be opened also to individual accommodations; and such openings could in turn take into consideration perhaps even religious requirements on the grounds of the principle of equality, although following this generic option would make everything less certain. Nevertheless, this blindness not only blurs any distinction between public and private spheres, making the former (institutional) sphere prevalent, but it also inevitably tends to subordinate accommodations to mainstream orientations. Moreover, a general blind-approach will not only undermine the present level of protection of religious freedom through its absorption under the much weaker umbrella of the 'right to culture', but it would also introduce an attention to specificities prevalently through a discrimination lens, with the risk of

35 Consequently, social actors eager to keep their autonomy and identity tend to take refuge in the more intimate private sphere: it is the case of school where duality is today between 'public' (state or private) schools and homeschools, often kept at the margins of the 'public system' for their orientation which is too far from the mainstream.

encouraging an often ex post protection, which requires a very good use of public-administrative and private discretion and a particularly attentive and sensitive system of checks and balances. More in general, this blindness based on direct relationships between individuals and the State once again underestimates both the needs and the value of the right to religious freedom. It underestimates its needs, in particular by devaluing religious communities, trying to totally absorb them into a secular framework and trivializing their autonomy, which is an expression of their more intimate experiences. But it also underestimates its value by not only forgetting the concrete – even sometimes State-functional – role played by religious communities as social actors in integrating groups and individuals into a wider societal framework,[36] and at the same time forgetting the role played by religions not just in a sort of desperate attempt to capture and overlap State and secular 'human universal rights', but also in co-producing and making the latter effective.

The European Mission

To conclude three main points are briefly emphasized:

1. the importance of keeping modern liberal cornerstones to achieve an effective multiculturalized constitutional secularism;[37]
2. the central role played by schools in making communication between traditional and new identities possible and, consequently, to enforce a culture favourable to this multiculturalized constitutionalism;
3. a more involved role of the European Union in giving the right to religious freedom more substance and efficacy, making it a real paradigm of a pluralistic society, the result of the confluence of the interpretations of States, individuals and communities.

About the liberal heritage: the distinction and not a confused mixture of different – public and private – spheres is the guarantee of the public recognition of real 'interconnected differences'.[38] A balanced use of classical liberal instruments is simultaneously the real precondition for not falling into a sort of homogeneous

36 The role played by Catholic schools in France in 'integrating' Muslim veiled students has shown a more universalistic ability than the French *catho-laïcité* itself. The same role, sometime intelligently recognized by States, is also often played by religious communities in the matter of family law.

37 Cf. Tariq Modood, *Is there a Crisis of Secularism in Western Europe?*, in http://blogs.ssrc.org/tif/2011/08/24/is-there-a-crisis-of-secularism-in-western-europe/ (accessed 4 October 2011).

38 Cf. the lecture of the Archbishop of Canterbury given at the British Council of New Delhi on 15 October 2010 in www.archbishopofcanterbury.org/articles.php/569/

post-modernity but instead to finally enter a multicultural modernity consisting of different communities with different languages and living in different spheres. Keeping a specific consideration for religion and, consequently, keeping the substance of a separation principle enforced through specific laws able to 'see' religion is functional, and not contradictory, to the ability to pay attention to the dynamics of this reality and to the lively experience of individuals and communities also beyond the classic Western paradigm of religion. Actualized liberal contents also work in favour of a balanced relationship between individual and associative freedoms in relation to which States, following a real 'principled distance', play the role of common guarantor of constitutional rights. At the same time, the possibility for States to play an active and legitimate role is directly connected with their real ability to foresee multi-level and participated decisional processes, which means the ability to promote local and specific decisions with universal feelings and to use the universalistic approach of the post-Second World War Constitutions to avoid the temptation of too 'morally thick' identitarian decisions. This hope is strictly connected to the second point, concerning the role of school systems. Also in this case we are not confronted with a novelty. Schools have always been absolutely central in the European tradition where educative objectives have always constituted the core of national Constitutions. Schools play an essential role in 'communication' between different identities (see Wolton 2009: 45–57), it is from school that both the desire to be together or a fragmenting frustration can influence future European societal stability above all for the role played by schools in relation to the 'second generation' of post-modernity. In particular, the explosion of de-structured religious identities in school reflects not only the de-structuration of the religious field but also the difficult balance between Nation-State and State-Nation, between local and universal identities. From a rapid glance at some legal cases, it is interesting to note a preference for majoritarian religion, which is nothing new, but also a tendency to ask schools to respect religious pluralism not only as a constitutional duty but as the condition of survival of majoritarian positions themselves. It is what seems to emerge, for example, even if not without ambiguity, from the Lautsi case but also from other different national decisions.[39] Looking closely, it seems that these cases represent a transposition, on a more reduced scale, of the *Darby* v. *Sweden*[40] approach, which justifies a national/dominant Church only when individuals and groups are not discriminated against. It is, once again, a recognition of a particular tradition, but within universal limits.

archbishops-chevening-lecture-at-the-british-council-new-delhi (accessed 4 October 2011).

39 Cf. the Multani case in Canada and, among others, *R. (on the application of Watkins-Singh)* v. *Aberdare Girl's High School Governors* in the UK or, but in a negative way, the German Federal Administrative Court in a decision concerning a veiled teacher: the two last quoted from Augenstein (2009a: 6 and 17).

40 Cfr. ECtHR, *Darby* v. *Sweden*, Report of 9 May 1989, paragraph 45.

Finally, this need to accept States' traditions but also to anchor universal limits is an important mission especially for the European Union. For the latter multiculturalism and national traditions together are, at the same time, the antidote to the temptation to become a new 'supra-Nation State', emphasizing the quest for clear and mono-cultural roots or a new 'supra-State Nation' indulging in a too decontextualized approach. In this sense, the capability to accommodate and overlap single national traditions with the universalistic contents emerging both from national constitutions and from the documents of the Council of Europe would constitute an obligation and an opportunity for the EU to fulfil its 'integrative attitude' (see Kastoryano 2009: 2–23; Hersant 2009: 69; Augenstein 2009b). Moreover, such an attitude will be articulated not only in the relationships between the EU institutions and single Nation States, but also, and arguably especially, in the relationships between EU and local public powers, starting from municipalities, the place where local and universal concretely meet, social cohesion has its roots and from where new national policies can be originated. Attention and active support to the concrete attempts of European cities to implement in their specific contexts universalistic guidelines drafted both by national constitutions and by the Council of Europe has to be seen as a fundamental mission of EU policy, above all if it effectively wants to get over its bureaucratic and scarcely 'democratic' image. Doing this will perhaps help European public opinion to discover that, even under strong mono-identitarian narratives, for European cities 'religious diversity is less and less seen as a threat, and more and more perceived as a pragmatic tool, among others, which could help to promote better ways to live together'.[41]

More in general, the European Union legal system has two main specific and closely connected rails to follow, both reflecting at once a liberal and a multicultural approach, and both already within its competences. The first is the ability to 'see' religion and to maintain a public–private divide by recognizing identity and the specific contribution of religious communities: it is what is required by article 17 of the Treaty on the Functioning of the European Union. The second is the promotion of a non-blind anti-discrimination policy, with the courage to raise the level and areas of its direct intervention and, consequently, of the European Court of Justice jurisprudence (see Augenstein 2009a and Neuwahl 2009). It is important to note, in any case, that even authors not so disposed to enlarge direct EU competences emphasize the necessity 'of a *human rights policy* with everything this entails' (Weiler 2009: 111ff.).

---

41 Sebastian Fath, *Regulating Religious Diversity in the Parisian Area*, Draft paper presented on the 14th of June 2011, in http://frenchwindows.hautetfort.com/media/01/01/2833096528.pdf (accessed 26 October 2011).

About city policies in managing religious and cultural differences cf. for example, the work of the European network of cities for local integration policies for migrants, in www.eurofound.europa.eu/areas/populationandsociety/clip.htm (accessed 26 October 2011).

Making it effective, at the same time as the 'Constituent moment' of the other side of the Mediterranean, should not be delayed: there is not a second chance, but only another lost opportunity.

References

Ahdar, R. and Leigh, I. (2005), *Religious Freedom in the Liberal State* (Oxford and New York: Oxford University Press).

Augenstein, D. (2009a), 'Religious Pluralism versus Social Cohesion? Normative Fault Lines of Human Rights Jurisprudence in Europe', *Working Papers Series*, 23 (University of Edinburgh School of Law).

Augenstein, D. (2009b), 'The Contested Polity: Europe's Constitutional Identity between Religious and Secular Values', *Working Papers Series*, 13 (University of Edinburgh School of Law).

Basdevant Gaudemet, B. and Jankowiak, F. (eds) (2009), *Le droit ecclésiastique en Europe et à ses marges (XVIII-XX siècles)* (Leuven: Peeters).

Danchin, P.G. (2011), 'Islam in the Secular Nomos of the European Court of Human Rights', *Michigan Journal of International Law*, 32:663, 663–747.

Doe, N. (2011), *Law and Religion in Europe. A Comparative Introduction* (Oxford and New York: Oxford University Press).

Ferrari, A. (2009), 'De la politique à la technique: laïcité narrative et laïcité du droit. Pour une comparaison France/Italie', in Basdevant Gaudemet, B. and Jankowiak. F. (eds), 333–345.

Gaudreault-DesBiens, J.-F. (ed.) (2009), *Le droit, la religion et le 'raisonnable'. Le fait religieux entre monisme étatique et pluralisme juridique* (Montréal: Éditions Thémis).

Hersant, Y. (2009), 'Against Euroculture', in Kastoryano, R. (ed.), 59–70.

Kastoryano, R. (ed.) (2009), *An Identity For Europe. The Relevance of Multiculturalism in EU Construction* (New York: Palgrave Macmillan).

Lefebvre, S. (2009), 'La liberté religieuse modelée par les effets paradoxaux de la modernité', in Gaudreault-DesBiens, J.-F. (ed.), 195–212.

McRea, R. (2010), *Religion and the Public Order of the European Union* (Oxford and New York: Oxford University Press).

Mégret, F. (2009), 'Le Canada à la pointe de la tolérance? L'accommodement raisonnable à l'aune du droit international des droit de la personne', in Gaudreault-DesBiens, J.-F. (ed.), 263–302.

Moyn, S. (2010), *The Last Utopia. Human Rights in History* (Cambridge, MA and London: The Belknap Press of Harvard University Press).

Neuwahl, N. (2009), 'Secular or Saint? Religion and Reforming the European Union', in Gaudreault-DesBiens, J.-F. (ed.), 359–379.

Sartori, G. (2000), *Pluralismo, multiculturalismo e estranei. Saggio sulla società multietnica* (Milano: Rizzoli).

Weiler, J.H.H. (2009), 'Human Rights, Constitutionalism, and Integration: Iconography and Fetishism', in Kastoryano, R. (ed.), 103–114.

Wolton, D. (2009), 'Communication and Europe: From Multiculturalism to Cultural Cohabitation', in Kastoryano, R. (ed.), 45–57.

Chapter 6
The 'Public' and the 'Private' in the Common Law and Civil Law Traditions and the Regulation of Religion

Jean-François Gaudreault-DesBiens and Noura Karazivan

Introduction

From an archetypical standpoint, there are two distinct historical moments to which the contemporary division between the public and private spheres can be traced back (Taylor and Maclure 2010: 49–50).

The first trace of that division is to be found in Roman times, where a separation was established between 'public' matters that pertained to the State, on the one hand, and matters that were deemed to belong to the private realm (such as the family), on the other. It is during that era that the notion of *res publica* was conceptualized (ibid.). The 'public sphere' eventually became associated with the political realm. Such a vision has persisted to this day, for example in Rawls' conception of the 'public reason' (Rawls 1993: 213), which, precisely by focusing on political institutions and on the citizens' relations to what is deemed to belong to the *polis*, excludes associational realms (Audard 2007: 206) that are, in other accounts such as Habermas', included in a broader public sphere, albeit divisible into an informal one and an institutional one (see, *inter alia*, Habermas 1989).

The second significant moment dates back to the Reformation and the rise of humanism, which entailed the recognition that each individual enjoys his own 'absolute' sphere of autonomy, a space both distinct from the State and inviolable by it. Previously, the Church and political power had been united, forming a 'political *universum*' (Schmitt 1993: 296). With the Reformation, the privatization of religious worship was instigated, and, coupled with the rise of humanism that characterized the Renaissance, the individual started being envisaged as the holder of an absolute right based on his autonomy. Carl Schmitt argues in this respect that the elevation of the individual as the 'absolute value' led to a conception under which the State is reduced to a mere 'relative value'. It is in this context that the public sphere somehow became incidental to the private sphere, and that a dynamic of privatization of religion ensued. The nexus between this privatization dynamic and the remaining influence of religion as a variable to reckon with, sociologically and politically, led to the recognition of freedom of religion as the very first fundamental right (Schmitt 1993; Zoller 2008: 264). All these evolutions more or less took place at the time the Westphalian model of the State was consolidated. Yet, in spite of a certain recess of this model, today's conception of the interplay between the private and public spheres remains influenced by the debates that took place in the early modern era, as well as in Roman times. Of course, there are competing narratives of the emergence of the modern division between the public and the private spheres, such as that rooting it in the rise of the bourgeois class (Habermas 1989), but for the sake of this chapter, the account discussed shall suffice.

What is more important to note is that, as a legacy of Western political thought and practice, the division between the public and private spheres still matters today, even though it has been deconstructed since the 1960s, primarily by feminists and post-structuralists (see Zaretsky 1994: 198). It is a construct, for sure, but a construct which has a certain philosophical and sociological thickness: whether we like it or not, this divide continues to inspire the State's regulatory endeavours, as well as the behaviour of many citizens, who actually play with the boundaries between the two spheres. As Jeffrey Alexander puts it:

> The symbolic representation of traditional public functions is a regulating idea, one that carries with it an obvious force. But it is not the concrete public as a face-to-face association that is fundamental to contemporary civil societies. It is the idea of that public as it has inserted itself into social subjectivity as a structure of feeling. In order to gain influence, actors must speak the language that makes the democratic public into a regulative ideal. The normative reference of the public sphere is a cultural structure, the discourse of civil society. (Alexander 2006: 72)

As components of a cultural structure, it is inevitable that what is deemed to belong to the public sphere and what is presumed to belong to the private realm varies, even within a shared macro-cultural normative environment such as the so-called 'Western world'.

For instance, when it comes to law – itself a cultural construct – the scope occupied by public *law* varies according to the legal tradition in which one finds himself. In the common law tradition, for example, the very existence of a separate body of public law is debated, and even when its existence is recognized, the relevance of maintaining the distinction is under attack and needs to be defended.[1] In such an intellectual context, the State predictably remains relatively under-theorized (Prosser 1982), the emphasis being placed instead on determining the appropriate mechanisms to monitor its action, an approach that speaks volumes about the very conception of the 'public' as incidental to the 'private'. All this contrasts starkly with the rich literature theorizing the State in the civil law tradition – just think of the works of Duguit, Carré de Malberg, Hauriou, Kelsen, Schmitt, etc. – but which seems less preoccupied with concretely monitoring its action.

---

1 See the contributions in Auby and Freedland (2004).

The discussion that follows underscores comparative elements in both the common law and the civil law traditions which may explain the historic reluctance towards a separate public law in the common law tradition. It also highlights the often different and unstated premises upon which these legal traditions rely when attempting to distinguish the public sphere from the private realm. These remarks will inspire, in conclusion, developments regarding the space that each legal tradition confers to freedom of religion and the latitude each allows to the State in regulating religion.

The common law and civil law traditions will be contrasted along three axes: the relative importance of the State in each tradition; the consequence on the treatment of fundamental rights; and the impact on certain legal doctrines such as that of *abus de droit* (abuse of rights). Examining how each legal tradition conceives of these intellectual pillars should provide some insight in view of better understanding how each tradition conceptualizes the divide between the public and private spheres.

An important caveat is warranted at this stage, however. This account as to how the common law and the civil law traditions deal with the 'public' and the 'private' is largely ideal-typical, and to some extent relies on representations coming from insiders of these traditions. Moreover, the ideal-types examined are French and English law, and the common law and civil law traditions are not reducible to them. For instance, it is known that, despite family resemblances (Wittgenstein 1961: 148), the current state of the common law in Britain cannot be assimilated to that in the United States, notably as a result of systematization attempts through, for example, the US Code, and of the long-standing primacy of the principle of constitutionalism in the latter country. Also in spite of family resemblances, the *Code civil des Français*, with its universalistic ideology, is different from Germany's *BGB*, with its more particularistic ideology. The style of legislative drafting is also markedly different between the two. Beyond these legal variables, broader societal variables may also account for differences between the legal cultures, both internal and external,[2] of countries formally sharing a similar legal tradition. For example, in spite of both partaking in the civil law tradition, France and Italy remain quite different from each other, particularly as regards to the strength of the statist ideology. Whether such differences can be explained by reference to the respective circumstances of the construction of the French and Italian States, or as a consequence of the resilience, in the latter, of a stronger associational life beyond formally recognized socio-political actors such as political parties and unions, they possibly lead to divergences in regulatory patterns, notably with respect to religious issues.[3]

2 Friedman (1975: 223): 'The external legal culture is the legal culture of the general population; the internal legal culture is the legal culture of those members of society who perform specialized legal tasks'.

3 The authors are grateful to Alessandro Ferrari for pointing out, at the Como conference, the remaining strength of various formal or informal communities within Italy,

Bearing this caveat in mind, it remains that French and English law both had a significant reach beyond their borders, through colonialism, imperialism but also voluntary legal transplants. As such, their ideal-typical nature is hardly debatable. Although one must be cautious about inferring consequences from a normative model without actually examining how it has concretely influenced a particular State, relying on ideal-types may help identifying broader normative dynamics and 'deep social conventions' (Marmor 2009: 171–175) about what is possible or not in a legal system. Indeed, the intellectual pillars of a legal tradition may provide an analytical template – often internalized by both legal professionals and non-professionals as a form of 'tacit knowledge'[4] – from which one approaches a debate. One of the authors of this chapter has referred to such templates as 'reasoning templates', which encompass both the modes of reasoning and the basic jural conceptions underlying a legal tradition.[5] Understood in that manner, a legal tradition is more than 'a loose conglomerate of data' (Glenn 2007: 15). It can actually partake in the broader identity reference of a nation,[6] and it certainly frames the legal-cultural identity of jurists.[7] In sum, it is constitutive of an *episteme*,[8] which may sometimes determine how one ends up knowing material facts or normative proposals.

However, examining the intellectual pillars of a legal tradition does not and cannot tell the whole story.[9] It is important to stress, in that regard, that other variables may indeed be equally, or more, influential than legal tradition in order to explain the particular division between the public and the private spheres in a given jurisdiction. And, in all likelihood, one can surmise that these other variables will sometimes be more influential than legal tradition-related ones, especially considering that the intellectual pillars of legal traditions are often located at a rather deep level of legal consciousness. All this is to say that the aim is to avoid at all costs the determinism that characterizes the negative comparativism emanating from, say, 'legal origins' scholars (see Djankov 2003; Glaeser and Shleifer 2002) who occasionally oversimplify or caricature the origins of legal traditions and their influence on how States are governed and how they perform

which would account for the lesser influence of individualism in this country than in France.

4 On this type of knowledge, see Polanyi (2009).

5 On legal traditions as providing reasoning templates, see Gaudreault-DesBiens (2006: 178).

6 This may be particularly true for civil law: according to Rémy Cabrillac, the French *Code civil* 'a été délibérément voulu par ses concepteurs comme le socle fondateur de la nouvelle société, l'élément fédérateur de la Nation, tant du point de vue social que géographique' (citation omitted). See Cabrillac (2005: 245–251).

7 Gaudreault-DesBiens (2010: 683–704). As Legrand points out, law is part of a tradition 'qui forme l'arrière-plan et donc la condition de possibilité du connaître du juriste, de ses jugements de valeur et de ses opinions critiques'. See Legrand (1999: 1053–1071).

8 Legrand (1999: 1056). See also Samuel (2003: 15–17 and 111–113).

9 On the use of ideal-types in comparative law, see Lallement and Lima (2009: 379).

economically and politically.[10] This does not mean, however, that their initial intuition that legal traditions may matter at a deeper level is wrong, as there is surely something to be found in the genealogy of legal traditions. This highlights the gist of the present argument, which can be summarized as follows: when the analysis shows that no other variable is susceptible of strongly determining the outcome of a political debate about which regulatory approach should be adopted towards a particular phenomenon, looking at the reasoning template provided by the relevant legal tradition, as internalized by a particular legal system, might prove instructive.

It is with this further caveat in mind that this chapter should be read. The ideal-typical background provided should therefore be used as a springboard for launching more specific comparative research projects and obtaining finer analyses. Such analyses could reveal both similarities and differences between ideal-types and actual regulatory patterns. Our use of ideal-types thus serves a primarily heuristic purpose.

The Relative Importance of the State in the Common Law and the Civil Law Traditions

The notion of the State has been central to the development of modern French law. In the civil law tradition, the separation of public and private law stems from the 'deep belief that the cases dealing with the *res publica* are not of the same nature as those concerning the multitude of private interests. It exists only because of the belief in a public interest distinct from the numerous private interests of the people' (Zoller 2008: 259). On the other hand, in dominant representations of the common law tradition, the State has traditionally played a smaller role. Society, as a collective construct protected in civil law jurisdictions by 'public order' and from which stems a 'public interest', also has an ambiguous status in common law countries. Many reasons account for this difference: historical, institutional, legal, etc. Some pertain to the idea of sovereignty, others to the relationship between the individuals and government, and others relate to the characteristics of each legal tradition.

The Crown vs. l'État

Maurice Hauriou famously referred to the French State as a territorially-based *entreprise* which is aimed at furthering the common good.[11] Zoller describes the French notion of the 'State' as 'an ideal carried by a political will, a public

10 See Gaudreault-DesBiens (2010).

11 Hauriou (1933). According to Hauriou, the development of this *entreprise* is due to a combination of factors which increased the *étatisme* in France, defined as the intervention of the community in the sphere of private life irrespective of (and detrimental

power in charge of leading society toward a common end defined in a manifesto, a program of government' (Zoller 2008: 190). The Sovereign is the nation, composed of the people of France viewed in its unity and defined by liberty, fraternity and equality. The individual will is subsumed into the general will, the public interest, the common good. Civil codification projects illustrate this idea of the State as a societal leader. Indeed, a Civil Code is not a mere statute; it is regarded as the 'constitution of civil society'.[12] As such, it posits a *jus commune* from which particular laws derogate, which explains its pre-eminent status as a source of law. Granted, the law in civilian jurisdictions cannot be reduced to the image of a legislator handing down the 'tables of the law' to a passive society. This image nevertheless evinces the State's predominant role both as a law-giver and as a beacon to which one turns to determine where lies the common good in a plural society. From this follows this conclusion: because the ends of the State justify the means taken to further common interests, a distinct body of rules applies only to the State, and particular administrative authorities, as opposed to regular 'common law' courts, are responsible for monitoring its action. Prerogatives are an intrinsic part of these rules; hence the threads of a certain form of authoritarianism – which, it bears noting, is *not* synonymous with totalitarianism – are sown into this Republican model.[13] Why this authoritarian potential is realized in jurisdiction A and not in jurisdiction B raises questions that cannot answered solely by relying on the legal tradition variable.

In England, as a matter of principle, absolute sovereignty is exercised by Parliament,[14] and attitudes towards the 'State' are lukewarm. The relationships between Crown, Parliament and people lie at the root of the lack of distinction between public and private law. From the Magna Carta and on, there has been a progressive erosion of Crown sovereignty in favour of Parliamentary sovereignty. Moreover, the trend has been one towards the personification of the Crown. Far from embodying the State, the Crown is rather the illustration that the State 'barely existed in England'. As Allison points out, citing Barker, '(o)ur State is on its executive side a bundle of officials, individually responsible for their acts, and only united by a mysterious Crown which is responsible for nothing and serves chiefly as a bracket to unite an indefinite series of 1+1+1' (Allison 2000: 77). And as Dicey would later illustrate, the rule of law meant that public officials ought to be subjected to the ordinary law of the land, even though they could still invoke shrunken iterations of prerogatives and immunities dating back to the era of absolute monarchy. In such a context, a separate body of rules called 'public

to) individualism (ibid.: 5). This enterprise is, 'essentiellement, une entreprise de gestion d'affaires' (ibid.: 18).

12 Carbonnier (1984: 293–309). On the sociological rather than legal scope of Carbonnier's famous expression, see Cabrillac (2005: 245).

13 As such, and perhaps ironically, the French republican state ends up rather close to the Hobbesian model of the state, as expounded in his *Leviathan*.

14 Obviously, the UK's integration into the European Union has altered this dynamic.

law' almost looks like an oxymoron, and the very theorization of the 'State', a futile endeavour. To some extent, the common law tradition indeed encapsulates a vision of a 'droit sans l'État' (Cohen-Tanugi 1992).

The way in which the powers and prerogatives exercised by the monarch were transferred to (or appropriated by) Parliament is also telling. That transfer was, for the most part, gradual and pragmatic, not sudden and principled. As a result, 'it has not approximated to a developed concept of the State or its administration with the passing of time' (Allison 1997: 77–78). Of course, as will be seen in the next section, English law caught up with its French counterpart when, in the nineteenth and twentieth centuries, administrative centralization became unavoidable.

Private Interests v. l'État-Providence

According to E.C.S. Wade, the common law is a system based on the protection of individual rights which is 'not readily comparable with legislation which has for its object the welfare of the public' (Wade 1965: ciii). Traditionally, the British people viewed with a suspicious eye the neighbouring 'well-fed' States:

> (I)n the eighteenth century, when the kings and princes of continental Europe were occupied with making their people happy, the British rejoiced that they did not live under the rule of continental public law ... Nothing could be more alien to the English spirit than the well-ordered Police-State then thriving on the continent ... England was not a 'well-fed' continental state that promulgated happiness among the people by exacting laws. England was a land of freedom. (Zoller 2008: 85)

Locke's heritage can be recognized here, more precisely in the idea that the State 'exceeds its legitimate function' if it endeavours to go beyond what is strictly necessary to prevent individuals from harming one another or jeopardizing the freedom that each person is endowed with (Harlow and Rawlings 1997: 10).

If theoretically the role of the State in the Lockean tradition was merely to ensure that individuals do not infringe each other's rights, practice showed otherwise. The growth of the welfare state in England came much later than its French counterpart, but it did occur.[15] From the early nineteenth century to the end of the twentieth century, a 'change of ideology' culminated in a centralized, welfare state. In line with the British tradition of pragmatism, this steady but progressive explosion of administrative law and institutions was made, according to some views, almost unbeknownst to Parliament (see Harlow and Rawlings 1997: 10). On the face of these developments, one could not hold anymore that the State 'exceeds its

15 When calls for decentralization were being held in France, England was still in the process of centralizing its own administration, a process which was slowed down by the doctrine of *laissez-faire* still very present at the time: see Allison (1997: 76).

legitimate function' if it went beyond what was strictly necessary according to the Lockean heritage (ibid.). But such an evolution does not necessarily undermine the relevance of ideal-types, nor does it affect the resilience of reasoning templates evincing deep social conventions.

The French and English Revolutions determined the respective roles that the 'State' would play in their aftermath. In France, the administrative centralization was secured by the French Revolution, contrary to the case prevailing in England. The *Loi des 16-24 août 1790* provided that:

> Les fonctions judiciaires sont distinctes et demeureront toujours séparées des fonctions administratives; les juges ne pourront, à peine de forfaiture, troubler de quelque manière que ce soit, les opérations des corps administratifs, ni citer devant eux les administrateurs à raison de leur fonction.[16]

Such separation is explained in part by the notion of general will, which is woven into the Rousseauist theory of sovereignty. In France, the belief was that if the State is to be able to fulfil the interest of the nation, and to carry out the reforms needed to fill the gap left by the abolition of feudalism, it had to be able to act freely, *outside of the purview* of the judicial branch. In other words, it had to be 'freed from the judges and endowed with the power necessary to enforce the needed reforms' (Zoller 2008: 253).

The birth of public law in France is thus attributed to the need, for the administrative judge, to apply a distinct body of rules, one that would take into account the 'particular purpose of empowering (the administration) to carry out its enterprise' (ibid.: 255). And the underlying justification for this special law was the idea that the 'enterprise' aimed at achieving the common interest through public service.

In contrast, the English revolution 'did not express a theory of popular sovereignty conducive to administrative centralisation and comparable to the Rousseauist theory of the general will' (Allison 1997: 76). It rather strengthened the role of Parliament, clothed it with sovereignty, and enshrined the supremacy of ordinary courts. By doing so, it reinforced both 'legislative and judicial centralisation' (ibid.).

An interesting hypothesis attributes the hesitant achievement of public good by the 'State' to the gradual fading of the Royal prerogative. According to Zoller, in England, the idea of the public good was traditionally associated with the Royal prerogative, which was progressively absorbed by Parliament. As a result, 'the executive must obtain authorization from Parliament to carry out the public good. The principle of the rule of law pre-empts any governmental initiative to that end, no matter how well-intentioned that initiative may be' (Zoller 2008: 110). Under that view, the fact that the Royal prerogative came under Parliament's control contributed to slowing the emergence in England of

16 Cited in Théry (2004: 47).

an idea of the public good. As Zoller further contends, 'the realization of the public good – this common good that was formerly contained in the prerogative – is subject to parliamentary authorization and under the control of the common law, which is principally interested in the protection of *individual interests*' (ibid., emphasis added). One could construe this evolution as an acknowledgment of the contested and deliberative nature of the public good in the common law tradition. It also highlights the bottom-up process that characterizes the definition of what pertains (or not) to the public good in that tradition.

Rule of Law v. Droit administratif

In a well-known exercise in negative comparative law, A.V. Dicey cited French *droit administratif* 'as a model of what English constitutional law and practice should not do, and as illustrating features which it was a matter for rejoicing that English law did not display' (Freedland 2004: 103). In so doing, Dicey was not merely reflecting legal assumptions; he was pursuing a nationalistic agenda: '[w]hat is left is an assertion of national authority, an assertion of Englishness which, for Dicey, constrasted immeasurably with the deficiencies of the French and, especially, the Belgians. Inconvenient domestic entities which did not fit Dicey's scheme, like Scotland, were relegated in a blend of evasion and bluster' (Fitzpatrick 1992: 115). Thus, the

> classic thesis of the common law's superiority promotes an image of the civilian methodology as a machine that transforms the law into a formalist and authoritarian mechanism. Codes are criticized as unduly abstract juridical constructions which leave too much space between norms and facts, this at the risk of undermining the legal certainty that ensures the prevalence of the rule of law. The intellectual rigidity associated with the codification of key concepts possessing an immutable and predetermined content (such as that of 'property') is also deplored. With its preference for concepts and their integrity, the civilian tradition coerces facts to fit with concepts, which reflects, according to this view, the primacy of formalist reasoning in the civil law tradition as opposed to the common law's pragmatism. Last, the primarily deductive (and incidentally analogical) reasoning mode that is privileged in the civil law tradition renders unduly difficult non-syllogistic reasoning and precludes legal and, a fortiori, judicial creativity. In sum, the civilian tradition prohibits any genuine form of interpretation and legitimizes instead a naively rationalistic and mechanistic conception of legal application. Thus, rigidity and authoritarianism define that tradition, thereby considered as inferior to a common law one depicted as flexible and evolutionary, and produced organically and, first and foremost, liberally. (Gaudreault-DesBiens 2007: 59–60 [authors' translation])

As noted earlier, this form of negative comparativism remains well and alive today, albeit in a different tone.[17]

That said, Dicey's idea that public officials ought to be treated as ordinary citizens is commonly associated with the reluctance, in English law, to recognize a separate body of public law. More specifically, according to Dicey's second element of the rule of law definition, every person in England, whether public official or simple citizen, ought to be subject to the ordinary law of the land and is under the jurisdiction of regular courts. Dicey believed that administrative law and administrative tribunals were 'utterly unknown to the law of England' and 'fundamentally inconsistent' with the common law tradition (Dicey 1915 [1982]: 121). Equality before the law is a component of the rule of law which emphasizes the absence of special treatment for public officials, hence the absence of a different body of rules called administrative law.

Many pointed out the logical shortcuts in Dicey's analysis. Dicey himself revisited his position in a later edition of his *Introduction to the Study of the Law of the Constitution,* acknowledging the substantial convergence in French and English law regarding the treatment of public officials.[18] Yet, even at the time of writing, Dicey seemed to ignore the doctrine of Crown immunity which more or less isolated public officials from the realm of the common law (see Freedland 2004: 104). Of course one may hold that Crown immunity in England did not create a *different* body of law for public officials, but merely put those public officials *above* the law. But that distinction is perhaps too formalistic to stand scrutiny.

Adversarial v. Inquisitorial

As Anna Grear suggests, the *ideal-type* of private law relies on the notion of individual autonomy while that of public law revolves around the notion of control: 'public law (paradigmatically) centers on the control of a relationship of power and imposition, while private law (paradigmatically) centres on giving effect to a bilateral relationship of liberty and choice between ... individual actors' (Grear

17 Economists belonging to the 'New Comparative Economics' or 'Legal Origins' movement, who strongly inspired the World Bank's famously controversial *Doing Business* reports, occasionally fall into that trap. See Djankov, Glaeser, La Porta, Lopez-de-Silanes and Shleifer (2003: 595). See also Glaeser and Shleifer (2002: 1193).

18 According to Jean Rivero, there is substantial convergence in administrative law and *droit administratif*: 'les solutions concrètes apportées aux conflits qui s'élèvent entre administration et administrés sont, le plus souvent identiques des deux côtés de la Manche, parfois même plus efficaces sur la rive anglaise, où le *contempt of Court* garantit l'exécution de la décision du juge. Parallélisme des résultats, diversité des concepts: droit administratif et *administrative law* parviennent ainsi à concilier les traditions juridiques propres à chacun des deux pays et les réponses que le Droit se doit d'apporter aux questions posées, dans l'un et dans l'autre, par l'évolution, identique ici et là, de la société contemporaine' Rivero (1986: 18).

2003). This logic is reflected in the common law's adversarial model, especially when one considers litigation involving a private party against the Crown. Though in exercising judicial review, Courts will not hesitate to *control* the legality of the state action, they will abstain from interfering with the equality of bargaining powers between litigants. In other words, the adversarial model is adapted to the idea that public officials are also persons, and that private parties do not need extra help to sue them.

On the other hand, French law rather seems premised on the idea of the inequality of bargaining power between the individual and the State, an inequality of means which ought to be corrected by attributing the judge a significant investigative role. French law, more paternalistic than English law, embraces the inquisitorial model of adjudication, which is adapted to the perceived difficulty of private parties to access the evidence 'necessary to prove administrative illegality' (Allison 1997: 73). The inquisitorial model thus assumes the inequality of bargaining powers between the private party and the State, an assumption perhaps based on the impossibility to exercise sufficient *control* over the administrative authority, such as demonstrated by the impossibility to enforce administrative decisions against the State.[19] This gives rise to a paradox, however, which lies in the fact that the recognition of this inequality through the creation of a specific government-monitoring stream may actually end up privileging this government's interests over the citizens'.

Two Conceptions of the State–Individual Relationship

In the following part, the discussion moves towards conceptualizing how the private–public divide in each tradition influences how rights or liberties come to be recognized and exercised. The first section addresses the concept of fundamental rights in each tradition, while the second section discusses doctrines (or lack thereof) devised by each tradition in order to limit the exercise of private rights for the sake of public good.

The Concept of Fundamental Rights

Is the common law in a better position to protect fundamental rights because, contrary to continental systems of law, rights are somehow inherent in the common law and can hardly be limited on account of supra-individual values such as the common good? That hypothesis brings us back to one of Dicey's famous displays of negative comparative constitutional law (see Dicey 1915 [1982]: 116–119) to which this section is devoted.

19 According to Léon Duguit: '(l)e sujet actif n'a pas de voie d'exécution forcée contre l'État' (Duguit 1921: 548).

One of the legacies of the English revolution was the recognition that the people enjoyed individual human rights which no monarch could violate lest he run the risk of losing his legitimacy and being overthrown by the people. According to Locke, the sovereignty is vested in the people but it is exercised by Parliament; a loss of legitimacy empowers the people, through Parliament, to overthrow the monarch. As mentioned earlier, the sole function of the State, at least in Locke's theory, is to prevent individuals from infringing each other's liberties. The protection of inalienable rights which pre-exist the State was thus the backbone of Locke's work and warranted a vision of the State, and of the government, that is necessarily limited.[20]

That rights pre-exist the State is perhaps another way of saying that rights are merely recognized at common law rather than being created by courts or some constituent. These rights exist irrespective of any legislative enactment, regardless of any declaration. As such, they are pre-political, quasi natural. The American Declaration of Independence of 1776, with its emphasis on 'inalienable rights' and the government's duty to 'secure' these rights, enshrines this view. So does Dicey's third element of his definition of the rule of law. Dicey opposed to the catalogue of rights 'guaranteed' in continental constitutions, arguing that the unwritten protection of rights, as found in England, provided a better level of protection than the former. Because in England individual rights flow not from a text but from a tradition of judicial decisions which devise remedies by which these rights will be enforced, these rights are more secure than in continental systems. While appearing blameless, laying down general principles of law, as continental jurists do, may obscure the 'absolute necessity for the provision of adequate remedies by which the rights they proclaimed might be enforced' (Dicey 1915 [1982]: 117–118). Since in the common law *ubi jus ibi remedium*, the focus is put on the remedy rather than on a formal declaration which contains no enforcement mechanisms. The consequence of this distinction is, for Dicey, the relative facility with which rights in continental traditions can be 'suspended or taken away' (ibid.: 120). Conversely, in the common law tradition, the rule of law makes such suspension of rights impracticable, given the role of the judiciary in guarding and enforcing the common law, in which are rooted the fundamental rights of individuals. In light of this, can it be assumed that rights are more easily suspended in continental traditions? In other words, is Dicey's look over the Channel persuasive?

---

20 Locke (2002: Chap. IX, paragraph 131). On the distinction between rights as limiting the *State*, and rights as self-imposed limitations on *government* actions that the State adopts in order to achieve its goals, see Steinberger (2004: 186): 'The doctrine of limited government is thus completely and entirely consistent with the omnicompetence of the state'. Referring to Hobbes' vision of an unlimited State, Steinberger adds: 'whereas Hobbes's insistence on unlimited power is a part of his account of the state, his minimalism – like his preference for monarchical government – is merely a pragmatic or prudential claim about the particular mechanisms that the state might best employ in order to achieve its goals' (ibid.).

True, continental law contains catalogues of rights. But as Carl Schmitt argues, fundamental rights ought to be distinguished from other constitutionally-guaranteed rights. The Constitution lists both, both are said to be 'rooted in the Constitution', but only the former pre-exist the State. Thus, in Schmitt's view:

> dans l'État de droit bourgeois les droits fondamentaux ne sont que les droits qui peuvent être considérés comme *antérieurs et supérieurs à l'État*, que l'État n'octroie pas dans les conditions prévues par les lois … mais qu'il reconnaît et qu'il protège comme antérieurs à lui, et auxquels il ne peut porter atteinte que d'une façon mesurable en principe et seulement selon une procédure réglementée. (Schmitt 1993: 301)

Fundamental rights such as the right to personal liberty, freedom of expression, etc., can thus be said to pre-exist the State in the continental traditions as well as the common-law ones.[21] The sole purpose of the State, with regards to those rights, is the protection of their exercise free of restraints. And writing down those rights, for Schmitt, merely serves the purpose of recognizing their existence; it does not define the content of those rights. For some other continental authors, however, declaring clearly what the natural rights are and where the limits on the legislative power lie, avoids the English vagueness which was seen as providing opportunities for abuse.[22] In any event, and whatever added value *is* given to the written text, continental authors do not argue that the text creates the right, as Dicey implied.

But even if this conception seems to contradict Dicey's analysis of the catalogue of rights, the following part of Schmitt's theory confirms Dicey's apprehension, however. Schmitt stresses the unlimited individual freedom and the limited '*mesurable et contrôlable*'[23] ability of the State to limit those rights. Discussing what those measurable limits may be, Schmitt refers to normal activities meant to secure peace and order; if those normal activities are not sufficient, we fall back on

21 *Contra*: see Hogg (1987: 89–90): 'I do not believe in "natural rights". If that makes me a positivist, so be it. I do not know how to identify natural rights, from whence they derive their authority, or what the legal effect of their breach could be … To me, rights are creatures of the law. The rights guaranteed by the *Charter of Rights* are legally enforceable because they are contained in a supreme constitutional instrument, not because they reflect the natural rights of man (or woman)'.

22 Cornu (2004: 163) summarizes as follows the semantic analysis of the Déclaration des droits de l'homme et du citoyen: 'En effet, à la prendre dans son contenu explicite, tout son ressort consiste à dire, (y compris pour Brissot et Condorcet): (a) il existe des "lois naturelles"; (b) aucune nation ne peut les créer ni les décréter, l'Assemblée se borne à les déclarer, c'est-à-dire à les reconnaître, alors qu'elles existent déjà (etc.)' (ibid.: 176).

23 Schmitt (1993: 302).

the *état d'exception*, for which a temporary suspension of fundamental rights can be operated by a legislative act.[24]

The question that remains unsolved in legal theory is that of the power of the State to limit rights considering, on the one hand, theories that support the inalienable right of the individual, and, on the other, theories that support the emergence of a common will creating a political order, itself autonomous, and hence carrying the seeds of unlimited action. That paradox, as Rainer Nickel observes:

> is by no means only a problem of constitutional orders with a written catalogue of rights; the common law tradition of parliamentary sovereignty only vested the dispute in different terms and its intense discussion of the rights-related essentials of the common law and the content of the principle of the 'rule of law' reflects the unclear heritage of enlightenment thinking. (Nickel 2007: 147–152, footnote 7)

Consequently, the hypothesis that in common law systems, fundamental rights are more secure, i.e. that they are less easily limited by the State, because they are inherent to the individual and are not 'given' by the State, remains to be demonstrated. Perhaps the difference in the level of protection lies not in the conception of rights (as both traditions believe in the inherent rights of men), but in the existence of an efficient remedy to sanction violations. Judicial review of administrative action may be a more powerful indicator of the level of rights protection.

'Private' Rights and Private Law

Suppose that private law and public law are indeed separate areas of the law and coexist in a legal system. What about areas *within private law* which involve elements of the distinction between public and private? Are they treated differently? As the next sections briefly expound, even in areas of 'private law' such as the law of contracts, the distinct approach to the public–private dichotomy cannot be avoided.

The narrower scope of public policy as compared to ordre public Dubbed as an 'unruly horse',[25] the concept of public policy does not fare well in the common law

24 See (ibid.: 313–314 and 248). See also Dyzenhaus (2006). On the distinction between Dicey and Schmitt and the right of the Sovereign to decide on the exception, see Karazivan and Crépeau (2009).

25 *Richardson v. Mellish* (1824) 2 Bing. 229, 252, per Burrough J. In *Egerton* v. *Brownlow* (1853) 4 HLC 1, public policy was described as 'that principle of law which holds that no subject can lawfully do that which has a tendency to be injurious to the public, or against public good'.

tradition. Since the common law has a tendency to privilege freedom of contract, which has its roots in the individualism that characterizes the tradition, there is a clear reluctance to resort to public policy and more generally to broad principles with uncertain contours. Conversely, in French civil law, good mores or *l'ordre public*, the latter referring to a set of general principles which may be codified or not, cover a vast array of improper conduct. According to Gutteridge, 'les principes supérieurs des bonnes moeurs et de l'ordre public jouent un beaucoup plus grand rôle dans le droit du continent que la "morality" et la "public policy" dans notre common law' (Gutteridge 1953: 133). That difference may be explained by the prudent attitude of the common law judge 'toutes les fois que les circonstances rendent nécessaire de faire appel à quelque principe général pour éviter une injustice qu'entraînerait l'application d'une règle de droit positif' (ibid.: 134). Ironically, Gutteridge's chosen example of what constitutes a public policy rule in common law England is the rule against the 'unreasonable restraint of trade'.[26]

It also bears noting that, in addition to being given a broader application in contracts law than its common law bedfellow, the doctrine of *ordre public* applies beyond that field. Perhaps counter-intuitively, civil law judges thus enjoy a margin of discretion almost unknown to their common law counterparts. Domestic arbitration is one area where debates commonly arise as to what is encompassed by public policy or *ordre public* (Gaudreault-DesBiens 2011: 159, 172–173). International arbitration law also regularly struggles with this thorny question.[27] Moreover, the concept of *ordre public* is mentioned in international and regional treaties (Goodwin-Gill 1978: 354), raising the question of the predictability of state-parties conduct, especially as regards the implementation of that concept. In other words, the seemingly ambiguous relation between the concepts of *ordre public* and public policy has ramifications that go beyond the civil law-common law debate as it is traditionally envisaged.

That being said, what must primarily be borne in mind for the sake of our discussion is that a concept, i.e. that of *ordre public*, which seeks to legally materialize societal concerns deemed consensual and important enough to justify a restriction to the private freedoms of particular social actors, is given a broader interpretation in the civil law tradition than that afforded to its functional equivalent in the common law tradition, i.e. the public policy doctrine.

The absence of a theory of abus de droit Another consequence of the public–private divide is the acceptance of the idea that private rights are not absolute; they ought not to be exercised in a way that willingly diminishes the rights of others

26 Ibid.: 132. The equivalent of an 'unreasonable restraint of trade' is against *bonos mores* in French law.

27 See the Final Report of the International Law Association – International Commercial Arbitration Committee – on public policy as a bar to the enforcement of international arbitral awards: Conference Report New Delhi, 2002, www.ila-hq.org/en/committees/index.cfm/cid/19.

in the absence of a serious or legitimate interest on the part of the right holder. It bears noting that contractual abuse of rights is only one aspect of the general abuse of rights doctrine[28] which applies in property law, administrative law, etc. To grasp its general meaning, one can quote Voltaire, as the Supreme Court of Canada did in *Houle* v. *National Bank*, when he said that 'A right taken too far becomes an injustice'.[29]

While the abuse of rights doctrine may be understood in more than one sense, in the matter of relevance here, the absence of a theory of *abus de droit* has been related to the discreet role played by the notion of 'public interest' in the common law tradition. In fact, public interest seldom comes in the way of a right, however ill-exercised.[30] 'A right is a right is a right' is an oft-quoted maxim in the common law world. The idea that a right is a legally valid claim, which is also typical of the common law mindset, somehow presides over the demise of the very possibility that a right be abused, since it would amount to giving moral considerations precedence over legal ones proper. According to Michael Taggart, no matter how 'harmful to the public interest' the exercise of a right may be, the common law generally refuses to 'investigate the motives or reasons for the exercise of lawful powers' (ibid.).

Although a theory of *abus de droit* may not be found strictly speaking in the common law tradition, the doctrines of nuisance, public policy, bad faith in the performance of a contract, duress, and others refer to concerns similar to those raised by the civil law doctrine.[31] According to Tony Weir, English law is 'not supposed to have any doctrine of abuse of rights (but it is only the doctrine which is lacking)'.[32] Similarly, Gutteridge refers to the doctrines of good faith, equity and public policy as acting in lieu of the abuse of rights doctrine, though they are

28 *Houle* v. *National Bank of Canada* (1990) 3 S.C.R. 122, 136. It is to be noted that the Supreme Court of Canada decided this case on the basis of Quebec's civil law, which is largely derived from French civil law.

29 Ibid., the Court citing Voltaire, p. 138.

30 See Taggart (1997: 16), on the absence, in the common law, of a doctrine which 'prevents a right-holder abusing the right by exercising it for the sole purpose of harming another or for a purpose other than that for which it was granted or in an unreasonably disproportionate fashion'.

31 On American law, see Perillo (1995).

32 Weir (1998: 97–124, footnote 140). At a conceptual level, Ernest Weinrib argues that although the notion of abuse of rights tends to be viewed as introducing considerations of morality (for some) foreign to the idea of rights, and although it seems to 'contain the contradictory impulses of recognising the right yet limiting the right holder's freedom', this conception is mistaken. If one holds on to an idea that 'participants in the system of rights' commit only 'purposive actions', i.e. actions which are not intended to merely create obstacles to someone else, but which are rather aimed towards the achievement of one's self-chosen goals, then to require that one exercises his rights while avoiding adverse consequences to others is not at all incompatible with the common law (or, for that matter, the civil law tradition). Otherwise, 'if the freedom to perform an act merely to frustrate the

much more circumscribed than their French counterparts given the common law's historical reluctance towards *principes supérieurs* (Gutteridge 1953: 129–134). It is important not to forget that good faith has been aptly characterized by Gunther Teubner as an 'irritant' in the dialogue between the common law and the civil law in the European context (see Teubner 2000).

Yet, one question lingers: is the presence of a doctrine of *abus de droit* necessary, after all, in the common law? According to Pierre Catala and Tony Weir, the characteristics of the common law, and more particularly the pragmatic judicial recognition of rights make that doctrine superfluous:

> A doctrine of abuse of rights is necessary only if the rights are proclaimed in generous terms; if they are initially hedged with qualifications, it may not be required at all. The former is the French legislative method; the latter is peculiar to the common-law tradition of England, which affects the style of legislation as well as its construction. If a right arises at common law, the authority for it will be a judicial decision in typically narrow terms, obiter and unauthoritative in so far as it goes beyond the facts under review; English statutes also make every effort to avoid appearing to grant a broadly stated right, and even when a right is indubitably conferred, the judges are there to state that the legislature has at the same time impliedly restricted it. (Catala and Weir 1964: 221)

The common law, which sees itself as casuistic and pragmatic, does not easily lend itself to the iteration of general principles of public interest. Hence, perhaps having an abuse of rights doctrine is not of the utmost importance.

To sum up, while some of the themes examined in Part I and Part II of this chapter demonstrate a deep division between the civil law and the common law paradigms, others show that the presumed differences are, in fact, differences in form, not substance. The use of metaphorical language to refer to the distinctions between both traditions is, on the other hand, here to stay. For example, considering the lack of a categorical approach to law, Allison speaks of the introduction of the distinction between private and public law in the common law as similar to that made by a Trojan-horse.[33] Taggart suggests, for his part, that French law is a 'motorway' and English law is a 'maze', yet, producing better 'practical results' (Taggart 1997: 19). This last value judgment quite obviously reveals his author's own assumptions about both practicality and the quality of results. As such, it remains debatable.

---

purposes of another were legitimate, rights would be transformed from markers of mutual freedom to instruments of subordination'. See Weinrib (2008: 3, 29–30).

33 See generally Allison (2000).

Conclusion: Implications for the Regulation of Religion

What to make of these ideal-typical differences when reflecting on the State regulation of religion?

While their explanatory power should not be exaggerated, especially given the relative blurring that is currently taking place between legal traditions as a result of the globalization processes affecting law, they shed some light on implicit presuppositions underlying State regulation in that area. Robert Cover aptly noted that a legal tradition

> includes not only a corpus juris, but also a language and a mythos – narratives in which the *corpus juris* is located by those who will act upon it. These myths establish the paradigms for behaviour. They build relations between the normative and the material universe, between the constraints of reality and the demands of an ethic. These myths establish a repertoire of moves – a lexicon of normative action – that may be combined into meaningful patterns culled from the meaningful patterns of the past. (Cover 1983: 9)

As such, they constitute 'reasoning templates' that may provide deep reasons for adopting one broad regulatory approach over another. At the very least, they may explain some observable tendencies in the State regulation of religion. The most important ones are summarized hereunder.

Firstly, the power balance between the State as the guardian of the public interest and individuals as rights bearers varies according to each tradition. Within each tradition, this balance may be significantly altered, depending of the society involved, by the presence (strong or weak), or the absence, of intermediate and politically salient layers of solidarity which express themselves through formally or informally constituted groups. These groups provide a buffer between the atomized individual and the omnipotent State. Depending on the State's level of formal recognition of these groups, religious freedoms, both in their individual and collective dimension, may be more or less easily restricted. This refers here not only to groups generally thought of as belonging to 'civil society',[34] such as religious ones, but also to groups which, given the specific fabric of a society, may end up being formally recognized in law as deserving a form of special status, such as national minorities in some countries.

As well, the power balance between the State and individuals as it is established at a certain moment in time always has an *historicité*, which accounts for the sometimes very significant differences that are observable between States sharing the same legal tradition. In order to fully understand certain regulatory patterns, reference to history is often mandatory. For example, France's current regime of *laïcité* cannot be understood in all of its complexity without further examining the interactions between the Church and the State in the centuries before the

34 For a genealogy of the concept of 'civil society', see Thériault (1985).

1905 separation law. Such an examination would reveal that a process of legal secularization, which had begun with the Revolution, had deeply affected the enactment, a few years later, of the *Code civil des Français*.[35] It would also bring to light a general normative dynamic of diversity reduction after the Revolution, at least in the realm of public law.[36]

Secondly, the dominant representation of the State and of its officials within a particular legal tradition may also influence the shape that the regulation of religion will take in a State belonging to that tradition. Is the State abstractly envisaged as the bearer of sovereignty, thereby giving it primacy over individuals? Or is it instead conceptualized, in both internal and external legal cultures, as the formal legal embodiment of a particular political community with a shared trajectory? If the former conception prevails, restrictions to individual freedoms risk being easier to justify, be it on the ground of public order or of *raison d'État*. If the latter dominates, regulatory patterns might be quite different. Arguably, the State is more likely to be considered as an end in itself in the civil law mindset, while it will tend to be considered as a means in the common law tradition. Important consequences might flow from this premise. For example, the civil law's more abstract and 'finalist' conception of the State might induce a government to strongly insist on the religious neutrality of its civil servants, especially those interacting with citizens, and to prohibit them from wearing visible religious signs at work. On the contrary, if a legal tradition adopts the more instrumental and concrete conception of the State that is promoted within the common law tradition, it might be more inclined to allow its employees to wear such signs because they are deemed not to represent an abstractly-defined sovereign State, but a particular community, with its tapestry of colours, that must be *served* and *represented* by the State.[37]

Thirdly, and as a consequence of the above, the civil law tradition seems more prone to accept intrinsic limitations to fundamental rights, with a conception of these rights that is more objectivist than the more subjectivist one adopted in common law jurisdictions.[38] A subjectivist conception of rights is, by definition, more sensitive to one's own self-definition of identity, be it religious or otherwise, than an objectivist one, which evaluates that self-definition in light of criteria that are external to the claimant, and that often refer to majoritarian conceptions that may even be consciously rejected by that claimant. These conceptions may either refer to a dominant strand within a particular community, for example a religious

35 Jean Carbonnier characterized the Civil Code as a 'code laïque'. See Carbonnier (2008: 1384–1385).

36 On this dynamic, see Rouland (1995).

37 The authors would like to thank Adam Seligman for his very useful comments on this difference at the Como conference.

38 We are not referring here to the distinction, often found in civil law systems, between 'objective law', i.e. the entire body of positive norms, and 'subjective rights', i.e. the rights that legal persons can claim for themselves.

one, or to the majoritarian values of the global community. In this respect, Pierre Langeron notes that:

> l'idéal politique et les valeurs communes sont définis dans la culture latine par une majorité, et la diversité n'est qu'une étape vers l'intégration dans un modèle commun; la culture anglo-saxonne est beaucoup plus ouverte à la diversité et à la liberté des individus et des groupes, elle tend à fédérer plutôt qu'à assimiler. (Langeron 2011: 169–172)

This means, concretely, that a civil law State will tend to enjoy more leeway than its common law counterpart when it wants to impose constraints on one's exercise of individual liberties.[39] As anecdotal evidence of this, think of the relatively easy acceptance in some civil law countries of a legal distinction between (legitimate) religions and (illegitimate) cults, or of bans on signs that are seen by some as having a religious dimension,[40] and the reluctance in common law ones to adopt a similar path.

Fourthly, the public sphere tends to be broader in civil law jurisdictions than in common law ones, resulting in a larger space of State regulation. Here 'public sphere' is taken to refer to all the loci, generally open to the public, where individuals interact concretely or symbolically with others envisaged as non-proximate others. In any event, the concepts of 'public sphere', 'public good', 'public interest', or 'public order' are all generally given a broader interpretation at civil law than at common law.

Now, if we assume that the account above accurately reflects basic cultural traits that can be associated to the common law and civil law traditions, which variables are likely to reinforce these traits and which are instead susceptible of undermining their influence?

What about, for example, the influence of language as a vector of ideology? The example of Quebec, in Canada, is quite interesting in this regard. While the formal legal framework governing freedom of religion is the same across Canada, resistance to the subjectivist conception of that freedom, which is very close to that adopted in other common law countries, is much stronger in Quebec than in other provinces. Interestingly, public opinion in this predominantly French-speaking province with close cultural ties to France is heavily influenced by the French conception of secularism, even if it this particular conception has no legal

39 Another important variable, which is not per se related to a particular legal tradition, is whether or not a given State has integrated the principle of constitutionalism into its positive constitutional order, especially if this principle is implemented through a concrete and a posteriori judicial control of the constitutionality of State action.

40 See for example, the opinion of the French Constitutional Council upholding the *Act prohibiting the concealing of the face in public*, Decision no. 2010 – 613 DC of 7 October 2010, www.conseil-constitutionnel.fr/conseil-constitutionnel/root/bank/download/2010613DCen2010_613dc.pdf.

resonance strictly speaking in Canada. For example, Bill 94, which was tabled in the National Assembly in 2010 but has yet to be adopted, seeks to prohibit the delivery of public services to persons, or by government employees, covering their face (i.e. wearing a full veil). Should it be adopted, Quebec would join France and Belgium, all civil law jurisdictions, in enacting that type of legislation. Interestingly, the province is a mixed jurisdiction where private law is of French origins and public law of British origins, but, here, language as a vector of ideology is possibly more potent than legal tradition as a potential explanation of the 'stronger' type of regulation privileged. The ideology in question interestingly reveals most, if not all, of the features described earlier about the civil law's 'statist' ideology.

Then, what about the influence of religion itself? For instance, can the State regulation of religion be affected by a 'Catholic' conception of religion, which may induce one to search for a correspondence between a religious claim and some official doctrine when appraising the seriousness of such a claim, as opposed to a 'Protestant' conception of religion, which is more likely to emphasize the subjective nature of religious choices and their intimate connection with personal identity?[41]

These are mere examples of inquiries that could be made in view of isolating the actual impact, if any, of the legal tradition variable on the regulation of religion in a particular State. Clearly, much more remains to be said about the intersection of legal tradition and other variables in view of explaining regulatory patterns concerning religion. And if most of these patterns arguably result from a complex nexus of influences, researchers should nevertheless make sure to integrate the legal tradition variable in their analyses, be it only to discard it *after* a fully-fledged examination of its potential impact.

References

Alexander, J.C. (2006), *The Civil Sphere* (Oxford: Oxford University Press).

Allison, J.W.F. (1997), 'Theoretical and Institutional Underpinnings of a Separate Administrative Law', in Taggart, M. (ed.), 71–89.

Allison, J.W.F. (2000), *A Continental Distinction in the Common Law: A Historical and Comparative Perspective on English Public Law* (Oxford: Oxford University Press).

Aroney, N. and Adhar, R. (eds) (2011), *Shari'a in the West* (Oxford: Oxford University Press).

Auby, J.-B. and Freedland, M. (eds) (2004), *La distinction du droit public et du droit privé: regards français et britanniques; The Public Law-Private Law Divide: une entente assez cordiale?* (Paris: Panthéon Assas).

Audard, C. (2007), *John Rawls* (Montreal and Kingston: McGill-Queen's University Press).

41 For that type of argument, see Moon (2005: 202).

Benoist O. and Isar, H. (eds) (2011), *Pluralisme, pluralismes* (Aix: Presses Universitaires d'Aix-Marseille).

Cabrillac, R. (2005), 'Le code civil est-il la véritable constitution de la France?', *Revue juridique Thémis*, 39:2, 245–251.

Calhoun, C. (ed.) (1994), *Social Theory and the Politics of Identity* (Oxford: Blackwell).

Cane, P. and Stapleton, J. (eds) (1998), *The Law of Obligations: Essays in Celebration of John Fleming* (New York: Oxford University Press).

Carbonnier, J. (1984), 'Le Code civil', in Nora, P. (ed.), 293–309.

Carbonnier, J. (2008), 'La sécularisation du droit civil par le Code civil des Français', in *Écrits* (Paris: Presses Universitaires de France), 1384–1394.

Catala, P. and Weir, J.A. (1964), 'Delict and Torts: A Study in Parallel, Part II', *Tulane Law Review*, 38, 221–236, 221.

Choudhry, S. (ed.) (2006), *The Migration of Constitutional Ideas* (Cambridge: Cambridge University Press).

Cohen-Tanugi, L. (1992), *Le droit sans l'État. Sur la démocratie en France et en Amérique* (Paris: Quadrige/Presses Universitaires de France).

Cornu, L. (2004), *Une autre république: 1791, L'occasion et le destin d'une initiative républicaine* (Paris: L'Harmattan).

Cover, R.M. (1983), 'Foreword: Nomos and Narrative', *Harvard Law Review*, 97, 4–68.

Dicey, A.V. (1915), *Introduction to the Study of the Law of the Constitution*, originally 8th edn (London: MacMillan; reprinted in Indianapolis: Liberty Fund, 1982).

Dicey, A.V. (1959), *Introduction to the Study of the Law of the Constitution: with Introduction by E.C.S. Wade*, 10th edn (London: MacMillan, 1965).

Djankov, S., Glaeser, E., La Porta, R., Lopez-de-Silanes, F. and Shleifer, A. (2003), 'The New Comparative Economics', *Journal of Comparative Economics*, 31:1, 595.

Duguit, L. (1921), *Traité de droit constitutionnel*, vol. 1, 2nd edn (Paris: Broccard).

Dyzenhaus, D. (2006), 'Schmitt v. Dicey: Are States of Emergency Inside or Outside the Legal Order?', *Cardozo Law Review*, 27:5, 2005–2011.

Fitzpatrick, P. (1992), *The Mythology of Modern Law* (London and New York: Routledge).

Flogaïtis, S. (1986), *Administrative law et droit administratif* (Paris: L.G.D.J.).

Freedland, M. (2004), 'The Evolving Approach to the Public/Private Distinction in English Law', in Auby, J.-B. and Freedland, M. (eds), 93–112.

Friedman, L.M. (1975), *The Legal System: A Social Science Perspective* (New York: Russell Sage Foundation).

Gaudreault-DesBiens, J.-F. (2006), 'Underlying Principles and the Migration of Reasoning Templates: A Trans-Systemic Reading of the Quebec Secession Reference', in Choudhry, S. (ed.), 178–208.

Gaudreault-DesBiens, J.-F. (2007), *Les solitudes du bijuridisme au Canada. Essai sur les rapports de pouvoir entre les traditions juridiques et la résilience des atavismes identitaires* (Montréal: Éditions Thémis).
Gaudreault-DesBiens, J.-F. (2010), 'La critique économiste de la tradition romano-germanique', *Revue trimestrielle de droit civil*, 4, 683–704.
Gaudreault-DesBiens, J.-F. (2011), 'Religious Courts, Personal Federalism and Legal Transplants', in Aroney, N. and Adhar, R. (eds), 159–180.
Glaeser, E.L. and Shleifer, A. (2002), 'Legal Origins', *The Quarterly Journal of Economics*, 1193–1229.
Glenn, P. (2007), *Legal Traditions of the World*, 3rd edn (New York: Oxford University Press).
Goodwin-Gill, G. (1978), 'Ordre Public Considered and Developed', *Law Quarterly Review*, 94, 354–358.
Grear, A. (2003), 'Theorizing the Rainbow? The Puzzle of the Public-Private Divide', *Res Publica*, 9, 169–182.
Gutteridge, H.C. (1953), *Le droit comparé: introduction à la méthode comparative dans la recherche juridique et l'étude du droit,* traduction sous la direction de René David (Paris: Librairie générale de Droit et de Jurisprudence).
Habermas, J. (1989), *The Structural Transformation of the Public Sphere: An Inquiry into a Category of Bourgeois Society* (Cambridge, MA: MIT Press).
Harlow, C. and Rawlings, R. (1997), *Law and Administration*, 2nd edn (Butterworths: London).
Hauriou, M. (1933), *Précis de droit administratif et de droit public*, 12th edn (Paris: Sirey).
Hogg, P. (1987), 'The Charter of Rights and American Theories of Interpretation', *Osgoode Hall Law Journal*, 25, 87–113.
Karazivan, N. and Crépeau, F. (2009), 'Le rôle des tribunaux dans l'affirmation de la primauté du droit en temps d'insécurité: l'affaire Arar', in Scherrer, A. et al. (eds), 32–48.
Lallement, M. and Lima, L. (2009), 'Idéal-type et convention: complémentarité ou concurrence?' in Legrand, P. (ed.), 379–403.
Langeron, P. (2011), 'Le pluralisme au Québec; un modèle en crise?', in Benoist, O. and Isar, H. (eds), 169–172.
Legrand, P. (1999), 'Analyse différentielle des juriscultures', *Revue internationale de droit comparé*, 51:4, 1053–1071.
Legrand, P. (ed.) (2009), *Comparer les droits, résolument* (Paris: Presses Universitaires de France).
Locke, J. (2002), *The Second Treatise of Government and A Letter Concerning Toleration* (Mineola: Dover Publications Inc.).
Loughlin, M. and Walker, N. (eds) (2007), *The Paradox of Constitutionalism: Constituent Power and Constitutional Form* (Oxford: Oxford University Press).
Marmor, A. (2009), *Social Conventions: From Language to Law* (Princeton: Princeton University Press).

Moon, R. (2005), 'Religious Commitment and Identity: Syndicat Northcrest v. Amselem', *Supreme Court Law Review*, 29 (2d), 201–220.

Nickel, R. (2007), 'Private and Public Autonomy Revisited: Habermas' Concept of Co-originality in Times of Globalization and the Militant Security State', in Loughlin, M. and Walker, N. (eds), 147–152.

Nora, P. (ed.) (1984), *Les lieux de mémoire*, v.2, t.2 (Paris: Gallimard).

Perillo, J.M. (1995), 'Abuse of Rights: A Pervasive Legal Concept', *Pacific LJ*, 27, 37–97.

Polanyi, M. (2009), *The Tacit Dimension* (Chicago: University of Chicago Press).

Prosser, T. (1982), 'Towards a Critical Public Law', *Journal of Law & Society*, 9:1, 3.

Rawls, J. (1993), *Political Liberalism* (New York: Columbia University Press).

Rickett, C.E.F. (ed.) (2008), *Justifying Private Law Remedies* (Oxford and Portland: Hart Publishing).

Rivero, J. (1986), 'Préface', in Flogaïtis, S., 15–19.

Rouland, N. (1995), *L'État français et le pluralisme. Histoire politique des institutions publiques de 476 à 1792* (Paris: Éditions Odile Jacob).

Samuel, S. (2003), *Epistemology and Method in Law* (Aldershot: Ashgate).

Scherrer, A., Guittet E.-P. and Bigo, D. (eds) (2009), *Mobilité(s) sous surveillance. Perspectives croisées UE/Canada* (Montreal: Athena).

Schmitt, C. (1993), *Théorie de la Constitution* (Paris: Presses Universitaires de France), coll. Léviathan.

Snyder, F. (ed.) (2000), *The Europeanisation of Law: The Legal Effects of European Integration* (Oxford: Hart Publishing).

Steinberger, P.J. (2004), *The Idea of the State* (Cambridge: Cambridge University Press).

Taggart, M. (ed.) (1997), *The Province of Administrative Law* (Oxford: Hart Publishing).

Taylor, C. and Maclure, J. (2010), *Laïcité et liberté de conscience* (Paris: La Découverte).

Teubner, G. (2000), 'Legal Irritants: Good Faith in British Law, or How Unifying Law Ends Up in New Differences', in Snyder, F. (ed.), 243–268.

Thériault, J.-Y. (1985) *La société civile ou la chimère insaisissable* (Montreal: Québec/Amérique).

Théry, P. (2004), 'Droit public et droit privé: l'évolution du droit processuel', in Auby, J.-B. and Freedland, M. (eds), 39–47.

Wade, E.C.S. (1965), 'Introduction', in Dicey, A.V., xvii–cxcviii.

Weinrib, E. (2008), 'Two Conceptions of Remedies', in Rickett, C.E.F. (ed.), 3–32.

Weir, T. (1998), 'The Staggering March of Negligence', in Cane, P. and Stapleton, J. (eds), 97–138.

Wittgenstein, L. (1961), *Investigations philosophiques* (Paris: Gallimard).

Zaretsky, E. (1994), 'Identity Theory, Identity Politics: Psychoanalysis, Marxism, Post-Structuralism', in Calhoun, C. (ed.), 208–213.

Zoller, E. (2008), *Introduction to Public Law: A Comparative Study* (Leiden: Martinus Nijhoff).

Chapter 7

Contested Normative Cultures: Gendered Perspectives on Religions and the Public/Private Divide[1]

Hanne Petersen

Tribulations and Reinterpretations

The German legal historian Franz Wieacker wrote in 1985 that no 'planetary legal culture' yet exists, but that a plurality of ancient and contemporary often very old legal cultures exist – also outside of Europe. Wieacker had given a lecture on the conditions of a European legal culture, which he also called an 'Atlantic-European' legal culture, and had spoken about challenges to law:

> In its external form of power law's mightiness is only outdone through the pure violence of inner or outer wars as *ultima ratio regis*; towards its inner side it is only outdone through religions as long as they still stay alive and have force, or through the not only proclaimed but also believed ideologies, which irresistibly drive human beings to the bad or to the good (also against their own interests or even their own existence). (Wieacker 1985: 7; my translation)[2]

Wieacker's speech was held at the onset of the glasnost[3] era starting in the mid 1980s with the elections of Gorbachev. Since then we have witnessed further decades of challenges to Western (European) state law both through wars and through challenges from religions, particularly Islam. The Soviet Union collapsed

1 A part of the research leading to this chapter has received funding from the European Commission's Seventh Framework Programme (FP7/2007-2013) under the grant agreement Religare (project no. 244635).

2 The original text: In seiner äusseren Machtgestalt wird Recht an Mächtigkeit nur noch überboten durch die reine Gewalt der inneren oder äusseren Kriege als *ultima ratio regis*; nach seiner inneren Seite nur durch die Religionen, solange sie noch Leben und Kraft haben, oder durch die nicht nur verkündeten, sondern auch geglaubten Ideologien, welche die Menschen unwiderstehlich (auch gegen ihre eigenen Interessen oder gar ihre Existenz) zum Bösen oder zum Guten treiben.

3 Glasnost is Russian for openness and indicates the reform period leading up to the collapse of the Soviet Union in 1991.

and both former Eastern and Western European (and other) states have been weakened by globalization. This has had a clear effect on the trust in state laws and their possibilities of delivering the goods for their populations. Ferrari claims that globalization, by reducing any particular culture to a regional custom, has engendered a sense of alienation and disorientation that has fostered the need of a common identity, which states have not been able to meet (Ferrari 2006: 626). Contemporary European Christian communities and organizations have by and large not been able to meet this need of European majority populations, even if religions have again become more public (Casanova 1994).

After the euphoria following the end of the Cold War we have also witnessed growing fear and uncertainty (see Baumann 2007; Høilund 2010), policies of fear and more or less orchestrated 'phobias', particularly Islamophobia, particularly since 9/11. Since the collapse of the Soviet Union, European culture(s) have re-evaluated their Christian historical heritage alongside the importance of secularism – also in a legal context. Belgian law professor Isabelle Rorive writes in a recent article that it is worth keeping in mind that until 1992 the European Court of Human Rights did not issue a single judgment 'where the right to religious freedom was given a full and proper consideration. For more than thirty years, these applications were deemed inadmissible as "manifestly ill-founded"'. This happened in spite of the fact that numerous complaints based on Article 9 of the European Convention of Human Rights were raised (Rorive 2009: 2673).

What we have been witnessing can be understood as a reinterpretation of the European past and of the importance of religions and religious cultures. They have for about two centuries been considered belonging to the so-called private sphere in a secular normative culture.[4] The Christian influence is increasingly acknowledged, and the latest example of this can be seen in the *Lautsi* case decided by the European Court of Human Rights in March 2011. In the twenty-first century the importance of a secular worldview and a secular organization of the state are especially stressed in France and Turkey. Both countries formally and strongly underline the importance of *laïcité*.[5]

The 'return of religion' to the European public sphere has coincided with a period of extra-European migration, often in the form of family reunification. The influx of especially Muslim migrants has overlapped with an increasing move (migration/mobility) of women (both secular, Christian, Muslim and other) during the last decades from the private sphere of family life to the public sphere of

4 Isabelle Rorive writes that most of the 16 lawsuits decided in Strasbourg (until 2008) in cases concerning individuals banned from wearing religious symbols in various circumstances, were filed after 2000 (Rorive 2009: 2671). This jurisprudence is thus a twenty-first century phenomenon.

5 Of the 16 cases discussed by Rorive, 14 were filed against Turkey (nine cases) and France (five cases).

politics, education and the labour market. The interrelation and intersectionality[6] between these two spheres and their consequences for men and women living in Europe at the beginning of the twenty-first century still needs to be studied.

This chapter will first consider religious and secular normative cultures from a gendered perspective. Monotheistic religions are based on distinct gender hierarchies and divisions, which are inherited by secular state organizations and regulations. The 'Atlantic-European' inspired secular normative culture introduces a division in public and private spheres, which continues a tradition of gender division and class privilege. However, this division between spheres is challenged by women moving from the private to the public sphere – by religion becoming more public, and by new media. Some claim that the division is collapsing. The final section discusses issues concerning 'gender display' and gender performance in the twenty-first century as a field, where 'religion', 'public', 'private' and 'gender' overlap, interact, and possibly take on new forms and new meanings and changes all the involved actors.

Religions as Gendered Normative Cultures

Religions are normative communities and cultures, which may prescribe for their members and adherents certain (often quite contested) norms, values, attitudes and behaviour. These directives are of differing strength according to historical period and context, community power and pressure and local conditions. Norms and values differ according to the actual strength of the relevant religious traditions. In a European context the monotheistic religions have historically been of particular importance. Judaism, Christianity and Islam all emerged in the south-eastern part of the Mediterranean area over a period of several thousand years, Islam being the youngest emerging only about 1,500 years ago. Christianity and Islam have spread over the planet from their beginnings. During the last decades much of the European debate has focused primarily upon the differences between these religions.

From a gendered perspective the monotheistic religions share a number of characteristics (see for instance Petersen 2010a). They all imagine a (male) God – also often understood to be a GodFather – whose abode is seen to be in the sky.[7] They share a strong distinction and hierarchical relation between gender and species which may be illustrated in the Figure 7.1.

---

6 The term intersectionality was coined by African-American law professor, Kimberlé W. Crenshaw, in an article in a law journal in 1989.

7 The Pakistani psychologist, Durre S. Ahmed, writes that 'God in Islam is beyond gender', but that all religious fundamentalisms can be understood as 'hypermasculine approaches to text, interpretation, meaning(s) and expression which negates and devalues the Divine Feminine' (2010: 64). D.S. Ahmed has on several occasions dealt with important

GOD

I

MAN

I

WOMAN

I

CHILD

I

NATURE

Figure 7.1 Monotheistic hierarchies

This hierarchy is an integrated part of the religions, and it has implications for historical and contemporary gender divided practices in different parts of religious community life – some(times) depending upon specific interpretations. Since monotheistic religious *texts* are generally considered of a superior authority, the texts as such are rarely subject to change, but they are subject to translations and (re)interpretations, which may challenge and even change their local and sometimes general understandings and the adhering practices. During the last decades many women have undertaken reinterpretations of and reflections on these texts (see for a few examples Mernissi 1998; Moltmann-Wendel 2000; Mahmood 2005; Graetz 2005).

The dominant parts of these monotheistic religions uphold the gendered and anthropomorphic images of the male deity. They also maintain an organizational structure, where only men can be rabbis, priests or imams. Women are thus excluded from servicing their religious communities as holders of the highest religious authority in Orthodox Judaism, Orthodox Christianity, Roman Catholicism and Islam. This structural characteristic influences all major aspects of these normative communities.[8] The awareness of being privileged whether because of gender, religion, race, age, class or other characteristics often goes unnoticed amongst those who benefit from such privileges, and privileges also

feminist perspectives on gender and religion: see also her book *Masculinity, Rationality and Religion: A Feminist Perspective* (1994).

8 This is reflected in the RELIGARE project, which has embarked upon an empirical investigation of the views of representative contemporary leaders of European religious communities. These leaders are predominantly male.

shift over time and space (Pateman 2011; Petersen 2007). Bourdieu describes male dominance as comparable to 'masculine nobility' (Bourdieu 1998: 74–82) which produces a 'radical asymmetry in the valuation of male and female activities' (79; my translation). It is characteristic of the dominant 'that they are able to secure acknowledgment of their particular way of being as universal. The definition of excellence is in any way loaded with masculine implications, which do not become visible as such' (82; my translation). Views presented by all-male leadership in monotheistic religions are thus likely to reflect a continued but often unrecognized exclusivist gender hierarchy of these normative communities. This of course influences both female and male self-perception.

The dominant part of Europe belongs either to cultures influenced by Orthodox Christianity or by Roman Catholic Christianity. Here the likelihood of a change in the gender of the leadership structure appears to be very distant. The consequence of this is that these important normative cultures will continue to present themselves as highly gender exclusive on the management level. As normative cultures they are thus not in accordance with the professed (global and) European values of equality. This may not be a serious legal problem due to the continued cultural and legal privileges, but it may over time become a problem of declining legitimacy and relevance. The experience of a decrease in both membership and adherence to basic norms and values seems to be common to both Catholics and Protestants.

The European Parliament in July 2011 advised EU businesses to hire women in their executive boards by 2012 or face a mandatory quota of 40% modelled on the Norwegian experience.[9] It remains to be seen whether the EU Parliament will also scrutinize the gender composition of management in belief communities, or whether these predominantly 'all male' management organizations can continue to be legitimized by tradition, custom and religious authority.

Secular Normativity and its Heritage

From a gendered perspective there are similarities between monotheistic religions and societies, but there are also similarities between religious (monotheist) societies and (European) secular societies. Roughly speaking one might claim that secularism removed God from the hierarchical relations presented above but kept the rest of the hierarchy, and perhaps reordered it somewhat:

9 Valentina Pop, 'EU Parliament Backs Female Quotas for Top Corporate Jobs', http://euobserver.com/9/32598 (accessed 8 July 2011).

SECULAR

MAN

PRIVATE / **PUBLIC**

WOMAN
I
CHILD
I
NATURE

RELIGIOUS

Figure 7.2 Secular hierarchies of gender and species

In this model man is no longer subordinated to God. Man has become secular and public. However woman is still subordinated to man. She is now considered belonging to a private sphere, which is governed by tradition. This tradition is still strongly influenced by religious worldviews and norms, which have been relegated to the private sphere. The model above is obviously unsophisticated and does not reflect a dynamic and very complex 'reality', which has over the last decades undergone considerable adjustments. The model is however supported by observations by many feminist and female researchers, as for instance the Finnish historian, Anu Pylkkänen:

> The so-called neutral and secular laws on family life, in fact, allow the traditional Christian teleological/functional notions of family institutions to live on. The secular laws might not have many coercive norms anymore as to what kind of lifestyle is preferred, and neither do they intervene in the families, but they nevertheless allow the social and religious norms to form the normative expectations of family life and values. (Pylkkänen 2010: 539–540)

> In sum, secular law has been so much intertwined with religious norms and understandings that it does not make sense to discuss the relation of law and religion as if they were two separate systems. (541)

This intertwinement has been particularly felt by women. The values of equality have been considered secular, and have especially been influential in Europe since the French Revolution of 1789. As is well known gender equality was not considered part of these values until after further fights, wars and revolution. The First World

War and the Russian revolution and its reverberations in Europe brought political rights to many women, especially in Northern Europe, including Germany where women got the vote in 1918. Gender equality has been particularly underlined in Europe after the Second World War, which brought political rights and the right to vote to women in several of the founding member states of the EEC. When the European Economic Community was established in 1957 women had only very recently gained suffrage in the majority of the founder countries. The Netherlands and Luxemburg had already granted women suffrage in 1919, but in Italy and France women only gained full suffrage in 1945 and in Belgium in 1948. The uneven political and historical heritage of women's suffrage has undoubtedly had an effect on both national and European political and legal cultures as well as on Europe's secular and religious cultures. It may be noted that Turkish women got the vote already in 1930.

A gender exclusivist and gender static approach of Europe's leading religious majority cultures has for centuries interacted with a similarly patriarchal political and legal culture.[10] This history has also influenced 'secularism' – a term that has been understood in many different ways. Both minority and majority religious and normative cultures in Europe share this heritage of male dominance. However the inconsistency between a European secular (and in practice male dominated) political culture which formally emphasizes gender equality and a religious majority and minority culture which practices formal gender exclusion in religious leadership leads to difficulties for believing women in both majority and minority cultures.

Over the last decades to half a century, women in (Western) Europe have in very high numbers moved from the private sphere dominated by religious norms into the public sphere in principle considered to be secular in order to gain paid work. This move has challenged all existing 'public' and 'private' authority structures and created new problems and challenges. Men have not undertaken similar dramatic moves from the public to the private sphere anywhere in the world.

It seems that it is especially (believing) women who are suffering from the 'mixed blessings' of the coexistence of secular and religious normative cultures in general (Whiting and Evans 2006) and also in Europe. The cases from the first decade of the twenty-first century of *Lucia Dahlab* v. *Switzerland* (42393/98, ECHR 2001-V), of *Leyla Sahín* v. *Turkey* (44774/98, ECHR 2005) and the case of *Soile Lautsi* v. *Italy* (30814/06, ECHR 2011) could be seen as examples of this.

In an article on 'Gender Equality Jurisprudence of the European Court of Human Rights', Ivana Radacic writes that the European Court of Human Rights has consistently held that equality of sexes is one of the major goals of the member states of the Council of Europe. However, she criticizes the Court for being both

10 The media case and legal case concerning alleged sexual abuse by the former male French director of the IMF, DSK led to a heated debate in France and internationally about the gender culture both in the IMF and particularly in France, and has demonstrated that France scores very low in the Gender Gap Index. See Lizzy Davies (2011).

inconsistent, formalistic and (in the headscarf cases) 'paternalistic and insensitive to intersectionality of discrimination' (Radacic 2008: 842).

The countries influenced by less radical Anglican or Lutheran secularism (Berg-Sørensen 2010) have experienced a stronger domination of the state over religion including religious leadership. Danish feminist theologian Bodil Koch (1903–1972) played an important role for the revitalization of female influence in Nordic political life in general during and after the Second World War. In 1947 she became a member of parliament for the Social Democrats. In 1950 she became the first female minister of Ecclesiastical Affairs in the world (Possing 2007). In 1947 the Social Democratic government had by law guaranteed the right of women to become ministers in the Church of Denmark, the Danish 'Folkekirke'. In 1948 three female priests were ordained. About 60 years later female priests constitute about half of all priests in the Church of Denmark, and have thus secured a 'modernization' and contemporary legitimacy of the Church[11] – also reflected in a high – but passive – membership. However, there are still conservative male Danish priests who will not shake hands with female priests, and this rejection is permitted.[12]

The possibility for women to be ordained to the clergy of the Church of Norway was opened through statutes in 1938 and 1956. Within the Church, however, the resistance against female clergy was great. When, in 1961, the first female minister was ordained it resulted in negative reactions from conservatives (Modéer and Petersen 2010a).

The Public/Private Divide – Gendered Perspectives

> The distinction between public and private realms arose out of a double movement in modern political and legal thought. On the one hand, with the emergence of the nation-state and theories of sovereignty in the sixteenth and seventeenth centuries, ideas of a distinctly public realm began to crystallize. On the other hand, in reaction to the claims of monarchs and, later, parliaments to the unrestrained power to make law, there developed a countervailing effort to stake out distinctively private spheres free from the encroaching power of the state. (Horwitz 1981–1982: 1423)

In his article on 'The History of the Public/Private Distinction', American legal historian, Morton J. Horwitz, underlines how recently 'a distinctively public realm came to be a generally understood part of political and legal consciousness' (1981–1982: 1424). It was a central goal of nineteenth-century legal thought to

11 Ekspertvinkel: 60-året for kvindelige præster i folkekirken, http://teo.au.dk/nyheder/pressearkiv/ekspertewp/.

12 I recently learnt that this led one of my close female friends, a medical doctor, to leave the Church.

create this distinction, and according to Horwitz there was 'a virtual obsession with separating public and private law, both conceptually and practically' and the concern that caused this obsession was above all:

> the effort of orthodox judges and jurists to create a legal science that would sharply separate law from politics. By creating a neutral and apolitical system of legal doctrine and legal reasoning free from what was thought to be the dangerous and unstable redistributive tendencies of democratic politics, legal thinkers hoped to temper the problem of 'the tyranny of the majority. (Horwitz 1981–1982: 1425)

The areas of life which belonged to the private sphere were thus protected from 'the tyranny of the majority'. These were property law and contract law, but also family life and religious life.

The tyrannical majority was not only the bourgeoisie, who secured the change from absolutist regimes to constitutional monarchies in Europe, but later also the upcoming underclass or 'dangerous classes' whose voting power would be considerable in the parliamentarian democracies. Horwitz describes how America's 'most brilliant and original legal thinkers' in the beginning of the twentieth century exposed the 'conservative ideological foundations of the public/private divide' (1981–1982: 1426).

In the latter part of the twentieth century a considerable number of feminist thinkers from different parts of the world have continued to criticize the division between public and private. Carole Pateman wrote in her article on 'Feminist Critiques of the Public/Private Dichotomy' that feminist criticism was primarily directed at 'the separation and opposition between the public and private spheres in liberal theory and practice' (Pateman 1987: 103). The public and the private are central categories in liberal theory, but they are not clear, nor is it clear why they are crucial.

> The way in which women and men are differentially located within private life and the public world is, as I shall indicate, a complex matter, but underlying a complicated reality is the belief that women's natures are such that they are properly subject to men and their proper place is in the private, domestic sphere. Men properly inhabit, and rule within, both spheres. The essential feminist argument is that the doctrine of 'separate but equal' and the ostensible individualism and egalitarianism of liberal theory, obscure the patriarchal reality of a social structure of inequality and the domination of women by men. (Pateman 1987: 105)

What Pateman describes here is a Western understanding of the relationship between public and private, which the Australian law professor Margaret Thornton takes further in her chapter on 'The Cartography of Public and Private'. Here she reminds us that the state is not a unitary entity, but 'a pervasive and fluid force' and that, for women, neither the polity nor the market have been realms of freedom or self-realization, but realms of hostility (Thornton 1995: 7). Women have been – and to an important degree still are – confined to sex-segregated jobs, their authority is not recognized, and it is only very recently that issues such as domestic violence have been outlawed by public parliaments in Western states. The domestic sphere is considered inferior to the public sphere, which has been seen as the sphere of rationality, culture and intellectual effort.

> The public sphere, mediated through law, has enabled benchmark men to construct normativity, like God, in their own image. The seeds on invidiousness associated with the domestic sphere attach to women, who have been marked as its indigenous inhabitants. The stigmata of affectivity continue to detract from the rationality and authority of women and others in public office. Conventionally, a 'public woman' was a prostitute, a figure of derision, in contrast to a 'public man', a figure of approbation who acted in and for the universal good. (Thornton 1995: 13)

The different versions of criticism of the public/private divide presented by Horwitz, Pateman and Thornton (and many others) relate to the context and conditions of which they are part. Horwitz and Pateman wrote during the era of the Cold War, and Thornton wrote a few years after the end of the Cold War before Western societies had begun to focus on the political influence of religions and the fears emerging from a new geopolitical global landscape – issues of globalization and migration were hardly on the agenda before the end of the twentieth century.

In the twenty-first century Turkish-French professor of sociology, Nilüfer Göle, writes about the 'authoritarian modernism' in the Turkish context, which means that here 'women's participation in public life, corporeal visibility and social mixing with men all count as modern' (Göle 2002: 177). Nilüfer Göle has on several occasions dealt with the relation between private and public spheres (see also Göle and Ammann 2006), which are central for the relationship between religion and the state as well as for contemporary modern Turkish and Muslim women.

> The ways in which Islam provides new definitions of self and intimacy in public is at the intersection of culture and politics. Especially in contexts of secular and modern publics, *the coming out of Islam from the private to the public sphere takes place with performative acts, such as veiling and segregation of sexes, which underpins religious difference and Muslim habits but also expresses resistance to assimilative and secular modernity*. The redesigning of the frontiers between private and public spheres and the control of gender socialization becomes a central stake for islamist politics. Through these micro-practices and gendered frontiers between the private and public spheres, an Islamic social imaginary is at work generating new definitions of religious Islamic self in counterdistinction

> with liberal and emancipatory definitions of modern subject. (Göle 2003; italics here)

The idea of a public/private divide is Western, but has spread beyond the West. Göle writes about the impact of this public space in an Islamic context and the changes this leads to:

> Islam carves out a public space of its own as new Islamic language styles, corporeal rituals, and spatial practices emerge and blend into public life. On the one hand, public Islam testifies to a shift in the orientation of the Islamic movement from macropolitics toward micropractices, and on the other hand, it challenges the borders and the meanings of the secular public sphere.
>
> As Islam makes a move into national public spheres, the consensual principles and homogeneous structure of the national public spheres are unsettled, but so are those of the Islamic movement. (Göle 2002: 173)

Gendered performativity, control of gender socialization and challenges of the borders and meanings of a secular public sphere are elements underlined by Göle a decade ago. The perception of a challenged division of spheres has increased since then.

The Collapse of Public and Private? And its Consequences?

A recent example of the clash between 'secular state law' and 'religious norms' and traditions which especially Muslim women have to deal with in the European context is the French legal ban on niqab and burqa in force from 3 March 2011.[13] This is an intervention in issues related to religious and personal life, belonging to a gendered (private) sphere. It may be no coincidence that this intervention will especially be felt by women, who have in the twentieth and twenty-first centuries increasingly undertaken a move from the 'private' sphere characterized by subordination to male authority, to a public sphere, be it in education or in the labour market, not least in order to be able to maintain themselves economically in a world where family life and marriage no longer secures female maintenance.

In a way we might speak of a contemporary 'virtual obsession' (to borrow Horwitz's phrase) with female ('religious') dress in the twenty-first century. It seems as if traditions, religions and states (and not to forget markets) want to dictate to women what (not) to wear. The decisions of women themselves as regards dress and choice of dress seem to be subjected to interests of both organized state and religious interests. Secular organizations and states seem especially concerned

13 Circulaire du 2 mars 2011 relative à la mise en oeuvre de la loi no 2010-1192 du 11 octobre 2010 interdisant la dissimulation du visage dans l'espace public.

about female dress. Monotheistic religious institutions seem especially concerned about the possibility of (male) same-sex marriage.

Several investigations in Europe have demonstrated that it is only a tiny minority of women who are wearing a niqab and especially a full burqa. In France about 2,000 women are expected to wear the burqa or 'integral veil', many of whom are converts.[14] A Danish study from 2010 estimated that between 100 to 200 women or less than 0.2% of Muslim women wear the niqab.[15] However it is also well known that 'small numbers' may give rise to considerable uncertainty and fear. Arjun Appadurai writes that modern nation states recognize their common belonging to what he calls the vertebrate world, and like the last dinosaurs, see that they are in a desperate struggle for survival as a global formation (Appadurai 2006: 21). The European legislators, who are representing the 'vertebrate world', have banned the wearing of 'integral veils' by (Muslim) women, in the hope to survive by exploiting the fears of terrorism and consequences of migration.

> For now, let us note that terror in the era of globalization cannot be divorced from certain deeper crises and contradictions that surround the nation-state. One such crisis … concerns the link between minorities *within* the modern nation-state and the marginalization *of* the nation-state by forces of globalization. (Appadurai 2006: 33)

The discussion about the weakened nation states (and consequently the weakened legislations of these states) and of 'the end of the world as we know it' is not new (Wallerstein 1999). In a European context both states and organized majority religions are weakened (Petersen 2010b). Thus when states try to uphold strict separations between (secular) public and private (religion) by means of austere regimes of dress for (migrant and minority) women this may clearly lead to both practices of exclusion against and feelings of being excluded by the minorities concerned. But it may also produce a certain sense of absurdity amongst populations in general. States seem to be upholding and underlining their own importance and 'power' by 'fighting wind-mills', 'shooting sparrows with cannons' or, in the English version, 'using sledge hammers to break nuts':

> minorities are the major site for displacing the anxieties of many states about their own minority or marginality (real or imagined) in a world of a few megastates, of unruly economic flows and compromised sovereignties. Minorities, in a word, are metaphors and reminders of the betrayal of the classical national project. (Appadurai 2006: 43)

Jill Walker Rettberg sees the dramatic shift in the balance between private and public as highly related to the development of participatory media, and argues that

14 Information by Prof. Mohamed Kerrou, 29 September 2010.

15 Johansen et al. (2010).

the spread of 'instantaneous publication and social, shared, conversational media such as blogs is intimately linked with the collapse of private and public' (Rettberg 2007).[16] This will come as no surprise to anybody after the Arab Spring of 2011. But if the boundaries between private and public that were seemingly clear in the nineteenth and mid- and late twentieth century are collapsing in the twenty-first century, then what?

Ihsan Yilmaz writes about the 'adaptive strategies to cope with the challenges of modern life' employed by young Muslims, who surf the Internet to find answers to their everyday life dilemmas. 'They select, eclectically and also pragmatically, a convenient answer from one of the mainstream, that is Sunni madhabs'. Thus a Muslim becomes his/her own mufti, he writes.[17]

Rettberg compares the development of social media to the emergence of print media and literacy related to this tool. The specificities of the media affect the ways of communication. She claims that the many parallel and later social developments in participatory and social media show that 'the urge to share our ideas, opinions, thoughts and desires is strong', and she also claims that we are beginning to see how alternative markers of authority are developing in these new forms of media. She introduces the ideas of another author/actor, Tom Pewitt, who claims that we are at the end of the 'Gutenberg Parenthesis' – the 400 years 'dominated by print and its attendant norms such as the idea that you can have an autonomous, fixed text, or the idea that a text or cultural object is originally composed once, and thereafter passively reproduced by readers, musicians or performers' (Rettberg 2007: 8).

These ideas of the autonomous fixed text are exactly what theologians, religious people 'of the book' and modern positivist lawyers hold in common.

> What will happen, then, when we move away from this relatively brief historical interlude – parenthesis – where print and print literacy dominated our culture? Pewitt argues that we will return to the pre-Gutenberg privileging of the performance as a fluid happening that relies on other performances and will influence later performances, but also stated that there will, of course, be differences between the pre-parenthetical and post-parenthetical. (Rettberg 2007: 8)

If young Muslim women are wearing what Mohammed Kerrou has called the *new veil* (2010) as a post-parenthetical performative act, then they might be at the forefront of the changes related to a collapse of the divide between the public and the private, the religious and the secular, and the written and the 'happened'.

---

16 I would like to thank Cecilie Brito Cederstrøm for having drawn my attention to this article, and for interesting conversations on the topic of this article.

17 Yilmaz (2005) discusses the dangers of fragmentation stemming from this process, but also its potentials. Thanks to Prakash Shah for drawing my attention to this article. Quotes are from p. 198.

This will create considerable challenges for all the custodians of the print culture including theologians, priests, imams, lawyers, judges, politicians and modern lawmakers of written laws. Are the court cases from the twenty-first century by the European Court of Human Rights which involve issues concerning women and belief an example of this? Perhaps they are.

Performing Gender and 'Gender Display' in the Twenty-First Century?

Figure 7.3 Al Masson: woman cycling[18]

In 1976 Canadian born sociologist, Erving Goffman (1922–1982) wrote about what today might be called 'market norms' in a publication called *Gender Advertisements* (1976). Ritually speaking, he writes, 'females are equivalent to subordinate males and both are equivalent to children' (Goffman 1976: 5). He writes about gender display that

> Displays thus provide evidence of the actor's *alignment* in a gathering, the position he seems prepared to take up in what is about to happen in the social situation. Alignments tentatively or indicatively establish the terms of the contact, the mode or style or formula for the dealings that are to ensue among the individuals in the situation. (1976: 1)

Later he writes that one might as well say that there is no gender identity. 'There is only a schedule for the portrayal of gender' (1976: 8). Displays are symptoms,

18 Al Masson is born in France but has lived and worked as an artist in Copenhagen, Denmark since 1996, see www.almasson.com.

not portraits. The veiled woman cycling in the drawing above by French-Danish artist Al Masson, may be interpreted as a representation of a gender display. In Copenhagen you will see veiled women cycling, indicating an alignment to important local norms of 'mobility' in the public sphere by using vehicles considered to be of both practical and symbolic importance.

Modern European women are by now expected to enter the public sphere, and to participate in public life. However, their entrance is, in practice, only approved if they submit themselves to the dominant though (somewhat) diverse surface-secular norms governing life in the particular sphere they enter. This includes adhering to existing but mostly tacit dress codes. These norms and values are constructed by and modelled on what Margaret Thornton calls 'benchmark men'. Western women, who want to enter the still highly male dominated world of politics, business or higher learning, have to adapt to these mostly 'unwritten' behavioural codes to be successful.[19]

For an example of this display of women aligning themselves to male norms of dress, formally perceived and presented as 'neutral', one may visit the website of the European Court of Human Rights which presents the judges of the court.[20] On a very small and long picture all judges are presented dressed in their formal attire, a loose black dress and white formal neck scarf. It is very hard to distinguish gender on this long and narrow image. But on the individual images of the judges, where they all wear their formal dress, this can of course be done. By June 2011 18 of the 47 judges were women, most of them from 'new' post-communist and often small countries (Armenia, Bosnia-Herzegovina, Bulgaria, Croatia, Georgia, Latvia, Lithuania, The Former Yugoslav Republic of Macedonia and Ukraine – the biggest of them). Turkey and Germany are the other big countries who have female judges in Strasbourg. The last six Western European countries which have female judges are also rather small (Austria, Belgium, Ireland, Monaco, San Marino, Sweden). On average the female judges are about seven years younger than the male judges. The Belgian judge, Francoise Tulkens, is vice-president of the Court.

Achieving and upholding authority in a male-dominated environment is a challenge for all women. Carole Pateman writes that legal and political reform has been easier to achieve than changes in social practices, beliefs and attitudes

19 In May 2011 I participated in a 'debate-service' between Sørine Gotfredsen, a highly profiled and conservative female priest-cum-journalist and Pernille Vigsø Bagge, a female priest and member of the Danish Parliament for the Socialist People's Party. The title of the event was 'Can women fully execute authority?'. In the public debate following the religious service, where the two women were debating, both women reflected extensively on issues of dress and voice as part of performing authority. Sørine Gotfredsen, herself a highly intellectual woman, considered that men were better thinkers and philosophers than women, because there were many more male philosophers.

20 www.echr.coe.int/ECHR/EN/Header/The+Court/The+Court/Judges+of+the+Court/ (accessed 29 May 2011).

including in understandings of masculinity and femininity (Pateman 2011: 2). But changes are taking place, perhaps not least in the Muslim world.

In September 2010 professor Mohamed Kerrou from the Faculty of Law and Political Sciences of Tunis, Université de Tunis El Manar, gave a lecture in Copenhagen about 'Islamic Veils, Identities and Public Spheres'.[21] Professor Kerrou claimed that what had been witnessed in Tunisia (four months before the uprisings in Tunisia hit the world news) was not a use of the 'same conventional veil' but 'a trans-social and trans-generational piece of clothing'.[22] These veils were '*new veils*', stylish, colourful and not Islamic veils and they were very different from the 'old veils', which were communitarian and forced on women. He claimed that these veils were at the intersection of politics, religion and sexuality, and went beyond simplistic explanations. A wide variety of veils and ways to wear them gave rise to multiple meanings of this piece of headdress, and words had little effect on practices of veiling and unveiling. According to Kerrou the message of these veils could be seen as consisting of the following three elements: I exist; I am Muslim; I am veiled. This implicit and political symbol of identity and otherness was 'less religious than political, less political than cultural and less cultural than symbolic'. This new veil was 'a symbol of individual choice in a globalized and inter-linked world' and Kerrou saw it as an example of a 'rise of female power in the public sphere' and as an intersection between market and morality.

The existence of conflicting and sometimes paradoxical norms and practices is not something only women experience. The late Japanese professor of sociology of law, Masaji Chiba, wrote in an article on 'Legal Pluralism in Mind' about the difficulties of Japanese people, who have had to adjust to a combination of transplanted modern European law with Japanese traditions (Chiba 1995). This conflict is spelled out not only in public and private spheres, but also in the minds of individual people. In a similar way (Muslim) women in Europe have to grapple – both in practice and also in their minds – with the conflicts emanating from differences and clashes between traditional secular norms about (gendered) behaviour in public and private on the one side and traditional religious norms and demands towards public and private 'performance' on the other side.

In a Europe which considers itself presently secular but historically Christian, this becomes a challenge particularly for (minority) women who want to, choose to or feel they have to display both femininity and belief according to the local normative cultures, of which they are (or were) part. Women in general, including Muslim women, have increased their educational level considerably over the last

21 The lecture took place on 29 September 2010 and was announced with the following text: 'The veil, complete or partial, raises questions about the status of the woman in society, citizenship and civil society. The discussion must also focus on how the Muslim women understand their own identity. Aesthetic, political and economical perspectives will be included in this discussion of a new reading of the veil'.

22 The following résumé of professor Kerrou's speech is based on the printed version (Kerrou 2010) and on my handwritten notes from the lecture.

decades, and are everywhere trying to enter the labour market, however with varied success.[23] As with European women with a Christian background, Muslim women have also been considered belonging to the private sphere, and the cultural, religious and legal restrictions on the move between spheres has often been even stronger than has been the case for 'modern' Western women.

In a Danish context some believing Muslim women (may) choose to adapt to the dominant secular norms of their local environment, and thus do not cover their hair in public but perhaps do so in private. They may choose to go against the norms of their own religious communities, by specifically underlining their religiosity in private. Other pious young women may wear the hijab in public – and do also keep their heads covered in the privacy of their own homes.[24]

If the dress women decide to display under these conditions of normative pluralism can be understood as a symptom, then what is it a sign of? Is it a sign of a 'turbulent' subjectivity[25] – acting not as 'a revolutionary' or 'a reformer' but performing an under-cover activity and resistance both in relation to religious and secular cultures?

Wearing the veil (or the formal judge dress?) may help in overcoming internal and local cultural obstacles related to female public performance. It may support and underline the authority of the individual in a non-private context. It may make it possible for the Muslim woman to be more physically mobile and thus become a 'cycling woman' and take a job, which is something which is highly valued for women in Europe's mobile cultures – and beyond. However, displaying and performing gender in a formalized way in the public sphere may also lead to a feeling of unease in both public and private relations. The monotheistic cultures – whether religious or secular – have not been used to public performance of female authority for very long. Female public performance may challenge existing value hegemony (including male dominance) whether women wear traditional 'headscarf and loose-fitting clothes' indicating 'allegiance to a particular faith'[26] or whether they wear loose-fitting judge robes or other 'gender neutral' business attire.[27]

---

23 Prof. Madawi Al-Rasheed told in continuation of a lecture on 'Saudi Women Novelists: Cosmopolitan Fantasy against Religious Nationalism' in Copenhagen in May 2011 that 78% of unemployed women in Saudi Arabia have a university degree.

24 Information by law student Badar Shah, who is assistant at the RELIGARE project in Copenhagen (May 2011), and with whom I have had several discussions about whether the categories of public and private are (becoming) outmoded.

25 Enrica Capussotti et al. discuss 'the appearance of new types of working subjectivities that could be characterized as "turbulent" rather than as "revolutionary" in the old sense' in an article on 'Migrant Women in Work' (2007: 134).

26 Quotes from *Dahlab* v. *Switzerland*, ECHR App 42393/98.

27 It is well known among young (Danish and many other) women that they should avoid appearing too bright if they want to find a date in the public sphere. The present popularity of stilettos and shoewear fashion for young female professionals might perhaps be interpreted as a need to underline and display 'proper femininity' in a highly competitive

Is the *virtual obsession* with the way (some) women dress in the so-called 'public' sphere a sign of the collapse of earlier divisions which have served vested interests – often of privileged elites?

It seems that the 'public sphere' is becoming 'privatized', while the 'private' sphere is becoming more 'publicized' and that religions are going public, while states are privatizing. New orientations, performances and authorities may be expected to emerge.

References

Ahmed, D.S. (1994), *Masculinity, Rationality and Religion: A Feminist Perspective* (Lahore: ASR Publications).

Ahmed, D.S. (2010), 'Penetrations: A Psycho-Cultural View of Modernity, Fundamentalisms and Islam', in Foblets, M.C. and Carlier, J.-Y. (eds), *Islam and Europe: Crises are Challenges* (Leuven: Leuven University Press), 53–69.

Appadurai, A. (2006), *Fear of Small Numbers: An Essay on the Geography of Anger* (Durham, NC and London: Duke University Press).

Baumann, Z. (2007), *Liquid Times. Living in an Age of Uncertainty* (Cambridge: Polity Press).

Bourdieu, P. (1998), *Den maskuline dominans* (Copenhagen: Tiderne Skifter).

Berg-Sørensen, A. (2010), 'The Politics of Lutheran Secularism: Reiterating Secularism in the Wake of the Cartoon Crisis', in Christoffersen, L., Raun Iversen, H., Petersen, H. and Warburg, M. (eds), *Religion in the 21st Century: Challenges and Transformations* (Farnham: Ashgate), 207–214.

Capussotti, E., Laliotou, I. and Lyon, D. (2007), 'Migrant Women in Work', in Passerini, L., Lyon, D., Capussotti, E. and Laliotou, I. (eds), *Women Migrants from East to West: Gender, Mobility and Belonging* (New York: Berghahn Books), 122–137.

Casanova, J. (1994), *Public Religions in the Modern World* (Chicago and London: The University of Chicago Press).

Chiba, M. (1995), 'Legal Pluralism in Mind: A Non-Western View', in Petersen, H. and Zahle, H. (eds), *Legal Polycentricity: Consequences of Pluralism in Law* (Aldershot: Dartmouth), 71–83.

Crenshaw, Kimberlé W. (1989), 'Demarginalizing the Intersection of Race and Sex: A Black Feminist Critique of Antidiscrimination Doctrine, Feminist Theory, and Antiracist Politics', *The University of Chicago Legal Forum*, 139–167.

Davies, L. (2011), 'How Dominique Strauss-Kahn's Arrest Awoke a Dormant Anger in the Heart of France's Women', *Guardian* and *Observer*, 21 May 2011, www.guardian.uk (accessed 27 May 2011).

world where gender characteristics may tend to disappear – and thus lead to gender insecurity in intimate relations.

Ferrari, S. (2006), 'Nationalism, Patriotism, and Religious Belief in Europe', *University of Detroit Mercy Law Review*, 83:5, 625–639.

Goffman, E. (1976), *Gender Advertisements* (New York: Harper Colophon Books).

Göle, N. (2002), 'Islam in Public: New Visibilities and New Imaginaries', *Public Culture*, 14:1, 173–190, www.havenscenter.org/files/gole_1_2.pdf (accessed 19 May 2011).

Göle, N. (2003), 'The Voluntary Adoption of Islamic Stigma Symbols', *Social Research*, 'Islam: The Private and Public Spheres', 70:2, published online, www.socres.org/vol70/issue703.htm (accessed 19 May 2011).

Göle, N. and Ammann, L. (eds) (2006), *Islam in Public. Turkey, Iran, and Europe* (Istanbul: Bìlgì University Press).

Graetz, N. (2005), *Unlocking the Garden: A Feminist Jewish Look at the Bible, Midrash and God* (Piscataway: Gorgias Press).

Høilund, P. (2010), *Frygtens ret* [Law of Fear] (Copenhagen: Hans Reitzels Forlag).

Horwitz, M.J. (1981–1982), 'The History of the Public/Private Distinction', *University of Pennsylvania Law Review*, 130, 1423–1428.

Johansen, Birgitte Schepelern, Warburg, Margit and Østergaard, Kate (2010), 'Det tilslørede ansigt – frivillighed eller tvang?', *Kristeligt Dagblad*, 3 March.

Kerrou, M. (2010), *Women, Veils and Public Spheres* (Lecture held as part of The Copenhagen University Islam Lecture Series organised by the Centre for European Islamic Thought and the New Islamic Public Sphere Programme, http://islam.ku.dk/lectures/Kerrou290910.pdf/ (accessed 8 July 2011).

Mahmood, S. (2005), *The Islamic Revival and the Feminist Subject* (Princeton and Oxford: Princeton University Press).

Mernissi, F. (1998), 'A Feminist Interpretation of Women's Rights in Islam', in Kurzman, C. (ed.), *Liberal Islam: A Source Book* (Oxford: Oxford University Press), 112–126.

Modéer, K. and Petersen, H. (2010), *Believing in Norway. Beliefs in Norway. A 'Humanitarian Great Power' under Globalization.* Norwegian Centre for Human Rights & Norwegian Helsinki Committee, http://www.jus.uio.no/smr/om/aktuelt/arrangementer/2010/docs/believing.pdf (accessed 19 May 2011).

Moltmann-Wendel, E. (2000), *Wach auf, meine Freundin. Die Wiederkehr der Gottesfreundschaft* (Stuttgart: Kreuz Verlag).

Pateman, C. (1987), 'Feminist Critiques of the Public/Private Dichotomy', in Phillips, A. (ed.), *Feminism and Equality* (Oxford: Basil Blackwell), 103–126.

Pateman, C. (2011), 'Securing Women's Citizenship: Indifference and Other Obstacles', *Eurozine* www.Eurozine.com (published online 7 March 2011) (accessed 19 May 2011).

Petersen, H. (2007), 'Transformations of Legal Subjectivity in Europe: From the Subjection of Women to Privileged Subjects', in Passerini, L., Lyon, D., Capussotti, E. and Laliotou, I. (eds), *Women Migrants from East to West: Gender, Mobility and Belonging* (New York: Berghahn Books), 68–83.

Petersen, H. (2010a), 'Women, Secular and Religious Laws and Traditions: Gendered Secularization, Gendering Shari'a' in Nielsen, J.S. and Christoffersen, L. (eds), *Shari'a As Discourse. Legal Traditions and the Encounter with Europe* (Farnham: Ashgate), 77–87.

Petersen, H. (2010b), 'Beyond National Majority/Minority Dichotomies. Towards Legal Traditions & Religions of World Society – A Local Example' in Christoffersen L., et al (eds), *Law & Religion in the 21st Century – Nordic Perspectives* (Copenhagen: Djøf Publishing), 321–344.

Pop, V., (2011), 'EU Parliament Backs Female Quotas for Top Corporate Jobs', http://euobserver.com/9/32598 (accessed 8 July 2011).

Possing, B. (2007), *Uden omsvøb. Portræt af Bodil Koch* (København: Gyldendal).

Pylkkänen, Anu (2010) Feminism and the Challenge to Religious Truths on Marriage. In Lisbet Christoffersen. Kjell Åke Modeer & Svend Andersen (eds), *Law & Religion in the 21st Century – Nordic Perspectives* (Copenhagen: Djøf Publishing), 525–545.

Radacic, I. (2008), 'Gender Equality Jurisprudence of the European Court of Human Rights', *The European Journal of International Law*, 19:4, 841–857.

Rettberg, J.W. (2007), 'Blogs, Literacies and the Collapse of Private and Public', *Digital Arts and Culture*, 15–18 September, Perth, Australia.

Rorive, I. (2009), 'Religious Symbols in the Public Space: In Search of a European Answer', *Cardozo Law Review*, 30:6, 2669–2698.

Thornton, M. (1995), 'The Cartography of Public and Private', in Thornton, M. (ed.), *Public and Private: Feminist Legal Debates* (Melbourne: Oxford University Press), 2–16.

Wallerstein, I. (1999), *The End of the World as We Know It: Social Science for the Twenty-First Century* (Minneapolis: University of Minnesota Press).

Whiting, A. and Evans, C. (2006), *Mixed Blessings: Laws, Religions, and Women's Rights in the Asia-Pacific Region* (Boston: Martinus Nijhoff).

Wieacker, Franz (1985), *Voraussetzungen europäischer Rechtskultur* (Bursfelder Universitätsreden herausgegeben von Lothar Perlitt, Abt von Bursfelde, Verlag Göttinger Tageblatt GmbH & Co.).

Yilmaz, I. (2005), 'Inter-Madhab Surfing, Neo-Ijtihad, and Faith-Based Movement Leaders', in Bearman, P., Peters, R. and Vogel, F.E. (eds), *The Islamic School of Law. Evolution, Devolution, and Progress* (Cambridge, MA: Islamic Legal Studies Program, Harvard University Press), 191–206.

Chapter 8

Religion in the European Public Spaces: A Legal Overview

Silvio Ferrari

Introduction

In Europe religions have a prominent and very visible position in the public sphere: almost everywhere religion is taught in State schools (frequently in the form of denominational teaching), in many countries religions are financed by the State and in some of them there is even a State religion.[1]

This strong presence of religions in the public space is increasingly challenged by the transformation of the religious landscape of the Old Continent. Two developments, in particular, are to be taken into consideration: first, a growing number of Europeans are not members of any religion and therefore question the support offered by the State to religious communities (Berger et al. 2008: 11);[2] second, a similarly increasing number of Europeans follow religions that are not traditional in Europe (first of all Islam) and that are excluded from the support reserved by the State to majority religions.[3] While the first group – those who do not profess any religion – want to reduce the presence of religious communities in the public sphere, the second group – those who profess non-traditional religions – want to enlarge this presence so that they can enjoy the same advantages reserved to mainstream religions. The first group support a neutral public sphere, without any religious connotation; the second is in favour of a plural public sphere that is inclusive of different religions. Finally, some traditional religions oppose both the neutrality and the plurality of the public sphere because, in the first case, they are afraid of being confined in the private space and, in the second, of losing their dominant position. For these reasons a complex and lively debate about the place of religions and beliefs in the public sphere is taking place in Europe.

1 For an overview of the Church–State systems in Europe see Robbers (2005).

2 The decline both in Church attendance and in belief in God is confirmed by the data collected by Pollack (2008: 83–100).

3 On Islam in Europe see Cesari (2009). More in particular on the legal status of the Islamic communities in the European countries, see Ferrari (2003: 219–254); Ferrari (2007b: 35–60).

Three European Patterns of Relations between States and Religions

Although it is very much influenced by the specific national backgrounds, this debate has a few common features and three basic patterns can be identified.

The first pattern is particularly evident in some Catholic and Orthodox countries. It is based on the conviction that traditional religions can still play a central role in granting the national cohesion that, in the opinion of many, is required to deal with the process of globalization and pluralization: therefore they deserve a special position in the public space. In this perspective the dominant religion of a country is seen as a central component of the civil religion, that is of the set of principles and values that all the citizens of that country are required to accept and defend. Italy is a good example of this trend. The central core of the Italian pattern is the attempt to govern the growing ethical, cultural and religious plurality of the country through the values of Catholicism, raised to the rank of civil religion (Ferrari 2010: 397–420). More precisely, Catholicism supplies the cultural and ethical principles on which full citizenship[4] is based: provided they are ready to accept these principles, non-Catholics can fully enjoy religious freedom rights (although not religious equality rights). Governing diversity by stressing (Catholic) identity is the narrow and arduous path Italy is trying to follow.

The debate about the crucifix is the best example of this way of understanding the place of religions in the public sphere. In Italian State schools a crucifix has to be hung on the walls of every classroom. Two years ago the European Court of Human Rights decided that the compulsory display of the crucifix violated the freedom of religion of the students and their parents.[5] The Italian government appealed against this sentence, arguing that the crucifix is not only a religious symbol but also the symbol of Italian identity: it manifests the historical and cultural tradition of the country and is a sign of a value system based on freedom, equality, human dignity and tolerance.[6] As citizenship is founded on these same values, which are to be respected by everybody, the presence of the crucifix in the classroom is and must be compulsory, because it shows a set of values that everybody who wants to live in Italy has to accept and defend. As a consequence the crucifix cannot be removed from the classroom wall, nor can its presence be made dependent on the

4 That is not only legal citizenship. Full citizenship is not only a matter of status and rights but also of shared values: to be a good citizen does not mean (only) not to commit crimes but also entails feeling part of a common narrative, partaking in some foundational myths, developing a sense of belonging, solidarity and commitment. The different dimensions of citizenship are underlined by Joppke (2008: 37).

5 See the Second Section decision in the case *Lautsi* v. *Italy*, 3 November 2009 (Application no. 30814/06). On this decision see also Mancini (2010a).

6 See Mémoire du Gouvernement Italien pour l'Audience devant la Grande Chambre de la Cour Européenne des Droits de l'Homme, in www.governo.it/Presidenza/CONTENZIOSO/contenzioso_europeo/grande_camera/Memoria_Rappresentanza_Lautsi_Grande_Camera.pdf.

choice of the students and the teachers. These arguments express in legal terms the idea – supported by a large part of the Catholic hierarchy, the governing political coalition and public opinion – that only the Catholic tradition can perform the role of civil religion of Italy and can provide the set of fundamental principles and values on which social cohesion is founded. This model is not exclusive to Italy. The Italian appeal against the decision of the Strasbourg Court has been supported by other Catholic and, more interestingly, Orthodox countries:[7] an unprecedented alliance between Catholic and Orthodox States was formed to counter the trends of the European Court, which are considered detrimental to both national sovereignty and religious tradition.

The second pattern answers the same need in the opposite way. It is based on the conviction that national identity and social cohesion can no longer be granted by the traditional religions which have become too weak to serve as a unifying factor. A common citizenship can be built only around a set of secular principles – liberty, equality, tolerance and so on – that every individual and group must embrace independently from his origins, preferences, creed. These principles are assumed to be religiously and culturally neutral: in this way secularism can claim the right to govern the whole public sphere, where every citizen can feel at home exactly because this space is without any reference to the particular values and symbols of the different religious, racial, ethnic, cultural and political communities living in the country. The French laws that forbid the wearing of religious symbols at school and the full-face veil in all public places, including the streets, are a good example of this approach.[8] Of particular interest is a passage of the French Constitutional Council decision that declared the constitutional legitimacy of the law. It affirms that the self-determination of women is irrelevant: even if their decision to wear the *burqa* or the niqab is taken freely and consciously, they are in an objective 'situation of exclusion and inferiority that is clearly incompatible with the constitutional principles of freedom and equality'.[9] Beneath this statement there is the conviction that, if national identity has to be built around the notion of *laïcité*, 'it is the role of the State to create laïque citizens' (Berger et al. 2008: 77) by educating them to the values of secularism and shielding them from the competing values upheld by religions. This approach to the place of religion in

7 Ten countries asked to intervene in the judgment in support of the Italian position. They are Lithuania, Malta, Monaco, San Marino (all countries with a Catholic majority), Bulgaria, Cyprus, Greece, Romania, Russia (all countries with an Orthodox majority) and Armenia (see *Grand Chamber Hearing Lautsi* v. *Italy – press release issued by the Registrar, 30 June 2010.*). It is significant that no country with a Protestant majority of citizens is part of this group.

8 See 'Loi 2004-228 du 15 mars 2004 encadrant, en application du principe de laïcité, le port de signes ou de tenues manifestant une appartenance religieuse dans les écoles, collèges et lycées publics', in *Journal Officiel de la République Française*, 15 March 2004; 'Loi 2010-1192 du 11 octobre 2010 interdisant la dissimulation du visage dans l'espace public', in *Journal Officiel*, 12 October 2010. See also Bowen (2006) and Joppke (2010).

9 Décision no. 2010-613 du 7 octobre 2010, in *Journal Officiel*, 7 October 2010.

the public space is shared by some international organizations, like the Council of Europe and the European Court of Human Rights: it is no coincidence that all the applications against the ban of religious symbols in the French and Turkish schools have been rejected by the Court of Strasbourg (Evans 2010: 109–115; Ringelheim 2012).

The third pattern is best exemplified by the United Kingdom, which is probably the most advanced European country in the pursuit of an extensive multicultural organization of society. The United Kingdom is a common law country where, as in many countries of this type, the central role in shaping the legal system is not played by the State and its laws but by the courts and their judgments. In the task of striking a balance between the different ethnic, religious and cultural groups coexisting in British society the courts are guided by the respect of fundamental human rights. But sometimes human rights are interpreted and applied in a way that ends up restricting one of them: freedom of religion. An example of this approach is provided by the British Supreme Court ruling in the case of the Jewish Free School.[10] This school had an admission policy that privileged Jewish students and, more specifically, in accordance with the principles of Orthodox Judaism, students born to a Jewish mother: these admission criteria led to the exclusion of a student born to a non-Jewish mother who had converted to Judaism according to the rites of a non-Orthodox branch. The Supreme Court judged that the school admission policy, focusing on the maternal descent of the student, was based not on religion but on ethnicity and therefore violated the Race Relations Act 1976 that forbids any discrimination on this ground (Mancini 2010b).

This judgment has far-reaching consequences as it implies that the membership rules of a religion are subject to the scrutiny of State courts. By applying the principle of non-discrimination, they can overrule the decisions of the religious authorities about membership in the religious group, thus limiting its collective religious freedom right. The application of a fundamental right – non-discrimination – collides with the respect of another fundamental right, religious freedom. This contrast exemplifies the potential tension between human rights and religious rights (Ballard 2009: 299–330): the former, as codified in the declarations of the last two and a half centuries, have a rational/ethical foundation and a universal scope that can easily clash with the religious foundation and the more particular scope of the rights claimed by religious individuals and groups.[11] As Oftestad underlines, 'the liberal democracy has its own fundamental ideology rooted in universal human rights' and 'the ideological goal of the democratic state is to implement individual freedom and cultural and social equality among all members of the society'. Such a goal places some religious communities, whose doctrine and organization is not entirely consistent with these principles

10 See *R* v. *The Governing Body of JFS* (2009 UKSC 15).

11 Religions cannot compete with fundamental rights on the ground of universality. Even large supra-national religions – Islam, Christianity, Buddhism, etc. – are not as universal as human rights claim to be. See Ferrari (2007a: 3–14).

(think of the Catholic Church teaching and practice on ordination of women and homosexual marriages), on a collision course with these democratic ideals. 'Until now the State has avoided a concrete confrontation with the Church on these issues, because the State is obliged to respect the ideal of religious freedom not only for the individual, but for the religious institutions as well. But how long the State will maintain an attitude of reserve towards the 'discrimination' in the Church is a delicate question' (Ofenstad 2010: 473). A 'fundamentalistic' interpretation of human rights is another – perhaps less evident but equally insidious – way to affirm the dominance of secularism in the public sphere.

Each of the three models described has its limitations. The 'Italian' pattern is based on the gamble that citizenship and social cohesion can be built around a particular religious and cultural tradition. In the short term, this strategy may work, yet nobody knows how long it will be able to deal with the challenge of the increasing immigration of non-Christian communities. The weakest point of the 'French' pattern is the assumption that not only the State and its institutions, but also society and politics, have to be independent from particular traditions and conceptions of life.[12] To attain such a goal these traditions are to be pushed to the margins of public life. Yet the privatization of religion is being met with growing resistance by many historical religions of Europe and it is rejected by a substantial part of the immigrant communities, especially those that come from countries where law and politics are intermingled with religion. Finally, the 'British' model is flawed by an internal contradiction: it has the stated aim of securing and developing religious pluralism but ends up using human rights to compress the differences and promote cultural homogenization.

These models are little more than 'ideal types' that do not exist, in a 'pure' form, in Italy, France, the United Kingdom nor in any other European State. Moreover they are far from being static: the British Prime Minister has recently advocated 'muscular liberalism' as the best way to tackle the multiculturalist drift,[13] while the French President is taking the lead in Europe as a supporter of 'positive' and 'open' *laïcité*.[14] Nowadays British multiculturalism and French *laïcité* are no longer inviolable dogmas which must be blindly reaffirmed without taking account of social changes. However, these models foreshadow three different ways of understanding the place and the role of religion in the public sphere. It makes little sense to ask which of them is the best in abstract terms. It is more appropriate to ask in which direction each of them should progress to deal with

12 This assumption emerges clearly in the *Déclaration sur la laïcité* prepared by Jean Baubérot, Roberto Blancarte and Micheline Milot and published on 9 December 2005 (see its articles 4 and 9). For the text see Baubérot (2006: 247–265).

13 Cameron's speech of 5 February 2005 can be read at www.number10.gov.uk/news/speeches-and-transcripts/2011/02/pms-speech-at-munich-security-conference-60293.

14 See the speech delivered by Sarkozy in Rome on 20 December 2007, in www.elysee.fr/president/les-actualites/discours/2007/allocution-de-m-le-president-de-la-republique.7012.html.

the changes that are taking place in Europe. The French model has evolved in a context characterized by a strong State and a declining religion, while the Italian one has arisen from a situation where, ever since its creation, a relatively young and weak State has had to deal with a strong religion. These different starting points have to be taken into account in order to understand what can be reasonably expected from each national tradition regarding the accommodation of religion in the public sphere.

The Changing Religious Landscape of Europe

One of Europe's main assets is its internal diversity and it is wise to try to make the most of it, giving up from the very beginning any dream of assigning to religion the same space and relevance in the public sphere all over Europe. The existence of different national systems of relations between States and religions is not in contrast with the unification process of Europe, provided they stay within a broad framework defined by the respect of human rights. That said, we can briefly mention the two processes that are challenging the traditional conception of public sphere in many European States.

The first is the cultural, religious, ethnic and ethical pluralization of contemporary Europe. Due to immigration and globalization, individuals and groups are now present in Europe (physically or virtually) who do not recognize the primacy of individual religious liberty as it has been established in European history: in different ways, they are in favour of a communitarian approach that questions the centrality of individual rights and therefore the distinction between the public and private sphere.

Second, there is the publicization of religion. In most of Europe (and with the exception of the Communist regimes) religion was never privatized, in the sense of being excluded from public recognition and support: but there was a clear distinction between the spiritual and the temporal sphere and it was widely assumed that, in the latter, religions had a duty of self-restraint. In the last 20 to 30 years the boundaries between spiritual and temporal have become much more blurred and religions have been able to influence the public discourse on matters from which they were previously excluded. Alberico Gentili's 'silete theologi in munere alieno' has gone out of fashion and an increasing number of citizens claim that they have the right to publicly follow the tenets of their religion in matters of dress codes, gender relations, dietary rules and so on.[15]

These two processes take place in a context dominated by the fear that Europe has entered a phase of demographic, economic, political and military decline. This feeling has instilled many doubts in European minds about being able to manage the pluralization and publicization of religion with the tools available in the store

15 The analysis of this phenomenon goes back to Casanova (1994).

of human rights.[16] This lack of confidence results in a constant oscillation between the impulse to confine religion more strictly to the private sphere, excluding it from the process of building the national identity, and the desire to strengthen national identity through the revitalization (and therefore the re-publicization) of the majority religion(s) only. In the first case the arsenal of human rights is rigorously applied without fear of marginalizing and alienating a substantial part of the population and, in certain cases, of obtaining illiberal results. In the second case a limited application of human rights (particularly when equal treatment is at stake) is adopted with the aim of maintaining the privileged status of the majority religion(s). The French law that forbids wearing religious symbols at school is a good example of the first trend; the laws that mandate the display of the crucifix in the Italian classrooms,[17] that prevent teachers from wearing religious symbols other than Christian ones in some German *Länder* (Fogel 2006/2007: 619–653), or the Swiss referendum that forbids the building of minarets (Stüssi 2008: 135–153; Chapter 17 in this volume) are a good example of the second trend.

To overcome this impasse, the common law model (of a 'light' State and no inclination to marginalize religion from the public sphere) could be appealing. But – apart from the fact that it is hardly exportable beyond the English Channel – this model too presents some dangers. Judging from some court decisions, the price religions have to pay to be admitted to the public sphere is the respect for human rights within their own doctrinal and organizational system. If rigidly applied, this principle can start a process of cultural homogenization that, in the end, undermines the specificity of religious communities and the contribution they can give to building a plural society: a much more dangerous result than their marginalization from the public sphere (as in the case of the 'French' model).

According to some, these difficulties foreshadow 'the end of a secular order based on principles – however inadequately they may operate in practice – of consensual rationality', the decline of the distinction between public and private sphere and 'the fusion again ... of those relatively distinct spheres' (Frow 2006: 87).[18] In the opinion of this author this outcome is not inevitable or even desirable. Liberal democracy has sufficient resources to govern the transformations of contemporary society without calling into question the fundamental principles on which it is based.

To find a way out, the notion of public sphere has to be re-thought so that it is made hospitable to individuals and groups who want to manifest their religion or belief; accessible to all individuals and groups (not only to a select few) who are ready and able to accept the plurality, on an equal footing, of different religions and beliefs in this same sphere (this is the access card required from all subjects

16 Tariq Modood defined this process as the passage from a 'pluralism of hope' to 'a pluralism of fear' (see 'We Need a Multiculturalism of Hope', *Guardian*, 21 September 2009).

17 See *supra*, footnote 5.

18 On this perspective see Petersen (2010: 321–344).

that want to enter it); respectful of human rights but open to the accommodations that are necessary to safeguard the internal autonomy of religion and belief communities. This strategy presupposes a better understanding of the multiple spatial and personal dimensions that are hidden under the notion of public sphere.

Public, Private, Plural: Introductory Notes

Before starting any discussion on the public and private divide, a few preliminary remarks are required. From many quarters it has been pointed out that such a distinction is ideologically tainted, in the sense that 'the classic liberal public/private dichotomy hides lots of publics and tries to keep lots of political or public issues (e.g. structural power-asymmetries) "private", i.e. off the public/political agenda' (Bader 2008). Hanne Petersen believes that the private/public dichotomy is connected to the monotheistic way to conceive religion, 'inherited by secular state organizations and regulations. The "Atlantic-European" inspired secular normative culture introduces a division in public and private spheres, which continues a tradition of gender division and class privilege' (Chapter 7 in this volume), while others identify a direct link between the public/private divide and Christianity (in particular Protestant Christianity), where religion is seen as something that primarily affects the spiritual (versus the material) side of human existence, the *forum internum* as opposed to the *forum externum*.[19] In both cases it is highlighted that the private/public distinction is culturally biased and far from being universal.[20] Finally, it is also a crude and imprecise distinction: a sharp line neatly dividing these two dimensions of human life cannot be drawn and, whatever definition of public and private is adopted, it is impossible to remove a large grey area in which public and private overlap and mingle (Hénaff and Strong 2001: 23). These criticisms cannot be overlooked but, on the other hand, the public/private distinction is deeply ingrained in our way of understanding the social fabric and plays a positive role in building and maintaining a democratic society (Parkinson 2009): a world where private is public and vice versa would probably be a totalitarian or a theocratic world. As underlined by Gaudreault-DesBiens and Karazivan (Chapter 6, this volume), 'the division between the public and private spheres still matters today … whether we like it or not, this divide continues to inspire the state's regulatory endeavours, as well as the behaviour of many citizens'. For these reasons, a careful and prudent use of these two categories can still provide useful hints to reflect on the place to be assigned to religion and on the role it can play in either area.

---

19 The legal implications of this way of conceiving religion are discussed by Danchin (2011).

20 However, the fact that the public/private distinction is culturally-specific does not exclude it from playing a positive role in the Western political and legal context and be a resource Europe can use in the dialogue with other civilizations.

In Chapter 2 of this volume Kjell Modéer provides an interesting historical perspective on the public/private divide. In his view, this divide is a matter of power and regards who is in charge of what. He supports this view with three examples – family, education and poor relief. Family and its law was, and still largely is, part of the private domain where individuals are the main actors. Education underwent a process of 'publicization': for a long time it was regarded as a private matter but, starting from the eighteenth century, it increasingly became a responsibility of the State, although parents still have an important directive role in it. Finally, poor relief has become an almost exclusive task of the welfare state, with private actors playing a subsidiary role.

Religion was never an exclusively private or public matter. In the Christian tradition (Judaism and Islam may have a different approach) faith is a personal matter that concerns the most private part of human life, the *forum internum*, the conscience. 'My kingdom is not of this world' said Jesus and, as correctly underlined by Modeér, this persuasion supported the idea that State and Church have distinct spheres of influence. But the evangelical dictum 'Render unto Caesar the things that are Caesar's, and unto God the things that are God's', which translates the previous principle into operative terms, was never interpreted by the Church authorities in the sense that Caesar is public and God is private. The public dimension of religion was always upheld by the Christian Churches and they strongly opposed the attempt to privatize religion that was pursued in particular throughout the nineteenth century: this opposition explains why the privatization programme was never completed in Europe so that, even in the most 'separatist' countries like France, religion never lost its public role (as shown by the persistence of religious chaplaincies in the Army, the legal status of the Catholic places of worship, etc.).

Now, as it has been shown in the first part of this chapter, the public/private divide seems to be again on the move, at least as far as religion is concerned. The privatization process has lost much of its impetus and re-publicization of religion has become the new catch phrase in many academic circles. But this re-publicization cannot simply be a repetition of the past because something new has been happening in Europe: religion has become plural and, differently from the past, this plurality involves many non-Christian religions and a growing number of Europeans who have no religion. Categories and language are inevitably more diversified and this difference has an impact also on the definition of public and private: how these two notions can be reformulated to fit this plurality is the subject of the second part of this chapter.

The Manifestations of Religion or Belief in the Private and Public Sphere

Many international and national legislative texts affirm the right to manifest one's religion or belief in private and in public.[21] Both in the private and in the public domains, manifestations of religion or belief have to respect some limits: even in the most private places and areas of life (at home, in the family or in the religious community), religion or belief convictions are not a valid justification for behaviours that infringe some fundamental human rights such as, for example, the right to life. But the limitations that apply to the first and second areas differ in type and intensity: in the public field limitations are usually more extensive and intrusive than in the private one. For example, according to the UK Racial and Religious Hatred Act, 2006, stirring up religious hatred is not a crime when the offensive words are pronounced or the unlawful behaviour takes place 'inside a dwelling'[22] and the French prohibition to wear a full-face veil does not apply at home.[23] The problem derives from the fact that it is impossible to define a priori and once and for all what is public and what private: as a consequence it is not always easy to determine in which cases a manifestation of religion or belief can be legitimately limited. Some laws ground the distinction on the notion of accessibility,[24] others provide a definition of public space case by case, in relation to a specific text of law.[25] Faced with these different definitions, we need to find a firmer ground for distinguishing the private and the public domain. This ground is not provided by a spatial (public/private places) or personal (individuals acting in a public/private capacity or providing a public/private service) element. Although these elements are not irrelevant, a better way to distinguish public and private

21 See for example art. 9 of the European Convention of Human Rights; art. 18 of the International Covenant on Civil and Political Rights; art. 19 of the Italian constitution; art. 16 of the Czech Charter of Fundamental Rights and Freedoms; art. 2 of the Bulgarian Religious Denomination Act, 2006. The reference to the public space has a historical explanation due to the fact that, in the past, manifestations of religion or belief were frequently restricted to the private sphere.

22 *Racial and Religious Hatred Act 2006*, 29B(2).

23 See footnote 8.

24 Art. 5,3 of the *Bulgarian Religious Denomination Act*, 2006: 'Religious beliefs are expressed in private when they are performed by a member or members of the religious community or only in the presence of persons belonging to that community, and in public—when their expression may become accessible to people who do not belong to the respective religious community'.

25 Art. 2 of the French *Loi interdisant la dissimulation du visage dans l'espace public*: 'Pour l'application de l'article 1er, l'espace public est constitué des voies publiques ainsi que des lieux ouverts au public ou affectés à un service public'. A detailed description of the places falling into the category of 'public space' is provided by the *Circulaire du 2 mars 2011 relative à la mise en œuvre de la loi n° 2010-1192 du 11 octobre 2010 interdisant la dissimulation du visage dans l'espace public*, in *Journal Officiel de la République Française*, no. 0052, 3 March 2011, 4128.

is offered by the content and aim of the communication that takes place in the two fields (Chapter 4, this volume): in the public sphere citizens discuss, debate and share information about affairs of collective interest. From this point of view places that are always and only private or public – as well as individuals who always and only act in a public or private capacity – do not exist: this qualification depends on the type of communication that is carried out in these places or by these persons.

It has already been said that religion does not pertain only to the private or the public sphere. Now it is possible to add that, applying these criteria to distinguish public and private, religious communication can have a public or private dimension independently from the space where it takes place or the subjects involved in the communication process.

Deconstructing the Public Sphere

The European Union motto 'Unity in Diversity' requires that, when trying to identify a viable and 'shareable' notion of public sphere, we make reference to a conceptual framework that is strong enough to guarantee the respect of the common principles upon which European democracies are based and, at the same time, open enough to include the different national identities of the EU Member States. The building of this framework requires first of all a better understanding of the different dimensions and functions that are implicit in the expression 'public sphere': this can be done through distinctions regarding the space and the individuals or organizations that inhabit it.

(1) *The spatial dimension.* The first distinction is based on the conviction that, within the public sphere, it is helpful to distinguish between common space, political space and institutional space.[26] It is of fundamental importance to understand from the outset that these three spaces are not physically or temporally separated: they coexist and overlap. The square is a space that can be common, political or institutional depending on the use made of it; the school is a space that is common, political and institutional at the same time.[27] With this caveat, it is possible to identify some characteristics of these three dimensions of the public sphere.

The common space is the physical space that people have to enter to meet their basic needs: in this sense it is inescapable. This space is not accessed with

26 See Wolton (2011): 'l'espace commun concerne la circulation et l'expression; l'espace public, la discussion; l'espace politique, la décision'. Although this chapter employs a different terminology to identify these three spaces, their content and function are defined along the same lines.

27 Wolton (2009) insists on the fact that 'ces trois espaces … naturellement sont synchrones dans le fonctionnement quotidien'. However, their distinction is important from a legal point of view, as different rules apply to different spaces.

the intent to participate in a political debate but simply to get to work or to buy what is needed for daily life.[28] The communication process that takes place in this space is not primarily political. Of course, wearing a cross, a *kippa*, a turban may convey a message concerning the belief of an individual even when that individual is going to buy bread and butter: but the same message can be conveyed by his/her haircut, or earring, or tattoo and there is no reason why religious symbols should be regulated more restrictively than other symbols. From a normative point of view this common space must be kept as accessible as possible to avoid segregating in their homes people who do not feel able to enter it without manifesting their religion or belief. This is the problem raised recently by the French and Belgian laws that banned the full-face veil in the streets. General prohibitions of this type can be problematic not only because they limit the freedom of religion and expression of individuals but primarily because they affect their daily and, in a sense, 'pre-political' life. No doubt, public authorities have the duty to ensure that the decision to wear the *burqa* or the niqab is a matter of free choice and not imposed by the family or the religious community; moreover the wearing of the full-face veil can be prohibited when it creates real and actual difficulties to an orderly enjoyment of the common space. But once individual freedom and common interest are safeguarded, wearing clothes that manifest the religious and cultural convictions of a person cannot be limited in the common space if the actual damage caused to the 'usability' of that space by other people is not proven.[29]

The political space is the space of debate and discussion where the public discourse takes shape. It should not be understood only as a space of intellectual 'argumentation about the truth value of propositions', but more broadly as 'a realm of creativity and social imaginaries in which citizens give shared form to their lives together, a realm of exploration, experiment, and partial agreement' (Calhoun 2011: 129): in Robert Cover's words, it is the space where new 'normative worlds' take shape.[30] It is a metaphorical space, although it can have physical materializations (Hyde Park Corner, or a political rally in a square, for example).[31] In order to perform its creative function, the political space should be free and plural: the

28 See Parkinson (2009: 1), about the accessibility and inescapability of this space; see also Hénaff and Strong (2001: 4), who underline that it 'is not a space where one goes to speak with others' and 'is not a human construct' (differently from the political space).

29 On the issue of the *burqa* see, besides the text indicated in footnote 8, Ferrari (forthcoming).

30 According to Cover (1983: 4–9), any person lives in a normative universe that is defined as 'a world of right and wrong, of lawful and unlawful, of valid and void'. Religious communities are a good example of these normative worlds: they are places where new legal meanings are created through the personal commitment of the community members, who apply their will to transform the 'extant state of affairs' according to their 'visions of alternative futures'.

31 This description of the political space (and of the institutional one mentioned a few lines below) corresponds largely to Habermas' characterization of the informal and institutional public sphere (Habermas 2006: 1–25).

visible presence of different religions and beliefs in this area is indispensable for the pluralism on which a democratic society is based.[32] Much attention has been devoted to the conditions required to participate in the political debate that takes place in this space: while there is significant agreement on the opportunity to accept different types of discourses (including those based on comprehensive doctrines),[33] a call to responsibility is also present. Differently expressed (Lafont 2007: 236–256), it underlines the need that a public discourse – even when it manifests a particular experience and vision of life – takes into account social complexity and plurality. This point has recently been made by Ino Augsberg who, building on the works of Luhmann and Teubner, highlights that 'every social system forms part of the social environment of the other social subsystems', so that 'its task is also to establish a sensible relationship of compatibility towards the specific functions and characteristics of the other systems'.[34] Therefore not only freedom (as in the case of the common space) but also responsibility are the principles that should be borne in mind, from a normative point of view, when giving a legal configuration to this space.

Finally, the institutional public space is the place where coercive deliberations, which are compulsory for all, are taken (parliament, the law courts, public administration, etc.). It is not (only) the space of debate and discussion, it is the space of decisions that, once they have been taken, have to be respected by everybody.[35] The law court is not a TV talk show: one does not go there to have a nice chat with a judge, one goes to court to obtain an enforceable sentence that decides who is right and who is wrong. In order to gain the general respect and recognition that is required for the enforcement of such binding decisions, this space must not only be, it must also be seen to be, fair and impartial. That is why some doubts are raised, for example, by the legal provisions that require a crucifix to be displayed in the courtrooms of some European States (like Italy for example): these provisions could give the impression that the administration of justice is biased, as it is influenced by a specific religious doctrine. However, these principles of fairness and impartiality do not mean the automatic exclusion of all religious references, manifestations and symbols from the public institutions. The presence of religious symbols can be unsuitable in some of them and not in others, particularly if the principle of neutrality of the institutional space is

32 See the European Court of Human Rights decision in the case *Metropolitan Church of Bessarabia* v. *Moldova*, 2001.

33 The 'Babel of voices in the informal flows of public communication' evoked by Habermas (2006: 22).

34 Quoting Teubner's *Reflexives Recht*, Augsberg concludes that 'it is the task of reflexive structures in any social subsystem to resolve conflicts between function and performance by imposing internal restrictions on given subsystems so that they are suitable as components of the environment of other subsystems' (Augsberg 2011).

35 Wolton 2011 writes that in the political space (what I call institutional space) 'il ne s'agit ni de discuter ni de délibérer, mais de décider et d'agir'.

applied in a way that includes different religions and conceptions of life: when appropriate and possible, the quest for solutions that consent the coexistence of different religious symbols in the same physical space can be the best way to educate towards responsible and accountable pluralism.[36]

The public (i.e. State) school provides a good testing ground for understanding the differences and the overlaps between political and institutional space. The school is primarily a space of the first type, where a process of communication and exchange between different conceptions and experiences of life takes place: from this point of view it is essential to ensure the freedom of expression and the plurality of experiences. The prohibition of wearing religious symbols at school, which is in force in some European countries, affects this political space: it limits the students' freedom to manifest their religion and can be justified only on the ground of the protection of a legitimate and pressing social need that requires to be assessed case by case.[37] But the public school is at the same time an institutional space, which must be characterized by neutrality towards different religious (or non-religious) convictions of students and teachers: from this point of view the compulsory display of a religious symbol (for example a crucifix) can be problematic, as it indicates the preference of the public institution for a specific religion.[38]

(2) *The personal dimension.* The second distinction regards the individuals or the organizations that inhabit the common, political and institutional spaces. All these spaces are populated by subjects that act in a different capacity: a public school, for example, is attended both by students and by teachers but only the latter are employees of a State institution. They share the same space but act in a different capacity. Therefore, the degree of freedom that is granted to students may be greater than that accorded to teachers. For example, in many European countries students can wear religious symbols that teachers are not allowed to wear because they represent the State.[39] The religious symbol is the same but the

36 An example of good practice of 'inclusive neutrality' in the institutional space is offered by the legal discipline of the oath that is in force in some countries where, when an oath is required, it is possible to take it in a secular or religious form and, in the second case, according to different religious creeds.

37 For this reason the rules that were in force in France before 2004, when the school principal had the power to prevent student from wearing religious symbols if they caused an actual perturbation of the school life, were more in line with the approach supported in the text than the actual discipline, based on a general prohibition.

38 On this issue the European Court of Human Rights pronounced two conflicting decisions (see the Second Section and the Grand Chamber decision in the case *Lautsi and Others* v. *Italy*, 30814/06).

39 This point was made by the European Court of Human Rights in the case *Dahlab* v. *Switzerland* (a teacher who wanted to wear an Islamic headscarf at school). The Court decided that 'as a civil servant, she represented the State; on that account, her conduct should not suggest that the State identified itself with one religion rather than another'

subjective position of the person who wears it is different: therefore limitations that are unacceptable in one case can be legitimate in the other.

The picture becomes more complex when a private subject performs a public service. With a good dose of approximation human activities can be defined 'public' when responding to a general interest, 'private' when responding to a particular interest. But not all public activities are performed by public subjects: in many cases, services of general interest – that is, public service – are provided by private individuals or entities (and vice versa). As in the previous examples, it is not a matter that can be addressed in spatial terms: when driving in a car one share the same space in which a taxi driver operates, but he/she performs a public service and therefore cannot refuse transportation to an individual because of his/her religion (which other drivers could do without problems).

Once more, school is a good example. Education is a service of general interest that can be provided both by public and private schools. But the rules that apply to the former do not correspond to those that regulate the activity of the latter. For a State school, for example, a teacher's religious faith is irrelevant for the purpose of his/her hiring or dismissal; for a religiously-oriented private school, on the contrary, this element can legitimately be taken into account. Both schools provide the same educational service and operate within the same public space (which can be common, political or institutional depending on the circumstances), but in one school the teacher has the right to wear religious symbols, in the other he/she cannot do so.

Correctly identifying the type of public space where a manifestation of religion takes place (which can already be a tricky affair) is not enough: the role performed by the different actors who play in that space and the services they provide have to be taken into consideration too.

Conclusion

There are no easy answers to the problems posed by the changes affecting the relationship between law and religion in Europe. As was to be expected, the transformations that are ongoing in this field have made obsolete the old models of the legal government of religions without replacing them with convincing alternatives.

The de-construction of the notion of public sphere according to its spatial and personal components can provide some useful guidelines for dealing with the problems raised by the process of re-publicization and pluralization of religion mentioned at the beginning of this chapter. First, it restrains the adoption of general and uniform solutions that fail to consider the coexistence of many overlapping public spaces and neglect the specific role that each of them plays in the promotion

(no. 42393/98, at no. 1 of the section 'The law'). In the same sense see also the decision in the case *Kurtulmus* v. *Turkey*, 65500/01.

of a vital and democratic society. Second, it is functional to a pragmatic approach, focused on a practical and case-by-case evaluation of the problems deriving from the manifestations of religion or belief in the public sphere. It is exactly the opposite of what happened in the discussions about the full-face veil, monopolized by those who believe that the *burqa/niqab* – always and in any case – offends women's dignity, public order and gender equality and those who consider it a manifestation of faith, personal self-determination and freedom of expression that must be guaranteed without exceptions. Such an ideological debate completely overlooked a functional approach to the limits to be imposed on the manifestations of religion or belief in the common space, omitting to consider whether banning the *full-face veil* from the streets meant segregating women in their homes.

Deconstructing the notion of public sphere helps to accommodate the manifestations of religion and belief in this area of life in a way that maximizes the freedom of religion and belief enjoyed by individuals and groups and, at the same time, respects the different social functions of the common, political and institutional space and the different roles played by the individuals and organizations who operate within it.

A final warning. The framework outlined in the previous pages does not apply to a deserted land: it applies to countries that have their own historical, cultural and religious characteristics. The need to respect them has been affirmed by the European Court of Human Rights through the 'margin of appreciation' doctrine: although it has not always been applied in a consistent way, it introduces an element of flexibility that is required by the different heritages of the European countries (where difference has to be seen as an asset and not a burden). A State where secularism is a constitutional principle can adopt an approach to manifestations of religion and belief in the public sphere that is more restrictive than the approach followed by a country with a State religion: both approaches can be legitimate provided they do not exceed the boundaries of the framework and respect freedom of religion and equal treatment of religious groups.

References

Augsberg, I. (2011), 'Religious Freedom as "Reflexive Law"', paper presented at the McGill University, Faculty of Law, *Conference on Religious Revival in a post-Multicultural Age*, Montreal, 28–29 January 2011.

Bader, V. (2008), 'Eurospheres? Fragmented and Stratified or Integrated and Fair? A Conceptual and Pre-Theoretical Mapping Exercise', *Eurospheres working papers series*, no. 9, paper available at: http://dare.uva.nl/document/115557 (accessed 31 May 2012).

Ballard, R. (2009), 'Human Rights in Contexts of Ethnic Plurality: Always a Vehicle for Liberation?', in Grillo, R. et al. (eds), 299–330.

Baubérot, J. (2006), *L'intégrisme républicain contre la laïcité* (Paris: Aube).

Berger, P., Davie, G. and Fokas, E. (2008), *Religious America, Secular Europe? A Theme and Variations* (Aldershot: Ashgate).
Bowen, J.R. (2006), *Why the French Don't Like Headscarves: Islam, the State, and Public Space* (Princeton: Princeton University Press).
Calhoun, C. (2011), 'Afterword: Religion's Many Powers', in Mendieta, E. and Vanantwerpen, J. (eds), 118–134.
Casanova, J. (1994), *Public Religions in the Modern World* (Chicago: University of Chicago Press).
Centre de droit civil et comparé du Québec (2010), *Convictions philosophiques et religieuses et droits positives* (Bruxelles: Bruylant).
Cesari, J. (ed.) (2009), *Handbook of European Islam* (Oxford: Oxford University Press).
Christoffersen, L., Modéer, K.A. and Andersen, S. (eds) (2010), *Law & Religion in the 21st Century – Nordic Perspectives* (Copenhagen: Diøf Publishing).
Cover, R. (1983), 'Nomos and Narrative', *Harvard Law Review*, 97, 4–68.
Danchin, P.G. (2011), 'Islam and the Secular Nomos of the European Court of Human Rights', *Michigan Journal of International Law*, 32, 663–747.
European Parliament (2007), *Islam in the European Union: What's at Stake in the Future?* (Brussels: European Parliament).
Evans, C. (2010), 'Individual and Group Religious Freedom in the European Court of Human Rights: Cracks in the Intellectual Architecture', *Journal of Law and Religion*, XXVI:1, 345–370.
Ferrari, A. (ed.) (forthcoming, 2013), *The Burqa in Europe* (Farnham: Ashgate).
Ferrari, S. (2003), 'The Legal Dimension', in Maréchal, B. et al. (eds), 219–254.
Ferrari, S. (2007a), 'Tra geo-diritti e teo-diritti. Riflessioni sulle religioni come centri transnazionali di identità', *Quaderni di diritto e politica ecclesiastica*, 1, 3–14.
Ferrari, S. (2007b), 'Juridical Profiles and Political Management of Muslims' Presence in Europe', in European Parliament.
Ferrari, S. (2010), 'The Italian Pattern of Law and Religion Relations: Catholicism as the Italian Civil Religion', *Convictions philosophiques et religieuses et droits positives*, 397–420.
Fogel, S. (2006/2007), 'Headscarves in German Public Schools: Religious Minorities are Welcome in Germany, Unless – God Forbid – They are Religious', *New York Law School Law Review*, 51, 619–653.
Frow, J. (2006), 'Waiting for the Antichrist', in Ribeiro, 71–89.
Grillo, R., Ballard, R., Ferrari, A., Hoekema, A.J., Maussen, M. and Shah, P. (eds) (2009), *Legal Practice and Cultural Diversity* (Farnham: Ashgate).
Habermas, J. (2006), 'Religion in the Public Sphere', *European Journal of Philosophy*, 14, 1–25.
Hénaff, M. and Strong, T.B. (eds) (2001), *Public Space and Democracy* (Minneapolis: University of Minnesota Press).
Isin, E.F., Nyers, P. and Turner, B.S. (2008), *Citizenship between Past and Future* (London: Routledge).

Joppke, C. (2008), 'Transformation of Citizenship: Status, Rights, Identity', in Isin, E.F. et al., 36–47.
Joppke, C. (2010), *Limits of Restricting Islam: The French Burqa Law of 2010*, unpublished paper available at: http://igovberkeley.com/content/limits-restricting-islam-french-*burqa*-law-2010-0 (accessed 31 May 2012).
Kepel, G. (1990), *La revanche de Dieu* (Paris: Seuil).
Lafont, C. (2007), 'Religion in the Public Sphere', *Constellations*, 14:2, 236–256.
Mancini, S. (2010a), 'The Crucifix Rage: Supranational Constitutionalism Bumps Against the Counter-Majoritarian Difficulty', *European Constitutional Law Review*, 6, 6–27.
Mancini, S. (2010b), 'To Be or Not to Be Jewish: The UK Supreme Court Answers the Questions', *European Constitutional Law Review*, 6, 481–502.
Maréchal, B., Allievi, S., Dassetto, F. and Nielsen, J. (eds) (2003), *Muslims in the Enlarged Europe: Religion and Society* (Leiden and Boston: Brill).
Mendieta, E. and Vanantwerpen, J. (eds) (2011), *The Power of Religion in the Public Sphere* (New York: Columbia University Press).
Motzkin, G. and Fischer, Y. (2008), *Religion and Democracy in Contemporary Europe* (London: Alliance Publ. Trust).
Ofenstad, B. (2010), 'Presence and Mission. The Social-Ethical Engagement of the Catholic Church within the Nordic Context 1970–2006', in Christoffersen, L. et al. (eds), 451–476.
Parkinson, J. (2009), 'Holistic Democracy and Public Space', in Turmel, P. and Kingwell, M. (eds), 71–84.
Petersen, H. (2010), 'Beyond National Majority/Minority Dichotomies: Towards Legal Traditions & Religions of World Society – A Local Example', in Christoffersen, L. et al. (eds), 321–344.
Pollack, D. (2008), 'Religious Change in Europe: Theoretical Considerations and Empirical Findings', in Motzkin, G. and Fischer, Y., 83–100.
Ribeiro, A.P. (2006), *The State of the World* (Manchester: Carcanet and Fundacao Calouste Gulbenkian).
Ringelheim, J. (2012), 'Rights, Religion and the Public Sphere: The European Court of Human Rights in Search of a Theory?' in Ungureanu, C. and Zucca, L., 283–306.
Robbers, G. (ed.) (2005), *State and Church in the European Union* (Baden-Baden: Nomos).
Stüssi, M. (2008), 'Banning of Minarets: Addressing the Validity of a Controversial Swiss Popular Initiative', *Religion and Human Rights*, 3:2, 135–153.
Turmel, P. and Kingwell, M. (eds) (2009), *Rites of Way: The Politics and Poetics of Public Space* (Waterloo: Wilfrid Laurier University Press).
Ungureanu, C. and Zucca, L. (2012), *Law, State and Religion in the New Europe. Debates and Dilemmas* (Cambridge: Cambridge University Press).
Wolton, D. (2011), *Espace public*, available at: www.wolton.cnrs.fr/spip.php?article67 (accessed 31 May 2012).

PART II
Religion and the Dress Codes

Chapter 9

From Front-Office to Back-Office: Religious Dress Crossing the Public–Private Divide in the Workplace

Katayoun Alidadi

Introduction

This chapter explores the relationship between the concept of the public space and the wide array of workplaces in real life and considers the implications of different degrees of 'publicness' of workplaces and job positions in the adjudication of labour relations conflicts involving religious dress.

The defining of the 'public space' has significant consequences for legal practice, including which rules apply and what approaches are taken towards the labour market. It must be observed that most concrete workplaces and job positions have both private and public dimensions, so that 'the workplace' defies straightforward categorization in either the public or the private space. It is argued that this multifaceted nature is reflected in the assortment of cases regarding religious dress in the workplace, and it is proposed that the distinction between *front-office* positions (with direct public visibility and interaction) and *back-office* positions (with little or no public contact) plays a significant – even if sometimes unwitting – role when it comes to dealing with religious dress in the workplace.

In order to illustrate the distinct role that the 'public' nature of a job position or a workplace plays in practice, this chapter draws from European (Belgian and French) and US case-law regarding the headscarf and other religious dress in employment conflicts. In the two European countries discussed, wearing religiously distinct dress often means restricted employment opportunities, particularly when it comes to front-office positions. Since the United States has a long experience dealing with (religious) diversity in the employment area, it could function as a good point of departure for a comparison with Europe. However, it seems that even in the US the consideration given to employers' public image concerns in the case-law – which can sometimes be based on (perceived) discriminatory customer preferences or bias – also implies the 'routing' of religiously dressed employees, as it were, 'from the store counter to the stockroom'. Thus, the (contested) idea that religion is first and foremost a matter of conscience and belongs to the private sphere has clear implications in this area.

Routing and hiding religiously dressed employees to less visible jobs and workplaces has harsh consequences for the opportunities of religious minorities. It is also bad for society and a missed opportunity to engage productively with the increasing religious diversity in many places. Even if accommodating a particular visibly distinct employee by assigning him or her to back-office duties – away from customers' sight – might appear as a good compromise in individual situations, especially if the only alternative seems rejection or dismissal, the principle and effects of the *back-office tendency* or *backstage routing*[1] of visibly religious staff and their distinctiveness clearly remains problematic. This concern raised by the analysis of the case-law is discussed in the conclusion.

In what follows, the introduction continues on a more anecdotal note, attempting to illustrate show how well-intentioned business owners can struggle with various tensions of their own in shaping their responses towards religion and religious dress in the workplace.

Hema and the Headscarf: Conforming to Local Customs

It must have been on his mind when he called to meet up for some coffee since I remember it as one of the first things he brought up that day. 'Have you heard about this Hema case?' he prompted, eager to share his stance with me. 'I was thinking what *I* would do if a woman with a headscarf applied to work in the restaurant. *Very unlikely* of course', he went on.

My friend, the proud but habitually fraught owner of a trendy restaurant, usually tried to avoid all things religious, so it surprised me he had not diverted his attention elsewhere when it came to the latest media frenzy starring the headscarf.

I knew what he was referring to. The story surrounding Hema, the Dutch high street retailer, firing[2] a 21-year-old Muslim saleswoman from one of its Belgian

1 This is not to disregard that businesses can also adopt strategies explicitly going against this pattern. Following the Danish Supreme Court judgment in the Føtex case, Danish supermarket chain COOP adopted a strategy to hire headscarved women to improve their integration and to reflect the existing diversity present in Danish society, see EU Agency for Fundamental Rights, Annual Report 2010, 53–54, at http://fra.europa.eu/fraWebsite/attachments/AR_2010-conf-edition_en.pdf (accessed 5 October 2011).

2 As the woman was recruited by a temp office and worked on a short-term contract, her contract was not renewed after she refused to remove her headscarf on the job. Hema had offered a permanent position if she were willing to do so. P. Lesaffer, 'Hema ontslaat winkelbediende voor hoofddoek' [Hema Fires Shop Employee for Wearing a Headscarf], *De Standaard*, 8 March 2011, at (accessed 5 October 2011). In March 2012, one year after, the Belgian Centre for Equal Opportunities and Opposition to Racism announced that negotiation and mediation attempts had failed and it was pursuing the case in court, suing HEMA for discrimination on the basis of religion, see Y. Delepeleire, 'Hema voor rechter na ontslag voor hoofddoek' [HEMA before the court after dismissal because of headscarf], *De Standaard* 6 March 2012. The case is currently pending before the Labour Tribunal in Tongeren.

branches for wearing a headscarf on the job had been in most Belgian newspapers and even on national television.[3] The native Belgian woman – who according to the newspapers had converted as a teenager and was newly-married to a Moroccan man – had been recruited by a temp agency to work for the retailer.[4] She had kept on her habitual *hijab* the first day on the job,[5] refusing to take it off when asked to do so, and the matter had apparently gone away. As she would later explain to the press, 'they needed all the help they could get during the busy sales days'.[6] A few days later, however, she was dismissed, with Hema referring to numerous negative customer comments and complaints regarding her headscarf.

I told my friend I was surprised he had taken an interest in this matter. I reminded him that in an earlier conversation he described the headscarf as an example of an overzealous stance towards religion standing in the way of successful integration. He continued with a paradigmatic 'everyone is entitled to his or her religion of course' and told me he had recently hired a new waitress, who was a Muslim convert. 'The other day I warned her not to eat the spaghetti sauce since it's made with pork', he said – perhaps thinking this was some sort of a reasonable accommodation. 'It's also reassuring I know she won't be drinking behind the bar', he laughed.

But a *visibly* religious waitress would be different, and I was curious as to why exactly.

He brought up that none of the other restaurants in town had any personnel donning a headscarf. 'And I will not be the first to scare customers off that way. Relationships with the local business council are already tense and that would

3 P. Lesaffer, 'Hema ontslaat winkelbediende voor hoofddoek' [Hema Fires Shop Employee for Wearing a Headscarf], *De Standaard*, 8 March 2011, at (accessed 5 October 2011).

4 X., 'Hema "schikt zich naar gewoonten van het land"' [Hema is 'Conforming itself to the Customs of the Country'], *De Standaard*, 8 March 2011, at (accessed 5 October 2011).

5 The accounts of Hema and the employee differed on this point: Hema had stated that she had started to work without a headscarf but later received permission to wear it, while the employee stressed she had always worn a headscarf, as without it she would not have been the same person. P. Lesaffer, '"Hoofddoek is mijn vrijheid," Joyce Van Op den bosch over haar ontslag bij Hema' ['Headscarf is My Freedom', Joyce Van Op den Bosch on her Dismissal from Hema], *De Standaard*, 10 March 2011, at http://altahrir.wordpress.com/hoofddoek-is-mijn-vrijheid/ (accessed 5 October 2011).

6 P. Lesaffer, '"Hoofddoek is mijn vrijheid," Joyce Van Op den bosch over haar ontslag bij Hema' ['Headscarf is My Freedom', Joyce Van Op den Bosch on her Dismissal from Hema], *De Standaard*, 10 March 2011, at http://altahrir.wordpress.com/hoofddoek-is-mijn-vrijheid/ (accessed 5 October 2011). The turn of events must have come as some surprise: the employee had received a headscarf in the company colours and logo, ordered for her from the main office in the Netherlands, something she stated that she much appreciated.

only make it worse, in particular since I am an immigrant myself. The message a headscarf represents is one I am not prepared to send out', he said.

I had not realized that – besides an obvious fear for potential customer backlash – relations with the local entrepreneurial circle would also be on his mind, and could explain the conservative disinclination to draw outside the lines set by local consensus.

Himself an immigrant, my friend was not oblivious to the existence of anti-discrimination laws. In fact, the difficulties he had faced in various jobs triggered him to start his own business. Having opted for a non-ethnic restaurant and a menu to fit the local customer base, his staff turned out to be particularly ethnically diverse. Although this was not the result of any conscious diversity policy, it would imply some favourable attitude towards hiring minorities.

Yet, the idea that he could be discriminating *on the basis of religion* if he rejected an applicant *because of her headscarf or other dress* seemed hard to swallow.[7] After all, religion and dress involved plain personal choices, and these by nature carry consequences. 'Plus, if that were the case, then all the restaurants in this town must be discriminating', he considered.

Workplace Amalgam: From Front to Back

It occurred to me that besides the waiting staff, who mingled with the patrons inside the restaurant and on the outside terrace, there were other restaurant positions with a lot less public contact, or even none at all. In other words – using typical office terminology – there were a number of 'back-office' positions available.[8]

Would there be an equal reluctance when it came to one of these less 'public' job positions? Would my friend be more comfortable hiring a religiously distinct employee to work 'backstage'?

He had to think about this. 'Well, if there is no customer contact, I don't care. If I need staff and a woman with a headscarf appears the best-qualified person, I would take her on', he sounded convinced. But then he changed his mind since he considered 'she would probably not work well in the team'.

---

7 This is not to be taken as to state that a rejection of a veiled candidate for the position of waitress would necessarily amount to unlawful discrimination or that such discrimination could be easily proven and compensated under the existing Belgian legal framework.

8 At least in his restaurant, the bartenders only stepped out in very busy moments, for instance to help clear some tables while new patrons were waiting to be seated. The head chef and the sous-chef could be seen by the people since there was an 'open kitchen' set-up but really only when one paid close attention. The dishwasher worked upstairs, outside the vision of patrons, which however did not prevent my friend's insistence on the same team dress – a bright-green polo shirt with the name of the restaurant and black slacks. Also, there was a cleaning lady who came by after closing time, whom I had never seen in the team uniform.

As the press dug deeper into the developing Hema controversy, I paid close attention. It appeared to me that when it came to allowing religion to enter the mainstream workplace my friend's attitude and concerns were commonplace amongst many Belgian employers.

Sometime after the affair had been widely reported in the media, Hema made an official statement. Regretting having become the centre of a political controversy, Hema in its statement pointed to the 'local attitudes in Belgium' in an attempt to justify the dismissal. The company argued that its decision 'was not directed towards the wearing of headscarves in specific but applies to all forms of expression that go against the neutral and discreet image of Hema'.[9] But interestingly, Hema had integrated the headscarf in the work uniform for its staff in the Netherlands. This seemed to imply that not only did local acceptance of the headscarf vary depending on the particular setting and the local customs, but also what could be considered a 'neutral and discreet' image changed accordingly. Apparently, it was not seen as contradictory that in one country the headscarf is part of an inclusive dress policy while in the neighbouring country it leads to excluding religious minorities from the workplace.

The idea of *routing religion out* of the public space seemed to be common amongst Belgian employers, both big and small. Local attitudes on the role of religion and in particular Islam in the public sphere seemed to have permeated the often unwritten employer dress policies, with concrete responses cloaked in local customs and taken-for-granted attitudes, which differed from country to country and even from city to city.[10] The extent to which these local attitudes are also taken

9 X., 'Hema 'schikt zich naar gewoonten van het land' [Hema is 'Conforming itself to the Customs of the Country'], *De Standaard*, 8 March 2011, at www.standaard.be/artikel/detail.aspx?artikelid=DMF20110308_100 (accessed 5 October 2011).

10 X., 'Hema 'schikt zich naar gewoonten van het land' [Hema is 'Conforming itself to the Customs of the Country'], *De Standaard*, 8 March 2011, at www.standaard.be/artikel/detail.aspx?artikelid=DMF20110308_100 (accessed 5 October 2011). In a statement, Hema justified its decision by stating that: 'In Belgium it is obviously not customary to wear a headscarf in shops, supermarkets and in public functions … Hema conforms itself to the customs of a country. For that reason, we cannot compare Belgium or other countries where Hema has branches with the Netherlands where people generally look differently on wearing of a headscarf. In the Netherlands the headscarf is part of the company uniform (optional) and in Belgium and France it is not'. A number of organizations replied that Hema should 'give a clear signal that discrimination is not accepted instead of following the discriminatory attitude of its customers'. S. De Graeve, 'Ontslag werkneemster met hoofddoek door Hema flagrante discriminatie' [Dismissal of Employee with Headscarf by Hema is Outright Discrimination], *DeWereldMorgen.be*, 8 March 2011, at www.dewereldmorgen.be/artikels/2011/03/08/ontslag-werkneemster-met-hoofddoek-door-hema-flagrante-discriminatie (accessed 5 October 2011); Y. Delepeleire, 'Hema mocht niet zwichten onder druk klant' [Hema Should Not Have Caved in under Customer Pressure], *De Standaard*, 9 March 2011, at http://dagelijksnieuws.be/hema-mocht-niet-zwichten-onder-druk-klant-de-standaard/ (accessed 5 October 2011); The Belgian Centre for Equal

into consideration by courts, e.g. in interpreting concepts such as proportionality, can however be problematic. Such 'conforming' interpretation (i.e. conforming to the prevailing customs and attitudes) erodes the importance of equality and anti-discrimination norms of which the ultimate aim is exactly to *change* existing societal prejudices and biases.[11]

Hema's decision to prohibit its front-office staff from wearing a headscarf on the job confirmed the –disintegrating- business consensus in the city of Genk which notably presented itself as a 'multicultural city'. In contrast to other Belgian cities such as Antwerp, and in stark contrast to the Netherlands, a newspaper investigation showed headscarved staff were entirely absent from the city's main street shopping stores. Instead headscarved Muslim women were to be found working in backstreet ethnic minority stores which they sometimes owned.[12]

While attention for the Hema case faded, the topic of religious dress remained in the public arena. Less than two months later the Belgian Chamber of Representatives voted – almost unanimously – the so-called *burqa* ban, prohibiting women from wearing the full Islamic face veil in public.[13] Much has been debated and written on the place of religion in the European 'public space'. Human rights organizations have generally opposed *burqa* bans for being divisive and counter-productive.[14] One way of connecting this debate to that concerning religious dress in the employment market is to consider where actual workplaces

---

Opportunities and Opposition to Racism also referred to the Feryn case of the ECJ, see ECJ, Case C-54/07, *Centrum voor gelijkheid van kansen en voor racismebestrijding (Centre for equal opportunities and combating racism)* v. *Firma Feryn NV*, [2008], ECR I-5187 (this racial discrimination case followed after the owner of a company which installed garage doors was quoted as saying during an interview that he did not and would not recruit Moroccans in order to meet customers' wishes. The ECJ held that giving in to discriminatory customer preferences can amount to direct racial or ethnic discrimination).

11 On the aims of non-discrimination and equality norms, see Hepple (2011: 1–6).

12 E. Bergmans, '"Niet ik, maar mijn hoofddoek was het probleem", Hoofddoeken zijn zeldzaam bij Genks winkelpersoneel' [Not Me, but My Headscarf was the Problem', Headscarves Rare amongst Genk's Store Personnel], *De Standaard*, 9 March 2011, at http://dagelijksnieuws.be/niet-ik-maar-mijn-hoofddoek-was-het-probleem-de-standaard/ (accessed 5 October 2011) (a young Turkish woman who recently started her own business selling Turkish quality tableware stated she had wanted to work for Zara or Hema, but that that the temp agencies had informed her that was impossible with her headscarf).

13 BBC, 'Belgian Lawmakers Pass Burka Ban', 30 April 2010, at http://news.bbc.co.uk/2/hi/8652861.stm (accessed 5 October 2011).

14 Thomas Hammarberg, Human Rights Commissioner of the Council of Europe, in a statement on the council's website argued: 'Much deeper problems of intercultural tensions and gaps have been sidetracked by the burqa and niqab discussions. Instead of encouraging this unfortunate discourse, political leaders and governments should take more resolute action against hate crimes and discrimination against minorities'. See Council of Europe, 'Human Rights Comment: Penalising Women Who Wear the Burqa does not Liberate Them', 20 July 2011, at http://commissioner.cws.coe.int/tiki-view_blog_post.php?postId=157 (accessed 5 October 2011); see also X., 'EU Rights Body Blasts Veil Ban',

fit in the public–private divide roster, a question that is not easily answered. One could reasonably expect ideas on the appropriate place of religious dress in the public space to have crossover implications for the participation of religiously dressed employees[15] in the workplace. First of all, the place where some people work forms part of the public sphere so that applicable dress regulations have a direct effect on their ability to perform work duties. When the *burqa* is banned from the streets or while driving a vehicle,[16] this means women in *burqas* are effectively disqualified from positions that are to be performed even partially in the public sphere (e.g. delivering mail, transportation …), or even from any employment that is outside their home.

It is proposed that the distinction between *front-office* and *back-office* positions can be constructive as it bears an intuitive relation to the public–private divide. This front-office/back-office distinction is inspired by the American case of *EEOC* v. *Alamo Rent-A-Car*, which will be discussed further,[17] but it can form a useful framework to view various case-law decisions on the place of religious or otherwise distinctive dress in the workplace. Front-office in this context refers to positions or workplaces where employees have direct personal[18] contact with clients or customers who wish to buy products or make use of services, whether it be in the public or private sector.[19] Employees in back-office positions remain outside of customer view, and are considered as less connected with the public sphere. Front-office positions bear much more 'publicness' and relation to the public sphere,

Islam Online, 21 July 2011, at http://www.onislam.net/english/news/europe/453159-eu-rights-body-blasts-veil-ban.html (accessed 5 October 2011).

15 The focus in this chapter is on the position of civil servants and private sector employees and not on self-employed individuals, even though it must be recognized that restrictions on religious expressions and dress can lead to a move to self-employment. See introduction and comment in footnote 11.

16 J. Voelcker, 'Should Driving While Wearing Burqas Be Illegal? How About Helmets?', *The Car Connection*, 26 April 2010, at www.thecarconnection.com/news/1044516_should-driving-while-wearing-burqas-be-illegal-how-about-helmets (accessed 5 October 2011) (discussing the case of a woman fined in Nantes for wearing a full-face veil while driving and the question whether 'driving while veiled' involves a 'safety risk').

17 *EEOC* v. *Alamo Rent-A-Car, LLC*, 432 F. Supp. 2d 1006 (D. Ariz. 2006), 1016; see Solieman (2009: 1084–1085).

18 Positions that only involve contact with customers via other communication means (phone, Internet) without being seen by customers are for the purposes of this chapter considered as back-office.

19 E.g. locations such as city hall desks, bank branches, travel agencies and grocery stores can be considered typically front-office. However, most of these locales also have back-office positions, e.g. stockroom staff in a grocery or clothing store. In the case of a hotel, receptionists have front-office positions, while cleaning and cooking staff work in back-office jobs. Back-office positions can be high-end positions, such as managerial production, logistics, warehousing, sales, accounting, human resources management, etc.

irrespective of whether the work is performed for a government employer and in a government-owned public space. Local customs and ideas about appropriate dress can in particular limit employment opportunities for employees who seek to wear their religious dress in front-office positions, even though issues are not entirely absent with regard to some back-office positions.

The next section inquires into the public–private nature of real-life workplaces, observing the complex relationship between the public space and the workplace. Subsequently, the following section considers the role that the 'publicness' of work positions plays in case-law on religious dress in the workplace. Finally, the conclusion discusses some implications and the message sent out by a tendency to route religious employees to the background in many mainstream workplaces.

Exploring the Relationship between the Public Space and Real-life Workplaces

Defining the Public Space: Implications for the Workplace

Historically, the idea of a distinct public space crystallized when productive processes moved from the domestic sphere to factories and other collective settings (Glorieux 1995). When the home also formed the main place of production and work, the distinction between public and private was much less relevant in people's lives. While things have evolved, the concept of 'public space' often remains defined in relation to its antipode, the private space, for instance:

> A broad definition could be that public space is space that is open to the general public. Another could be that public space is space that is owned by the public, meaning the government. Perhaps public space is the space that is between private spaces … It is theoretically open to everyone, and is thus accessible to all, the opposite of private space. (Levine 2006: 278)[20]

It is said that the 'public space' should be seen as an 'elusive' concept.[21] Indeed, 'it is less a specific concept than it is a malleable idea that changes with the passage of time and is continually dependent upon one's perspective' (Levine 2006: 278). Since the characterization of public versus private space has real and sometimes far-reaching consequences for legal practice, the critical demarcation is never merely descriptive but often ascriptive and normative as well.[22] For instance,

20 On the public–private divide see generally Weintraub and Kumar (1997).

21 Weintraub and Kumar (1997: 278); see also Chapter 3 in this volume noting 'the very diverse and sometimes opposing meanings and definitions attribute to' the concepts of public and private spheres.

22 Ferrari (2011), noting that the organization of the respective realms of public and private space 'is connected to a specific way of conceiving religion and cannot be

in arguing for better constitutional protection of free speech and association in 'privately owned spaces [that have] become a substitute for the traditional spaces used by the public', Levine makes a case for including locales such as shopping malls and gated communities within the definition of public space. Under US law, free speech is better protected in the 'traditional' – i.e. government-owned – public space, and less so in privately owned places.[23] Stressing the transformation of ownership of public spaces, he writes:

> As Americans have drifted from cities to suburbs, our public spaces have become less municipal and more commercial. Our town squares have become shopping malls. Our open neighborhoods have become gated communities. Our public basketball courts have become private health clubs. It appears that the ownership of the space where the public is, has been transformed. (Levine 2006: 279)

He urges the US judiciary to no longer 'ignore this change in the ownership', and extend the freedom of speech.[24] Within his discourse, Levine sees 'public space' as referring to 'the idea of space that functions in ways that resemble the traditional notion of public space, regardless of whether a governmental entity holds title to the geographic location' (Levine 2006: 279). Under this viewpoint, many workplaces should be considered as part of the 'public space', at least for free speech purposes.[25]

In contrast, Gilman would designate workplaces as 'quasi-public spaces' to distinguish them from public spaces owned by the government and thus, by implication, the larger public:

> The public/private distinction includes the *clearly* private sector and the *purely* governmental public sector. However, it also includes *quasi*-public settings that are not governmental but act as *semi*-public spaces, such as the workplace, private schools, and shopping malls.[26]

---

understood without taking into consideration how some religions – first of all, Christianity – have contributed to shape it'.

23 Levine (2006), pointing to the landmark Lloyd Corp. Opinion of the Supreme Court (denial of injunctive relief to allow leafleting in a privately owned shopping mall because it was held that 'any public street, on any public sidewalk, in any public park, or in any public building in the city' was available, see *Lloyd Corp.* v. *Tanner*, 407 U.S. 551, 564 (1972).

24 Levine (2006: 280). For a similar argument, see Alexander (1999).

25 His position could also be seen as favouring a more permitting regime with regard to the display of religious symbols as a form of free speech in the workplace: since traditional public spaces are becoming more and more scarce or less meaningful, the workplace where people spend much of their time has to pick up that role.

26 Gilman (2001: 60; own emphasis).

This distinction serves her position that the government should not be able to dictate language rights outside of the 'traditional' or government-owned public space.

> In general, the U.S. legal system and international human rights law recognize negative rights precluding government intervention regarding languages to be spoken in the workplace. In the United States, the government has not attempted to dictate language use in *the private workplace, which is a quasi-public space*. The government has apparently assumed a negative right.[27]

It is clear that in attempting to define and demarcate the 'public space', implications for the labour market become apparent. Similarly, the debate on religion in the public space is intertwined with that on the issue of religion in both the public and private sector workplace. In particular, the role awarded to the criterion of ownership in the definition of the public space has important ramifications for the place of religious dress and display in the private sector: if places such as malls and grocery stores are to be considered part of the public space, as Levine argues, then in principle the same (speech) rules and protections should be extended to these locales, even if additional restrictions would apply to emloyees. But if, on the other hand, as Gilman argues, private workplaces can at best be considered 'quasi-public spaces', then a different legal regime and different restrictions form the starting position.

The Conceptual Public Space and Real-Life Workplaces

Despite potentially important legal implications, the relation between the concepts 'workplace' and 'public space' is rarely explicitly considered or analysed in various academic writings. Often the idea seems to be that 'the workplace' as a collective notion is either a(n integral) part of 'the public space' or closely associated with it, for instance when the two terms are connected by an 'or' or an 'and'.[28] An appraisal of the combined usage of the two terms in legal texts shows that commentators in a wide array of legal fields indeed view 'the workplace' as part of the (larger) 'public place', albeit largely unconsciously.[29]

---

27 Gilman (2001: 62; own emphasis).

28 'Workplace *or* public place'; 'workplace *and* public place'; 'public place (e.g. workplace ...)'.

29 This is apparent in the statement that '[i]t is common, for example, for individuals to first meet their sexual partners *in public places* (*such as* on the streets, in *workplaces*, or in bars)'. See Ball (2008: 56); or when, in a text on the need for government pandemic influenza plans, there is talk of 'mass quarantine, travel restrictions, and social distancing – for instance, closure of *public places* (schools, childcare, *workplaces*, mass transit) and cancellation of public events (sports, arts, conferences)'. See Gostin (2008: 355) (here it

Similarly, in a number of areas regulators have adopted this view that 'the workplace' is a subfield of the larger 'public space'. One reason is that the same concerns[30] are raised, and the workforce is (sought to be) protected *as a particular constituency of the general public*. Anti-smoking laws are a good example. In Belgium, a 2009 law prohibits smoking in closed spaces accessible to the wider public and in workplaces.[31] One of the aims of the law is to protect employees from the health detriments of second-hand smoke so smoking is banned in work areas, personnel facilities like canteens and toilets, and during group transportation to and from work.[32] The law also considers that workplaces can extend to private homes, and prohibits smoking in the case of exclusive professional use and when personnel are employed there.[33]

Workplaces are therefore not clearly confined to the public space but are transversal and can be –completely or partially- situated in the prototypical private sphere of the home. Thus, when we try to fit the array of real-life workplaces in the broad definition of a 'public place' and its antipode 'the private space', this transversal nature of the workplace becomes apparent. Within the 'public space', in addressing the formal and substantive neutrality of the public space, Ferrari distinguishes between the common space, the political space and the institutional space (Ferrari 2011). The various public places which can be counted amongst these are to some extent and for some individuals also a place for work (without necessarily being their only workplace, e.g. doing office work or checking business reports in the station or on the train), while not all workplaces are necessarily (completely) situated in the 'public space'.

The public sector–private sector dichotomy, itself having become somewhat blurry as a consequence of privatization and government outsourcing, plays a part

---

can be noted that in fact all the specific public places listed in the quote – schools, childcare, mass transit – are also workplaces).

30 On the other hand, sometimes public concerns justify different approaches in certain workplaces such as schools and government buildings as opposed to public places such as sidewalks, squares and parks, where the right to freedom of speech is more strongly protected.

31 Art. 3, §1 and art. 11,§1 of the Law of 22 December 2009 concerning a general regulation for smoke-free closed places accessible to the public and for the protection of employees against tobacco smoke, *Belgian State Gazette*, 29 December 2009 (hereafter 'Belgian Anti-smoking Law'). The Belgian Constitutional Court on 15 March 2011 however found all these exceptions to be unconstitutional so that they no longer apply beyond 30 June 2011 (e.g. art. 5 the gaming exception; art. 4§1 on cafés where no food was served), see Belgian Constitutional Court, judgment nr. 37/2011, 15 March 2011, at www.const-court.be/public/n/2011/2011-037n.pdf (accessed 5 October 2011) (considering that smoking in gaming workplaces harms the health of staff and customers in the same way as it does in other workplaces so that the difference is not justified).

32 Art. 13 of the Belgian Anti-smoking Law.

33 Art. 11, §2, 2° of the Belgian Anti-smoking Law. This means house staff do not benefit from the protection of the law.

in situating a particular workplace within the public–private roster but does not in itself determine it. In other words, not all public sector jobs are in the public sphere nor are all private sector jobs are in the private sphere. Both public and private sector employees can be employed to work in what could be a formal or governmental public space. For instance, police officers patrol the streets and commercial leaflets distributors or ice-cream vendors take on the streets and squares as their main location of work.

Rather, the distinction between front-office and back-office seems relevant here, the former involving direct personal customer or public[34] contact and the latter lacking a similar visibility through direct interaction with clients or the public. Both public and private sector jobs (potentially in the same organizations) can entail much, little or no public visibility or contact, determining their front-office or back-office nature.[35] As for in-between positions that take place predominantly in one sphere or another, there are innumerable variations.[36]

The 'workplace' can be seen as a physical location, but it is also possible to consider the potentially multiple settings in which an individual performs her or his professional duties. The nature of the workplace setting and of job positions can change over time, and with the general evolution of work and its organization,[37] so that an *in concreto* evaluation of a position or workplace at a given time (e.g. in the case of a conflict) is advisable to assess both its nature and the relevant implications.

34 This does not preclude contact with the employer and co-workers in the workplace.

35 Some examples are the gardener who takes care of another individual's yard on a regular basis, the house maid of a wealthy family or personal chef of a celebrity.

36 See Court of Appeal Paris, 22nd Chamber, Section A, 23 January 2008 (this case concerned the dismissal of a social worker by a socio-cultural association for wearing a headscarf. The main place of work of the employee was in the homes of various families she was assisting).

37 The office worker who traditionally worked from an office or cubicle could be given the permission to work from his own home a few days a week or could move further from work and commute by train to the office, taking the commute time to draft reports or review documents. The receptionist who serves hotel customers can be asked to help in other areas during a short renovation phase of the building. University professors might concentrate on research and public service during summers but when the academic year comes along fill most of their days with teaching students, reviewing papers and correcting exams. An attorney might study files and draft briefs in the office most of the time, but appear in court a few days a week, and the work organization could alter as (s)he climbs the seniority ladder.

Schizophrenic Dress Rules for Religion Teachers in State Schools

It is clear that *the particular location* where a job is performed – outdoors, indoors, private home, formal or casual office setting, government building – has an influence on proscribed dress rules or what is considered acceptable work wear. Thus, different dress customs or rules apply to different settings. The particular position and tasks of the employee could also influence the applicable dress 'code' and these are not necessarily identical for various aspects of the same position or profession. In the case of an attorney wearing a Muslim headscarf or a Jewish *kippa*, the wearing of headgear will be much more relevant and possibly problematic when appearing in court but less so when studying and analysing files in the office or even in client meetings or conferences. Attorneys, judges and professors have to wear togas only in particular settings, such as in court or during ceremonial gatherings, so not during the bulk of their professional time.[38]

The fact that different dress customs and rules apply to work in various settings[39] can lead to odd situations. For instance, a Muslim teacher who taught Islam in a Flemish public school was summarily dismissed for gross misconduct because she dared wearing a headscarf *outside of* her class.[40] The school's internal regulations provided an exception to the general ban on the display of religious or philosophical signs and symbols for religion teachers, but this applied only so far as they stayed *in their own classrooms*. The Islam teacher in question was fired for keeping her headscarf on *outside of her classroom*, something which the school board considered to be an act of insubordination. A commentator aptly described the incongruity of the affair as follows:

> Once the school bell rang and she thirstily hurried herself to the teacher's room, her headscarf had to be taken off unrelentingly. Quickly to the restrooms in-between classes? Headscarf off and then hop on again. Called via the intercom to 'come see the principal'? The same. At a certain moment the teacher refused

38 For an argument that attorneys should generally be allowed to wear full face veils in court, see Bakht (2009: 115–134); for an argument that attorneys should be able to wear a headscarf in court, see Lamon (2009: 10) (referring to the decision of the French-speaking section of the Brussels bar to ban attorneys from wearing headscarves during oral pleadings. The author is surprised by this decision and argues in favour of the freedom of attorneys – as opposed to judges – to wear religious headgear or symbols as a client is free to choose his representation and there is no religion that could not play a role in that decision).

39 The most flexible work dress atmosphere must be the home office, where one can work 'in pyjama bottoms and slippers', however see K. Ross, 'Dress for Success: Even Working from Home Requires a Dress Code', no date, at www.womans-work.com/NewsInd/work_from_home_dress_code.htm (accessed 5 October 2011).

40 Belgian Council of State, 18 oktober 2007, case nr. 175.886, *X.* v. *Vlaamse Gemeenschap en Gemeenschapsonderwijs*, www.raadvst-consetat.be; see Van Den Broeck (2007: 14).

> to take part in this play of dress-up after which she, upon the second violation, was decisively fired.[41]

In 2007, the Council of State suspended her dismissal, holding that it was not up to the individual school to decide on a ban on all religious, political and philosophical symbols.[42] In 2009, when it annulled the dismissal of another Islam teacher[43] the Council of State confirmed the inconsistent and impracticable situation with regard to religion teachers and their religious dress code by stating that:

> By allowing the wearing of a headscarf during the classes of Islam religion, the school regulation recognizes that this is in keeping with the neutrality declaration ... [The school] does not point to any convincing element that would suddenly negate this when the same Islam teacher shows herself veiled outside of her classroom.[44]

Thus, the schizophrenic nature of school dress rules applying to religion teachers has been recognized. But teachers (including religion teachers) and Muslim women with front-office positions continue to face pressures and hostility in Belgium when they seek to wear a headscarf on the job (Amnesty International 2012).

Locking Religion in the Back-Room: The Nature of Workplaces or Job Positions and Restrictions on Religious Dress

Front-office and Back-office in the US: Alamo Rent-A-Car

In the US, cases concerning religious dress are judged under the reasonable accommodations for religion framework. Under Title VII of the US Civil Rights Act, an employer with more than 15 employees is, once on notice, under a duty to reasonably accommodate an employee's religious observances or practices unless he can show that this would amount to an 'undue hardship on the conduct of the

41 Van Den Broeck (2007: 14; own translation). He also notes the 'schizophrenic' nature of the policy subsequently adopted by the Flemish community education net with regard to the exhibiting of religious symbols by public school teachers.

42 Belgian Council of State, judgment nr. 175.886, 18 October 2007.

43 Belgian Council of State, judgment nr. 195.044, 2 July 2009, 13 (dismissal was annulled, after the Council had refused to suspend it in 2006 and 2007 because the position was temporary, see judgment nr. 162.161, 30 August 2006, and judgment nr. 175.887, 18 October 2007).

44 Belgian Council of State, judgment nr. 195.044, 2 July 2009, 13 (own translation).

employer's business'.[45] Religious dress such as the headscarf of Muslim women falls under 'religious observances or practices'.

In the Alamo case (2006), a Muslim female employee who was dismissed by the car rental company for wearing a headscarf in violation of the company's official dress was successful in establishing a prima facie case of religious employment discrimination in violation of Title VII. Alamo failed to convince the court that it had either made a good faith effort to offer a reasonable accommodation to the employee or that such accommodation would amount to an undue hardship on its business.[46] Either of these showings would have defeated the employee's case.[47]

When the employee asked for permission to keep on her headscarf on the job during the Islamic Ramadan holiday, and this was found in apparent conflict with the 'Dress Smart Policy',[48] she was given permission to wear the headscarf but only when working 'in the back of the office'.[49] When serving customers at the rental counter, however, she would have to abide by the dress policy.[50] The problem for the District Court was that the employee was still required to serve customers, so that there was no talk of an actual reasonable accommodation.[51]

The court thus took issue with the fact that Alamo had *not* exempted the employee from serving customers, rendering the 'accommodation' illusory for at least part of employee's working time. The question is whether one can infer from this that the court would *a contrario* have been satisfied that Alamo did offer a suitable and reasonable accommodation if it had allowed or instructed the employee to avoid any customer contact.[52] In other words, would routing the religiously distinctive employee back-office and outside of customer view meet the reasonable accommodation duty?

There is no clear answer to this in the Alamo holding. The Equal Employment Opportunity Commission guidelines on religious accommodations do offer some help to approach this question. In those guidelines, 'lateral transfer and change of

45 US Civil Rights Act of 1964, §§ 701(j), 703, 42 U.S.C.A. §§ 2000e(j), 2000e-2.

46 *EEOC* v. *Alamo Rent-A-Car, LLC*, 432 F. Supp. 2d 1006 (D. Ariz. 2006), 1013.

47 *EEOC* v. *Alamo Rent-A-Car, LLC*, 432 F. Supp. 2d 1006 (D. Ariz. 2006), 1013.

48 This dress policy did not explicitly prohibit the wearing of head coverings, but Alamo interpreted the policy as prohibiting the wearing of any 'garment or item of outer clothing not specifically mentioned'. *EEOC* v. *Alamo Rent-A-Car, LLC*, 432 F. Supp. 2d 1006, 1016 (D. Ariz. 2006), 1008.

49 *EEOC* v. *Alamo Rent-A-Car, LLC*, 432 F. Supp. 2d 1006 (D. Ariz. 2006), 1009.

50 *EEOC* v. *Alamo Rent-A-Car, LLC*, 432 F. Supp. 2d 1006 (D. Ariz. 2006), 1009.

51 *EEOC* v. *Alamo Rent-A-Car, LLC*, 432 F. Supp. 2d 1006 (D. Ariz. 2006), 1013.

52 It is clear that an employee could not reasonably request to be exempted from all customer contact as that would entail too much of a burden on the employer. *Noesen* v. *Medical Staffing Network, Inc.*, 232 Fed. Appx. 581, (7th Cir.2007) (a Roman Catholic pharmacist was terminated after he refused to have any contact with customers who asked to have birth control prescriptions filled. The employer, Wal-Mart, had already accommodated the pharmacist in substantial ways but was not required to go so far as to relieve him of all telephone and counter duties as well).

job assignments' are discussed as ways to meet the reasonable accommodation duty:

> When an employee cannot be accommodated either as to his or her entire job or an assignment within the job, employers and labour organizations should consider whether or not it is possible to change the job assignment or give the employee a lateral transfer.[53]

While the principle implications of this 'backstage routing' are not considered in the EEOC guidelines, it is recognized that:

> Some alternatives for accommodating religious practices might disadvantage the individual with respect to his or her employment opportunities, such as compensation, terms, conditions, or privileges of employment. Therefore, when there is more than one means of accommodation which would not cause undue hardship, the employer or labor organization must offer the alternative which least disadvantages the individual with respect to his or her employment opportunities.[54]

Thus, *only if allowing a deviation to the dress codes would entail undue hardship*, should a job re-assignment be considered. Accommodations requested and hardship arguments are assessed case-by-case.[55] In the end, the issue came down to whether allowing the employee to wear a headscarf during counter duty (thus exempting her from the dress policy) would in fact have entailed an 'undue hardship'. In this respect Alamo failed to convince the court. The court adhered to the standard that the US Supreme Court had adopted for assessing 'undue hardship' in the case of religious accommodations:

> '[u]ndue hardship' is created when an accommodation 'results in more than a *de minimis* cost to the employer … A claim of undue hardship cannot be supported by merely conceivable or hypothetical hardships; instead, it must be supported by proof of 'actual imposition on co-workers or disruption of the work routine'.[56]

The court found that Alamo's 'faulty understanding of Title VII's protections', namely the concern that one deviation from its uniform policy would lead to other employees requesting the same and the impossibility to enforce a dress code at

53 Equal Employment Opportunity Commission Guidelines on Discrimination Because of Religion, 29 C.F.R. 1630, § 1605.2 (d) (iii) (own emphasis).

54 Equal Employment Opportunity Commission Guidelines on Discrimination Because of Religion, 29 C.F.R 1630, §1630.2(d) (1) (own emphasis).

55 *Noesen* v. *Medical Staffing Network*, 232 Fed.Appx. 581 (7th Cir.2007), 1194.

56 *EEOC* v. *Alamo Rent-A-Car, LLC*, 432 F. Supp. 2d 1006 (D. Ariz. 2006), 1014–1015 (footnotes in original left out).

all, was groundless and 'based on a hypothetical scenario'.[57] Thus, this should not have stopped Alamo from being more flexible with its dress policy.

The depositions of Alamo's representatives made clear that their concern was to guarantee the formal equal treatment of all staff and they feared 'flood-gate requests' from other workers. There was no explicit wish for a 'neutral corporate image'. While there is some indication of this concern for adverse customer reaction in the file, the court does not consider this.[58]

It remains a question, however, whether the court would have accepted a business or image concern as constituting an 'undue hardship', namely in the argument that the display of religious (Muslim) affiliation would have been detrimental to its corporate image or its business profits, in particular as the incident took place just a few months after the 9/11 attacks.[59]

Customer preferences are generally not accepted as a defense under US anti-discrimination law:[60]

> During the early Civil Rights era, Southern employers often argued that hiring blacks would be financially ruinous; white customers would go elsewhere. In rejecting such customer preference defenses, Congress and the courts recognized that the most effective way of combating prejudice was to deprive people of the option to indulge it. (Rhode 2009: 1065)

Still, a more clear focus on image arguments or potential negative business outcomes could have been more successful in establishing the existence of a *de minimis* undue hardship.[61]

In the area of religious dress, it has been held that to allow a Muslim substitute teacher to wear a headscarf on the job would constitute undue hardship under Title VII because this would go against the 'compelling interest in maintaining

57 *EEOC* v. *Alamo Rent-A-Car, LLC*, 432 F. Supp. 2d 1006 (D. Ariz. 2006), 1017.

58 See deposition of Alamo's Human Resource Manager for the Western Region, Heather Phillips, in *EEOC* v. *Alamo Rent-A-Car, LLC*, 432 F. Supp. 2d 1006 (D. Ariz. 2006), 1015–1016; the Court refers to the testimony of an Alamo representative who 'did not believe that allowing Ms. Nur to wear a head covering at the rental counter would affect the impression she would make on customers, nor would it negatively impact customer expectations concerning the level of service or quality of the product they would receive, or otherwise create any type of negative expectations with customers'.

59 Solieman (2009: 1084) noting 'it is no leap to assume that the defendant's concern with the appearance of the hijab was closely related to the events of September 11th'.

60 Rhode (2009: 1065); but *contra* see *Brown* v. *F.L. Roberts & Co.*, Inc., 419 F.Supp.2d 7, D. Mass., 2006, 18 ('Even assuming that the defendants' justification for the grooming standards amounted to nothing more than an appeal to customer preference, which is not the case, *it is not the law that customer preference is an insufficient justification as a matter of law*' [emphasis in original]).

61 *Trans World Airlines, Inc.* v. *Hardison*, 432 U.S. 63, 97 S.Ct. 2264 (U.S. 1977).

the appearance of religious neutrality in the public school system'.[62] Similarly, the Philadelphia police department was held to face undue hardship if it was required to allow a female Muslim police officer to wear a *khimar*.[63] In the latter case, it was held that:

> Prohibiting religious symbols and attire helps to prevent any divisiveness on the basis of religion both within the force itself and when it encounters the diverse population of Philadelphia. [The Police force's uniform dress code] is designed to maintain religious neutrality, but in this case in a para-military organization for the good not only of the police officers themselves but also of the public in general. Under the circumstances, it would clearly cause the City an undue hardship if it had to allow plaintiff to wear a khimar.[64]

Similarly, in a case brought by a Rastafarian employee of an automobile lubrication service, who did not shave or cut his hair because of his Rastafarian religion, it was accepted that the employer would suffer undue hardship if it allowed a waiver of its new grooming policy that required all employees with public contact be clean shaven with short haircuts.[65] The employer had reassigned the Rastafarian employee to the lower bay[66] of the facility, and away from public eye, but the employee argued he was deprived of public contact, the work was less interesting and working conditions were worse in the lower bay.[67] The District Court, viewing the record 'in the light most favorable' to the employee,[68] held that a reasonable jury could find that the employee had not been reasonably accommodated:

> Accepting the facts the Defendant's accommodation restricted Plaintiff to a cold, uncomfortable, isolated work site, with significantly diminished responsibilities, as the price of maintaining his bonafide religious practice. A ruling that the

62 *U.S.* v. *Board of Educ. for School Dist. of Philadelphia*, 911 F.2d 882 (3rd Circ. 1990), 898.

63 'The khimar is a traditional garment worn by Muslim women which covers the hair, forehead, sides of the head, neck, shoulders, and chest and sometimes extends down to the waist. Plaintiff intended to wear the lower portion of the khimar tucked inside of her police shirt and to wear her police hat. Although some Muslim women also cover their faces leaving only a slit for their eyes, plaintiff was not seeking to do so at that time'. *Webb* v. *City of Phila.*, 2007 WL 1866763 (E.D.Pa. 2007), 1.

64 *Webb* v. *City of Phila.*, 2007 WL 1866763 (E.D.Pa. 2007), 4.

65 *Brown* v. *F.L. Roberts & Co., Inc.*, 419 F.Supp.2d 7 (D.Mass. 2006), 10.

66 *Brown* v. *F.L. Roberts & Co., Inc.*, 419 F.Supp.2d 7 (D.Mass. 2006), 10. According to the employer, 'both upper and lower bay technicians "carry the same levels of responsibility", and their jobs differ only in that "the technicians work on different parts of the vehicle"'.

67 *Brown* v. *F.L. Roberts & Co., Inc.*, 419 F.Supp.2d 7 (D.Mass. 2006), 11.

68 Pursuant to motion for summary judgment standards, in which the evidence should be viewed 'in the light most favorable' to the non-moving party.

> accommodation offered on these facts was reasonable as a matter of law would constitute too drastic a limitation on the protections offered under Title VII to sincerely held religious beliefs.[69]

Still, the Court found that a *wholesale exemption* from the grooming policy would entail an undue hardship.[70] It pointed to the well-known opinion of the Court of Appeals in *Cloutier* v. *Costco*,[71] in which the First Circuit held that the 'outright exemption' from a neutral dress code 'would be an undue hardship because it would adversely affect the employer's public image',[72] since '"employees reflect on their employers," especially where the employees "regularly interact with customers"'.[73] It was also held that the measure of hardship or the 'cost' to the employer in this context was not to be assessed in mere economic terms.[74]

The District Court noted the 'skeptical legal climate'[75] for religious discrimination claims in the United States but in light of 'controlling authority' awarded the employer summary judgment, albeit with 'a sense of uneasiness':

> It is impossible to make this ruling dismissing Plaintiff's case here without a sense of uneasiness. If *Cloutier's* language approving employer prerogatives regarding 'public image' is read broadly, the implications for persons asserting claims for religious discrimination in the workplace may be grave. One has to wonder how often an employer will be inclined to cite this expansive language to terminate or restrict from customer contact, on image grounds, an employee wearing a yarmulke, a veil, or the mark on the forehead that denotes Ash Wednesday for many Catholics. More likely, and more ominously, considerations of 'public image' might persuade an employer to tolerate the religious practices of predominant groups, while arguing 'undue hardship' and 'image' in forbidding practices that are less widespread or well known … An excessive protection of an employer's 'image' predilection encourages an unfortunately (and unrealistically) homogeneous view of our richly varied nation.[76]

While the employer in Alamo had responded *in promptu* to the request of an employee to wear a headscarf, other American companies have adopted more

69 *Brown* v. *F.L. Roberts & Co., Inc.*, 419 F.Supp.2d 7 (D.Mass. 2006), 15.

70 *Brown* v. *F.L. Roberts & Co., Inc.*, 419 F.Supp.2d 7 (D.Mass. 2006), 9.

71 *Cloutier* v. *Costco Wholesale Corp.*, 390 F.3d 126 (1st Cir. 2004). In *Cloutier*, an employee of the large supermarket chain Costco argued that as a member of the Church of Body Modification she had to display facial piercings, seeking an exemption under the company dress code.

72 *Cloutier* v. *Costco Wholesale Corp.*, 390 F.3d 126 (1st Cir. 2004), 136.

73 *Brown* v. *F.L. Roberts & Co., Inc.*, 419 F.Supp.2d 7 (D.Mass. 2006), 16 referring to *Cloutier* v. *Costco Wholesale Corp.*, 390 F.3d 126 (1st Cir. 2004), 134.

74 *Cloutier* v. *Costco Wholesale Corp.*, 390 F.3d 126 (1st Cir. 2004), 134.

75 *Brown* v. *F.L. Roberts & Co., Inc.*, 419 F.Supp.2d 7 (D.Mass. 2006), 9.

76 *Brown* v. *F.L. Roberts & Co., Inc.*, 419 F.Supp.2d 7 (D.Mass. 2006), 17–19.

targeted recruitment priorities and strategies to route distinctly ethnic and religious-looking job candidates backstage. In particular, clothing retailer Abercrombie & Fitch is considered'a leading example of what many industry experts and sociologists describe as a steadily growing trend in American retailing', namely by 'hiring [good-looking] workers to project an image'.[77] The company is said to hereby be 'skirting the edges of antidiscrimination laws'. Abercrombie & Fitch has already been involved in a number of religious anti-discrimination lawsuits amongst others filed by job seekers and former staff who wanted to don a headscarf on the job.[78] A number of ethnic minority plaintiffs involved in (now settled) anti-discrimination lawsuits lodged against the company had testified that 'when they applied for jobs, store managers steered them to the stockroom, not to the sales floor'.[79] Thus, steering 'otherness' systematically to the back is a consciously adopted strategy.

This 'growing trend' –which is thus also present in the US- has important and worrying implications, as will be further discussed.

From the US to Europe, Belgium and France

Under the EU Employment Equality Directive, which is transposed in national law in the EU Member States, the duty of reasonable accommodation is only provided for people with disabilities and does not extend to accommodations for

77 S. Greenhouse, 'Going for the Look, but Risking Discrimination', *New York Times*, 13 July 2003. It is also noteworthy that Abercrombie has even expressed concerns about celebrities tarnishing its image by wearing its clothes as it offered the cast of the popular MTV reality show 'Jersey Shore' a 'considerable sum' to stop wearing its clothes. S. Clifford, 'Abercrombie Wants Off "Jersey Shore" (Wink-Wink)', *New York Times*, 17 August 2011, at www.nytimes.com/2011/08/18/business/abercrombie-offers-jersey-shore-cast-a-paid-non-product-placement.html?_r=1 (accessed 5 October 2011).

78 S. Gregory, 'Abercrombie Faces a Muslim-Headscarf Lawsuit', *Time Business*, 23 September 2009, at www.time.com/time/business/article/0,8599,1925607,00.html (accessed 5 October 2011) (discussing the suit filed by the EEOC against Abercrombie for failing 'to accommodate her religious beliefs by making an exception to the Look Policy' on behalf of Samantha Elauf, a 19-year-old Muslim student from Tulsa, Oklahoma); J. Dearen, 'Worker Sues Abercrombie & Fitch over Hijab', *Associated Press*, 27 June 2011, at www.msnbc.msn.com/id/43552854/ns/business-personal_finance/t/worker-sues-abercrombie-fitch-over-hijab/ (accessed 5 October 2011) (discussing the case of a 20-year-old former stockroom worker Hani Khan from San Mateo who was asked to take off her headscarf).

79 S. Greenhouse, 'Going for the Look, but Risking Discrimination', *New York Times*, 13 July 2003, at www.nytimes.com/2003/07/13/us/going-for-the-look-but-risking-discrimination.html?pagewanted=all&src=pm (accessed 5 October 2011); a recent suit, however, concerns a former stockroom worker who was fired after refusing to take off her headscarf.

reasons of religious beliefs or practices.[80] However, direct and indirect[81] workplace discrimination based on religious or ideological beliefs and practices is banned in all Member States.[82] The terms of the game when it regards religious dress in the workplace is thus often whether there is talk of an (in)direct religious discrimination or whether the freedom of religion has been violated.[83] The prohibition of indirect discrimination in the EU is certainly affiliated with a positive duty of reasonable accommodation (see Tobler 2008: 52–53). De Vos even argues that the prohibition of engaging in indirect religious discrimination implies more extensive and burdensome duties for employers than a duty of reasonable accommodation such as in the United States and Canada (De Vos 2004: 81). However, while in theory this may be a defendable stance, the situation on the ground is that there are significant differences in the case-law of the EU Member States and many countries have not adopted a 'dynamic interpretation' of the prohibition of indirect religious discrimination.[84]

In the relatively rare Belgian case-law involving religious dress in the workplace,[85] conflicts with regard to front-office positions take a prominent place. Perhaps unsurprisingly, it is also in these cases that employers often come out ahead: in addition to any health and safety or hygiene concerns, or concerns with regard to the reactions of co-workers, these employers have an additional 'first line of defense'. In order to ban religiously distinct or 'strange' dress for front-office employees, employers can point to image and bottom-line concerns: allowing religious symbols to be present in their sphere of business would damage

80 Art. 5 Council Directive 2000/78/EC of 27 November 2000 Establishing a General Framework for Equal Treatment in Employment and Occupation, *OJ* 303 L, 2 December 2000, 16–22 (hereafter EU Employment Equality Directive); Waddington (2011: 186–198) (arguing against the adoption of an explicit duty of reasonable accommodation for religion).

81 There is talk of an 'indirect discrimination' when 'an apparently neutral provision, criterion or practice would put persons having a particular religion or belief … at a particular disadvantage compared with other persons', unless it can be objectively justified. See art. 2, 2, (b) EU Employment Equality Directive.

82 Art. 1 EU Employment Equality Directive; see EU Press Release, Memo 08/69 The Employment Equality Directive, Brussels, 31 January 2008, at http://europa.eu/rapid/pressReleasesAction.do?reference=MEMO/08/69&format=HTML&aged=1&language (accessed 5 October 2011) ('the Member States have now transposed the Directive into national law').

83 Besides equality law, human rights should be considered. In particular, the European Convention on Human Rights protects the freedom of religion in art. 9. However, the case-law of the Strasbourg organs seems to have rendered this protection largely ineffective and devoid of meaning for employees who are considered 'free to resign'. See Knights (2009: 283–298).

84 See, for example, on the remarkable differences in Belgian and Dutch case-law with regard to the prohibition of indirect discrimination on the basis of religion or belief in the workplace: Alidadi (2012).

85 For a more elaborate discussion, see Alidadi (2012).

their 'neutral or discrete image' leading to the loss of customers and business. The European Court of Justice (ECJ) has held in a racial/ethnic discrimination case that employers cannot take into account the 'discriminatory preferences' of their customers.[86] Belgian judges have, however, given effect to employers' desire to create or adhere to a 'neutral image', which is sometimes motivated by actual or perceived customer bias.[87]

The situation is somewhat different in the public and in the private sectors, although there are important spill-over effects. As in most European countries, the issue of headscarves for public school teachers has been hotly debated in Belgium.[88] The Belgian Council of State has accepted the legality of bans on the display of headscarves and other religious symbols for these civil servants with front-office visibility,[89] except when it concerns the case of teachers of religious courses as discussed above. Its position echoes the jurisprudence of the European Court of Human Rights.[90]

Dress and grooming standards in the private sector are generally determined by the employer. There have been a number of conflicts involving employees' religious dress, in particular regarding the *hijab* in front-office positions. The judgment of the Antwerp Labour Tribunal of 27 April 2010 serves as a good example.[91] The employee in question was a Muslim woman who was engaged as a

86 See ECJ, Case C-54/07, *Centrum voor gelijkheid van kansen en voor racismebestrijding (Centre for equal opportunities and combating racism)* v. *Firma Feryn NV*, [2008], ECR I-5187.

87 See introduction, on the Hema case.

88 See the Belgian Roundtables on Interculturality, Committee report delivered to the Belgian Vice-Minister, Minister of Work and Equal Opportunities on 8 November 2011, at www.interculturalite.be (accessed 5 October 2011), 78 (Dutch and French).

89 Belgian Council of State, judgment nr. 210.000, 21 December 2010; in the public sector, a number of Belgian cities have banned the wearing of headscarves and all other religious or political symbols by municipal employees directly engaged in dealing with the public, amongst which the city of Antwerp in 2007: D. Hermans, 'Scheldestad bant hoofddoek. 150 moslima's protesteren tevergeefs tegen verbod' [Antwerp Bans Headscarves. 150 Muslim Women Protest to no Avail], *Het Nieuwsblad*, 16 January 2007, at www.nieuwsblad.be/article/detail.aspx?articleid=GCK16VTL3 (accessed 5 October 2011) (it was subsequently reported that of the seven personnel members working at the city counter, three decided to take their headscarves off and other positions were sought for the others).

90 *Dahlab* v. *Switzerland*, ECtHR, App. nr. 42393/98 (2001) (dismissal of primary school teacher at a public school in Switzerland did not violate art. 9 ECHR); see also landmark case of *Sahin* v. *Turkey*, ECtHR, Appl. nr. 44774/98 (2005) (Turkish ban on headscarves for university students fell within margin of appreciation, and did not violate art. 9 ECHR).

91 Antwerp Labour Tribunal, 27 April 2010, A.R. 06/397639/A, unpublished decision, discussed in Alidadi (2010: 1–2); this was confirmed by the Antwerp Labor Court of Appeals which found that the employer had not abused its right to dismiss the employee who refused to work without a headscarf, see Antwerp Labor Court of Appeals

receptionist by a large multinational offering reception and security services. She was outsourced by her employer to work in other locations, and for three years she did not wear a headscarf on the job.[92] Her request to wear the headscarf on the job led to her dismissal and triggered the employer to adopt an explicit dress policy prohibiting the display of any visible political, philosophical or religious symbols. Before the Tribunal, the employer stressed the 'strict neutrality' it strived for 'both internally within the company and externally towards customers'. The Antwerp Labour Tribunal held that while the freedom to wear a headscarf, even though it is a disputed precept of Islam, fell under the freedom of religion protected under art. 9 ECHR, this provision was not violated. It also held that the employer had neither directly[93] nor indirectly discriminated against the employee.

In particular, there was no indirect discrimination as the ban was considered proportionate with the legitimate aim of creating 'a neutral and discreet image towards customers' and to 'guarantee a peaceful and tolerant co-existence within the company', which could only be done by showcasing neutrality. The Tribunal noted the employer was a 'multicultural enterprise' that hired people of all faiths, including many Muslims. The argument that the neutrality policy was motivated by the discriminatory preferences of customers – put forward by the Belgian national equality body, the Centre for Equal Opportunities and Opposition to Racism, which saw this as an important test-case – was rejected.[94]

In the 2008 'Club' bookstore case, the Labour Court of Appeal of Brussels[95] held similarly that the bookstore's workplace 'neutrality policy' prohibiting the wearing of religious symbols by personnel that came into contact with customers was justified in light of the company's 'open, available, sober, family-oriented, and neutral' image. Therefore, the dismissal of a saleswoman (upon her return from an extended leave) who sought to wear a headscarf on the job was justified.

---

23 December 2011, case nr. AR/2010/AA/453 and 2010/AA/467. The Belgian Centre for Equal Opportunities and Opposition to Racism has brought this case before the Cour de Cassation, where it is pending at the time of writing.

92 Until then, she had taken off the headscarf when she arrived on the job and put it back on after her shift ended.

93 The Tribunal noted the contradiction between the prohibition against direct discrimination on the basis of religion or belief (which lacks a possibility of justification under EU law) and the freedom of religion under art. 9 of the ECHR (under which manifestations could be restricted when certain conditions are met). In casu, the Tribunal held there was no direct discrimination since the 'wearing out' of religious symbols did not fall within the protected criterion of 'religion or belief' under the Belgian anti-discrimination law. See Alidadi (2010: 1–2) (arguing that this interpretation limits the anti-discrimination law's protective scope considerably, making it irrelevant for many fundamental aspects of religions apart from adherence).

94 ECJ, 10 July 2008, Case C-54/07, *Belgian Center for Equal Opportunities* v. *Feryn NV*, [2008], ECR I-5187.

95 Labour Court of Appeal Brussels (4th ch.), judgment nr. 48.695, 15 January 2008, *JTT* 2008, nr. 1003, 140.

It is noteworthy that the employee had herself welcomed another position which would not involve customer contacts, but the company had not considered such an accommodation and the Court stated clearly that it had no duty to do so. The fact that even a back-office accommodation was rejected only makes this case more problematic and harsh.

While the neutral image argument has been accepted by Belgian courts, the concern with regard to loss of business requires 'more than a subjective fear'. The Labour Tribunal of Charleroi on 26 October 1992[96] found the discharge for gross misconduct of a shoe saleswoman wearing 'long and wide robes and skirts' for religious reasons to be abusive. The employer argued the style of dress did not fit in with the 'commercial lifestyle of the city' but the Tribunal noted the lack of indications of actual financial loss, and the fact that no customer had ever complained. This seems to imply that *a contrario* the dismissal could have been justified in the case where the employer's concerns could have been substantiated, such as in the Hema case with customers complaining.

In neighbouring France, with formal bans on religious symbols in place in the public sector and in public schools, the right of the employer to judge the appearance of personnel that comes in contact with the public is confirmed 'as long as this is exercised respecting public order and good morals and is based on an objective reason connected with the interest of the company (l'intérêt de l'entreprise)'.[97] A number of cases show that in practice the religious interests of employees and the commercial interest of employers are reconciled by permitting 'attenuated' forms of the *hijab* in front-office positions with public interaction, for instance in the form of a bandanna or bonnet cap.

In 2001, the Paris Court of Appeal[98] held that the 'very tolerant' employer was justified to dismiss a grocery saleswoman who sought to wear a full headscarf instead of the acceptable bonnet she had previously donned and which met her religious needs as well. The Court found that the employer's concerns for repercussions on customers and co-workers and desire for a level of neutrality were justified, in particular since the store was located 'in the heart of the commercial center of La Défense' and there was contact with a very large and diverse public. The front-office positioning of the job as well as the actual location of the workplace played an important role in the ruling.

Back-Office Employees and the Headscarf

Workplace dress conflicts are not confined to employees with personal interaction with customers. When it comes to cases involving back-office positions that lack public interaction, concerns often relate to more 'objective' concerns such

96 Labour Tribunal Charleroi, 26 October 1992, *Chr. D. S.*, 1993, 84–85.

97 Besançon Court of Appeal (Social Chamber), 9 October 2009.

98 Paris Court of Appeal, 16 March 2001, *Madame Charmi, Semaine Juridique E*, 1339.

as health, safety and hygiene. The need for a neutral image can also be raised by employers but seems less successful as an argument. In back-office cases, employers miss the all important 'first line of defense'.

For instance, the Labour Tribunal of Hasselt in 1995[99] held that a Muslim woman wearing a headscarf had legitimate reasons to resign from her job picking mushrooms when she was prohibited to wear her veil. The court could not see any good reason to restrict the woman from wearing a headscarf on the job. Another case concerned a Muslim woman who had applied to work in a stitchery. During the job interview, she wore her headscarf and clearly indicated she would be unwilling to take off her headscarf when working on the machines. The employer decided not to hire her because of safety concerns for herself and other staff, which the court later considered a genuine and justified reason. In the procedure following her denial for unemployment benefits, the Court still held that the employee should not be penalized as she had only rejected a non-suitable position and remained available for the general labour market.

Here also the French case of Dallila Tahri is noteworthy, where the employer sought to justify banning the wearing of a headscarf for a back-office employee based on allegedly negative reactions from co-workers. The employee's headscarf had led to her dismissal from her job as a telephone marketing employee with a telemarketing firm.[100] She had worn the headscarf since she started work for the employer in 2001, but after a transfer to the head office she was repeatedly asked to adjust how she wore her headscarf and then finally fired for refusing to take it off. Her lawyer argued she was fired 'largely as a result of the "atmosphere of suspicion" in which French Muslims have had to live since Sept. 11, 2001'.[101] Under the French labour code the rights and freedoms of employees can only be limited if the limitations are justified in light of the tasks to be performed and stand in proportion towards their goals.[102] The telemarketing firm had argued that the *hijab* offended other workers. The Prud'hommes labor court, however, considered

99 Labour Tribunal Hasselt, 1 March 1995, *Chr. D.S.*, 1996, 409; *T. Vreemd.* 1997, 432; Palumbo and Radermecker (1996).

100 See also Davies (2009); Finkin (2006); for a Dutch case before the Equal Treatment Commission where a call centre wanted phone operators to take off their headscarf, see ETC 2006-215, 27 October 2006 (the concern of the call centre that the sound transition over the headset would be of lesser quality when worn over a headscarf could be met by asking employees to wear the headset *under* their headscarf).

101 P. Michaud, 'Court Allows French Muslim Woman to Wear Headscarf at Work', *Arab News*, 19 December 2002, at http://archive.arabnews.com/?page=4&section=0&article=21212&d=19&m=12&y=2002 (accessed 5 October 2011).

102 Art. L.120-2 Labor Code (FR), Law No. 92-1446 of 31 December 1992, Official State Gazette of France, 1 January 1993, 19 ('Nul ne peut apporter aux droits des personnes et aux libertés individuelles et collectives de restrictions qui ne seraient pas justifiées par la nature de la tâche à accomplir ni proportionnées au but recherché').

she had worn a headscarf for some 18 months and ordered her reinstatement, with headscarf, and reimbursement of lost salary.[103]

Perhaps it is a coincidence that in these back-office cases, the courts found in favour of the employees. Still, on the basis of the few cases that could be discussed within the confines of this chapter, it appears there is a difference with more 'public' or 'visible' positions that could affect the employers' image to the outside world. Clearly, there can be various justifications for requiring staff, even those without any public interaction, to abide by certain dress and grooming rules, e.g. to create a general professional environment[104] or a relaxed work environment. However, when there is no 'publicness', employers miss an important 'first line of defense' and must base their decisions on more limited, often 'objective', grounds. In contrast, employees stand in a weaker legal position when fighting their dismissal or removal from front-office positions for wearing religious garb, even though meaningful protection is crucial considering that not only the employers' toleration, but also that of customers and the public, play a role.

Conclusion

In the midst of a media frenzy surrounding the Hema case, the company admitted its error of judgment by sending out conflicting messages about the acceptability of the headscarf in the workplace and offered to re-hire the former employee.[105] In her new position, the woman would be able to wear her headscarf but would no longer have any customer contact. She rejected the offer. Having expressed a desire to return to her old job, she stated she enjoyed the customer contact and disputed that the offer was for 'the same job'.[106]

103 P. Michaud, 'Court Allows French Muslim Woman to Wear Headscarf at Work', *Arab News*, 19 December 2002, at http://archive.arabnews.com/?page=4&section=0&article=21212&d=19&m=12&y=2002 (accessed 5 October 2011).

104 See Rhode (2009: 1093) (discussing the UK case of *Dep't for Work & Pensions* v. *Thompson*, [2004] I.R.L.R. 348 ('a male administrative assistant whose job involved clerical, mail, and related secretarial duties, but no public contact' was required to appear 'professional and business-like' with coat and tie and avoid more casual items of clothing. Rhode criticizes the appellate decision, which did not evaluate any 'business justification for requiring a clerical worker with no public interaction to conform to such a standard')).

105 X., 'Hema biedt ontslagen werkneemster job aan' [Hema Offers Fired Employee Job Back], *Het Nieuwsblad*, 11 March 2011, at www.nieuwsblad.be/article/detail.aspx?articleid=DMF20110311_103 (accessed 5 October 2011). The experience also triggered the adoption of a written dress policy banning the wearing of religious symbols by staff in all Belgian branches.

106 X., 'Protestactie in Genk na ontslag om hoofddoek' [Protest in Genk after Headscarf Dismissal], *De Morgen*, 13 March 2011, at www.demorgen.be/dm/nl/989/Binnenland/article/detail/1234856/2011/03/12/Protestactie-in-Genk-na-ontslag-om-hoofddoek.dhtml (accessed 5 October 2011); besides the objection to 'being cooped up

In contrast, the opportunity to 'work in the shadows' would have been welcomed by the employee in the Alamo case, who would have accepted a complete exemption from having to serve customers at the car rental counter. Obviously, employees have varying personal preferences, and public contact (or lack thereof) in a job can play a role in choosing a job or profession, but to the extent possible employees should have that choice. From their side, employers have (and should have) the autonomy to decide who they will hire, but the choice should generally relate to the ability to get the job done and not be motivated by (vicarious) discriminatory bias. As the District Judge in *Brown* v. *Roberts* aptly considered:

> it would be distasteful to suggest that employers can legally single out employees who assert inconvenient but bonafide religious beliefs and isolate them in unappealing work environments ... Pay scales and formal job titles are only part of the conditions of a job; anyone who has worked knows that opportunities for variety in day-to-day tasks and reasonably palatable physical surroundings may make the difference between a tolerable and a flatly unbearable working environment.[107]

Indeed, the different treatment and standards for front-office and back-office employees compromises the equal treatment of employees and leads to exclusion. Prohibiting front-office staff from dressing religiously can mean that Muslim women wearing the headscarf in particular, or other individuals who wear particularly conspicuous religious clothing and symbols, have limited opportunities and are paying too high a price for their nonconformity. Still, what Hema seemed naïve enough to make explicit may be a leading inclination amongst many employers, at least in certain places ore sectors, namely 'playing it safe' by restricting front-office jobs to employees who conform to what are considered 'acceptable standards'.

In the Belgian public sector, it can be an explicit and overt policy to prohibit (only) front-office civil servants from displaying religious symbols.[108] This policy is mainly motivated by State neutrality concerns, with 'neutrality' being understood in an exclusive, non-pluriform, fashion. Considering the limitations the application

---

in the stockroom', the former employee also noted that Hema was merely offering her a temporary contract, not the long-term position that was offered had she been willing to take off her headscarf.

107 *Brown* v. *F.L. Roberts & Co., Inc.*, 419 F.Supp.2d 7 (D.Mass. 2006), 13–14.

108 E.g. in the city of Antwerp, municipal employees directly engaged in dealing with the public since 2007 are prohibited from wearing any religious or political symbols. D. Hermans, 'Scheldestad bant hoofddoek. 150 moslima's protesteren tevergeefs tegen verbod' [Antwerp Bans Headscarves. 150 Muslim Women Protest to no Avail], *Het Nieuwsblad*, 16 January 2007, at www.nieuwsblad.be/article/detail.aspx?articleid=GCK16VTL3 (accessed 5 October 2011).

of such conception of State neutrality carries for the employment opportunities of religiously dressed individuals, one can argue it is best to restrict its scope, for instance by limiting the strict duty of neutrality to front-office civil servants only. Recently, the applicability of the strict duty of neutrality for civil servants was debated by a Committee of experts appointed by the Belgian government with the task to formulate recommendations on how Belgium should respond to the various challenges created by a multicultural society. In fact, the issue of religious dress figured prominently in the work of the so-called 'Roundtables for interculturality', which – amongst others – formulated recommendations in the areas of employment and public service.[109] The Committee considered four potential options when it came to the fiercely debated issue of regulating religious symbols in the public service, namely (1) prohibiting all State employees from displaying symbols, (2) restricting the ban to civil servants who come into contact with the public (i.e. front-office workers), (3) restricting the ban to the State's representatives in positions of power (police, judiciary, army), and (4) allowing all civil servants to display religious symbols in all circumstances. The option to restrict only those civil servants in front-office positions from displaying religious affiliations was explicitly rejected as this would 'compromise the equality amongst civil servants without guaranteeing the neutrality of the public service'.[110]

In the European context, the problematic socio-economic status of certain ethno-religious communities (including low participation rates and occupational segregation) gives good reason for a careful consideration of subtle but structural barriers that exclude minorities from mainstream participation, including in the public service. The idea that (all or some) civil servants must 'exhibit neutrality', if that were possible, should also be evaluated in that light. Limiting the scope of application of that duty – to only front-office staff – may In the short run open up opportunities for some, but such delineation has perverse effects of its own and cannot discount the harsh consequences of an exclusively understood State neutrality for employment opportunities of individuals visibly identifying with various religions.

In the United States, decisions do not reject single incidences of appearance-motivated back-routing in the workplace, but concerns about its cumulative effect

109 Roundtables on Interculturality, Committee report delivered to the Belgian Vice-Minister, Minister of Work and Equal Opportunities on 8 November 2011, at www.interculturalite.be (accessed 5 October 2011), at 8–9. The Roundtables, presided by Marie-Claire Foblets and Christine Kulakowski, organized a large number of dialogues, meetings and events and supported local diversity initiatives from September 2009 to September 2010. I thank Prof. Foblets for pointing out this important aspect in the debates and in the final report.

110 Roundtables on Interculturality, Committee report delivered to the Belgian Vice-Minister, Minister of Work and Equal Opportunities on 8 November 2011, at www.interculturalite.be, 79–80; instead the Committee (as a compromise) recommended restricting a prohibition to civil servants in positions of power only (police, judiciary, army).

have been made.[111] Indeed, while individual examples of the *back-officing pattern* may keep a number of employees active and participating in the labour market, in its cumulative effect it undermines equal opportunities for individuals and groups which already face various obstacles to employment and societal participation, diverts attention from character and capabilities, confirms the existence of social stigma, leads to a level of self-selection and self-disqualification, causes a dispersed but sweeping form of occupational segregation, and sends out the wrong message about the values of tolerance and diversity.The role of the, even if somewhat rudimentary, distinction between front-office and back-office positions in delineating opportunities for certain non-standard-conforming individuals illustrates the role of the 'public' and the 'private' in structuring our societies, in particular by inclusion and exclusion of religious dress in certain positions and workplaces.

From the point of view of a business owner, the question remains. How is (s)he to respond to the business needs of society when customer preferences reflect and reinforce precisely the attitudes that anti-discrimination law is seeking to eliminate? In the Belgian case-law discussed, customer preferences and image ideals were given deference and sometimes too readily accepted as a defence. This implicates cultural attitudes as one reason behind structural barriers and exclusion in the Belgian labour market. In such a setting, there are obvious limits to how much the law can achieve. But should the law single out some supposedly ill-fated employers who go with the flow of the prevailing customs and attitudes, or should employers, or at least public employers, be held to more responsibility? This choice is present in the interpretation of relatively new anti-discrimination norms. An audacious consideration of anti-discrimination law has to ask itself what remains of the relevance of norms if they are merely interpreted to coincide with the prevailing customs and attitudes. A firm commitment to equal opportunities implies the rejection of defenses based on assumptions of the public's toleration level and the confirmation that for most jobs the 'appearance of neutrality' bears no demonstrable relationship to job performance. In fact the confirmation of a mainstream aspiration for the ideal-typical 'neutral-looking' employee, whether in a front-office position or not, can become untenable and counter-productive in the context of increasing diversity.

111 *Brown* v. *F.L. Roberts & Co., Inc.*, 419 F.Supp.2d 7 (D.Mass. 2006), 19 (in particular, '[a]n excessive protection of an employer's "image" predilection encourages an unfortunately (and unrealistically) homogeneous view of our richly varied nation').

References

Alexander, M. (1999), 'Attention Shoppers: The First Amendment in the Modern Shopping Mall', *Arizona Law Review*, 41, 1–47.

Alidadi, K. (2010), 'Werkgever mag hoofddoek verbieden op basis van ongeschreven regels' [Employer can Prohibit Headscarf based on Unwritten Rules], *Juristenkrant*, nr. 210, 1–2.

Alidadi, K. (2012), 'Muslim Women Made Redundant: Unintended Signals in Belgian and Dutch Case Law on Religious Dress in Private Sector Employment and Unemployment', in Alidadi, K. et al. (eds), *A Test of Faith? Religious Diversity and Accommodation in the European Workplace* (Aldershot: Ashgate), 245–282.

Alidadi, K., Foblets, M.-Cl. and Vrielink, J. (eds) (2012), *A Test of Faith? Religious Diversity and Accommodation in the European Workplace* (Aldershot: Ashgate).

Amnesty International (2012), 'Choice and Prejudice. Discrimination against Muslims in Europe' (London: Amnesty International Ltd.), 1–123.

Bakht, N. (2009), 'Objection, Your Honour! Accommodating Niqab-Wearing Women in Courtrooms', in Grillo, R. et al. (eds), 115–133.

Ball, C. (2008), 'Privacy, Property, and Public Sex', *Columbia Journal of Gender and Law*, 18, 1–59.

Davies, A. (2009), 'Judicial Self-Restraint in Labour Law', *Industrial Law Journal*, 38, 278–305.

De Vos, M. (2004), 'De bouwstenen van het discriminatierecht in de arbeidsverhoudingen' [the building blocks of discrimination law in labour relations], in De Vos, M. and Brems, E. (eds), *De Wet Bestrijding Discriminatie in de praktijk* (Antwerp: Intersentia).

Ferrari, S. (2011), 'Religare WP5: The Public Space', *Discussion Paper*, Brussels, CEPS, June, available at: www.religareproject.eu/content/state-art-report-public-space-formal-and-substantive-neutrality-public-sphere (accessed 14 June 2012).

Finkin, M. (2006), 'Life Away from Work', *Louisiana Law Review*, 66, 945–974.

Gilman, D. (2001), '"Bilingual" Approach to Language Rights: How Dialogue Between U.S. and International Human Rights Law May Improve the Language Rights Framework', *Harvard Human Rights Journal*, 24, 1–70.

Glorieux, I. (1995), *Arbeid als Zingever: een onderzoek naar de betekenis van arbeid in het leven van mannen en vrouwen* [Labour as meaning: and inquiry into the meaning of labour in the life of men and women] (Brussels: VUB Press).

Gostin, L. (2008), 'Meeting Basic Survival Needs of the World's Least Healthy People: Toward a Framework Convention on Global Health', *Georgetown Law Journal*, 96, 331–392.

Grillo, R., Ballard, R., Ferrari, A., Hoekema, A., Maussen, M. and Shah, P. (eds) (2009), *Legal Practice and Cultural Diversity* (Aldershot: Ashgate).

Hepple, B. (2011), *Equality: The New Legal Framework* (Oxford: Hart Publishing).
Knights, R. (2009), 'Approaches to Diversity in the Domestic Courts: Article 9 of the European Convention on Human Rights', in Grillo, R. et al. (eds), 283–298.
Lamon, H. (2009), 'Een advocate met een hoofddoek. Et alors?' [An attorney with a headscarf. So what?], *Juristenkrant*, nr. 195, 10.
Levine, J. (2006), 'Defending the Freedom to be Heard: Where Alternate Avenues Intersect Empty Public Spaces', *University of Memphis Law Review*, 36, 277–334.
Palumbo, M. and Radermecker, C. (1996), 'Le voile islamique, ou "l'éternel" conflit entre un impératif religieux et une norme étatique' [The Islamic Headscarf, or the Eternal Conflict between a Religious Imperative and a State Norm], *Soc. Kron.*, 409–410.
Rhode, D. (2009), 'The Injustice of Appearance', *Stanford Law Review*, 61, 1033–1101.
Solieman, I. (2009), 'Born Osama: Muslim-American Employment Discrimination (Note)', *Arizona Law Review*, 51, 1069–1096.
Tobler, C. (2008), *Limits and Potential of the Concept of Indirect Discrimination*, European Commission (Brussels: Directorate-General for Employment, Social Affairs and Equal Opportunities), 1–87.
Van Den Broeck, B. (2007), 'De hoofddoek: onze grootste kopzorg?' [The Headscarf: Our Biggest Headache?] *Juristenkrant*, nr. 160, 14.
Waddington, L. (2011), 'Reasonable Accommodation: Time to Extend the Duty to Accommodate Beyond Disability?', *Nederlands Tijdschrift Mensenrechten/ NJCM-Bulletin*, 36:2, 186–198.
Weintraub, J. and Kumar, K. (eds) (1997), *Public and Private in Thought and Practice: Perspectives on a Grand Dichotomy* (Chicago: University of Chicago Press).

Chapter 10
Religious Dress Codes: The Turkish Case

A. Emre Öktem and Mehmet C. Uzun

Introduction

> C'était une Turquie somptueuse et charmante, aux beaux costumes éclatants, aux turbans de formes étranges et de dimensions gigantesques, aux caftans roses ou bleu pâle, noisette ou vert tendre, aux riches pelisses bordées de fourrures précieuses. (Diehl 1917: 85)

In Turkey the regulation of religious attire is never discussed only from a human rights point of view, since the understanding according to which the use of religious attire is a matter closely related to the political ideology of the State is dominant in political life. In this sense, the European Court on Human Rights touches one of the fundamental principles of Turkish law on clothing and attire in the case of *Leyla Şahin* v. *Turkey*, stating that:

> At the time of the Ottoman Empire both the central government and religious groups required people to dress in accordance with their religious affiliations. The reforms introduced by the Republic on the question of dress were inspired by the evolution of society in the nineteenth century and *sought first and foremost to create a religion-free zone* in which all citizens were guaranteed equality, without distinction on the grounds of religion or denomination.[1]

Consequently, the regulation of that which is 'religious' has to be taken into consideration in direct correlation with the transformation processes of society's way of life from the old Ottoman Empire to the new Republic, whose primary policy consisted of a clear-cut cultural separation from the old in line with the principles of the Republican revolution. Under the multi-faceted debate on Turkish *laicism*,[2] the vast amount of legislation pertaining to attire always has aspects with religion-related implications, in the sense that it constitutes a considerable

1 Emphasis added. *Leyla Şahin* v. *Turkey*, Chamber, European Court of Human Rights [ECHR], App. No. 44774/98, 29.06.2004, par. 29.

2 For the purposes of this chapter, the term '*laicism*' will be used instead of secularism, due to the fact that Turkish *laicism* inspired by the French concept is distinct from secularism, and it is this distinction which characterizes the nature of the regime on religious attire. See in general Öktem (2003: 93–94).

element of the Westernization and secularization/laicization processes adopted by the State. Reshaping society in itself implies addressing all the potential problems that the society may create. It is this approach which defines the key issues at the core of the problems born from the casuistic, totalistic and complex nature of Turkish attire law.

In order to demonstrate these complexities, and taking into consideration the vast amount of existing regulations, the methodology of this chapter will consist of a two-level analysis. First of all, each section will primarily focus on the existing legal framework. Details will be provided, as it is believed that only through such a demonstration can the reader truly appreciate the all-encompassing nature of the Turkish regime – which in return may contribute to a sounder comparative analysis. Secondly, the chapter will underline contemporary issues related to religious clothing or symbols under the relevant regime. With this approach in mind, the first section of this chapter will analyse the regulatory framework on attire in daily public life. Following on, the second section will detail the regulatory framework with regard to governmental service, comprising the three branches of government. The third and the fourth sections are specifically reserved for the regulation of attire in education and in higher education separately; for not only is the ideological position of the State most clearly visible within the area of education, but also, due to the legal development of the principle of Turkish *laicism*,[3] in Turkey the use of religious attire and specifically the '*türban*'[4] continues to be a highly debated domain, in which public opinion is polarized.

Finally, it cannot be stressed enough that the legal framework on attire is vast to an extent that no paper alone may claim to represent more than the surface of the issues underlying it. Within this perspective, the reader should know that this chapter will consist of the analysis of only some of the major contemporary issues; claiming more would be overly-ambitious. Moreover, the authors would like to acknowledge that in its preparation they have profited largely from Prof. Dr. Gemalmaz's authoritative work, *Turkish Attire Law and the Türban* (Gemalmaz

3 See in general, Uzun (2010).

4 Due to the lack of central authority and historical reasons, the Muslim religion does not possess a general regime on attire. Various regimes have evolved around the cultural and socio-political progress of respective communities. In Turkey, the religious head cover for women, the Islamic veil, has manifested itself in numerous ways and fashions. The differentiation between the more traditional way of covering the head (*başörtüsü*) and the *türban* is a result of the policies of the Council of Higher Education (see *infra* p. 207). While the use of the *türban* initially manifested itself in middle-class conservative families, the structural power struggle in Turkey has morphed it into the symbol of political Islam for the secular segments of the society. This perception has been further supported by the rhetoric of conservative political parties. For example, the Turkish Prime Minister, Recep Tayyip Erdoğan, specifically criticized restrictions on the *türban*, stating 'even if it is worn as a political symbol, can the use of a political symbol be considered a crime?'. See *Zaman Newspaper*, 15.01.2008.

2005: 1–1526), doubtlessly the single most comprehensive compilation of regulations on attire in Turkish legal literature.

Religious Dress Codes in the Public Sphere

In Turkey some laws on attire apply to all citizens, regardless of race, age, sex, religion or profession. These laws, for the most part adopted during the Republican revolution, directly project the ideological shift of the new regime and enjoy specific constitutional protection.[5]

Law No. 671 on the Adoption of the Hat imposes the wearing of the '*şapka*' (hat) as 'the general headgear', not only for civil servants, but for the entire Turkish population.[6] The imposition of the Western headgear through legislative action carries in itself a highly symbolic value, since it replaces the previously worn '*fez*', recognized as an attribute of the Muslim elements of the Ottoman Empire. The Western hat, in contrast, was only worn during the Empire era by visiting or residing foreigners and by some non-Muslim elements of the general population. Therefore, the special legal emphasis adopted through Law No. 671 has a clear secularist and modernist (in the sense of Westernization) connotation. Historically, the Parliamentary debates before the promulgation of the law clearly confirm that the choice of the hat was viewed as a crucial issue, with the major aim of demonstrating that the new Turkish Republic was embracing the common attire of the 'civilized nations'.[7] This general obligation for the entire population is supported through a sanction regime under the Turkish Criminal Code, which foresees imprisonment from two to six months for violations.[8] Law No. 671 was severely implemented, mostly in education and in the civil service until the 1960s. However, although still in force, it is nowadays in complete desuetude. Examples of its implementation and the sanctioning of violations are rare, if any do exist. Nevertheless, its violations are still considered by some segments of the society as anti-revolutionary conservative reactionism.

Law No. 2596 on the Prohibition of Certain Attires,[9] another constitutionally protected law based on the principle of laicism and the protection of the freedom

---

5 Article 174 of the Turkish Constitution of 1982 affords these regulations a semi-constitutional value by excluding them from all forms of constitutional challenge.

6 Article 1, Law No. 671 on the Adoption of the Hat, 25.11.1925, Official Gazette [O.G.], 28.11.1925/230.

7 See Justification of the Draft Law Motion 2/479 on the Adoption of the Hat.

8 Article 222, *Turkish Criminal Code*, Law No. 5237, 26.09.2004, O.G., 12.10.2004/25611.

9 Law No. 2596 on the Prohibition of Certain Attires, 03.12.1934, O.G., 13.12.1934/2879.

of religion of others[10] and applicable to all citizens, prohibits under article 1 religious personnel of all confessions and denominations from wearing religious attire outside of their respective worship places. It also provides under article 2 that scouting, sportive and other types of associations, as well as schools, may adopt special attires, as long as these attires are in conformity with established regulations. Article 3 of the Law also foresees a prohibition for Turkish citizens as well as foreigners residing in Turkey from wearing clothes and insignia of foreign political and military institutions.[11] Originally these latter provisions were inspired by the developments in the West, specifically the surfacing of Italian and German paramilitary units; today any uniform with religious reference would fall within their scope. For example, an issue would arise under this law if private educational institutions adopted religious attire for their students. Cases have been observed in which students of private Koran courses (under non-formal education, *see infra* pp. 207ff.) have been sanctioned for wearing religious attire in public;[12] however, in practice the application of such sanctions are synchronous with socio-political struggles in Turkey. At present, restrictions on the use of religious symbols and attire in public are rarely, if ever, enforced. This coincides with the increase in the use of the Islamic veil by females in Turkey in the last decade.[13]

10 See Justification of the Law No. 2596 on the Prohibition of Certain Attires, TBMM Zabıt Ceridesi, vol. 25, D.IV, İ.4, 1935, Ankara, Turkish National Assembly Print, pp. 74–78, cited in Gemalmaz (2005: 756).

11 This regime was further limited through a general restriction brought under article 44/2 of the Law on Associations of 1983 adopted by the 1980 Coup Regime (Law No. 2908, 06.10.1983, O.G., 07.10.1983/18184) which foresaw a prohibition on special attire or uniforms or insignia for members of associations. The new Law No. 5253 on Associations of 04.11.2004 (O.G., 23.11.2004/25649) contains a similar restriction under article 30/c.

12 See Court of Cassation, 7th Criminal Chamber, 08.05.1969, E.5270, K.4949. The Court concluded that female students of a private non-formal education institution which provided courses on the Koran, detained during their visit to a mausoleum in the city of Konya due to being dressed uniformly in the same religious attire, yet acquitted by the lower court should have been sanctioned for violation of Law No. 2596 on the Prohibition of Certain Attires.

13 A research project in 2007 has revealed an increase in religiously motivated covering of the head in Turkey. According to the results, the number of covered females had increased from 64.2% in 2003 to 69.4% in 2007. Moreover, those preferring to use the *Türban* had also increased from 3.5% to 16.2%. See Konda Research and Consulting, 2007, "Religion, Secularism and the Veil in Daily Life Survey" available at: http://www.konda.com.tr/en/reports.php?tb=2.

Religious Dress Code in Government

Justifiably, governmental service may necessitate the use of specific attire, either due to the requirements of the service itself or due to the understanding under which all aspects of governmental service, including all elected and appointed positions, are considered as physical representations of the State. Consequently, in Turkey the regime on State attire is considered the visual incarnation of the official *laïc* State identity. This regime in return constitutes a domain of conflict with that which is 'religious'. In this respect, most controversial issues with regard to the attire regime in governmental service stem directly from the use of religious attire and symbols, specifically the use of the Islamic veil.

The Legislature

The legal framework The regime on attire for members of the legislative branch of government is specified under the 'Internal Regulation of the Grand National Assembly of Turkey' (hereinafter Regulation), dated 1973.[14] This Regulation was inspired by the previous Regulation of the Parliament of 1964[15] which specified that Members of Parliament (MPs) were obliged to attend the plenary sessions and commission meetings with a necktie and that the President and Vice-Presidents of the Senate (created under the 1961 Constitution yet abandoned under the 1982 Constitution) were to wear a tailcoat while on Parliamentary business. Moreover, the subsequent Regulation on the Joint Sessions of the Two Chambers of 1965 specified that the President of the Republic should wear a tailcoat with a black waistcoat and white necktie at the swearing-in ceremony.[16] Adopted after considerable effort and providing for the same code on attire for the President of the Parliament, the Regulation of 1973 for the first time contained a special provision for female MPs. Article 56 of the Regulation, entitled 'Attire', reads:

> The President at the Presidency Chair shall wear a tailcoat with a white tie and a black waistcoat. Commissioned clerk members shall wear a dark suit.
>
> Members of Parliament, Ministers, civil servants of the Grand National Assembly of Turkey and other public personnel are obliged to wear a jacket and a necktie. Women shall wear a tailor-made suit.
>
> The attire of officers shall be determined by the Presidency Council.

14 Decision No. 584, 05 March 1973, O.G., 13.04.1973/14506.

15 Article 179, Republic Senate Internal Regulation, 1964, O.G., 18.01.1964/11610.

16 Article 11, Turkish Grand National Assembly Joint Session Internal Regulation, 1965, O.G., 01.03.1965/11941.

Although the Regulation of 1973 was revised in 2001 and 2002 with the aim of harmonizing its provisions based on the two chamber system with the unicameral system adopted under the 1982 Constitution, the provisions on attire have been maintained.

Contemporary issues While the regulations on attire for the legislative branch of government do not foresee specific restrictions with regard to religious attire, the *a contrario* reading of the stipulation of acceptable attire restricts their use within the premises of the Assembly of the Parliament. The scope of these regulations, in the sense of 'limiting' the attire of elected public officials, has caused considerable debate. The most controversial subject has focused on the attire of women; especially the possibility for women MPs to wear the *türban* in Parliament.[17] With the existence of reference to specific attire and not headgear, conservative political actors have widely debated the possibility to enter into parliament with the *türban*. According to this approach, since rules provided for specific attire and contained no reference to headgear, a limitation was not established by law. In the national elections of 1999 Mrs Merve Kavakçı, elected as an MP for the conservative Virtue Party (*Fazilet Partisi*), entered the plenary session of 2 May 1999 for the parliamentary oath wearing a *türban*. Amid protest she was forced out of the plenary session and upon discovery of her non-notified US citizenship, she was later on deprived of her nationality by the Council of Ministers,[18] thus also depriving her of her position as MP. A similar debate has taken place before the recent national elections of 2011. Some NGOs and conservative female opinion leaders have demanded that covered women be announced as candidates for electable positions,[19] however none of the main political parties, including the governing conservative Justice and Development Party (*Adalet ve Kalkınma Partisi*) have done so. Since then the debate has lain dormant, doubtlessly until the next elections.

The Judiciary

The legal framework With regard to judicial personnel, the Westernization of the legal system in the early Republican era produced an immediate impact on the dress code of the judiciary staff, displaying a close parallel between the abrupt

17 Another example is the situation of Ms. Şafak Pavey, who due to an accident has had her left arm and leg amputated. She was elected in the National Elections of 2011. Having to wear a tailor-made suit, her prosthese are constantly exposed during plenary session. This has caused a public debate on the necessity to modify the regulations in order to allow trousers to be worn by female MPs.

18 Council of Minister's Decision No. 99/12827, 13.05.1999, O.G., 16.05.1999/23697.

19 For example see Öğünç Pınar, *Bazı Kadınların Seçilme Hakkı* [Certain Women's Right to be Elected], *Radikal Newspaper*, 25.03.2011. Also see in general Ka-der [Association for the Support and Training of Women Candidates], www.ka-der.org.tr.

ideological change of the State and its visual manifestations. The Instructions on Dresses and Headgears to be Worn by Judges, Judicial Civil Servants and Solicitors of 1926[20] provides the first signs of the prevailing tendencies which have later on characterized following regulations: heavy use of foreign, i.e. French, vocabulary (*doublure, manteau, diagonal, visière, bleu de Saxe, bombée, drap, reglane*), extreme obsession with details, meticulous descriptions of attire and an absolute restriction of the religious. This regulation was updated and simplified in 1967.[21] The 1983 Law on Judges and Public Prosecutors,[22] abrogating the previous legislation which had empowered the Ministry of Justice with regard to the dress regulation concerning judges and public prosecutors, provides that the dress of judges and public prosecutors and the modalities of their use will be determined by a regulation to be issued by the Supreme Council of Judges and Public Prosecutors. Although the Regulation on the Register for Service to be applied to Judges and Public Prosecutors, issued the same year, does not contain a clear provision with regard to the dress code, it does provide in its annex that judges are to dress in conformity with the dignity of the judicial profession and that their attire will be taken into account in their professional evaluation.[23] The Regulation on the Official Dress of Judges and Public Prosecutors issued by the Supreme Council in 1998[24] adopts quite a simplified dress code. Regarding the dress to be worn under the official togas, the 1998 Regulation refers to the 1982 Regulation on Dress of the Civil Servants' in Public Service.[25] Although the specification was omitted in previous regulations, the overall regulation for all civil servants had been de facto applied.

The 1961 Constitution created a Constitutional Court for the first time in Turkish political history. A special regulation was adopted for its judges in 1962, and then amended in 1964.[26] It required that special headgear should not be worn during hearings and official ceremonies in covered spaces. The 1982 regulation,[27] adopted after the Military Coup of 1980, provides that constitutional judges should wear a black suit with necktie and socks and shoes of the same colour

20 The Instructions on Dresses and Headgears to be Worn by Judges, Judicial Civil Servants and Solicitors, 1926, cited in Bora et al. (1956: 226–231).

21 Regulation on the Amendment of the Instructions on Judges, 1967, O.G., 11.02.1967/12525.

22 Law No. 2802 on Judges and Public Prosecutors, 24.02.1983, O.G., 26.02.1983/17971.

23 Regulation on the Registry Records to be used for Judges and Public Prosecutors, 1983, O.G., 05.08.1983/18126.

24 Regulation No. 2802 on the Official Dress of Judges and Public Prosecutors, O.G., 29.03.1998/23301.

25 See *infra* pp. 199ff.

26 Constitutional Court Internal Regulation, O.G., 03.08.1962/11171; Internal Regulation on the Addition of Paragraphs to the Additional articles of the Constitutional Court Internal Regulation, O.G., 06.04.1964/11675.

27 Constitutional Court Internal Regulation, O.G., 03.12.1986/19300.

and a white shirt under their togas during hearings and official ceremonies. The 2000 amendment[28] provides special provisions for female members of the Court, who still have to wear black. Although special laws and regulations are devoted to the Court of Cassation[29] and the Council of the State,[30] they do not display major differences from the regulations relating to other jurisdictions. The Supreme Military Administrative Court[31] has a specific regulation which specifies that the regular military judges wear the same togas as their civil equivalents over their uniforms in official ceremonies and over daily attire in court. In all of the cases cited above, religious attire, headgear or symbols are not allowed.

The 1938 and 1969 Laws on Solicitors require that solicitors appear before the court in their official dress.[32] The 1973 and 2002 Regulations for the implementation of the Law on Solicitors provide that, while pleading before the courts or assuming their functions at the Union of the Bar Associations of Turkey or at the disciplinary council of the bar associations, and while taking the solicitor's oath, they should wear their official dress determined by the Union.[33] The rules adopted in 1986 by the Union include, *inter alia*, that 'Male solicitors shall wear a necktie to the extent the climate and seasonal conditions allow doing so' with their 'heads uncovered' regardless of gender.[34]

Contemporary issues The general controversy with regard to the use of the *türban* has also pervaded the courtrooms. The Bar Associations' Union's Circular of 1994 necessitates sanctions against female solicitors who insist on working with the Islamic veil in court (it must be noted that it also forbids long hair and beards for male solicitors).[35] There are a number of disciplinary cases with regard to breaches of these rules.[36] There exists jurisprudence from both the Court of

28 Internal Regulation on the Amendment of the Constitutional Court Internal Regulation, O.G., 05.12.2000/24251.

29 See article 66 of Law No. 2797 on the Court of Cassation, 04.02.1983, O.G., 08.02.1983/17953; Regulation on Attire of the Court of Cassation, O.G., 22.08.2001/24501.

30 See article 94 of Law No. 2575 on the Council of State, 06.01.1982, O.G., 20.01.1982/17580; Regulation on Attire of the Council of State, O.G., 31.01.2002/24657.

31 See article 91 of Law No 1602 on the Supreme Military Administrative Court, 04.07.1972, O.G., 20.07.1972/14251; article 42 of Internal Regulation of the Supreme Military Administrative Court, O.G., 21.05.1979.

32 Articles 24 and 37, Law No. 3499 on Solicitors, 27.06.1938, O.G., 14.07.1938/3959; articles 34 and 49, Law No. 1136 on Solicitors, 19.03.1969, O.G., 07.04.1969/13168.

33 Article 40, Regulation on the Law on Solicitors, 1973, O.G., 20.02.1976/14454; article 20, Regulation on the Law on Solicitors, 2002, O.G, 19.06.2002/24790.

34 Turkish Bar Associations Union, Principles Decision No. 521-3, 25.11.1986.

35 Circular No. 1826/52, Turkish Bar Associations Union, 23.11.1994.

36 See Decision No. 318/4, Turkish Bar Associations Union, 26.05.1973, in Erem F., Meslek Şerhi/1995, p. 71, cited in Ankara Barosu Dergisi, 1973/3; Decision No. E.989/64, K.989/74, 04.11.1989 in Erem Faruk, Meslek Şerhi/1995, p. 71, cited in Ankara Barosu Dergisi, 1990/2.

Cassation[37] and the Council of State[38] approving the expulsion of female lawyers insisting on wearing the Islamic veil during court. Although the restriction of religious attire under professional disciplinary law is understandable, it is not the same with regard to restrictions on individuals who appear before the court as a party, accused or witness to a case.

For instance, in a case before the Court of Cassation in 2003, the expulsion from the courtroom of a female lawyer wearing the Islamic veil, who in that specific instance was the accused, turned out to be problematic and triggered a nationwide debate.[39] Although from a legal standpoint such a decision is in conformity with the aforementioned 1926 Instructions, which require that all people in the courtroom be bareheaded, in practice this rule – though normatively imperative – has been applied most irregularly: by and large according to the political and social circumstances of the specific cases. Moreover, this restriction is seldom applied in lower level courts.

The Executive

General regulations with regard to governmental service Law No. 657 on Civil Servants[40] regulating the regime concerning all personnel working in establishments which function under the general and annexed budget administrations does not provide a specific regime on attire. However, Additional article 19 of the Law, entitled 'Obligation on Attire', provides that all civil servants are under the obligation to obey the rules on clothing and attire established by laws and regulations. Moreover, article 125/g on disciplinary measures specifically determines acts violating the established rules on clothing and attire as punishable offences of the law.

The rules on attire have been laid out under the Regulation on the Clothing and Attire of Personnel working in Governmental Administrations or Establishments of 1982[41] adopted by the Military Coup regime of 1980. All governmental personnel, except those who are subject to a special attire regime under their own relevant laws, are bound by this Regulation. Article 1 of the Regulation states that:

> This Regulation aims to guarantee that public personnel be in civilized non-excessive, plain clothing and in attire conforming to Atatürk's revolution and principles and in unity and integrity with regard to clothing and attire.

---

37 Judgment, Court of Cassation, 8th Criminal Chamber, 05.11.1997, E.1997/13604, K. 1197/15032.

38 For example Council of State, 8th Chamber, 11.06.1998, E.996/5341, K.998/2204.

39 See *Milliyet Newspaper*, 07.11.2003; *Hurriyet Newspaper*, 07.11.2003.

40 Law No. 657 on Civil Servants, 04.07.1965, O.G., 23.07.1965/12056.

41 Regulation No. 8/5105 on the Clothing and Attire of Personnel working in Governmental Administrations or Establishments, 16.07.1982, O.G., 25.10.1982/17849.

Article 4 determines that in all instances, plainness, cleanliness and conformity to service is to be considered as the main principle on attire. However, article 5 depicts in detail the appropriate attire to be worn by personnel of both sexes. Paragraph a) of article 5 states that female personnel should

> be in a clean, plain and ironed dress or trousers, with plain and polished normal heel shoes and/or boots, with their heads uncovered at all times in the place of duty, hair orderly done or knotted, with normal cut fingernail.

In any case,

> sleeveless or very low necked shirt, blouse or dress and trousers such as tights or blue jeans may not be worn. The length of the skirt may not be higher then the knee and the skirt may not be vented. Sandal type shoes may not be worn.

Paragraph b) states that male personnel shall wear

> plain, clean, ironed and neat clothing; shoes shall be closed, clean and polished. Sandals or Mary-Jane style shoes shall not be worn. Within buildings and in places of duty the head shall be at all times uncovered. Sideburns below mid-ear are not allowed. Hair may be grown, as long as it does not cover the ears and the shirt at the back of the neck in normal posture, and should be clean and neat. Personnel shall shave daily and a beard shall not be grown. A moustache may be grown naturally, its length not surpassing the upper lip limit, the top parts of the mustache may not be shaved, its side limits should be aligned with the upper lip and its lower ends should be cut at the lip limit. A necktie shall be worn, and jumpers such as polo-neck jumpers which cover the necktie shall not be worn. If provided for duty, uniform attire shall be worn. It is forbidden to wander within buildings without a shirt, necktie and socks.

Article 9 prohibits the use of any pins, emblems or insignia except those of the administration currently worked at, of schools of graduation or pins produced by the government for special occasions. Thus, civil servants are not allowed to use pins, emblems or any other sign which might have reference to a specific religious denomination. Moreover, article 10 obliges all photographs to be used in official documents to conform to the rules set out by the Regulation. Thus, personnel are not allowed to provide for official documents identity photographs in which religious attire or symbols, such as the *türban*, are visible.

An issue which necessitates emphasis is that the provision of such an excessively detailed attire regime and its association with the disciplinary sanctions regime foreseen under Law No. 657 on Civil Servants is a somewhat recent development. Initially, the Law on Civil Servants of 1965 only foresaw a general disciplinary regime without enunciating specific acts constituting breaches of the law. The 12 March Transitional Regime (after the Military Intervention of

12 March 1971) amended the law,[42] producing a list of acts necessitating disciplinary action; yet violations of the rules on attire were not included in this list. This was established with an amendment to the law[43] adopted by the Military Coup Regime of 1980. Thus, the excessively detailed and strict regime on attire and the sanctions for their breaches are products of the Military Coup Regime of 1980. One can therefore agree with Gemalmaz who underlines the fact that the main aim of the civil servants' attire regime is to create, in a military understanding of the word, a uniform civil servant model.[44] The Regulation covers all civilian personnel working directly or indirectly for the government, and it moulds them into a single model which in form and in substance is 'purified' from all that is ideological, political, philosophical and religious.

Certain Governmental Services

The Armed Forces As can be expected, the regime on attire in the military is highly comprehensive due to the nature of the service. Consequently, mention of only a number of existing rules will be provided in order to demonstrate the level of detail. The Turkish Armed Forces is strictly *laïc* in the sense that it does not contain within its official structure a specific religious service, such as an army chaplaincy which might exist in other armed forces. Consequently, military codes on attire do not contain reference to religious attire per se.

Under article 34 on Attire of the 1961 'Internal Service Law of the Turkish Armed Forces',[45] all members of the Turkish Armed Forces are obliged to wear the military uniform during service. Civilian attire may only be worn during service if such has been authorized by a superior for the accomplishment of a special task. Members of the Armed Forces are under the obligation to protect the honor and dignity of the military uniform, which also imposes a strict prohibition on Armed Forces' members from entering brothels, bars and taverns in military uniform. While the Ministry of Defense is competent in determining the form of the uniform, members of the Armed Forces are forbidden to grow whiskers, moustaches or beards and breaches of these provisions are sanctioned as military crimes.

The attire to be worn during military ceremonies that take place at national and religious celebrations is regulated by a special regulation dated 1926.[46]

42 'Amendment of Law No. 657' Decree, KHK/2, 23.12.1972, O.G., 30.12.1972/14407.

43 Law No. 2670 on 'the Amendment of Law No. 657', 12.05.1982, O.G., 16.05.1982/17696.

44 Gemalmaz names this process the establishment of a 'civilian personnel uniform'. Gemalmaz (2005: 129, 131).

45 Law No. 211, 04 January 1961, O.G., 10.01.1961/10703.

46 Council of Ministers' Decision No. 3687 on Instructions on Navy Ceremonies and Protocol, 30.05.1926.

This regulation contains a large number of casuistic provisions. Under the law, different provisions (Great Uniform, Little Uniform and White Great Uniform) apply to various occasions such as: ceremonies attended by the President of the Turkish Republic, by other heads of States, the opening session of the Turkish Parliament, National Republic Day and other national days, official dinners, receptions, weddings, balls, etc. Moreover the sword, which differs according to the army and the navy, accompanies the ceremony uniform on different occasions. A Decision dated 1963 regulates specifically the attire of female officers.[47] This Decision, unlike previous regulations, also foresees for the first time the wearing of ceremonial uniforms during religious days.

The most controversial issue with regard to attire in the armed forces stems from the use of religious symbols and attire by civilians on military premises, such as military hospitals, officers' clubs, officers' messes, military schools and other compounds. Such compounds may be used by military staff, their relatives and their guests and entry into these compounds wearing the Islamic veil or with a beard has caused numerous issues. Under the Regulation of Officers' Clubs, Military Messes and Social Facilities,[48] rules on entry into such facilities is administered under the orders and directives issued by the Office of the General Staff. While for a long time the practice of the General Staff was to forbid the entry of women wearing the Islamic veil and men with beards into such facilities,[49] a tendency to relax such measures, especially with regard to some of the facilities (hospitals and Officers' Clubs) is observed.[50] However, the issue has not been definitively resolved and is still an area of tension and propaganda.

Religious personnel In Turkey the regulation of religious attire for religious personnel is full of conceptual contradictions. Although *laïc*, the State employs a vast number of Muslim religious personnel through the Directorate of Religious

47 Council of Ministers' Decision No. 6/1835 on Turkish Armed Forces Attire, 07.06.1963, O.G., 06.08.1963/11473.

48 Article 11, Regulation of Officers' Clubs, Military Messes and Social Facilities, O.G., 20.8.2000/24146.

49 Usually issues manifest with regard to hospital visits, marriage ceremonies held in Officers' Clubs and diploma ceremonies in Military Schools. However, from time to time even official ceremonies have caused problems of this nature to arise. The attendance of some Members of Parliament accompanied by their wives wearing the *türban* to the Republic Day reception organized by the Governorship of Kayseri at the Kayseri Officers' Club is one such example, after which the General Staff started an administrative inquiry for violation of regulations on attire on military premises (see General Staff Press Release No. 21/03 of 06.11.2003).

50 In 2010 the General Staff started to work on a formula which might ease the restrictions with regard to entry into such facilities with a beard. See *Radikal Newspaper*, 09.06.2010 (Internet edition, www.radikal.com). Moreover, in practice restrictions towards the Islamic veil have also been relaxed to a certain extent, especially concerning access to military hospitals.

Affairs.[51] The first regulation relating to religious personnel adopted during the Republican era was the Regulation on 'Religious Class and Religious Attire' dated 1925.[52] This regulation is theoretically still in force and forbids all individuals not of the religious class from wearing religious attire, in all circumstances. However, these provisions turned out to be problematic in application, especially after the early ideologically enthusiastic Republican era: faced with a vast number of individuals wearing religious or semi-religious clothing, public authorities scarcely applied the Regulation and mostly overlooked its breaches. Unlike many Christian denominations, the lack of a clear definition of religious attire in Islam, together with the conservative nature of Turkish society in general and the surrounding debates on the freedom of religion have contributed to the desuetude of the Regulation. The definition of religious attire established under the Regulation of 1925 is simply confined to a white turban and a black frock.

Law No. 677 of 1925 on the Closure of Dervish Monasteries and Tombs, the Abolition of the Office of the Keeper of Tombs and the Abolition and Prohibition of Certain Titles,[53] a cornerstone of the republican laicization process, abolishes all sorts of attire and titles proper to sheikhs, dervishes and their followers and provides imprisonment and pecuniary penalties for infringements. However, the use without hindrance of an endless variety of colourful pseudo-religious attires can be actively observed in present-day Turkey.

Under Law No. 633 of 1965 on the Foundation and Duties of the Directorate of Religious Affairs, the Directorate is empowered to 'regulate the attire worn by the religious personnel in function'.[54] This law should be taken into consideration in conjunction with the law on 'The Prohibition of Certain Attires' of 1934[55] which stipulates the prohibition of the wearing of religious attire by religious personnel, of whatever religion or denomination, outside of places of worship and apart from religious rituals. In addition, under this law the Government may issue provisory authorizations for the religious leader of each religious community to wear religious attire outside of places of worship. In practice, this privilege has been granted to various Christian denominations (Greek Orthodox, Gregorian Armenian, Protestant, Catholic), to the Jewish religious leaders and to the Director of Religious Affairs – the latter representing particularly the Sunni branch of Islam. This practice ignores the religious leaders of other Islamic denominations.

51 See in general Öktem and Uzun (2010: 707).

52 Council of Ministers' Decision No. 2413 on Religious Class and Religious Attire, 02.09.1925.

53 Law No. 677 on the Closure of Dervish Monasteries and Tombs, the Abolition of the Office of the Keeper of Tombs and the Abolition and Prohibition of Certain Titles, 30.11.1341 (1925), O.G., 13.12.1925/243.

54 Law No. 633 on the Foundation and Duties of the Directorate of Religious Affairs, 22.06.1965, O.G.,02.07.1965/12038.

55 See *supra* pp. 193ff.

The Law of 1934 is further implemented through a Regulation of 1935,[56] which defines religious attire as 'all sort of clothing, signs or ensigns adopted for distinguishing religious personnel of any religion or denomination'. The fact that a *laïc* State Regulation refers implicitly to the respective canonic rules of various denominations is noteworthy.

Religious Dress Code in Education

The Turkish education system was unified and laicized with the adoption of Law No. 430 on the Unification of the Educational System (Unification Law) of 1924,[57] which not only brought all existing educational institutions under the direct and sole authority of the Ministry of Education, but also established faculties of theology and vocational religious high schools in order to train religious personnel, making existing *Madrasahs* and other religious educational institutions obsolete.[58] This law, still in force and under constitutional protection, forms the moral and semi-constitutional basis of the Turkish education system.

This system, further elaborated under Fundamental Law No. 1739 on National Education, consists of two categories of education: formal and non-formal education. Formal education consists of Pre-Primary, Primary, Secondary and Higher education. Primary education is provided for children from the ages of six to 13, is compulsory for children of both sexes and is free at State-run schools. According to the Ministry of National Education, the aim of Primary education is to

> ensure that every Turkish child acquires the necessary knowledge, skills, behavior and habits to become a good citizen and is raised in accordance with the concept of national morals and that he/she is prepared for life and for the next level of education in accordance with his/her interests, talents and capabilities.[59]

Secondary education is optional and is free at State-run institutions. Higher education includes institutions which continue for at least two years after secondary education, such as Universities, Faculties, Institutes, Higher Schools,

56 Regulation No. 2/1958 on the Execution of the Law on the Prohibition of Certain Attires, 06.02.1935, O.G., 18.02.1935/2933.

57 Law No. 430 on the Unification of the Educational System, 3.3.1340 (1924), O.G., 03.03.1340(1924)/63.

58 Article 4, ibid.

59 National Education Statistics, Formal Education 2010–2011, Republic of Turkey Ministry of National Education Strategy Development Presidency, Publication of Official Statistics Program, p. XII.

Conservatories, Vocational Higher Schools and Research and Application Centers.[60]

With regard to the dress code for students in pre-higher education in Turkey, the legal framework can be summarized in three periods. Legislation directly concerning national education during the period of 1920–1960 did not foresee specific norms and most rules brought through regulations and institutional decisions specifically focused on the clothing and attire of the staff rather than students (Gemalmaz 2005: 96). The following period of 1960–1980 witnessed greater regulation of clothing and attire; however, this was similarly conducted mostly through institutional regulations and disciplinary codes. The common ground of the rules during this period was that they required students to be dressed cleanly and plainly, with no permission for 'extravagant' hairstyles, the wearing of civilian head gear or attire representing certain groups,[61] including in practice religious denominations.

The period after the Military Coup of 1980 witnessed a trend to regulate attire meticulously in national education. The Fundamental Law on National Education contains no specific rule on attire but does include direct reference to the principle of *laicism*. Articles 2, 10 and 12 state the principle of *laicism* as one of the major aims of national education governing its overall function. Having said this, article 32 of the Fundamental Law also foresees vocational religious high schools (*İmam-Hatip Lisesi*) with the aim of training religious personnel for the State.[62] Within this perspective, an exception clause for religious attire is provided for these schools, allowing for the use of the Islamic veil by female students during the courses on the Koran.

The main framework for clothing and attire for students was established with the adoption of the Regulation on Attire of Staff and Students in Schools Subject to the Ministry of National Education and Other Ministries (Framework Decree) on 22 July 1981.[63] Under article 6:

60 As of 2010, 10,981,100 students were enrolled in primary education, 2,676,123 in general secondary education, 2,072,487 in vocational and technical junior high and high schools and 3,332,559 in higher education institutions. Ibid., p. 11.

61 For example, article 113 of the Regulation for Hotel Management Schools of 1962 (Tebliğler dergisi, 03.12.1962/1232): 'the imitation of the attire of certain groups is forbidden'; article 152 of the Regulation on Secondary and Junior High Schools of 1964 (O.G., 28.11.1964/11868): 'Attire of students shall be plain and clean; cleanliness and attire shall be controlled regularly'.

62 Although these institutions were provided greater support during the years of right-wing conservative political rule in Turkey, measures adopted by the '*28 February Process*' – especially the entry into force of eight years of obligatory laïc primary education and the closure of the primary school sections of vocational religious schools – limited their scope to a large extent.

63 Adopted through Council of Minister decision No. 8/3349, 22.07.1981, published on 7 December 1981.

> Regarding the attire of the administrators, teachers, civil servants, contractors, temporary service personnel and workers of schools, plainness, cleanliness and appropriateness to service is principal.

However, this general principal is further elaborated under article 7 which provides that with regard to the attire of the personnel cited in article 6 the detailed rules enumerated in the Regulation on the Clothing and Attire of Personnel working in Governmental Administrations or Establishments of 1982 apply.[64] Concerning students, article 9 puts forth plainness, cleanliness and conformity to aim as the main principle ruling the attire regime. Articles 10, 11, 12 and 13 respectively elaborate in extreme detail upon the uniform style attire to be worn by male and female students at different levels of the education system. This central framework is moreover supported under article 14 recognizing local school authorities' discretion to further regulate in cases enumerated within the Regulation. Without entering into the substantial detail of the provisions, it is possible to state that the common theme that persists for the attire of all students is cleanliness, uniformity, non-extravagance and the dismissal of all that might have a political or religious connotation.

Taking all of the above into consideration, one cannot but agree with Gemalmaz's conclusion that the regime on attire is strict to the point that the only attire seemingly not regulated is underwear (Gemalmaz 2005: 83). Moreover, just as observed in the regime for civil servants, the main focus of the regime of attire in education is to establish a uniform and mono-type student model that, at least in appearance, is detached from all that is political, philosophical and religious. The only exception is for the use of the Islamic veil by female students during courses of Koran in vocational religious high schools under article 12(c) of the Regulation. Flexibility to a certain extent can be observed in practice, as long as clear breaches of regulations are not made public. However, even in cases of relaxation of the rules by school administrations, the use of religious symbols and attire remains strictly forbidden and attempts to bypass the regulations have met with rigorous media exposure.[65]

Concerning non-formal education, the governing regulation is the Regulation on Non-Formal Education Institutions affiliated to the Ministry of National Education.[66] As optional educational programmes outside of the formal education

64 See *supra* pp. 193ff. We must note that the regime for administrators, teachers, civil servants, contractors, temporary service personnel and workers in education establishments are detailed to the point of determining moustache length and the use of make-up and perfume by females.

65 For example see *Milliyet News Paper*, 'Hastanede ve Lisede Türbanlı Görüntüler' [Images of the *Türban* in Hospitals and Schools], 25.02.2008. Usually such media exposures end up with administrative inquiries into the respective school authorities; however, the results of disciplinary sanctions, if ever adopted, are rarely made public.

66 Regulation No. 2582, March 2006, O.G., 14.02.2006/26080.

system, non-formal education does not contain specific rules regulating the attire of participants. However, article 126 of the Regulation on Non-Formal Education specifies that 'Plainness, cleanliness and appropriateness to service is the core principal with regards to the clothing and attire of trainees in Non-Formal Education'. Except for this, it is within the discretion of non-formal education establishments to determine their proper dress codes, which in all cases have to be in conformity with the general rules on religious attire in the public sphere, including the rules with regard to associations.[67]

Religious Dress Code in Higher Education

The use of religious attire and symbols by students in higher education[68] has been a largely controversial issue in Turkey. As in other areas, the use of the *türban* by students lies at the core of the argument. However, the legal debate does not stem from the limitation of its use by law – for no such clear stipulation exists – but from the restriction on its use born from the judicial interpretation of constitutional principles. Within this context, the lack of regulation on the subject has morphed the issue from a legal one into a complex hub of the struggle between different political institutions and factions. Within this equation the *türban* per se is conceptually perceived by some as a threat to the political regime of the State. The polarized nature of the underlying social trends has until now blocked a clear legal solution. Although not loudly voiced at the present, the antagonistic debate about the regulatory framework on the use of religious attire in higher education is ongoing.

The Historical Perspective

The current regulatory framework of higher education is based on Law No. 2547 on Higher Education.[69] Until the 1990s neither the Law on Higher Education, nor its predecessors, contained a specific regulation on attire in higher education

67 See *supra* pp. 193ff.; for jurisprudence with regard to violation, see *supra* fn. 12.

68 The rules with regard to higher education staff are subordinate or similar to the general rules of governmental service, thus will not be mentioned separately. See *supra* pp. 195ff.

69 As underlined by Gemalmaz, all statutes regulating higher education since the establishment of the Republic have been adopted in extraordinary circumstances. The first Law on Universities (Law No. 4936, 13.06.1946, O.G., 18.06.1946/6336) was put into force before the adoption of multi-party democracy in Turkey. Major amendments to this law were brought after the Military Coup of 1960 and it was replaced by the Law on Universities (Law No. 1750, 20.06.1973, O.G.,07.07.1973/14587), adopted by the transitional government in power after the military intervention of 1971. Finally this law was replaced with the current Law on Higher Education (No. 2547, 04.11.1981, O.G.,06.11.1981/17506), adopted after the Military Coup of 1980. Gemalmaz (2005: 30).

institutions. This lack of regulation raised issues by the end of the 1960s, a time in Turkey's history that was deeply marked by a fairly violent socio-political struggle between various political factions. In conjunction with the increase in the social visibility of Islamist movements, anxiety spread amongst the *laïc* segments of society and within the State institution itself. This anxiety peaked due to the proliferation of female students in higher education preferring to wear the Islamic veil during their studies. In response, the first disciplinary measures were taken by the University of Ankara in the mid 1960s and similar measures rapidly spread to various other institutions. Moreover, these measures were generally supported by the judiciary which upheld their validity. Although such measures brought a period of lull, they did transfer the issue from the individual to the political sphere.

From non-regulation to legal ambiguity Following the adoption of the 1982 Constitution after the Military Coup of 1980 and the return to multi-party democracy, the use of the Islamic veil in higher education re-emerged as a common theme in politics. The 1982 Constitution established the Council of Higher Education (*Yükseköğretim Kurumu*), which under article 131 of the Constitution has amongst its duties to plan, establish, control and supervise higher education. On 30 December 1982, the Council adopted Decree No. 7327[70] which for the first time regulated attire in higher education. According to the Decree, students had to be of plain and simple attire, conform to Atatürk's reforms and principles and dress with modernity and in any case not be excessive. Under the Decree, female students of Faculties of Theology were allowed to cover their heads during Koran classes.

In 1984, the governing centre-right Motherland Party's (*Anavatan* Partisi) demand for a certain amount of relaxation resulted in the adoption of a new Decree, bringing a dichotomy to the veil issue. Under Decree No. 15,527,[71] female students of higher education institutions were free to use the 'türban in a modern manner'. Within this conception, the traditional way of wearing the Islamic veil (*Başörtüsü*) was perceived as a non-modern regressive symbolic statement, while the *türban* was foreseen as an acceptable practice.[72] As remarked by Altintaş,[73] this regulation is probably one of the first examples of a legal text which determines the permissibility of using religious symbols according to the socio-economic conditions of the individual; the inconsistency of the regulation is clear. However, this Decree was not upheld to the full extent by the judiciary. Similarly, the Council's decision of 10 October 1984 allowing students to use identification

70 Decree No.7327, 30.12.1982.

71 Decree No.15.527, 10.05.1984.

72 See *supra* fn. 4.

73 Altintaş (2002: 80). We must also remark that such a distinction in itself contains discrimination from a human rights law perspective and the non-definition of the difference between the traditional head cover and the *Türban* has caused vast differences in practice between various higher education institutions.

photographs with a *türban* 'as long as it did not hinder identification' (Altintaş 2002: 80) was not accepted by the judiciary which continued to enforce the ban.[74]

Under political and judicial pressure, the Council took a step back on the issue through the adoption of another Decree in 1986,[75] which concluded that wearing the Islamic veil in higher education, including the *türban*, should be considered a punishable disciplinary offence. It stated that 'the fact that the veils used by female students are uniform and of the same color, gives the impression that it may be the symbol of certain ideological movements', and concluded that the Decree of 10 May 1984 which permitted the use of the *türban* was no longer in force. This Decree was supported in implementation through a Regulation adopted on 8 January 1987[76] which added paragraph 'h)' to article 7 of the Regulation on Student Discipline in Higher Education, sanctioning:

> to be in non-modern appearing attire in the classrooms, laboratories, clinics, policlinics and corridors of higher education institutions.

However, 10 months later, with the adoption of another Regulation on 4 December 1987,[77] this approach was reversed. This Regulation amended article 7/h so that it read:

> to be in non-modern appearing attire (the neck and hair can be covered through a veil or türban due to religious belief) in the classrooms, laboratories, clinics, policlinics and corridors of higher education institutions.

This provision stayed in force for two years. This phrase was annulled and the Islamic veil was re-banned with another Regulation adopted in 1989.[78] In this sense, this period can be summarized as being marked by the incompetence or unwillingness of all relevant institutions and parties to properly arrive at a consensus on the democratic resolution of the issue.

Judicial regulation on religious attire in higher education It can be said that the crisis prevailing in the 1980s resulted from two counteracting forces. While

---

74 For example see *Şenay Karaduman* v. *Turkey*, Admissibility, European Commission on Human Rights, App. No. 16278/90, 03.05.1993.

75 Decree No. 38/23574 dated 24 December 1986.

76 'Regulation on the addition of a paragraph to an article of the Regulation on Student Discipline in Higher Education' (with regard to disciplinary measures), O.G., 08.01.1987/19335.

77 'Regulation on the addition of a paragraph to an article of the Regulation on Student Discipline in Higher Education' (with regard to disciplinary measures), O.G., 04.12.1987/20009.

78 'Regulation on the addition of a paragraph to an article of the Regulation on Student Discipline in Higher Education' (with regard to disciplinary measures), O.G., 28.12.1989/20386.

on one side right-wing political parties tried desperately to relax any kind of prohibition on religious attire in higher education, the judiciary and the *laïc* State establishment was to a large extent unfavourable towards any such initiative. Especially the Council of State (*Danıştay*) upheld in numerous instances the validity of disciplinary measures taken by higher education institutions against students insisting on the use of the Islamic veil.[79] We must remark that even the judicial stance was based more on interpretation of official State ideology than pure positive law. In this sense, the *türban* had been perceived by the State as a symbol that was more political than religious in nature.[80] The judicial approach thus seems based largely on a non-concrete, conceptual threat analysis with regard to the symbol itself.[81] For example, as expressed by the Council of State in a judgment in 1984, the veil should not be perceived as an 'innocent practice' but rather as a 'symbol of a world view contrary to the freedom of women and the fundamental principles of our Republic'.[82] This rationale reached a level of non-legal second guessing of foundational constitutive law in 1987, when the Council of State stated that:

> In the Directive on the Attire of General Civil Servants, signed personally by Atatürk, the covering of the head in institutions has been prohibited without distinction of sex.
>
> It would be impossible to consider that Atatürk, who had foreseen this appearance for civil servants would not have similarly foreseen it with regard to students in higher education institutions under the control and supervision of the State.[83]

In 1989, the Parliament finally tried to resolve the issue through legislation. Law No. 3511 was introduced, which added Additional article 16 into Law No. 2547 on Higher Education, which read:

> Within higher education establishments, classrooms, laboratories, clinics, and policlinics and in corridors it is obligatory to be in modern clothing and looks.

79 Council of State 8th Chamber, 23.02.1984, E: 207, K: 330; Council of State 8th Chamber, 03.10.1989, E: 84, K: 724.

80 In its judgment of 1984, the Council of State assumes that the insistence to use the Islamic veil in higher education stems from clear political motivations. The Court states that: 'the head veil has been detached from being an innocent practice and has become the symbol of a lifestyle opposing women's freedom and the fundamental principles of our Republic'. Council of State, 8th Chamber, 23.02.1984, E.1983/207, K.1984/330; also see Council of State, 8th Chamber, E.1984/636, 13.12.1984, K.1984/1574.

81 We must note that developments in Europe, specifically with regard to the tendency towards a general prohibition on the use of the Islamic veil or the full body veil, imply a similar conceptual threat analysis.

82 Council of State, 8th Chamber, 23.02.1984, E: 207, K: 330.

83 Council of State, 8th Chamber, 16.11.1987, E.1987/128, K.1987/486.

> The closing of the neck and hair with a cloth or with a türban due to religious reasons is unrestricted.

Taken to the Constitutional Court by the President, the legislation was annulled by 10 votes to one on 7 March 1989 due to violation of the Preamble and articles 2, 10, 24 and 174 of the Constitution.[84] The Court concluded that the invalidity of the abuse of religion for political aims was a subject which extended to the domain of education and instruction and that 'the necessity to refrain from the use of symbols that represent religious beliefs in classrooms and relevant places' in higher education establishments was the legitimate basis of the non-conformity existing between the Islamic veil and the scientific environment. Moreover, according to the Court, views on a democracy without restrictions, isolated from the concrete circumstances of the case, were constitutionally unsound, since, 'exploiting freedoms in order to cast down freedoms' was unacceptable; and in this sense, 'forcing people to dress in this or that manner and cover their heads [would] cause discrepancy between those who are of a different religions or even of the same religion'. In other words, 'freedoms that were not in conformity with laicism' would not gain validity and 'could not be defended or protected'.

In 1990 the Parliament adopted Law No 3670[85] which amended the Law on Higher Education, introducing Additional article 17, which read 'Without being contrary to the law in force, clothing and attire is unrestricted in higher education establishments'. Moreover, a Transitional article was introduced bringing an amnesty for students who had already received disciplinary measures due to religious attire. This law was also taken to the Constitutional Court, which however did not annul the law and found it conform to the Constitution.[86] Nevertheless, the Court did conclude that the phrase 'Without being contrary to the law in force' had to be construed as encompassing the Constitutional framework, including the Court's previous jurisprudence of 1989, since under article 153 of the Constitution 'the Constitutional Court Judgments ... are binding on the legislature, executive and judiciary, administrative offices, natural and legal persons'. In this sense, and under the Court's jurisprudence of 1989, the phrase had to be read 'as not including "the closing of the neck and hair with a cloth or türban due to religious beliefs"'.

After the 1991 judgment, the *türban* issue was used with success as a political argument by conservative political parties. In the 1995 National Elections, the pro-Islamist/conservative Welfare Party (*Refah Partisi*) won the majority and formed the 54th Government with the centre-right True Path Party (*Doğru Yol Partisi*). However, various practices of the government, which included opposition to the widespread civil protests against corruption and State–mafia relations, pro-*Sharia* rhetoric by party members and the Prime Minister's conduct during his official foreign visits to Egypt, Libya and Nigeria resulted in the intervention of the National

84 Turkish Constitutional Court, Judgment, 07.03.1989, E: 1989/1 K: 1989/12.

85 Law No. 3670, 25.10.1990, O.G., 28.10.1990/20679.

86 Turkish Constitutional Court, Judgment, 09.04.1991, E: 1990/36, K: 1991/8.

Security Council in politics. The '*28 February Process*',[87] named so after Decision No. 406 adopted by the National Security Council on 28 February 1997 (called by some a '*post-modern coup*'), provided the legal and political atmosphere necessary for the prohibition on the *türban* to broaden. Under article 1 of the decision the reinforcement of the principle of *laicism* was to be prioritized and under article 13 public authorities were to apply the Constitutional Court Judgments with regard to practices concerning '*regressive*' attire. After this Decision, and based on the Constitutional Court's judgments of 1989 and 1991, the prohibition of the Islamic veil in higher education was effectively applied nation-wide.

Current Situation

While no clear statutory stipulation existed on the restriction on religious attire and symbols in higher education, the Constitutional Court's judgment of 1989, in conjunction with its judgment of 1991, provided a constitutional basis for the application of the ban on the *türban*. Such an understanding elevated the problem into a constitutional one, thus necessitating a constitutional initiative.

Constitutional initiative to overcome the prohibition On 9 February 2008 the governing Justice and Development Party, with the support of the Nationalist Action Party (*Milliyetçi Hareket Partisi*), proposed the adoption of Law No. 5735 on the amendment of the Constitution. According to the proposed text, article 10 on the equality of receiving public services was to be reinforced through the introduction of the phrase 'and in all enjoyment of public services' into paragraph 4 of the article, and a new paragraph which would read, 'No one shall be deprived from using their right to a higher education for whatever reason unless clearly stipulated by law. The limitations on the use of this right are foreseen by law', was to be added to article 42 on the right to education. Since the limitation on the Islamic veil lacked a statutory basis, all relevant regulations, circulars and decrees would become null and void and the new constitutional norm would similarly override existing jurisprudence. The legislation was taken to the Constitutional Court which rendered its judgment on 5 June 2008, annulling the amendment.[88]

According to the Court, the *sedes materiae* of the amendment was clearly the annulment of the Court's previous jurisprudence and 'the recognition of the freedom to cover for religious reasons to those who enjoy the right to higher

87 The '28 February Process' ended with the dissolution of the Welfare Party by the Constitutional Court. See Turkish Constitutional Court, Judgment, 16.01.1998, E:1997/1, K:1998/1. Also see *Refah Partis and others* v. *Turkey*, Judgment, Grand Chamber, ECHR, App. Nos. 41340/98, 41342/98, 41343/98, 41344/98, 13.02.2003.

88 Turkish Constitutional Court, Judgment, 5 June 2008, E: 2008/16, K: 2008/116. We must note that the competence of the Court with regard to constitutional amendments, especially concerning their substance, is a controversial issue, and this aspect of the judgment has been deeply criticized. For a detailed analysis of this issue see Uzun (2010).

education as a public service'. For the Court, this amendment was brought without '*social consensus*' on the issue, which in return risked deepening the problem. The Court stated:

> The Constitution does not allow the abuse of religion, religious feelings and those considered holy by religion as an alternative to resolving social problems within the framework of the Constitution's clear provisions, through methods based on democratic peace and conciliation. Since all abuse of social problems dislodges the possibility for the problem to be resolved, it may cause the deepening of social conflicts and the nonfunctioning of democratic processes; consequently the belief that the state power will resolve social problems may be damaged.

In addition the Court concluded that the proposed text did not foresee sufficient safeguards for the protection of third party rights. For the Court, the lack of legal limitation with regard to attire in higher education in combination with the proposed constitutional norm would bind administrative authorities against any kind of measures on any form of attire. In this respect, this de-regulation carried the risk of religious symbols being used as instruments of social pressure in places of education and instruction in which students of different convictions, social backgrounds and lifestyles are obliged to work together. The Court concluded that the text would leave 'the adoption of legal precautions which protect other people's freedoms and the public order' to the legislature's discretion. However, taking into consideration that 'the majority of the country's population adheres to a specific religion', it would prove difficult for this discretion to be used for the legitimate restriction of the freedom of religion. Within this perspective, the protection of the fundamental human rights and freedoms of third parties could not be left to the discretion of political parties, but necessitated a constitutional basis. The Court concluded that such an approach had already been approved by the European Court of Human Rights.[89] Consequently, the Court found that:

> When the Constitutional Court's and the European Court of Human Rights judgments are observed, the conclusion has been reached that the provisions brought to articles 10 and 42 of the Constitution are clearly contrary to the principle of laicism, for they constitute in form, the use of religion for political means, and in substance, the violation of third party rights and the establishment of ground for the disruption of public order.

---

89 The Court specifically referred to the European Court of Human Rights following case-law: *Dahlab* v. *Switzerland*, Admissibility, ECHR, App. No. 42393/98, 15.02.2001; *Refah Partisi and others* v. *Turkey*, Grand Chamber, ECHR, op. cit.; *Leyla Şahin* v. *Turkey*, Grand Chamber, ECHR, App. No. 44774/98, 10.11.2005.

Non-application of constitutional jurisprudence After the initiative to amend the Constitution, and pending the Constitutional Court's judgment on the subject, the Presidency of the Council of Higher Education sent to the Presidents of all higher education institutions a 'notification', demanding that the amendment be applied and in a matter of few days, higher education institutions in Turkey were divided into those who continued to apply the Constitutional Court's jurisprudence and those who did not.[90] While the Council of State issued interim measures against the 'notification'[91] until the legality of the demand was determined, the status quo in universities remained. Moreover, in another notification issued by the Council directly addressed to the University of Istanbul due to a formal complaint by a student,[92] the Council stated that students were not to be removed from class for violations of discipline (which include breaches of the rules on attire) and that staff could only determine such violations, after which measures were to be taken by the respective deanships. Although case specific, this 'notification' has had as effect the abandonment of the prohibition in all higher education institutions in Turkey and a total desuetude towards existing judicial decisions.[93]

Given the dominant victories of the ruling conservative Justice and Development Party in the national elections of 2007 and 2011, the adoption of the constitutional amendment through Referendum in 2010 providing greater discretion with regard to the composition of certain high levels of the judiciary and the government's de facto monopoly in the appointment of the presidents of State-run higher education institutions, it would be near impossible at the present state for a university to adopt measures against a student for breaches of the rules on attire due to the use of the *türban* in higher education. In this sense, socio-political realities seem to have prevailed over judicial and legal authority. Even though the Constitutional Court annulled the constitutional amendment of 2008, its desired effects have been installed through non-legal practice and female students who adhere to using the *türban* in higher education are not restricted and no major incident has been recorded since. However, as witnessed elsewhere, without legal determination, a shift in political structures can easily reverse the existing status quo. Moreover, a de facto resolution of the problem also brings with it the possibility of future demands on the use of the *türban* in public service, a highly delicate question;

90 Presidency of the Higher Education Council, Circular No. 225, 24.02.2008.

91 Although the Higher Education Council claimed that this was a non-binding notification, the Council of State decided otherwise in instituting interim measures against the circular. See Council of State, 8th Chamber, 10.03.2008, E:2008/1501. While there is no need to remark that the legality of the application by Universities of a non-binding statement in open contradiction to the Constitutional Court's jurisprudence is highly debatable, one must also not underestimate the political nature of the problem.

92 Presidency of the Council on Higher Education, Notification No.025309, 27.07.2010. See *Radikal Newspaper*, 05.10.2010.

93 See *Gazetevatan Newspaper* (Internet edition), 'Üniversitede artık Türbana Engel Yok' [No Longer Any Restrictions on the *Türban* in Universities], 02.02.2011.

in some minds creating doubt with regard to the future of the republican regime based on the principle of *laicism*.

Conclusion

Upon detailed examination of the regulatory framework on attire, certain general themes emerge. First of all, Turkish legislation pertaining to clothing and attire is burdensomely detailed and in most cases linked closely to a sanctions regime, either under criminal law or under disciplinary law. However, the application of sanctions differs according to the given political conjuncture. Secondly, legislation pertaining to clothing and attire is formulated under the understanding that all aspects of public life are closely related with the 'public sphere' in which the State not only has the competence but also the duty to regulate. Consequently, Turkish legislation is comprised of rules on attire applicable to all individuals in the quasi-totality of everyday life situations, be it access to education, to justice or to the administration. In this sense, these rules manifest themselves both in the provision of public services and in their enjoyment by private individuals. Finally, close observation of legislation and judicial practice shows us that regulations with regard to clothing and attire are generally based on the presumption that in order to guarantee the non-regression of the regime from the foundational revolutionary ideology towards a religiously motivated socio-political order, marginalization of that which is religious from the public sphere is essential. Independent from the validity of such a claim, or of any counter claim, it is possible to state that the approach exhibited towards religious attire is closely linked with existing power struggles within Turkish political life. Restriction or relaxation of the use of religious attire, either through legislation or through practice, is generally not the result of a legal understanding, but rather is the manifestation of the current positions of the relevant power-holding structures.

As explained in the last section of this chapter, this struggle has clearly manifested itself with regard to the use of the *turban* in higher education. One can conclude that the polarization with regard to the use of the Islamic veil in higher education, especially the political connotation associated with the *türban*, is a direct consequence of the policies of the Council of Higher Education. As Gemalmaz puts it:

> The Council of Higher Education's inconsistent policies or the power struggle realized through the use of the türban between various forces has borne its concrete results upon those elements who have never been the 'principal actors' of the processes, i.e. upon university students. (Gemalmaz 2005: 79)

Moreover, it is interesting to observe that the painstaking obsession with detail is not the product of the Republican revolution itself, but instead of more recent initiatives adopted after the Military Coup of 1980. Consequently, it may not be too far-fetched to assume that the declared Westernization of Turkish society is an ongoing and updated process of formulating what is acceptable. Some of the legal provisions address directly religion-related issues, such as the prohibition of religious attires in daily public life or the regulation of the attire of religious personnel. Other provisions, especially those concerning the civil service and education, focus on refashioning the Republic's youth in a more Western and less Oriental way; thus consequently less Islamic. This transformational operation may be described as a kind of secular initiation ritual: in fact, in numerous religious traditions, reception of the novice into the religious class is marked by the wearing of religious clothes, i.e. the cloak of the monk, the '*hırka*' of the dervish, the freshly flayed sheepskin in pagan sacrificial rituals. In the Turkish case, the old Ottoman Empire yields the ample oriental robes and the fez and drifts towards Western costume with the adoption of the necktie and the hat, in order to show that the formal transformation of ideology reflects the substantial one. However, present doubts on the social change achieved through these policies and the inconsistency witnessed in their application leads one to question their substantial worth.

References

Altintaş, M. (2002), *YÖK ve Hukuk* (Ankara: Eğitim Sen Yayınları).

Bora, K., Soysal, B., Bora, P., Soysal, M., Köksel, S., Örcün, F. and Galatalı, A. (1956), *Ceza Hükümlerni Havi Tam Metinli Hususi Kanunlar*, vol. II (Ankara: Son Havadis Matbaası).

Diehl, C. (ed.) (1917), *Dans l'Orient Byzantin* (Paris: de Boccard).

Gemalmaz, M.S. (2005), *Türk Kıyafet Hukuku ve Türban* (Istanbul: Legal).

Öktem, A.E. (2003), 'La Spécificité de la Laicité Turque', *Islamochristiana*, 29, 93–94.

Öktem, E. and Uzun, M.C. (2010), *IACL National Report: The Republic of Turkey*, in Martinez-Torron, J. and Durham, Jr. W.C. (eds), *Religion and the Secular State: National Reports* (Provo: International Center for Law and Religious Studies; Brigham Young University), 701–719, available at: http://iclrs.org (accessed 14 June 2012).

Uzun, M.C. (2010), 'The Protection of Laicism in Turkey and the Turkish Constitutional Court: The Example of the Prohibition on the Use of the Islamic Veil in Higher Education', *Penn State International Law Review*, 28:3, 384–426.

Chapter 11
Religious Dress Codes in the United Kingdom

Javier García Oliva[1]

Introduction

During the last few decades immigration has transformed the demographic make-up of Europe and, despite being both financially and culturally enriching, it has also given rise to inevitable conflicts between mainstream society (overwhelmingly Christian) and the new incomers, 'who belong to very different cultural universes' (Castro 2004: 1). Immigrants have brought with them their own traditions, customs and religions, including their religious symbols. The 'newcomers', with their different religions, are seen in many quarters as a threat to Christian values and, even more strongly, as a threat to the liberal value of tolerance.

In the first few years of the last decade the European Union went through a process of self-discovery and tried to approve a Treaty Establishing a Constitution for Europe. This ambitious text, which never came into effect because of its rejection in referenda held in France and the Netherlands, and which was eventually replaced by the Lisbon Treaty, included an explicit mention of Christianity in the Preamble to its first draft. Its supporters regarded this as a fair acknowledgement of the religious heritage of the continent, whilst its opponents considered it unduly restrictive and unwelcoming towards members of other faiths, particularly Islam. In the pluralistic Europe of the twenty-first century the tensions between a Christian/secular majority and new religious groups should not be underestimated.

Because of the diverse approaches to identity and integration across the European Union countries and issues such as the different models of Church and

1 I am indebted to Frank Cranmer, colleague at the Centre for Law and Religion (Cardiff University), for his stimulating and thought-provoking ideas, as well as his invaluable assistance at all times, particularly in relation to the Scottish response to religious symbols. I would also like to extend my thanks to my colleague Dr Russell Sandberg, at the same Centre, for his thorough comments on the first draft of this paper. I am equally grateful to my colleague Dr Myriam Hunter-Henin (UCL), with whom I first thoroughly enjoyed the study of religious symbols in Europe.

State relationships[2] and the concept of citizenship (Taylor 1994), there has been no single European response to these social transformations and this diversity is undeniable in the field of religious symbols.

Religious Symbols in Europe and the Case Law of the European Court of Human Rights

This lack of uniformity is illustrated by the diverse treatment of religious symbols in public venues throughout Europe. This is not surprising, as the plurality within Europe is celebrated by both the European Union and the Council of Europe. However, Member States do not have unlimited freedom at their disposal and, as Evans has declared, 'the State must be mindful of the need to be neutral and impartial in its approach, but at the same time it should be acting in a fashion which encourages pluralism and tolerance' (Evans 2009: 103). Nevertheless, the entitlement of individual national authorities to deal with religious symbols is self-evident and indeed the same author has pointed out that States are fairly interested in these matters and it is right that they should be involved: 'since it is engaging with such issues on an ongoing basis from a variety of public law perspectives, there is no reason for a State to shy away from regulating matters concerning religious symbols. When religious believers and organized religion enter the public arena, their activities, in common with those of all other participants, are subject to the legislative and regulatory powers of the State (which are of course to be exercised in accordance with human rights law). Secondly, it shows that it cannot be seriously maintained that the duty of neutrality and impartiality means that religious symbolism is to be removed from the public space, generally understood' (Evans 2009: 61).

Broadly speaking, there are two main mechanisms for dealing with religious symbols in the European context (Cañamares 2009: 184):

- Enactment of a general law: France.
- Referral to the discretion of the judiciary or solution *ad casum*: e.g. the United Kingdom, Spain and Italy.

2 It must be taken into consideration that generally speaking European Ecclesiastical Law commentators consider that there are three models of Church/State in the European Union countries (see Robbers 2005); 1. National Church systems (e.g. England and Scotland), with one or more official faiths, but at the same time a recognition of religious freedom (see García Oliva 2010: 482–504); 2. Separatist systems (e.g. France) where no faith is official and religion is regarded as a private matter, as all faiths are on an equal footing; 3. Hybrid systems (e.g. Spain and Italy), where no faith is official but public authorities cooperate with religious bodies (García Oliva 2008a: 41–50).

The differences between these choices have been stressed by commentators: 'It seems undeniable that the UK is more multicultural and tolerant than France, both in the sphere of education and more widely. Furthermore, the UK has managed this without accepting the concept of group rights that is so feared by the French' (McGoldrick 2006: 204). Similarly, Bacquet has criticized the French approach: 'A blanket ban on religious symbols as in France would lead to more consistency, but would require some minorities to comply with the customs and habits of the Judeo-Christian, but mostly secular, majority and this could be perceived as discriminatory' (Bacquet 2009: 133). Obviously, no model can be exempted from criticism and it could be argued that the French response is more uniform and straightforward and, consequently, fairer and more certain. By the same token, it could be claimed that the British solution is maybe lenient and it lacks uniformity. This latter criticism is undeniable and, as argued afterwards, the lack of consistency in some judicial decisions is a cause for concern. Nevertheless, this is not a sufficiently powerful reason to dismiss the British model which comes across as more nuanced and sophisticated than its French counterpart. In effect, a legislative response which ignores or undervalues the circumstances of each specific case is unlikely to be sufficiently respectful of individual needs.

An analysis of religious symbols in the United Kingdom or any other jurisdiction requires a study of the European Convention on Human Rights which contemplates freedom of religion in its individual and communitarian dimension in Art. 9.1:

> Everyone has the right to freedom of thought, conscience and religion; this right includes freedom to change his religion or belief and freedom, either alone or in community with others and in public or private, to manifest his religion or belief and freedom, either alone or in community with others and in public or private, to manifest his religion or belief, in worship, teaching, practice and observance.

However, the right to manifest in Art. 9.1 is qualified by Art. 9.2:

> Freedom to manifest one's religion or beliefs shall be subject only to such limitations as are prescribed by law and are necessary in a democratic society in the interests of public safety, for the protection of public order, health or morals, or for the protection of the rights and freedoms of others.

The European Court of Human Rights has been willing to endorse public authorities' limitations on manifestation of religions (García Oliva 2008b: 880–883). This section does not aim to be a thorough study of the case law of the Strasbourg Court, because the scope of this chapter is the British response to religious symbols, and only two landmark decisions of the European Court will be analysed. Nevertheless, it is important to focus on them because the UK courts must take into account the case law of the Court of Strasbourg. Indeed, the Human

Rights Act 1998, which has incorporated most of the provisions of the European Convention on Human Rights into United Kingdom law, states that:

> S 2: 'A court or tribunal determining a question which has arisen in connection with a convention right must take into account any – Judgment, decision, declaration or advisory opinion of the European Court of Human Rights'.

In *Leyla Sahin*[3] the Strasbourg Court ruled that the University of Istanbul's restrictions in the interests of secularism on the wearing of Islamic headscarves and the measures taken to implement them had not breached the applicant's rights under Art. 9 ECHR; rather, they were justified in principle and proportionate to the aims pursued and, therefore, could be regarded as 'necessary in a democratic society'.

In *Sahin* the Court of Strasbourg applied the specific situation rule, which had already been invoked in several earlier cases.[4] According to this rule, the specific situation of the individual, who could be an inmate in a prison, a member of the Armed Forces or a student at a university, might justify some limitations of the protective nature of Art. 9 of the Convention.

Despite its widely accepted use in some quarters, the support to the specific situation rule is far from unanimous. In *Sahin* itself Judge Tulkens, the sole dissenting judge who argued eloquently that the prohibition of religious symbols tended to prolong prejudices and social injustices, challenged the applicability of the rule. Nor have criticisms of the rule been limited to judges in Strasbourg. In *Copsey*,[5] which involved an unfair dismissal claim brought by an employee obliged to work on Sundays contrary to his religious convictions, the Court of Appeal applied the specific situation rule with some reluctance, describing the Strasbourg rulings as 'repeated assertions unsupported by the evidence or reasoning that would normally accompany a judicial ruling' and 'difficult to square with the supposed fundamental character of the rights'.[6]

It can be argued that the specific situation rule is closely linked with the doctrine of margin of appreciation, a firm choice on the part of the Court of Strasbourg to embrace the legitimate differences across the Council of Europe's

---

3 See *Sahin* v. *Turkey*, App. No. 44774/98, 41 Eur. H. R. Rep. 8 (2005), available at www.echr.coe.int.

4 See *Kalac* v. *Turkey* (1997) 27 Eur. H. R. Rep. 552, 27 ('Article 9 ... does not protect every act motivated or inspired by a religion or belief. Moreover, in exercising his freedom to manifest his religion, an individual may need to take his specific situation into account'). The rule had been previously acknowledged, many years before, in a landmark case, *Ahmad* v. *United Kingdom* (1982) 4 Eur. H. R. Rep. 126, 11 ('The freedom of religion, as guaranteed by Article 9, is not absolute, but subject to the limitations set out in Article 9(2). Moreover, it may, as regards the modality of a particular religious manifestation, be influenced by the situation of the person claiming that freedom').

5 *Copsey* v. *WBB Devon Clays Ltd* [2005] EWCA Civ 932, [2005] ICR 1789.

6 *Per* Mummery LJ at paras 35–36.

countries. This is to be praised, but it should not be achieved at the expense of the non-negotiable protection of fundamental rights and freedoms. Unsurprisingly, commentators have highlighted these inconsistencies. *Sahin* has been criticized by Pedain, who has declared that 'the Court was certainly right to tread carefully in relation to this sensitive issue, and to leave it to the Member States to find a compromise which is acceptable to their communities. But one would have wished for a less ringing endorsement of the policy choices of the Republic of Turkey in this regard: whatever the reasons for the rise of Islamic fundamentalism in that country, one must be allowed to question whether Turkey's particular brand of militant secularism is really the best way to ensure freedom and democracy' (Pedain 2004: 540) and also by Gibson: 'it is questionable whether the Court, or indeed the Convention, is adequate to the task of securing respect for minority traditions in a multicultural Europe' (Gibson 2007: 696). This concern, however, has not led Gibson to question the relevance of the Court at this stage. On the contrary, in his view 'a strong Court is needed more than ever. With the trend in European society moving towards increasingly diverse societies, the need for effective and fair principles by which to navigate the appropriate course between individual and community interests is becoming correspondingly more pertinent. Individual rights should smooth the rough majoritarian edges (or excesses) of democracy' (2007: 695–696).

Nevertheless, in this dichotomy between universalism (enhancement of uniformity throughout the current 47 members of the Council of Europe) and subsidiarity (emphasis on the respect for the legitimate differences), the European Court of Human Rights has allegedly chosen the latter over the former. An analysis of the previous cases (*Ahmad*, *Kalac* and *Sahin*) illustrates the overall respect which is shown by the Court to the specific traditions and socio-legal cultures of Member States.

By way of the margin of appreciation the Court is prepared to allow Member States a degree of flexibility, which one Italian commentator, Susanna Mancini (2010: 6–27), has regarded as excessive deference. One of the most widely publicized judicial controversies in the last few decades has been the *Lautsi* litigation. This began when Ms Soile Lautsi, a Finnish-born Italian national, claimed that the presence of crucifixes on the walls of the classrooms in the Italian State school where her children were being educated was contrary to the principle of secularism as recognized by the Italian Constitution. In the course of the domestic proceedings the Administrative Court declared that 'the crucifix was both the symbol of Italian history and culture, and consequently of Italian identity, and the manifestation of the principles of equality, liberty and tolerance, as well as of State's secularism'.[7] Furthermore, a year later the *Consiglio di Stato* dismissed Ms Lautsi's appeal on the ground that the cross had become one of the secular values of the Italian Constitution and represented the values of civil life.[8]

---

7 Administrative Court, 17 March 2005.

8 *Consiglio di Stato*, 13 February 2006.

It is at least arguable that the Court of Strasbourg has been inclined to protect the rights of the majority at the expense of the position of the minorities and this approach led Prof. Mancini to welcome the judgment at first instance in *Lautsi*[9] on the legality of crucifixes in the classrooms of Italian state schools: 'the novelty of *Lautsi* is being able to go beyond the traditional deference towards the States' approaches to religious freedom. If this is confirmed in future judicial pronouncements, the rights of religious and ideological minorities will be taken seriously at last, despite the fact that this will require a new formulation of traditional national values' (see Mancini 2010: 6) but, as we now know, Mancini's rejoicing was premature.

At first instance the Strasbourg Court showed its disagreement with the compulsory presence of crucifixes in Italian State classrooms as they are impossible not to notice.[10] 'The Court considers that the compulsory display of a symbol of a particular faith in the exercise of public authority in relation to specific situations subject to governmental supervision, particularly in classrooms, restricts the right of parents to educate their children in conformity with their convictions and the right of schoolchildren to believe or not believe. It is of the opinion that the practice infringes those rights because the restrictions are incompatible with the State's duty to respect neutrality in the exercise of public authority, particularly in the field of education'.[11] Furthermore, it rejected the suggestion that the crucifix, a Catholic-Christian symbol, can 'serve the educational pluralism which is essential for the preservation of a "democratic society", as conceived by the Convention'.[12]

On appeal to the Grand Chamber,[13] however, that decision was reversed by 15 votes to two (Maliverni and Kalaydjieva JJ dissenting). The Grand Chamber did not accept Italy's contention that the obligation under Art 2 of Protocol No. 1 to 'respect the right of parents to ensure ... education and teaching in conformity with their own religious and philosophical convictions' related solely to the school curriculum and that the question of crucifixes in State-school classrooms was outside its scope. That Article bound signatories 'in the exercise' of all the 'functions' which they assumed in relation to education and teaching. Nevertheless, 'the Court concludes in the present case that the decision whether crucifixes should be present in State-school classrooms is, in principle, a matter falling within the margin of appreciation of the respondent State'.[14] Although the crucifix was above other meanings a religious symbol, the Grand Chamber found no evidence that 'the display of such a symbol might have an influence on pupils'.[15] It was rather

9 *Lautsi* v. *Italy*, application no. 30814/06, paragraph 54.
10 *Lautsi* v. *Italy*, application no. 30814/06, paragraph 54.
11 Paragraph 57.
12 Paragraph 56.
13 Case of *Lautsi and others* v. *Italy*, Grand Chamber, Application no. 30814/06.
14 Paragraph 70.
15 Paragraph 72.

a 'passive symbol' as opposed to active teaching on a certain religion or forced participation of students in religious activities.[16]

The decisions in *Sahin* and *Lautsi* are blatant examples of the Court of Strasbourg's commitment to avoid undue interference in national matters and the doctrine of margin of appreciation has been enhanced. Even though this may give rise to legitimate concerns about the respect for minorities' rights in Europe, a uniform response to religious symbols would not be desirable. Despite the weaknesses of the doctrine of margin of appreciation, it is an inevitable price to pay for the maintenance of a healthy plurality of the European continent.

Religious Symbols in the United Kingdom

In the course of the last 15 years the United Kingdom has gone through a transformation in so far as the protection of religious freedom is concerned. Traditionally, religious freedom was regarded as a negative right and individuals only enjoyed those liberties which were not restricted by public authorities. This situation has been significantly different since the enactment, in 1998, of the Human Rights Act. The Act made most of the provisions of the European Convention on Human Rights justiciable in domestic courts and religious freedom was duly acknowledged as a positive right. The effect of the Act is that the individual, rather than the State, has become the centre of the new legal framework or order.[17] Sandberg has highlighted that the historical religion law of the United Kingdom sought to protect Christianity in general (and the Church of England in particular), while providing other faiths with an increasing degree of tolerance: 'the new religion law, by contrast, is facilitative, seeking to protect religious freedom mainly as an individual right which needs to be balanced against other rights. No special protection is afforded to any one religion and protection is afforded to non-religious beliefs. The new legal framework affords utmost importance to the concept of religious neutrality as the State takes on the role of facilitating the religious market place' (Sandberg 2010: 361).

As the same author mentions (2010: 361), this new religion law comprises, amongst others, the Human Rights Act 1998, the recognition of religiously-aggravated offences, charities and equality law and this plethora of legislation has given rise to a significant increase of case law. This combination of legislation and case law must necessarily be taken into account when the United Kingdom's response to religious symbols is studied. Furthermore, the sociological religious make-up of the United Kingdom (see García Oliva 2004: 8–26) plays a key role. The 2001 census[18] shows that the UK is one of the most pluralistic societies in

16 Paragraph 72.

17 For further analysis of the historical development of religious freedom in the United Kingdom, see García Oliva (2008b).

18 The findings of the 2011 census have not been released yet.

Europe. The census did not include any breakdown within Christianity, but 71% of citizens in England and Wales regarded themselves as 'Christians'. In 2001 Muslims were already an important minority, representing almost 3% of the population in those two nations. However, their presence in England and Wales is far from evenly-spread and Knights has highlighted that 'the significance of the numbers of adherents to minority religions becomes even greater when looked at by region or city within a country. For example, 75% of the Muslims in the United Kingdom live in 24 cities or local authorities, including around 38% of the total in London. Within these cities and local authorities, the Muslim population may be highly concentrated in specific areas – a quarter of London's Muslims, for example, live in the London Boroughs of Tower Hamlets and Newham, where they make up 36 and 24 per cent of the Borough's residents respectively' (Knights 2005: 501–502). The importance of the Muslim community in the UK has been deliberately stressed, as many of the cases which will be analysed deal with this religious community.

Finally, the 2001 census figures show that the Muslims are followed in descending order of size by the Hindu, Sikh, Jewish and Buddhist communities. Interestingly, those people who declared that they did not have any religion were the second largest group altogether, representing approximately 15% of the population in England and Wales. All these data will be helpful in order to understand the responses of our judiciary in the various cases concerning religious symbols in public establishments.

Even though the British response to the presence of religious symbols does not emanate from Parliament but instead from the judiciary, the significance of the legislature should not be underestimated. In fact, the Human Rights Act plays a key role, because the judges clearly rely on this Act in their decisions. Nevertheless, there is no primary legislation in any of the three UK jurisdictions[19] concerning religious symbols (see Sherlock and Williams 2005: 214–215). In England and Wales the secondary legislation[20] empowers governing bodies to decide whether or not there should be a school uniform and other rules relating to appearance, and if so, what the dress code should be. Interestingly, although most cases have dealt with Islamic garments, there have also been important decisions concerning religious symbols of other faiths, such as Sikhism and Christianity. The English way of dealing with the conflict between religious symbols and school rules was somehow played down by commentators: 'In England, despite a recent High Court case, the issue is usually seen as one which raises no more fundamental questions than the violation of school uniform rules, and can be resolved by reaching

19 England and Wales; Scotland and Northern Ireland. However, due to the process of devolution of powers in Wales (Government of Wales Act 1998 and 2006) in the last few years there is an *emerging* – albeit embryonic – Welsh law that is becoming slightly different from its English counterpart in some particular fields.

20 See *DCSF Guidance to Schools on School Uniform Related Policies*, published by the Department for Children, Schools and Families in October 2007.

appropriate compromise solutions at an individual institutional level' (Pedain 2004: 538). Similarly, in Scotland the matter is left to individual schools. The Scottish Executive's Discipline Task Group recommended in 2001 that 'schools should consult with pupils, teachers and parents/carers in order to agree a dress code for children and young people. Local authorities should support schools in the implementation of their agreed dress codes' (Scottish Executive 2001). Riddell noted in the 2009 survey of religious education in Scottish schools that at one primary school which included a number of Muslim children, 'a meeting was held with parents to agree on the colour of the head scarf which girls would wear as part of their school uniform' (Riddell et al. 2009).

A landmark case, which unexpectedly became the focus of media attention, concerned a teenage student called Shabina Begum.[21] Denbigh High School[22] refused her permission to wear the long *jilbab* coat but offered her alternative uniform options of trousers, knee-length skirt or a *shalwar kameez*. The school had been accommodating and had held thorough conversations with the representatives of the Islamic community in the area about the appropriate religious garments of female Muslim students. Furthermore, Shabina Begum had voluntarily accepted the school's uniform policy in the first instance and only at a later stage had rejected it. On 13 February 2004, Shabina issued a claim for judicial review arguing that the decisions to prevent her from wearing the jilbab and to exclude her until she was prepared to dress in accordance with the School's uniform policy were contrary to her human rights.

The Administrative Court considered that Art. 9 was not engaged at all. Indeed Bennett J stated as follows: 'Although her refusal [to respect the school uniform policy] was motivated by religious beliefs, she was excluded for her refusal to abide by the school uniform policy rather than her religious belief as such'.[23]

At a later stage the Court of Appeal disagreed with Bennett J's decision. This judicial body declared that Shabina's rights had been involved (therefore Art. 9.1 was engaged) and that there was no justification under Art. 9.2 for such limitation. Brooke LJ expressed his views in the following terms: 'Shabina Begum's freedom to manifest her religion or beliefs may only be subject to limitations that are prescribed by law and are necessary in a democratic society in the interests of public safety, for the protection of public morals, or for the protection of the rights and freedoms of others. There was no suggestion that the protection of public morals had any relevance, and a justification on health and safety grounds was dismissed by the judge and not resurrected on the appeal, once evidence had showed that other schools (including the local school which the claimant now attends) had been able to accommodate girls wearing the jilbab without any serious concern

21 See *R (on the application of)* v. *Denbigh High School* [2006] UKHL 15 (22 March 2006).

22 For a very detailed analysis of this saga, see Le Sueur et al. (2010: 812–824).

23 *R (Begum)* v. *The Headteacher and Governors of Denbigh High School* [2004] EWHC 1389 (Admin) at [74].

being raised on that ground'.[24] Consequently, Brooke LJ stated that the onus lay on the school to justify its interference with the Convention rights.

Commentators have expressed their disagreement with this decision. Eloquently, Poole declared that 'proportionality is a test to be applied by the court when reviewing decisions of public authorities after they have been made (*ex post*). It is not a test which ought to mean that public authorities should themselves adopt a proportionality approach to the structuring of their decision-making *ex ante.* There is nothing in the Human Rights Act, the European Convention or Convention jurisprudence which would seem to require public authorities to act in this way' (Poole 2005: 690). Furthermore, on completely different grounds, this decision has been criticized for endorsing a particular vision of Islam and for not making a 'substantive assessment as to whether every form of religious expression in schools should be protected as an exercise of human rights' (Thio 2005: 576). Other commentators (Mazher Idriss 2006: 60) have considered that this decision 'demonstrates the conflict between Western norms (and values) and Islamic ideology in present times' and have regarded it as a source of reflection about the position of religious minorities, particularly Islam in twenty-first century Europe.

This decision was appealed by Denbigh High School before the House of Lords.[25] The House of Lords disagreed with the Court of Appeal's decision and reinstated the decision of Bennett J. Although the five judges reached the same conclusion, there were important differences in relation to whether Art. 9 had been engaged. Three out of five – Lord Bingham, Lord Hoffman and Lord Scott – considered that the decision of the school had not breached Shabina's rights either under Article 2 of the First Protocol ECHR (education) or under Article 9 (thought, conscience and religion): moreover, if there *had* been interference under Article 9, it would have been justified because it had the legitimate aim of protecting the rights and freedoms of others and was necessary in a democratic society. Lord Bingham even referred to the 'specific situation' rule and applied it to school pupils, in the same way the Court of Strasbourg had used it with university students. Having said that, the differences between university and school students are striking and such a comparison is bound to be problematic. Only two judges – Lord Nicholls and Baroness Hale – disagreed with the reasoning employed by their fellow Law Lords, considering that the requirement of a specific uniform was a limitation to freedom of religion, however necessary, under Art. 9.2 of the Convention.

The decision of the House of Lords has been criticized by Hill and Sandberg (2007: 495–497) who have contended that instead of avoiding the issue altogether by arguing that the school board's decision had nothing to do with religion, their Lordships should have squarely addressed the straightforward issue of whether or not, under Article 9, the school's actions were justified as a reasonable limitation

24 *Begum* v. *Denbigh High School* [2005] EWCA Civ 199; [2005] 1 W.L.R. 3372.

25 Since October 2009, and in compliance with the provisions of the *Constitutional Reform Act* 2005, the Supreme Court has replaced the Appellate Committee of the House of Lords and the latter has now become a purely legislative Chamber.

imposed for 'public order'. In a more recent publication Sandberg has made a key distinction between justification and interference: 'The preferable approach in *Begum* is that of Lord Nicholls and Lady Hale, who, although concurring with the ultimate disposal of the appeal, differed from the other three Law Lords in that they dealt with the appeal on the question of justification rather than the question of interference. They recognized that Article 9 had been engaged, but that the interference was justified under Article 9(2). Although their speeches did not explain why their approach was the consistent interpretation of the Strasbourg jurisprudence, their treatment of Article 9(2), together with the *obiter* treatment of Article 9(2) made by the majority, showed how the same decision could have been reached in a more satisfactory way by focusing on the question of justification rather than that of interference' (Sandberg 2011: 92). This reasoning is very persuasive because claiming persistently that Article 9 is not involved due to the specific situation rule and the existence of alternative possibilities for the claimant means, in practical terms, that Article 9 rights receive little protection, since in the overwhelming majority of occasions it would be very difficult to argue that 'there was no alternative'.

Moreover, the significant difference between interference and justification has been discussed by other commentators: 'the "interference" filter favours the respondent. First, it does so because the respondent avoids the burden of proving any "justification". Secondly, because having to assess whether an interference is proportionate (in terms of both scope and effect) is a more exacting, multi-faceted exercise than the single question of whether there has been interference. A proportionality assessment not only contributes to the task facing the respondent, but also requires more detailed analysis by the court' (Gibson: 662–663).

Despite the fact that the five Law Lords in the *Shabina Begum* case reached the same conclusion, the difference in their reasoning is far from insignificant in terms of protection of religious feelings, a commendable and indispensable aim of our democracies. Regarding the use of religious dress and symbols as a manifestation of religion is a much more persuasive stance. Obviously, on some occasions this manifestation must be limited for the sake of the rights of others and other justifiable circumstances, but the reason why those conflicts arise in the first place is a religious one and its denial is unhelpful.

Unfortunately, *Begum's curse* (Sandberg 2011: 198) has had an impact on subsequent decisions of lower courts. A similar case concerning a Muslim female student involved a 12-year-old Muslim girl who was refused permission to wear a *niqab* veil covering her entire face, save her eyes, while she was being taught by male teachers. The Court stated that the student had not suffered an interference with her rights under Article 9 ECHR (thought, conscience and religion)[26] and,

26 Silber J stated that there would be no interference either where a person has voluntarily accepted an employment or role that does not accommodate that practice or observance or where there are other means open to practise or observe that religion without undue hardship or inconvenience.

in any case, that such interference would have been justified under Article 9(2). Furthermore, it emphasized that there was nothing wrong with the procedure adopted by the school (the head teacher having carefully considered whether or not the claimant should be allowed to wear the *niqab*): the rule was necessary in a democratic society for the protection of the rights of others and any interference would have been proportionate.[27]

The following two cases (*Azmi* and *Noah*) show the importance of this 'interference/justification' distinction. On both occasions the courts have looked at justification rather than interference and the result has been more nuanced and sophisticated. There is therefore room for optimism. These two cases involved Muslim citizens. In *Azmi*[28] it was decided that a bilingual support worker at a Church of England school, dismissed for insisting on wearing the *niqab* veil, had not been directly discriminated against on grounds of religion or belief contrary to the Employment Equality (Religion or Belief) Regulations 2003 (SI 2003/1660). The Employment Appeal Tribunal considered that she had not proved that she had suffered less favourable treatment than others in circumstances which were materially the same: though the school's 'no face veil when teaching rule' constituted *indirect* discrimination in that it put both Muslims in general and the claimant in particular at a disadvantage, it was justified as a proportionate means of achieving the legitimate aim of children being taught properly. It is very difficult to challenge the contention that the process of communicating with students goes beyond the mere transmission of words; and although the use of the *niqab* is, undoubtedly, a manifestation of her religious freedom, its limitation can be justified for the sake of the learning process of the students.

Outside the school context, the use of Islamic religious dress has also reached the courts. In *Noah* v. *Sarah Desrosiers (t/a Wedge)*,[29] the Employment Tribunal considered that a Muslim hairdresser suffered unjustifiable indirect discrimination when her job interview with a hairdressing salon was terminated because she was wearing the headscarf. In fact she was informed that such a piece of clothing was not in compliance with the 'ultra modern' hairstyle policy of the company. Although the Tribunal declared that it was legitimate for the company to take the future of its business into consideration, it found for Ms Noah, on the grounds that too much weight had been given to that concern and awarded her £4,000 for injury to her feelings.

Though most recent 'religious symbols' cases have involved Muslim students, their use in British schools has also been raised in relation to Christianity and

27 See *R (on the application of X)* v. *Y school & Ors* [2007] EWHC 298 (Admin) (21 February 2007).

28 See *Azmi* v. *Kirklees Metropolitan Council* [2007] UKEAT 0009 07 30003 (30 March 2007).

29 [2008] ET Case Number: 2201867/07 (29 May 2008).

Sikhism. In *Playfoot*[30] *a devout member of a Christian group failed* to overturn the decision by the defendant school to prevent her from wearing a 'purity' ring (expressing a commitment to premarital chastity) at school because she was under no obligation, by reason of her faith, to wear the ring; and even if Art. 9 ECHR had been engaged, there would have been no breach since she had voluntarily accepted the school's uniform policy and there were other means open to her to practise her belief without undue hardship or inconvenience. Cranmer (Cranmer, forthcoming) suggests that what does not seem to have been considered was whether or not a belief in premarital chastity might *itself* have represented a philosophical belief (rather than a religious one) that met the *Campbell and Cosans*[31] test of 'a certain level of cogency, seriousness, cohesion and importance'[32] and was therefore worthy of protection under Art. 9 of the European Convention. Had the court come to *that* conclusion, it would then have had to decide whether or not the 'purity ring' was a manifestation intimately linked with Ms Playfoot's 'philosophical' belief in premarital celibacy rather than with her religious convictions.

As previously noted, the insistence on the non-interference with Article 9 – because the claimant had voluntarily accepted the school's uniform policy and there were other means open to her to practise her belief without undue hardship or inconvenience – has become a recurring (and it is suggested unfortunate) theme in the decisions of United Kingdom courts. In addition to this worrying tendency, *Playfoot* shows that some members of our judiciary regard themselves qualified to state whether or not the Christian faith requires some manifestations of religion and not others. In other words, it seems to be the case that judges in the UK – despite their protestations to the contrary – make judgments about religious manifestation in relation to doctrine. Although this is, of course, somehow understandable, as the majority of UK judges come from a Christian tradition and are more familiar with the values, practices and doctrine of that faith, it is nevertheless dangerous and a cause of concern: who are the secular authorities to state what Christians are expected or bound to wear in conformity with their beliefs?

Our concern about the lack of judicial understanding of Christianity would never justify the statement by the former Archbishop of Canterbury, Lord Carey of Clifton, in which he sought to lend his support to Gary McFarlane for his appeal to be heard by a specially constituted Court of Appeal comprising five Lords who had 'a proven sensitivity to religious issues'.[33] This is an inappropriate request and Hill's views about the bewildering nature of the former Archbishop's speech, which should inevitably – and rightly – lead to an outright rejection by the judiciary (Hill

30 See *R (on the application of Playfoot (a child)* v. *Millais School Governing Body* [2007] EWCH Admin 1698 (16 July 2007).

31 *Campbell and Cosans* v. *United Kingdom* (1982) 4 EHRR 293 Series A No. 48.

32 Ibid., paragraph 36.

33 *Macfarlane* v. *Relate Avon Limited* [2010] EWCA Civ B1 at para. 17. Mr Macfarlane claimed that he had been discriminated against for refusing, on religious grounds, to provide psycho-sexual therapy to same-sex couples.

2010: 265) could not be sounder. As Sandberg correctly points out, 'Lord Carey's call was particularly ironic given that Lord Carey was one of the most vocal critics of his successor's lecture in which Dr Rowan Williams suggested tentatively that more use could be made of religious courts. The nuance found in Dr William's lecture was clearly absent in Lord Carey's witness statement' (Sandberg 2011: 370).

A similar stance to *Playfoot* was taken in *Eweida* v. *British Airways*,[34] another widely publicized case, concerning an air hostess who was prohibited from wearing a silver cross because it was regarded as a breach of British Airways' uniform policy. The Court of Appeal declared that the claimant was not required by her religion to wear the cross.[35] All these cases seem to show, at worst, a lack of respect for the Christian faith or, at best, a careless consideration of its values, principles and doctrine. In *Eweida* Sedley LJ had even added a reason why religion and belief are different from other grounds: 'out of all of the other grounds of equality, religion and belief alone are matter of choice'.[36] Understandably, Vickers has respectfully disagreed with this statement and has declared that on many occasions the possibility to choose one's religion is clearly limited. In the same piece the author has declared that a hierarchy between discrimination grounds (particularly sexual orientation and religion and belief) seems to be emerging and, in her view, secular courts should be more sensitive towards religion, but certainly not going as far as a separate court structure (see Vickers 2010: 301–303). Vicker's stance is to be commended.

More recently this unfortunate secular 'temptation' to state whether or not Christianity requires a certain behaviour or a manifestation of dress or symbols has been repeated in *Chaplin* v. *Royal Devon & Exeter NHS Foundation Trust*.[37] This case referred to a nurse who wished to wear a crucifix and, although this had not been an isolated case as a colleague of hers had previously been in a similar situation, the judge declared that the views of the former were not so strong to lead her to refuse to comply with that policy.[38] Ms Chaplin, a member of the Free Church of England, was not at all helped by the evidence provided by the minister of her own congregation who stated that wearing a crucifix was not part of their Church's practice.

In terms of the right to manifest under Art. 9, it is difficult at first sight to reconcile the decisions in *Begum* and *R (on the application of X)* v. *Y School* with

---

34 [2010] EWCA Civ 80.

35 See Vickers (2010: 295). In *Ladele* v. *Islington Borough Council* [2009] EWCA Civ 1357, a case concerning a registrar that refused to conduct civil partnerships on religious grounds, the Court of Appeal stated that Ladele's beliefs about marriage and sexuality were not core to her Christian beliefs.

36 *Eweida* v. *British Airways* [2010] EWCA Civ 89 at para. 40.

37 [2010] ET Case Number: 17288862009 (6 April 2010).

38 Ibid., paragraph 27.

that in *Watkins-Singh*.[39] In this case refusal by a school to allow a Sikh girl to wear a bangle, on the grounds that it was contrary to its school uniform policy, was considered indirect unjustified race and religious discrimination, contrary to the Race Relations Act 1976 (as amended to give effect to Council Directive 2000/43EC) and the Equality Act 2006. Mr Justice Silber declared that the use of the bangle was an important element of Sikhism and the views of Ms Watkins-Singh were also shared by other faithful of that community (Howard 2009: 23). Therefore, they needed protection.

Although both cases are different from each other and *Watkins-Singh* is exceptional, because of the race element, they show that under the current circumstances litigants are more likely to be successful if they rely on discrimination law claims rather than on the protection of Art. 9 of the European Convention on Human Rights, at least as far the wearing of religious dress and symbols is concerned (see Sandberg 2011: 110). The truth is that the protective scope of Art. 9 has been unduly restricted and the decisions of the courts rely excessively on numerical issues, such as how many individuals profess a certain faith. Furthermore, although there is a commendable and praiseworthy attempt on the part of our judges to protect religious minorities who felt particularly left out in the past, this should never be done at the expense of the majority denomination.

However, members of minority denominations, such as Rastafarians, have failed to prove indirect discrimination on the question of interference rather than justification. In *Harris* v. *NKL Automotive Ltd and another*,[40] a Rastafarian driver was prevented from achieving a full-time position on the grounds of his untidy hair. Both the Employment Tribunal and the Employment Appeal Tribunal declared that there had been no discrimination, but at the same time emphasized that even if discrimination had happened, it would have been justifiable, as it was crucial for the successful management of a company to have employees with a presentable appearance.

More recently, in *G* v. *St Gregory's Catholic Science College*[41] it was held that a claimant of African-Caribbean ethnicity who had not cut his hair since birth and, in accordance with family tradition, had kept it in 'cornrows' or braids and who, as a consequence, was not allowed to take up his place at the school, had suffered unjustified indirect racial discrimination contrary to s. 71 of the Race Relations Act 1976.

The importance of *G* for the present discussion is this. It was submitted on behalf of the school that the boy's evidence 'does not meet the test which … following observations of Silber J in *Watkins-Singh*, requires that the wearing of cornrows is for him a matter of exceptional importance'.[42] The reference was

39 See *Watkins-Singh, R (on the application of)* v. *Governing Body of Aberdare Girls' High School & Anor* [2008] EWHC (Admin) 1865 (29 July 2008).

40 [2007] UKEAT/0134/07/DM; 2007 WL 2817981 (3 October 2007).

41 [2011] EWCH 1452 (Admin) (17 June 2010).

42 Per Collins J at paragraph 28.

to the passage in *Watkins-Singh* to the effect that there would be a particular disadvantage or detriment if a pupil was forbidden from wearing an item when 'that person genuinely believed for reasonable grounds that wearing this item was a matter of exceptional importance to his or her racial identity or his or her religious belief'.[43] Collins J concluded that 'with the greatest respect to Silber J, it may be that the need to show exceptional importance puts the threshold too high'.[44] Has that lowered the threshold set in *Watkins-Singh*? And if it has, how might a case on similar facts to *Begum* now be decided? Would the decisions of the courts be different if cases were argued on discrimination rather than human rights grounds?

Conclusion

The presence of religious symbols in public establishments, particularly schools, is one of the most fascinating debates which Europe currently faces. It has been the outcome of the inevitable tensions between the mainstream society and new religious minorities (e.g. Islam). Nowadays there is no completely homogeneous State in the European Union, if this ever was the case.

Although there are different ways to deal with this new emerging plurality in Europe, the United Kingdom's heterogeneous make-up and its moderate and accommodating response could become a pattern for other European countries. Despite the fact that some inconsistencies in the decisions of British courts have been identified, the judiciary should be praised, generally speaking, for attempting to recognize – and even celebrate – cultural and religious diversity within the United Kingdom. Arguably, the price to pay is the presence of contradictory statements amongst some of the members of the judiciary, as well as some worrying and regrettable attempts on their part to decide on purely doctrinal matters. However, if the alternative is a homogeneous and inflexible piece of law – as enacted in France in 2010 – the British shortcomings are all worth it.

Solutions to these inevitable tensions must be the outcome of a fruitful and everlasting dialogue between public authorities and religious communities, on the one hand, and the majority Christian denomination (including all its branches) and other minorities, as well as atheists and agnostics, on the other. The United Kingdom has two official faiths, but the significant development which religious freedom has experienced in these jurisdictions is far more important than the mainly symbolic confessional nature of the State. Religious freedom must be a protective umbrella for believers, atheists and agnostics. Many citizens happen also to be members of religious communities and this duality continues to justify a healthy collaboration between secular and religious authorities. The debate about religious symbols in Europe has just started and it is bound to continue for decades.

43 *Watkins-Singh*, per Silber J at paragraph 56.

44 At paragraph 56.

References

Bacquet, S. (2009), 'Manifestation of Belief and Religious Symbols at School: Setting Boundaries in English Courts', *Religion and Human Rights*, 4, 121–135.

Cañamares, S. (2009), 'Religious Symbols in Spain: A Legal Perspective', *Ecclesiastical Law Journal*, 11:2, 181–193.

Castro, A. (2004), 'Inmigración, Pluralismo Religioso-Cultural y Educación: la utilización de signos de identidad en la escuela', *Osservatorio delle Libertà ed Istituzioni Religiose*, www.olir.it (accessed 30 January 2012).

Cranmer, F. (2012), 'Beating People is Wrong: *Campbell and Cosans*, *Williamson* and their Aftermath', in Hunter-Henin, M. (ed.), *Law, Religious Freedoms and Education in Europe* (Aldershot: Ashgate), 283–306.

Evans, M.D. (2009), *Manual on the Wearing of Religious Symbols in Public Arenas* (Leiden/Boston: Council of Europe).

García Oliva, J. (2004), 'Sociology, Law and Religion in the United Kingdom', *Law and Justice*, 152, 8–26.

García Oliva, J. (2008a), 'Public Authorities and Religious Denominations in Italy and Spain', in Morris, R. (ed.), 41–50.

García Oliva, J. (2008b), 'Religious Symbols in the Classroom: A Controversial Issue in the United Kingdom', *Brigham Young University Law Review*, 3, 880–883.

García Oliva, J. (2010), 'Church, State and Establishment in the United Kingdom in the 21st Century: Anachronism or Idiosyncrasy', *Public Law*, 482–504.

Gibson, N. (2007), 'Faith in the Courts: Religious Dress and Human Rights', *Cambridge Law Journal*, 66:3, 657–697.

Hill, M. (2010), 'Editorial', *Ecclesiastical Law Journal*, 12, 1–2.

Hill, M. and Sandberg, R. (2007), 'Is Nothing Sacred? Clashing Symbols in a Secular World', *Public Law*, 495–497.

Howard, E. (2009), 'School Bans on the Wearing of Religious Symbols: Examining the Implications of Recent Case Law from the UK', *Religion and Human Rights*, 4:1, 7–24.

Hunter-Henin, M. (ed.) (2012), *Law, Religious Freedoms and Education in Europe* (Aldershot: Ashgate).

Knights, S. (2005), 'Religious Symbols in the School: Freedom of Religion, Minorities and Education', *European Human Rights Law Review*, 5, 499–516.

Le Sueur, A., Sunkin, M. and Krushal Murkens, J.E. (2010), *Public Law: Text, Cases and Materials* (Oxford: Oxford University Press).

Mancini, S. (2010), 'The Crucifix Rage: Supranational Constitutionalism Bumps Against the Counter-Majoritarian Difficulty', *European Constitutional Law Review*, 6, 6 27.

Mazher Idriss, M. (2006), 'Dress Codes, the Right to Manifest Religion and the Human Rights Act 1998: The Defeat of Shabina Begum in the House of Lords', *Coventry Law Journal*, 58–76.

McGoldrick, D. (2006), *Human Rights and Religion – The Islamic Headscarf Debate in Europe* (Oxford and Portland: Hart Publishing).

Morris, R. (ed.) (2008), *Church and State: Some Reflections on Church Establishment in England* (The Constitution Unit: University College London).

Pedain, A. (2004), 'Do Scarfs Bite?', *Cambridge Law Journal*, 63:3, 537–540.

Poole, T. (2005), 'Of Headscarves and Heresies: The Denbigh High School Case and Public Authority Decision-making under the Human Rights Act', *Public Law*, 685–695.

Riddell, S., Ahlgren, L., McCluskey, G. and Weedon, E. (2009), *Religious Education in a Multicultural Society: Scotland National Report* (University of Edinburgh: Centre for Research in Education Inclusion and Diversity).

Robbers, G. (2005), *State and Church in the European Union*, 2nd edn (Baden-Baden: Nomos).

Sandberg, R. (2010), 'Laws and Religion: Unravelling Mc Farlane v Relate Avon Limited', *Ecclesiastical Law Journal*, 12:3, 361–370.

Sandberg, R. (2011), *Law and Religion* (Cambridge: Cambridge University Press).

Scottish Executive, *Better Behaviour – Better Learning: Report of the Discipline Task Group* (Edinburgh: 19 June 2001).

Sherlock, A. and Williams, K. (2005), 'Islamic Dress, Institutions of Education and Freedom of Religion under the ECHR: A UK Perspective', *Wales Journal of Law and Policy*, 4:2, 214–230.

Taylor, C. (1994), *Multiculturalism; Examining the Politics of Recognition* (Princeton: Princeton University Press).

Thio, L.A. (2005), 'School Dress Codes, Religious Freedom and Human Rights', *Law Quarterly Review*, 121, 572–576.

Vickers, L. (2010), 'Religious Discrimination in the Workplace: An Emerging Hierarchy?', *Ecclesiastical Law Journal*, 12:3, 280–303.

Chapter 12
Religious Dress Codes: The Italian Case[1]

Sabrina Pastorelli

The Italian Landscape: Immigration and Religious Pluralization

Religious diversity has been constantly growing since the Second World War, combining different religious traditions from the East and the Americas. As a consequence of globalization – which is not only an economic phenomenon but also a symbolic movement – cultural and religious borders seem to be disappearing, painting a picture of a pluralized religious and cultural Europe. Faced with the pluralization of the religious belongings, European States have to deal with different religions not only from Christian traditions but also – thanks to immigration – Muslims, Hindus, Sikhs and Buddhists as well as new religious movements (Wilson 2000).

Within the European landscape, Italy shows a peculiar form of pluralism, the one of a Christian Catholic country facing growing religious pluralization from a cultural background recalling the 'popular religion'. Italians still think of themselves as Catholics, but they seem to increasingly understand their belonging in different ways to the large substrate of a *diffused religion* displayed in different sectors of Italian society and going beyond aspects of religion/faith (Cipriani 1988, 1993; Pace 2007). The peculiarity of Italian society is that it is a society where citizens still declare themselves as Catholics (87% of the population), while nevertheless practising a *do it yourself religion*: Italians have a pragmatic attitude towards issues such as divorce, abortion and contraception that are largely accepted by Italian Catholics even though they are condemned by the Catholic Church (Ricceri 2006).[2]

Italian religious pluralism is mainly the result of immigration flows. Immigration has increased 20 times in the last 20 years, up to five million immigrants – around one immigrant for every 12 residents. Italy increasingly appears as a multicultural country: more than 250,000 mixed marriages; more than 570,000 foreigners born in Italy; approximately 100,000 births by immigrant

1 This research is the result of the activity performed as postdoctoral research fellow within the RELIGARE project, funded by the EU Commission's Seventh Framework Programme: www.religareproject.eu. I would like to thank Professor Silvio Ferrari for his comments and suggestions on the first draft of this chapter. I would also like to acknowledge Cristiana Cianitto for clarifying some questions about the Sikhs.

2 On the Italian pluralism see more generally: Garelli, Guizzardi, Pace 2003.

mothers; more than 110,000 newcomers for family reasons (Caritas-Migrantes 2010).

Around half of the immigrant population come from Europe and the rest mainly from Africa and Asia (respectively 22% and 16%), with lower percentages from America and Oceania. For the most part, the Northern and Central regions host this population but 13% is also present in the South of Italy.

Half of the growing religious pluralization of the Italian context is due to Christian Orthodox immigrants – from Eastern European countries – with one-third of Muslims and 5% for other oriental religions.

The estimated Muslim presence is of over one million people that represent the second religion of the country. This population 'is made visible by newspapers' but also thanks to the growing number of places of worship (around 661 mosques on Italian territory) (Caritas-Migrantes 2007: 13; Allievi 2009: 23).[3]

Concerning the Indian population, it is estimated at about 47,000 individuals (2% of the immigrant population) and a considerable part of them are of the Sikh religion, although this figure is not easily measurable (Denti et al. 2005a): Italy has the second biggest Sikh population in Europe after the United Kingdom.

Religious Dress between the Media and the Courts

Italian contemporary society, like other European countries faced with increasing religious diversity, needs to regulate and/or accommodate the plurality of religious belongings on the basis of its historical tradition while taking into account some relatively new religious symbols and dress codes. Indeed, in recent times there have been heated debates at the EU level about the wearing of religious symbols in the public space. According to M. Evans, even though there is no universal legal definition of religious symbol, what is important is to focus on what is realized/understood as a religious symbol and this depends on the context and consequently on time and space (Evans 2009, 2010). In recent years, the wearing of a religious symbol such as dress, turban, *kirpan* or crucifix has attracted the attention of the media and public opinion, within a general reflexion on the visibility of religion, or new religions, in the public space of EU countries. While some of them try to regulate and limit in different ways the wearing of certain religious symbols (for example France or Belgium), others prefer not to enact a specific regulation in this domain (for instance the UK), with public policies varying from banning to accommodating attitudes.

In the Italian system, the right to wear religious dress is protected by articles 8, 19 and 21 of the Constitution. Any religious community can provide indications to its followers as regards dress codes and the individual is granted the freedom to profess freely his or her own religious faith, in private or in public (Manco 2006). The limitations to the right to wear religious dress are connected to those of the

3 On Islam in Italy, see also Allievi 2008; A. Ferrari 2008.

freedom of religion, 'in the interests of public safety, for the protection of public order, health or morals, or for the protection of the rights and freedoms of others'.[4] Thus, the freedom to wear any religious oriented dress code is only limited by the exigencies of public order and the freedom of individual self-determination that is the freedom from external conditionings, by the community or the family (Colaianni 2006a).

For the purposes of this discussion, the chapter shall distinguish *media cases* from *court cases*[5] – concerning Muslims and Sikhs – which deal with religious dress codes in the common, political and institutional public spaces.[6] The main purpose is to verify what the issues are concerning dress codes in the Italian context through the analysis of some court cases. However, considering that not all controversies arrive in the courts and that the media – generally attracting the attention of political parties and public opinion – do not always report only court litigations, one of the aims of this chapter is to verify whether some media cases could highlight other aspects of the issues related to religious dress codes.

Scholars generally recognize an increasing interest of the media in religious issues, due not only to current events but also thanks to particular politico-religious connections, to the religious leaders' strategies at the global level, and probably also to greater demand from the public: an autonomous individual choosing his or her own religion *à la carte* in a more or less regulated religious market (Bréchon 2000). On the one hand, one can observe a sort of *do it yourself religion*, a general decline in vocations for priesthood and in believers and phenomena of 'believing without belonging' (Davie 1994, 2000, 2002). On the other, religion enjoys increasing space in media reporting: great events such as the World Youth Days, the death or election of the Catholic Popes, and the globalized concerns about the *Jyllands-Posten* Muhammad cartoons controversy are examples of the place given to religious issues in the media (Beck 2009: 45–48). So if religion shows a decreased influence in the EU countries, it seems, nevertheless, to enjoy more space in the media.

Media, together with other agents, such as the legal system, 'the State, the school, the family, the religious organizations', can act as a regulator of religion in general, broadcasting and giving their own interpretation of the events and news related to religious issues and regulating religious communication itself (Campiche 2000: 274).[7] Indeed on the one hand the media can certify the pre-eminence of the established religious traditions, while on the other they can define and set out what is 'religious' in society, making religion credible or banal but defining what is 'religiously correct' by enhancing or demonizing some aspects instead of others of specific religions (Willaime 2000: 327).

4 ECHR, article 9.

5 Media cases generally attracted the attention of the political parties and the public opinion but did not necessarily require a court decision.

6 On this distinction see Chapter 8, this volume.

7 On religion and regulation see above all: Beckford and Richardson (2007: 396–418).

In 2002 the European Research Centre on Migration and Ethnic Relations (ERCOMER) recognized that mass media reporting on ethnic, cultural and religious issues has progressively increased in the EU Member States during the last 20 years (ter Wal 2002). In its report on racism and cultural diversity for the European Monitoring Centre on Racism and Xenophobia (EUMC), ERCOMER highlighted how sensitive media reporting is when it comes to ethnic and religious relations in society and how much the media can influence people's attitudes and common knowledge.

Concerning immigrants, the media and politics are considered as 'working together' as a consequence of the heavy use of political and institutional sources in this kind of reporting. Generally, media reporting focus on stereotypical portrayals of immigrants as marginal and deviant with little attention paid to the immigrants' daily life. Indulging in a certain degree of sensationalism, the news emphasizes more the situations of social emergency – leading 'to biased representations of immigrants and ethnic relations' – and gives little voice to denominations for immigrants, who are often excluded from the debate (ter Wal 2002: 240).

Finally, the media seem to deal with religion especially while reporting some particular events but in the case of daily news on religion, the accent is more on religion as a 'threat against the social or international peace' (Chartier 2009) with a general tendency to 'denounce than to make thorough analysis' (Pépin 2009).

The Sikh Community: From Punjab to Northern Italy

In Italy Sikhs are mainly concentrated in the regions of Veneto, Emilia and Lombardy. They are commonly represented as good workers and the community is often indicated as a 'good one'. They arrived in Italy during the 1980s and at the beginning of the 1990s as a consequence of the economic crisis of the Indian Punjabi region. Sikh pioneers arrived in Italy to work in circuses and fairs, but thanks to networks and community and family relations they are currently mainly employed in rural areas in animal husbandry enterprises (especially in Lombardy) and in some peculiar districts specialized in tanning and furniture factories (Veneto and Emilia). Often represented as an 'invisible community', the Sikhs live as a separated/segregated group residing in isolated farms, having few relations with the Italian population and not speaking good Italian, and they are very much linked to their religious community (Denti et al. 2005b).[8]

In Italy Sikhs are constituted as an association – 'Associazione Sikhismo Religione Italia' – which has yet to be recognized. They recently requested recognition of legal capacity on the basis of the 1929 law but received a negative answer from the Council of State. Their application ran into difficulties not only on the basis of some incongruence between the aims of the association and their available economic assets. Concerns were also expressed as regards the public

8 See also Restelli 1990.

safety laws which are potentially violated by the *kirpan* – a ceremonial sword or dagger that Sikhs, men and women, have to wear at all times.[9]

Sikhs in the Media: 'Indiani Padani'

Italian newspapers generally provide a 'fair' image of the Sikh community and if during the 1990s they were mostly cited as immigrants and included in the immigration debates, in the early years of the new millennium they have progressively been referred to as a good community living around their temple. What is interesting to point out is the representation of Sikhs as 'good workers': people mainly dealing with 'work' and 'religion'. The common image is that of a 'milker with a turban' who is much more integrated into his own community than into Italian society.

News stories mainly deal with these aspects, underlining the image of a very religious rural community (Compiani and Galloni 2005; see also Galloni 2002). Positive attention is also given to the building of their temples around which parties are organized, bringing together the Sikhs and the local Italian population who are all invited to enter the temple and share a meal (Denti et al. 2005b).

Concerning the political approach to this kind of immigration, the Lega Nord, which generally opposes immigration flows, seems to well appreciate these communities through their local representatives. The image circulating in the local newspapers is that of the Punjab being similar to the Lombardy region, of 'Indians as Padanians'.[10] At the local level, in some cases the Northern League has endorsed the Sikh cause requesting help for the community from the local administrations and the Catholic local dioceses in order to give them a place for their worship (Denti et al. 2005a).

---

9 Any initiated Sikh accepts a specific discipline and the wearing of the 5 K (the Kanga [comb], the Kara [bangle], the Karchera [breeches], the Kes [unshorn hair] and the Kirpan) is a constant reminder of not forsaking one's principles. On this issue see: British Sikh Consultative Forum (2004).

10 *Padania* is the area of the Po valley, in the North of Italy, traditionally indicated by the political party Northern League (Lega Nord) as a potential autonomous/secessionist region from the Italian state. *Padanians* are used to being called the inhabitants of this area belonging to the Lega Nord.

Turban and Kirpan Cases

In the selection of articles – from July 2010 to September 2011[11] – provided by the ANSA agency and which focus on religious dress codes issues, Sikhs are rarely in the news if compared with cases concerning Muslims. When they are mentioned, the Sikh community is generally referred to in relation to dress codes, such as the turban and the *kirpan*, and the places of worship: the *Gurdwara* (the Sikh temple).

The Sikh turban has been at the centre of several newspaper articles. Since 2000, the media have reported the refusal of some Sikhs to remove their turban in order to wear a safety helmet when driving a scooter. In this respect, no particular regulations or actions have been enacted at the moment even though, in 2000, a recall of the existing rules was made by the under-secretary Mauro Fabris who was in charge of road safety. In these cases, it seems that the traffic police have generally been rather tolerant with Sikh bikers who finally found some pragmatic solutions such as that of putting the helmet on the turban.[12]

More recently, cases have arisen about the treatment of Sikhs in Italian airports (Milan Malpensa and Linate, Verona, Rome) where they are forced to remove their turbans at the security checks.[13] Following the EC regulation 300/2008 and 185/2010, passengers shall be screened by:

(a) a hand search; or

(b) walk-through metal detection (WTMD) equipment.

11 Considering that newspapers and other media mainly depend on the press agencies that are becoming progressively more essential, we chose to collect newspaper articles from ANSA (Agenzia Nazionale Stampa Associata). The Italian news agency publishes and provides over 3,500 daily news items to companies, public administration and media (www.ansa.it/prodotti/eng/agenzia.jsp) (accessed 5 February 2012). Generally, the agency provides news to other media that select the news to publish and deal with. Therefore, the ANSA could be considered as a 'wholesaler' of the news which main national newspapers draw on for a great part of their articles. The news provided by ANSA are then 'revised following the editorial line' of the newspaper, at the national or local level, in order to interpret the fact and make the opinion (Meucci 2001: 33).

12 'Indiani padani', *Report*, RAI, 24 September 2004; 'Niente casco, siamo sikh'; 'I vigili alla guerra del turbante', *Repubblica*, 6 April 2000.

13 'India: turbante vietato, golfista Sikh "umiliato a Malpensa"', *ANSA*, 16 March 2011. In July 2011, the Italian Minister Frattini declared, after his meeting with the Indian foreign minister, SM Krishna, that Sikhs would be given a separate room with a mirror to remove their turbans and would not be asked to remove their turbans in public. See: 'Sikh terranno turbante in scali italiani', *ANSA*, 27 July 2011.

> Where the screener cannot determine whether or not the passenger is carrying prohibited articles, the passenger shall be denied access to security restricted areas or rescreened to the screener's satisfaction.
>
> When a hand search is performed it shall be carried out so as to reasonably ensure that the person is not carrying prohibited articles.
>
> When WTMD equipment alarms, the cause of the alarm shall be resolved.

These regulations recognize the right for Member States to apply more stringent measures and the detail of how hand searches shall be performed is left, under the principle of subsidiarity, to the Member States. Concerning headgear, standard procedures and praxis in the EU airports allow Sikhs not to remove the turban since it is considered as a religious article. Numerous Sikh associations provide detailed indications for Sikh travellers by specifying the conduct to be observed. According to these indications, in the case of alarm of the metal detector and/or the hand wand, a pat-down of the turban could be demanded and eventually its removal 'BUT in a private area'.[14] In September 2011 a Sikh awareness gathering called '*Dastar* Day'[15] took place in London and simultaneously in Brussels, Rome and Madrid, in order to ask European governments to investigate the treatment of Sikhs at airports.[16]

At the moment, no court cases have dealt with these issues in Italy but several Sikh communities have already taken up political and lobbying initiatives in order to solve the problem at the international EU level as well as at the UN level.[17]

---

14 Upper case in the original text. See Sikh Coalition, United Sikhs and SALDEF, *Airport Screening Procedures for Sikh Travelers*, http://www.sikhcoalition.org/documents/pdf/SikhAirTravelersGuideandBillofRights.pdf (accessed 30 September 2010).

15 *Dastar* is, in Punjabi, the Sikh turban.

16 'Sikhs in Airport "Disrespect" Demo', *Independent*, 25 September 2011.

17 As reported by the ANSA, the Delhi government will ask for a resolution at the UN General Assembly in order to demand the respect of the turban considered as a religious symbol. The demand followed the accident endured by a top Indian golfer forced to remove his turban by security officials at the Milan airport. 'Caso turbante, Governo chiede una risoluzione ONU', *ANSA*, 23 March 2011. The British MP Pat McFadden, interviewed during the Dastar manifestation, invited other EU countries to follow the British approach with the very long established Sikh community. Indeed, in the UK the Aviation Minister has recently taken charge of the situation. Recognizing the cultural and religious sensitivities surrounding the touching of a Sikh's turban, he reported the running of a trial of alternative searching methodology in a number of UK airports aiming to 'establish whether security standards can be maintained in respect of the screening of religious headwear without the need for a hand search'. 'Sikhs in Airport "Disrespect" Demo', *Independent*, 25 September 2011. See also: Minister of State for Transport, *Trial of alternative procedures for screening of religious/cultural headgear*, 1 June 2011, available at: http://www.parliament.uk/deposits/depositedpapers/2011/DEP2011-1603.pdf (accessed 30 September 2010).

Other media cases arose around the issue of the *kirpan*, the sword that baptized Sikhs must always wear.[18]

In this respect, media cases mainly report the court cases that have occurred in Italy during the last few years. In 2007 there was a case in Cremona, a city in Northern Italy. In a shopping centre an Indian national of Sikh religion was approached by a policeman because he carried a sword: the *kirpan*. The Criminal Court of Cremona acquitted him of the crime of carrying a weapon or an object,[19] though not conventionally a weapon, which can be employed as one. The Court considered the carrying of a *kirpan* as an expression of one's religious faith, granted by article 19 of the Italian Constitution as well as by several international conventions. In the decision, the religious character of carrying the *kirpan* was recognized as a justified reason for excluding the application of the public security law.[20] More recently, ANSA reported the case of a Sikh child wearing the *kirpan* in a junior high school in the province of Venice. The authorities promptly recalled the decisions of the Criminal Court and tried to calm down the concerns of the other children's parents.[21]

Other media cases deal with the issue of the building of places of worship. Generally, newspaper articles describe the parties and the festive atmosphere around the new temples. Recently the biggest European Sikh temple was inaugurated in Pessina Cremonese, in the province of Cremona.[22] The news was widely delivered by newspapers and several comments were made by political representatives who generally welcomed the event. However, at the local level some Northern League and Forza Nuova[23] political parties' demonstrations took place even though a clear official opposition of the Lega Nord was not manifested.[24]

---

18 On these aspects: 'Sikh circola con coltello, assolto perché simbolo religioso', *ANSA*, 13 January 2009; 'In Tribunale con pugnale "ornamento religioso", denunciato', *ANSA*, 21 April 2010. On the *kirpan*, see British Sikh Consultative Forum (2004).

19 Law 18 April 1975, Integrative norms of the in force discipline for the control of weapons, of ammunition and of explosives, no. 110, article 4, 2.

20 Criminal Court, Cremona, 19 February 2009, no. 799/08. See also: Criminal Court, Vicenza, Dismissal decree, 28 January 2009; Supreme Court, Penal section I, March 2007, no. 8879.

21 'Bimbo Sikh a scuola con pugnale, esposto. Ma forze ordine rassicurano, non e' un'arma e non e' pericoloso', *ANSA*, 12 April 2011.

22 'Nel Cremonese tempio Sikh più grande d'Europa', *ANSA*, 27 July 2011.

23 Forza Nuova is a far right political party.

24 Sikhs' Italian temples are generally funded by the community itself. This is the case of the Novellara temple, in Emilia, built in 2000. For more details see Bertolani (2000). This is also the case of the new temple of Pessina Cremonese, inaugurated in 2011, see 'Banca bresciana paga tempio sikh', *Qui Brescia.it. Giornale telematico*, 16 August 2011, http://quibrescia.it/cms/?p=61953 (accessed October 2011).

'Work is Worship'

Scholars generally refer to the social success of immigrants belonging to the Sikh religion. E. Pace develops the hypothesis of an elective affinity, on the basis of the Weberian model, between the Sikh scheme of things as regards religion and ethics and their sense of 'adaptation to the social and economic world' (Pace 2002: 119; 2008b). The notion 'work is worship' sums up well the idea that devoting one's life to work is a way to contribute to the glory of God by following his will. According to this belief, to adapt to the social and economic order of a specific country and to obtain economic success is a way, for Sikh immigrants, to 'achieve the union with God, in the world and through the world' (Pace 2008b: 88). This could explain the efforts of the Sikh Italian community, within a solid transnational network and with great solidarity among immigrants, to adopt the lifestyles of a society where their 'turbans do not disturb' (Pace 2008b: 91) and where, thanks to a system of belief marked by flexibility and adaptability, they generally adapt well, almost everywhere, to the rules and regulations of the country (Pace 2002).[25]

The Plural Muslim Community

In Italy Muslims are estimated to be a population of over one million people but it is a 'plural reality': there is no specific national or geographical majority even though the Moroccan community is the largest one. The Muslims in Italy are from the Maghreb, Middle East, Balkans, Africa and Asia, and are especially of the Sunni tradition. They identify themselves on the basis of their religion but also of their nationality, ethnic belonging, socio-religious organization or confraternity (Guolo 2011: 56). Islamic belonging can be:

- privatised and individualised without any claim in the public sphere;
- secularised as is the case of Muslims linked to a certain tradition but who do not practise their religion to a great extent, a sort of 'secularised Muslim';
- re-islamised openly claiming visibility in the public sphere (Di Motoli 2009: 47).

Muslims in Italy do not refer to a single organization but to a number of different bodies producing a sort of pluralism of fact as a consequence of the absence of a central authority providing a single interpretation of the religious tradition. As a consequence of the competition among different Islamic organizations, between an 'Islam of the State' and an 'Islam of the mosques', there is no single representative body in Italy and therefore an agreement has not yet been signed with the Italian State which has encountered many difficulties in dealing with so

25 On this see also: Osservatorio provinciale sull'immigrazione (2002).

plural a reality.[26] It is obvious that in this landscape the position of the Catholic Church and the choices of the Italian political parties could influence the situation. More particularly, one has to bear in mind the official opposition of the Lega Nord towards any agreement with the Muslim community (Guolo 2011: 61–62).

Burqa and Burkini: From the Media to the Courts

In the media the discussion on immigration seems to be closely linked to that on Islam (Schmidt di Friedberg 2003) and 'pernicious stereotypes are identified in the coverage of Islam' which is often associated with illegal immigration, fundamentalism, denial of rights – in particular women's rights (ter Wal 2002: 239). The media also seem to particularly focus on 'anti-Islamic mobilisations by the Lega Nord as well as on the positive pro-immigrant stance of the Catholic Church' (ter Wal 2002: 253).[27]

Indeed, the Italian media generally represents Islam as a 'public problem': the more this religion is given visibility in the public space the more the contradictions related to the Italian identity and citizenship are highlighted. The debates around the building of the Lodi mosque, in 2000, are an emblematic example of the media representation of Islam in Italy. At that moment, different actors were mobilized around this controversy and the media mainly gave space to political and institutional representatives, to the Catholic Church and to intellectuals, but the marginalized Muslims living in Italy, who were the subject of the debate, could not really take part in it (Perocco 2008).

During the summer of 2009, some media cases arose around the *burkini*, the swimsuit for Muslim women covering the whole body except the face. The cases were mainly concentrated in the North of Italy where some mayors of the Northern League adopted local decrees in order to forbid this kind of swimsuit not only for hygiene reasons but also for 'maintaining the public decency and serenity of the other bathers especially the children'.[28] The reason, explained one mayor, is that 'the sight of a masked woman could disturb, mainly kids, without taking into account the potential problems of hygiene'.[29] Media cases mainly arose in Piedmont and Veneto but the media also reported some cases from France concerning the prohibition to enter swimming pools wearing a *burkini*.[30] The accent is often put

---

26 On the representativeness of the Muslim communities see also: S. Ferrari (2008).

27 The Catholic Church through its representatives has however shown a plurality of approaches towards the Muslim communities and the building of places of worship. On these aspects see Perocco (2008).

28 City of Varallo, local decree, no. 99, 2009.

29 'Sindaco piemontese vieta burkini. 500 euro di multa', *ANSA*, 19 August 2009.

30 'Musulmana in piscina con burkini, stupore a Verona. Mamme protestano, l'incrocio burqa-bikini spaventa i bimbi', *ANSA*, 21 August 2010; 'Francia, vietata piscina a donna in burkini', *ANSA*, 12 August 2009.

on the hygiene problems and the rules of the swimming pools but media also highlighted that the sales of *burkini* grew all over Europe.

The *burkini* is only a part of the more general debate on the *burqa*, in the media and in society as a whole, which has led to several court cases.[31]

The municipality of Azzano Decimo undertook one of the first measures against the *burqa*. In 2004 the mayor enacted council decree no. 24 forbidding the headscarf covering one's face for public security reasons. The prefect, following the advice of the Minister of Interior, revoked the decree as illegitimate but the municipality of Azzano Decimo appealed to the regional administrative court of law that rejected the appeal.[32] The municipality finally appealed to the Council of State that gave its judgment in 2008 and rejected the appeal of the Azzano Decimo municipality.[33]

In order to ban the *burqa*, the council decree referred to article 85,1 of royal decree n. 773/1931 and to article 5 of law no. 152/1975. These two measures intended to forbid respectively:

- to appear disguised in public space, except during certain specific periods of the year;
- to use safety helmet in public space or private space open to public, without any justified reason or, in any case, during public manifestations.

The Council of State assessed the legitimacy of the revocation of the council decree made by the prefect. The Council recognized that the municipality, when referring to the headscarf covering the face, only sought to prohibit the *burqa* worn by Muslim women, the decree having a strong cultural and political bias. In fact, on the basis of article 85,1 of royal decree n. 773/1931, the Council considered that the *burqa* is not a mask but the traditional clothing of certain populations used on the basis of religious convictions. Concerning article 5 of law no. 152/1975, the Council explained that the *ratio* of this rule, originally conceived against terrorism, is to protect public order and to stop safety helmets or other means from preventing the recognition of a person. Moreover, the complete ban only applies during public manifestations. In all other cases, it is forbidden to use a safety helmet in any public space or private space open to the public unless there is a justified reason.

According to the Council, the *burqa* is not used to avoid recognition but it is worn as traditional article of clothing in some cultures and by some populations. The court did not intend to go to the heart of this matter or to verify whether the *burqa* is a religious or cultural symbol; it only recognized that it is not used to prevent the recognition of a person. Article 5 allows in fact the wearing of a veil for cultural or religious reasons when the public security exigencies are satisfied.

31 On the different kind of veil, such as *burqa, niqab* etc., see Chapter 14, this volume.

32 TAR Friuli Venezia Giulia, decision no. 645/2006.

33 Council of State, section VI, decision no. 3076/2008.

So if the veil is not used during public manifestations or the person wearing it accepts to be identified and to remove it in order to allow recognition by public authorities, it is fully allowed by the Italian system.[34]

Other municipalities enacted similar decrees, mainly in the North of Italy.[35]

Media cases and court cases focused the attention of the public opinion on the *burqa* and *burkini* issues and broadcasted the positions of some Italian political parties.[36]

'Assimilation without Assimilation' and the *Burqa* Ban

Since the 1990s, and as a consequence of the presence in the government of the Lega Nord, a political party with an anti-immigration and anti-Islamic policy, there is no general law referring to a model of cultural integration. Moreover, one can observe the absence of an organized national immigration policy focusing on the integration of the newcomers. Italy seems mainly to refer to an assimilative integration which, in practice, becomes a sort of multicultural approach. This 'assimilationism without assimilation', which does not easily give immigrants the possibility to obtain Italian citizenship, thus facilitates a de facto multiculturalism where there is no interaction with the immigrant who lives in a sort of parallel

34 On this issues, see also Colaianni (2006a: 163–176).

35 Drezzo, Varallo Sesia, Fermignano, Sassuolo, Chivasso, Novara, Cossato, Tezze di Vazzola, Sesto S. Giovanni. See also: Supreme Court, Penal Section, decision of 4 April 2006, no. 11919, concerning the attempt to remove the veil of a Muslim woman. Among media cases on the *burqa*, see also: 'Tunisina con burqa. Giudice di pace le cancella la multa 500 euro. Ragazza araba vince causa dopo divieto sincaco Lega', *ANSA*, 10 December 2010; 'Autista blocca autobus perché donna islanmica porta niqab. E' successo a Mestre, donna poi toglie velo per farsi riconoscere', *ANSA*, 31 December 2010; 'Dal burqa al 'burkini', multe, divieti e proposte legge', *ANSA*, 17 September 2010. In 2010, another media case concerned a mother that accompanied her child to school in a town close to Rome. Defined as the 'dark lady' by the other mothers, she and her husband were summoned by the school director. On this see: 'Mamme contro burqa: la dirigente, rassicureremo i genitori', *ANSA*, 18 September 2010. In 2009, a court case concerned a woman wearing a *burqa* in a Penal Court where her husband was being judged. Denounced for violation of article 5 of law no. 152 of 1975, she was acquitted because she accepted to be identified and as a consequence there was no reason to apply article 5. Tribunale di Cremona, 27 November 2008. On this judegment see Gatta (2009).

36 A survey confirmed that more than seven Italians out of 10 do not agree with the full veil which is considered as a barrier to integration. According to the collected data, Italians generally feel that each country has the right to autonomously deal with this kind of concern and the majority of the interviewees declared they agreed with a possible anti-*burqa* law. Panel data, 'Oltre sette italiani su dieci dicono no al velo islamico integrale nei luoghi pubblici: non rispetta la dignità delle donne e frena l'integrazione', available at: www.paneldata.it/newsite/wp-content/uploads/2011/09/36_comunicato_gli_italiani_e_il_velo_islamico.pdf (accessed 28 September 2011).

society, an 'identity ghetto' (Guolo 2011: 58 59). Finally, the lack of measures to promote the integration of the newcomers has led to a securitarian approach towards religious diversity as regards Islam, together with narratives in defence of the Catholic identity of the nation (Fiorita 2010: 127–147).

At State level there does not seem to be a central organized public policy concerning religious dress codes, neither at the national nor at the regional level.[37] However, several bills have been presented – not by the Government itself but by individual deputies – in order to ban the *burqa*.[38] Several of them explicitly refer to

---

37 In recent years, some attempts to deal with the Italian plural Islam have been made. In 2005, the Minister of Interior Pisanu (Il Popolo della Libertà, PdL) created a consultative board, Consulta per l'Islam italiano, with the aim to improve the dialogue between State authorities and the Muslim communities. Minister of Interior, decree 10 September 2005. The Consulta was the result of the policy of the center right governing coalition but several objections were made against the activity of this body. On these issues: Fiorita (2010). In 2007, a Charter of values of citizenship and integration was enacted by the Minister of the Interior Giuliano Amato (Ulivo – centre-left coalition), recalling the principles of human dignity. The document specifies that 'in Italy there are no restrictions on people's attire, as long as it is chosen freely and it is not detrimental to his/her dignity. It is not accepted to cover the face because this impedes the person's recognition and hinders establishing relations with the others'. Minister of Interior, *Charter of Values of Citizenship and Integration*, 23 April 2007, available at: www.interno.it/mininterno/export/sites/default/it/assets/files/14/0919_charter_of_values_of_citizenship_and_integration.pdf (accessed 25 September 2011). Several draft agreements between the State and the Muslim communities have already been introduced by different Muslim associations (UCOII, Centro Culturale Islamico di Italia, Associazione dei Musulmani Italiani, CO.RE.IS) but none of them directly mention the full veil, *burqa* or *niqab*. On these aspects: S. Ferrari (2000); Colaianni (2006b). The headscarf issues had already been at the centre of attention concerning *identity documents*. The general rule is that photos for identity documents have to be taken without any scarves or headdresses, but in Italy a dispensation is provided in the case of religious reasons, such as for the Sikh's turban, the Muslim headscarf or the nun's veil, following two circulars of the Minister of Interior stating that as long as the face is visible, the photograph wearing headgear is possible. Ministero dell'Interno, Circolare no. 4/95 del 14 marzo 1995 and Circolare no. 300.C/2000/3656/A/240159/1^Div., 21 luglio 2000.

38 Several bills have been presented during the XVI Legislature. *Chamber of deputies*: Binetti et al.,UDC (C. 627, 29/4/2008); Sbai e Contento, PdL (C. 2422, 6/5/2009); Cota et al., Lega Nord (C. 2769, 2/10/2009); Mantini e Tassone, UDC (C. 3018, 3/12/2009); Amici et al., PD (C. 3020, 4/12/2009); Bertolini, PdL (C. 3760, 11/10/2010); Garagnani et al., PdL (C. 3719, 21/9/2010); Lanzillotta, mixed group (C. 3183, 8/2/2010); Vassallo et al., PD (C. 3205, 11/2/2010); Reguzzoni et al., Lega Nord (C. 3715, 23/9/2010); Vaccaro et al., PD (C. 3368, 7/4/2010). *Senate*: Vicari et al., PdL (ddl 2342, 23/9/2010); Baio et al., Apl-FLI (ddl 289, 30/4/2008); Bianchi, PdL (ddl 1205, 13/11/2008); Spadoni Urbani, PdL (ddl 2343, 23/9/2010). A *consolidation Act* has finally been presented on 19 October 2011. It provides the modification of article 5 of the law 22 May 1975 and explicitly mentions 'clothing or accessories of any ethnic origin and culture, such as the burqa and the niqab'. The fine is of 1,000 to 2,000 Euros. Penal measures are provided in case of pressure in order

burqa and *niqab*, others simply mention 'clothings that can impede the recognition of the person', but all agree on the fact that it is not accepted to cover one's face, which needs to be uncovered and recognizable for the purposes of public order, no discrimination against women, combating terrorism, etc.[39]

Faced with the bills on the *burqa/niqab* ban, the Committee for Italian Islam was called upon for its advice. The Committee is an advisory board composed of 19 members.[40] Among them there are experts of religion and Islam in general and representatives of Muslim organizations. With the purpose to improve the integration of Muslim communities in the Italian context, the Committee is supposed to provide advice on questions concerning places of worship, imam training, *burqa*, etc. Recognizing the role of the media in transmitting and spreading the concerns about dress codes all over Europe, the Committee directly referred to the local decrees of the North Italian municipalities against *burqa* and *niqab*, largely reported in the Italian newspapers. For this consultative body these kinds of dress codes raise three main issues: public security, respect of women's dignity and freedom of religion. Recalling that the wearing of these garments is not the result of a Koranic prescription, and taking into account the dangers of terrorism and the public order concerns, the Committee substantially agreed with a law on *burqa* and *niqab* through a modification of the 1975 law, but it asked for a

---

to constrain somebody to cover the face and this can preclude acquiring citizenship. The consolidation Act has not yet been approved but is under examination of the Constitutional Affairs Commission of the Chamber of Deputies. For a detailed analysis on the legislation on burqa/niqab in Italy, see the paper delivered by A. Ferrari, 'The Burqa in Italy', at the RELIGARE/University dell'Insubria workshop: The Burqa Affair across Europe: between Private and Public, Como, 4–5 April 2011; in Italy and in Europe see Tirabassi (2011).

39 On this aspect, see: Cardia (2010: 59–64); S. Ferrari (2004a). See also A. Ferrari (2011). During the discussions on one of the most symbolic Bill, C. 2422 Sbai (Proposta di legge: Sbai e Contento: 'Modifica all'articolo 5 della legge 22 maggio 1975, n. 152, concernente il divieto di indossare gli indumenti denominati burqa e niqab' [2422] available at: www.camera.it/126?PDL=2422&leg=16&tab=1 (accessed July 2012)), several experts of Islam and religion as well as intellectuals and journalists participated at the official auditions at the Chamber of deputies. The bill C. 2422 proposed to modify article 5 of the 1975 law, no. 152, specifying the 'ban of women's garments, used by Muslim women, referred to as burqa and niqab'. Some researchers pointed out that the necessity to modify the article is a political one as generally judges, public authorities and officials do not need a clear specification of the garment, as results from the absolute correspondence of the judges' decisions at different levels (Domianello); others underlined that the original main *ratio* of the law to be modified was the fight against subversive terrorism, highlighting the necessity to refer to soft law methods in order to contribute to governance instead of a rigid regulation by law, in a more general approach enhancing education and mediation paths (Mazzola). See: Chamber of deputies, resoconto stenografico, 10 November 2009.

40 The Committee was created in 2010 by the Minister of Interior Maroni (Lega Nord). www.interno.it/mininterno/export/sites/default/it/sezioni/sala_stampa/televideo/2010/archivio/0995_2010_02_10_comitato.html (accessed 25 September 2011).

sort of 'deconfessionalization' of the law by avoiding explicit reference to religion and Islam in its text.[41]

Conclusion

In Italy, the legal framework of State/Church relations, as a result of the historical heritage, seems to provide a generalattitude towards religion that allows a quite flexible approach to *other religious realities* – other than the Catholic Church – and usually open to religious pluralization. Indeed Italian history, characterized by divisions and local arrangements – which did not contribute towards creating a strong sense of belonging to the Nation[42] and where the Catholic faith has always been a predominant element of the citizens' identity – has often been an example of pragmatic local solutions and arrangements as regards the effects of religious pluralization, such as the greater visibility of religious dress codes in the public spaces.[43] In this landscape, political parties can play a role in exacerbating the debates which are given much coverage by the media; and when reporting religious aspects of daily life, the media seem more open to sensationalism than to balanced information and meticulous analysis.

Some tendencies seem to be detectable in the cases outlined above and can raise some questions.

First, one can notice a sort of *Europeanization* of the issue: in a European context, characterized by the free circulation of individuals and workers, concerns related to dress codes spread from one country to another through the media (this is the case for the Sikh turban in the airport and the burkini/burqa issues in Europe) and debates, in a globalized world, become increasingly more European

41 Minister of Interior, *Burqa e niqab. Parere del Comitato per l'Islam Italiano*, available at: www.interno.it/mininterno/export/sites/default/it/assets/files/19/00036_Comitato_Islam_-_relazione_Burqa_07_10.pdf (accessed 25 September 2011). A. Ferrari, member of the Committee, made some critical remarks over the advice of the Committee. More particularly he alerted against the risks of: religious discrimination and violation of gender equality (the proposal only refers to a specific religious group and to women); the potential limitation of the freedom of religion of some specific groups; the possible ideological *bias* as far as the document explicitly refers to *burqa* and *niqab*. In conclusion he refers to a potential negative judgment of the European Court of Human Rights and to the real difficulties at the moment of the application of the law. Commissione Affari Costituzionali della Camera dei Deputati, modifica dell'articolo 5 della legge 22 maggio 1975, no. 152, Primo commento alle proposte di legge Cota e Sbai, A. Ferrari, 14 July 2010.

42 On these issues see: Galli della Loggia (1998, 2003); Garelli (1999: 169–188), Pastorelli (2012: 227–229); Pace 2008a.

43 On the local management of religion following the modification of the Title V of the Italian Constitution (18 October 2001) and the principle of subsidiarity, see Consorti (2003) and Pastori (2003).

than national. On the one hand, in this situation the European institutions adopt political actions, such as the resolution of the Council of Europe Assembly on *Islam, Islamism and Islamophobia in Europe*,[44] while recognizing at the same time that religious issues are a national matter. On the other, transnational religious movements can adopt legitimating strategies at the European level and not only at the national one.[45]

Second, one can observe a sort of *instrumentalization*/exploitation of the issue by some political nationalist parties such as the Lega Nord.[46]

Third, the *genderization* of the dress codes issues seems to target not only the religious aspects or the freedom of religion of individuals but the situation of women who are not free to wear whatever clothes they wish.

Fourth, there is the general balance between the *political securitarian approach* and the *judicial protection of the freedom of religion*. In all the cases mentioned here, public order and public security issues seem to be at the centre of the debates regarding the Sikh *kirpan* and the turban in the airports as well as the Muslim full veil, but the court decisions always refer to the freedom of religion principles.

This chapter has shown that the real issue is not the religious symbol in itself but what it reminds the public of: from the 'Islamic threat'[47] to the peaceful Sikh community that 'rescues the Italian parmesan',[48] the media give their own interpretation of the events and news related to religious issues, influencing people's attitudes and common knowledge.

Muslims – more numerous and as a consequence much more visible if compared with the *invisible* Sikhs – are generally reported by the media in relation to some problems. While newspaper articles try to explain the Sikh faith and traditions, often reporting successful court cases in which Sikhs appear justified in wearing a turban or a *kirpan*, when dealing with Muslim communities the accent is on 'masked', segregated women and the declarations made by the Lega Nord representatives. Indeed, in the cases concerning Islam, the media make considerable use of political and institutional sources. When reporting on Sikhs, the media refer to good workers and a happy community, while regarding Islam the accent is almost always on terrorism and fundamentalism.

---

44 Council of Europe, Parliamentary Assembly, *Resolution on Islam, Islamism and Islamophobia in Europe*, Resolution 1743 (2010), 23 June 2010, http://assembly.coe.int/Main.asp?link=/Documents/AdoptedText/ta10/ERES1743.htm (accessed 30 September 2010).

45 Pastorelli (2009); Willaime (2010).

46 See on this issue as regards the Bulgarian case: Chapter 13, this volume.

47 'Pericolo islamico in Italia', *Repubblica*, 24 August 1998; 'La Nato scopre il "pericolo" islamico', *Corriere della Sera*, 3 February 1995; 'Berlusconi, Pisapia e il pericolo islamico', *Il Messaggero*, 24 May 2011.

48 'Senza gli indiani addio Grana Padano', *Corriere della Sera*, 8 September 2011; 'In Italian Heartland, Indians Keep the Cheese Coming', *New York Times*, 7 September 2011.

Court cases show that the issue of dress codes always refers to respect of the freedom of religion – according to articles 19 of the Italian Constitution and 9 of the ECHR – which can represent a 'justified reason' to exclude the application of the public security law.

In the European landscape, the Italian case seems to constitute an alternative non-prescriptive model compared to other European realities like, for example, the French model. Accommodations seem to be possible and no legal measure has been applied yet to regulate the dress code issues, but it is certain that the Italian approach can still evolve in a different way.

References

(2009), *Les religions: espoir ou menace pour nos sociétés?* (Paris: Bayard).

(2010), 'La laïcité à l'épreuve du voile intégral', *Regards sur l'actualité*, 364.

Allievi, S. (2008), 'Islam italiano e società nazionale', in Ferrari, A. (ed.), 43–76.

Allievi, S. (2009), *Conflicts over Mosques in Europe Policy Issues and Trend* (NEF Initiative on Religion and Democracy in Europe).

Aluffi, R. and Zincone, G. (eds) (2004), *The Legal Treatment of Islamic Minorities in Europe* (Leuven: Peeters).

Barker, E. (ed.) (2008), *The Centrality of Religion in Social Life. Essays in Honour of James A. Beckford* (London: Ashgate).

Beck, U. (2009), *Il Dio personale. La nascita della religiosità secolare* (Bari: Laterza).

Beckford, J.A. and Demerath, N.J. III (2007), *The SAGE Handbook of the Sociology of Religion* (London: Sage).

Beckford, J.A. and Richardson, J.T. (2007), 'Religion and Regulation', in Beckford, J.A. and Demerath, N.J. (eds), 396–418.

Bertolani, B. (2000), 'I Sikh in provincia di Reggio Emilia: caste e network di parentela nei processi di ridefinizione dell'appartenenza religiosa', *Religioni e società*, 50, 31–38.

Bréchon, P. and Willaime, J.-P. (eds) (2000), *Médias et religion en miroir* (Paris: PUF).

British Sikh Consultative Forum (2004), *The Kirpan. A Submission to the Department of Communities and Local Government (UK)*, April 2009, available at http://bscf.org/documents/The_Kirpan_Final_version%5B1%5D.pdf (accessed 25 September 2011).

Campiche, R.J. (2000), 'Médias et régulation socioculturelle du champ religieux', in Bréchon, P. and Willaime, J.-P. (eds), 265–280.

Capelle-Pogacean, A., Pace, E. and Michel, P. (eds) (2008), *Religion(s) et identité(s) en Europe. L'épreuve du pluriel* (Paris: Presses de Sciences Po).

Cardia, C. (2010), 'Dire sì o no al burqa una scelta di valore ineludibile', *Libertà civili*, 4, 59–64.

Caritas-Migrantes (2007; 2010), *Dossier statistico immigrazione*, available at: www.dossierimmigrazione.it (accessed 5 February 2012).

Chartier, C. (2009), 'Les religions dans les médias et l'expression culturelle', in *Les religions: espoir ou menace pour nos sociétés?*, 178–179.

Cipriani, R. (1988), *La religione diffusa* (Roma: Borla).

Cipriani, R. (1993), 'De la religion diffuse à la religion des valeurs', *Social Compass*, 40:1, 91–100.

Colaianni, N. (2006a), *Eguaglianza e diversità culturali e religiose. Un percorso costituzionale* (Bologna: Il Mulino).

Colaianni, N. (2006b), 'La Consulta per l'Islam italiano: un caso di revisione strisciante della Costituzione', *Osservatorio delle libertà ed istituzioni religiose*, OLIR, available at: www.olir.it (accessed 5 February 2012).

Compiani, M.J. and Galloni, F. (2005), 'I Sikh in Lombardia', in Denti, D. et al. (eds), 143–161.

Consorti, P. (2003), 'Nuovi rapporti fra la Repubblica e le confessioni religiose? Sui riflessi ecclesiasticistici della riforma del Titolo V, parte seconda, della Costituzione', *Quaderni di Diritto e Politica Ecclesiastica*, 1, 13–36.

Davie, G. (1994), *Religion in Britain since 1945: Believing without Belonging* (Oxford: Blackwell).

Davie, G. (2000), *Religion in Modern Europe: A Memory Mutates* (Oxford: Oxford University Press).

Davie, G. (2002), *Europe: The Exceptional Case. Parameters of Faith in the Modern World* (London: Darton Longman Todd).

Denti, D., Ferrari, M. and Perocco, F. (eds) (2005a), *I Sikh. Storia e immigrazione* (Milano: FrancoAngeli).

Denti, D., Ferrari, M. and Perocco, F. (2005b), 'Scienze sociali e migrazioni', in Denti, D. et al. (eds), 7–16.

Di Motoli, P. (2009), 'L'Islam organizzato in Italia: un esempio di frattura organizzativa su linee nazionali', *Religioni e Societa*, 65, 47–52.

Dieni, E., Ferrari, A. and Pacillo, V. (eds) (2006), *I simboli religiosi tra diritto e culture* (Milano: Giuffrè).

European Research Centre on Migration and Ethnic Relations, ERCOMER (2002), *Racism and Cultural Diversity in the Mass Media*, available at: http://fra.europa.eu/fraWebsite/research/publications/publications_per_year/previous_publications/pub_mr_racism_diversity_media_02_en.htm (accessed 27 September 2011).

Evans M.D. (2009), *Manual on the Wearing of Religious Symbols in Public Areas* (Strasbourg: Council of Europe Editions).

Evans, M.D. (2010), 'Religious Symbols: An Introduction' in Ferrari, S. and Cristofori, R. (eds), 291–296.

Ferrari, A. (ed.) (2008), *Islam in Europa. Islam in Italia tra diritto e società* (Bologna: Il Mulino).

Ferrari, A. (2011), 'The Burqa in Italy', paper presented at the workshop: *The Burqa Affair across Europe: between Private and Public*, Como, 4–5 April 2011 (RELIGARE/Insubria University).

Ferrari, S. (ed.) (2000), *Musulmani in Italia. La condizione giuridica delle comunità islamiche* (Bologna: Il Mulino).

Ferrari, S. (2004a), 'Le ragioni del velo', *Osservatorio delle libertà ed istituzioni religiose*, OLIR, available at: www.olir.it (accessed 5 February 2012).

Ferrari, S. (2004b), 'Islam in Europe: An Introduction to Legal Problems and Perspectives', in Aluffi, R. and Zincone, G. (eds), 1–9.

Ferrari, S. (2008), 'Le questioni normative', in Ferrari, A. (ed.), 77–90.

Ferrari, S. and Cristofori, R. (eds) (2010), *Law and Religion in the 21st Century. Relations between States and Religious Communities* (London: Ashgate).

Fiorita, N. (2010), *L'Islam spiegato ai miei studenti. Undici lezioni sul diritto islamico* (Firenze: Firenze University Press).

Foret, F. and Itçaina, X. (eds) (2012), *Politics of Religion in Western Europe. Modernities in Conflict?* (Oxford: Routledge).

Galli della Loggia, E. (1998), *L'identità italiana* (Bologna: Il Mulino).

Galli della Loggia, E. (2003), *La morte della patria* (Bari: Laterza).

Galloni, F. (2002), 'Turbanti che non turbano: le immagini dei sikh nella stampa locale', in Osservatorio provinciale sull'immigrazione, 103–130.

Garelli, F. (1999), 'La religione civile e il problema dell'integrazione nelle società complesse', *Rassegna Italiana di Sociologia*, 1, 169–188.

Garelli, F., Guizzardi, G. and Pace, E. (2003), *Un singolare pluralismo. Indagine sul pluralismo morale e religioso degli italiani* (Bologna: Il Mulino).

Gatta, G.L. (2009), 'Islam, abbigliamento religioso, diritto e processo penale: brevi note a margine di due casi giurisprudenziali', *Stato, Chiese e pluralismo confessionale*, giugno 2009, available at: www.statoechiese.it (accessed 5 February 2012).

Guolo, R. (2000), 'La rappresentanza dell'Islam italiano e la questione delle intese', in Ferrari, S. (ed.), 67–82.

Guolo, R. (2011), 'L'Islam in Italia', *Il Mulino. Rivista bimestrale di cultura e di politica*, 1, 56–63.

Manco, M. (2006), 'Abbigliamento confessionalmente orientate fra diritti di libertà e laicità dello Stato', in Dieni, E. et al. (eds), 263–291.

Marechal, B., Allievi, S., Dassetto, F. and Nielsen, J. (eds) (2003), *Muslims in the Enlarged Europe – Religion and Society. Muslim Minorities*, vol. 2 (Leiden: Brill).

Meucci, A. (2001), 'Agenzie di stampa e quotidiani. Una notizia dall'ANSA ai giornali', *Working papers del dipartimento di Scienze Storiche, Giuridiche, Politiche e Sociali dell'Università di Siena*, 42, 3–35.

Mortensen, V. (ed.) (2006), *Religion and Society: Crossdisciplinary European Perspectives* (Aarhus: Univers).

Osservatorio provinciale sull'immigrazione (2002), *Turbanti che non turbano. Ricerca sociologica sugli immigrati indiani nel cremonese, rapporto di ricerca* (Università di Padova), Dicembre 2002.
Pace, E. (2002), 'Il misticismo intramondano della via dei sikh', in Denti, D. et al. (eds), 115–132.
Pace, E. (2007), 'A Peculiar Pluralism', *Journal of Modern Italian Studies*, 2:1, 86–100.
Pace, E. (2008a), 'Nation et religion en Italie', in Capelle-Pogacean, A. et al. (eds), 59–71.
Pace, E. (2008b), 'The Inner-World Mysticism and a Successful Social Integration of the Sikh Panth', in Barker, E. (ed.), 85–92.
Pastorelli, S. (2009), 'The European Union and the New Religious Movements', *Religion, State and Society*, special issue: 'Religion, Politics and Law in the European Union', 37:1–2, 193–206.
Pastorelli, S. (2012), 'Public Policies towards New Religions' in Foret, F. and Itçaina, X. (eds), 224–240.
Pastori, G. (2003), 'Regioni e confessioni religiose nel nuovo ordinamento costituzionale', *Quaderni di Diritto e Politica Ecclesiastica*, 1, 3–12.
Pépin, P. (2009), 'Les religions dans les médias et l'expression culturelle', in *Les religions: espoir ou menace pour nos sociétés?*, 177–178.
Perocco, F. (2008), 'L'enjeu "islam" en Italie', in Capelle-Pogacean, A. et al. (eds), 141–157.
Restelli, M. (1990), *I Sikh fra storia e attualità politica* (Paese: Pagus Edizioni).
Ricceri, M. (2006), 'Italians and the Church: Fait and Disobedience', in Mortensen, V. (ed.), 59–80.
Robbers, G. (ed.) (2005), *State and Church in the European Union. Second Edition* (Baden-Baden: Nomos).
Schmidt di Friedberg, O. (2003), *Building the Enemy: Islamophobia in Italy*, available at: http://inhouse.lau.edu.lb/bima/papers/Ottavia.pdf (accessed 5 February 2012).
ter Wal, J. (2002), 'Italy', in European Research Centre on Migration and Ethnic Relations.
Tirabassi, M.G. (2011), 'Alcuni paesi europei a confronto: burqa e spazio pubblico tra leggi e iniziative legislative', *Quaderni di Diritto e Politica Ecclesiastica*, 2, 351–381.
Willaime, J.-P. (2000), 'Les médias comme analyseur des mutations religieuses contemporaines', in Bréchon, P. and Willaime, J.-P. (eds), 299–329.
Willaime, J.-P. (2010), 'Le voile intégral: approches européennes et réactions nord-américaines', in 'La laïcité à l'épreuve du voile intégral', 53–65.
Wilson, B.R. (2000), 'Tolleranza religiosa e diversità religiosa', *Futuribili. Luci sull'immortalità. Religioni storiche, movimenti, New Age* (Milano: FrancoAngeli), 41–48.

Chapter 13

Religious Dress Codes: The Bulgarian Case

Maya Kosseva and Iva Kyurkchieva

The aim of this chapter is to outline the respective dress code strategies in Bulgaria within the boundaries of different public spaces, taking into account the role of individuals and communities as a whole. The delimiting of the functions is clearly evident in the institutional public space where individuals have different status due to the different activities that they perform. In the open public space the circumstances are more dynamic – the emphasis there is on the position which the individual holds or wants to attain within the respective social environment. It is necessary to specify that there are significant differences between the everyday dress code strategies and the festive ones (during holidays, family celebrations, town festivals, etc.). Often there is a demonstration of different identities at the personal and collective level.

Traditionally, in Bulgaria the various religious and ethnic groups have freely demonstrated their group affiliation through their clothing. It has been accepted throughout the ages and has never been a serious problem of social interaction.[1] However, in recent years the ongoing debate about Islam, the new immigrants and their activities in Europe and the rest of the world is becoming more of a hot topic in Bulgaria. It attracts public interest and provokes public discussion about the upcoming changes and the need for a reaction and a clear position on behalf of the institutions and civil society.

Until recently dress code policies and practices in Bulgaria did not incite any serious public debate. The media usually reported only extreme or controversial cases. Otherwise they mostly dealt with religious dress code when covering specific religious holidays or traditional customs of the respective ethnic or religious communities.

Dress code strategies in Bulgarian public and private spheres are reviewed in the historical and contemporary context of both the State regulation of the relations between the secular and the religious, and of the traditional ethnic and religious diversity of Bulgarian society in the European context.

1 There are notable exceptions in the periods of aggressive state interference with regard to the Muslim population during the twentieth century which will be mentioned in the study.

Historical Dimensions in State–Religion Relations

The specifics of the contemporary relations between the State and organized religion and the overall social structure are based on several historical milestones: Ottoman legacy, Orthodox affiliation, Communist and Post-Communist period and European identity. Due to the Ottoman legacy Bulgarian society has not been mono-religious since the establishment of the modern Bulgarian State in 1878. Considerable groups of Muslims (Sunni and Alevi), Jews, Armenians, Catholics and Protestants coexisted for centuries with the majority of Orthodox Bulgarians. Nevertheless, the perception of the official State policy was that Bulgaria was/or had to be a mono-ethnic and mono-religious nation-state. In the first Bulgarian Constitution of 1879[2] it is clearly stated that the Eastern Orthodox is the ruling religion and religious matters in the State are under the jurisdiction of the Holy Synod of the Orthodox Church (articles 37, 39). However, it is also mentioned that people from other religious affiliations could freely practise their religion as long as this did not contradict the State's legislation (articles 40, 41). Other confessions had their own religious structures but they were under the supervision of the corresponding Ministry (article 42).

The Communist period Constitutions (one from 1947[3] and another one from 1971[4]) treated religion and relations between the State and the Church in article 78 (1947) and article 53 (1971). According to the new regulations the Church was separate from the State. All citizens could freely practise their religion but with a special note that prohibits 'to misuse the church and religion for political reasons'. In this case 'The Church' referred to the Eastern Orthodox Church although it was not explicitly stated. However, it is mentioned that all other confessions had a right of autonomous management but it would be regulated by a special law[5] and supervised by a State institution. In practice these regulations did little to secure real freedom of religion within the totalitarian State and atheism was promoted in all spheres of social life.

The new Constitution of 1991 provided substance to the statements about freedom of religion contained in it since it was adopted after the democratic changes in the country.

Article 13 states that:

> (1) The practising of any religion shall be unrestricted
>
> (2) Religious institutions shall be separate from the State

---

2 www.kingsimeon.bg/downloads/Turnovska_Konstitucia.pdf (accessed 6 June 2012).

3 www.parliament.bg/?page=history&lng=bg&hid=5 (accessed 6 June 2012).

4 www.parliament.bg/?page=history&lng=bg&hid=6 (accessed 6 June 2012).

5 Religious Denomination Act from 1949, replaced in 2002. See: Peteva (2003: 40–41).

(3) Eastern Orthodox Christianity shall be considered the traditional religion in the Republic of Bulgaria

(4) Religious institutions and communities, and religious beliefs shall not be used to political ends.[6]

The autonomy of the confessions is, however, specifically guaranteed by a special Confessions Act (2002) (last amended in 2009). In the Act the attitude towards different religions and the position of the Eastern Orthodox Church is once again differentiated. On the one hand it declares the freedom of confessions and the independence of religious institutions: institutionally all confessional denominations are treated as equal and are eligible for State budget subsidies (article 28). On the other, it reconfirms the special position of the Eastern Orthodox Church based on tradition, history and significance to the State (article 10 [1]).[7] Moreover, while other denominations should register at the Sofia City Court as a corporate body (article 15), such status is acknowledged to the Bulgarian Orthodox Church by the law (article 10 [2]).[8] Despite this text, it is further on specified that article 10 (1) and (2) are not 'grounds for conceding of privileges or any preferences deriving from the law' (article 10 [3]).[9]

Thus, while all the confessions including the Orthodox are treated equally for the first time, the Eastern Orthodox is still declared to be the traditional one. So it once again retains its privileged position in Bulgaria. In comparison with other post-Communist Eastern European countries only Bulgaria has constitutionally defined Orthodoxy in terms of traditional religion of the State. This statement does not correspond to the declared strict separation between Church and State (Ferrari 2003: 414–415).

We could conclude that while the independence of the Orthodox Church and other religious institutions from the State is constantly and officially emphasized at all levels, the relations between the State and the religious bodies have always been ambiguous. For instance, a State institution – usually the Ministry of Foreign Affairs or the Ministry of Internal Affairs, always supervised all confessions in the past. Nowadays there is a Confessions Directorate at the Council of Ministers of the Republic of Bulgaria.

It should also be mentioned that in its history Bulgarian society was never characterized by deep religiosity in the canonical sense of the term. The experts usually refer to 'traditional Christianity' and 'traditional Islam' to describe the religiosity in Bulgaria, which is a mixture of pagan beliefs and various superstitions,

6 http://parliament.bg/en/const (accessed 6 June 2012).

7 'Traditional religion in the Republic of Bulgaria is the Eastern Orthodox. It has a historic role for the Bulgarian state and actual significance for its state life' (article 10 [1]) – http://lex.bg/laws/ldoc/2135462355 (accessed 6 June 2012).

8 http://lex.bg/laws/ldoc/2135462355 (accessed 6 June 2012).

9 http://lex.bg/laws/ldoc/2135462355 (accessed 6 June 2012).

covered by a thin layer of the official religions (Zhelyazkova et al. 1995). This process intensified substantially during the Communist period, when practising religion was discouraged and hindered by the State. After the democratic changes in 1989 many people again turned towards the traditional religions, above all in a reaction to the previous prohibitions. Nevertheless, religious affiliation is perceived more as a marker for ethnic identification.

Contemporary State Implementation of EU Strategy

Since the second half of the twentieth century Bulgaria has adopted all United Nations and European documents regarding the freedom of religion as an individual human right. It can be stated that issues of tolerance, civil and religious rights are adequately covered in the national legislation – the Constitution, the Confessions Act of 2002, the Political Parties Act, the Protection Against Discrimination Act of 2004, the Penal Code. There are also specialized bodies in place, which are involved in overseeing the implementing of the relevant legislation – National Council for Cooperation on Ethnic and Demographic Issues – NCCEDI (est. 1997), Ombudsman of the Republic of Bulgaria (est. 2003), Commission for Protection against Discrimination – CPD (est. 2005).[10] The European Commission against Racism and Intolerance (ECRI) is of the opinion that there are adequate texts in the current Bulgarian Constitution that guarantee the equal rights of the citizens. With regard to the Confessions Act and the Political Parties Act, the ECRI is of the opinion that religious and political rights are guaranteed but more effort should be invested in enforcing the legislation.[11] There are, however, numerous recommendations with regard to implementation of the Penal Code in race or religion related crimes. These comments mainly target the court of law practice, since no sentences have been passed based on the legislation articles regarding the above issues.[12]

10 CPD was established by the Parliament in 2005 in accordance with the Protection Against Discrimination Act (PADA) of 2004. It is a State administrative body, which can issue decisions according to PADA. The CPD procedure is expedient and free of taxes. The cases are investigated by CPD commissioners and there is also a public hearing. The decisions of the Commission are subject to appeal within 14 days before the Supreme Administrative Court (SAC) under the provisions of the Administrative Procedure Code. The Commission reviews the cases in specialized panels of which the Third is dealing with discrimination based on religion.

11 http://www.coe.int/t/dghl/monitoring/ecri/country-by-country/bulgaria/BGR-CbC-IV-2009-002-ENG.pdf (accessed 6 June 2012).

12 The activities of the CPD are most highly evaluated, since the Commission has reviewed the greatest number of complaints and has expediently issued the respective rulings. There is also mention of some documents which are not ratified (for example, European Charter for Regional or Minority Languages).

Throughout its entire existence the Bulgarian State has always strived to introduce and adopt its legislation in accordance with the tendencies in Europe and the rest of the world. Bulgarian legislation has adequately transposed the new relevant treaties, directives and other legislation documents. However, the implementation of the legislation often suffers from administrative obstacles and the lack of political will to enforce it.

Minorities and State–Religion Relations

According to the census of 2011, 76% of the Bulgarian population declared themselves as Eastern Orthodox Christians, 10% as Muslims (this includes Turks, Sunni and Alevi, Bulgarian Muslims – Pomaks and some groups of Roma). Catholics (including Uniates), Protestants, Jews, Armenian–Gregorian were less than 1% each. 4.7% declared that they did not belong to any denomination and 7.1% did not indicate their religious affiliation.[13]

It should be noted that according to a number of sociological surveys this religious self-identification is very often based on ethnic identification or family tradition and not so much on actually practising a certain religion (Peteva 2003: 38) or belonging to a certain confessional congregation. For example, not all of those who declared themselves as Eastern Orthodox Christians in the census were actually baptized or adhered to any prescriptions of the declared religion.

In 2010 the immigrants in Bulgaria were considered to be about 1.4% of the whole population.[14] The majority of Muslim immigrants (from Arabian, African, Turkish, Kurdish, Afghani, Iranian communities) are male. The reasons for this are the prevalent cultural and social norms in the countries of origin where female migration is considered appropriate only in the company of a male family member (BHC 2004: 21; Желязкова и др. 2005: 31–58). The overwhelming majority of foreigners with permanent residence live in larger cities which offer a more cosmopolitan atmosphere and better possibilities for employment and business (НСИ 2005: 307).

The official Bulgarian State policy towards the *traditional Muslim population* is very inconsistent. Periods of relatively liberal expression of traditional cultural identity were followed in turn by deliberate repression and assimilation attempts during the twentieth century. It should also be noted that the Muslim population in question lives in compact groups in peripheral, mainly rural, regions of the country.

During the totalitarian Communist regime after 1948 the goal was to gradually integrate all Muslims into the Socialist nation. The state imposed an excessive regulatory regime on religious denominations with a high level of administrative interference (Peteva 2003: 40). Muslim practices and tradition were subject to

13 www.nsi.bg/EPDOCS/Census2011final.pdf (accessed 6 June 2012).

14 http://esa.un.org/migration/p2k0data.asp (accessed 15 June 2012, no longer available).

pressure from two directions. As a principle, religion was officially persecuted as incompatible with Communist ideology. From another perspective Islam was seen to uphold an identity which was different from the Bulgarian identity. It should be noted that the internal denominations within the Muslim community (e.g. Sunni and Alevi) were never formally recognized and they were all subordinated to the institution of the Chief Mufti who is Sunni. This reflects the state policy towards the merging of all Muslims into one common group.

Claiming that it is necessary 'to overcome the backwardness in the lifestyle and the consciousness' among the Turks and the Bulgarian Muslims, the State undertook several assimilation campaigns during the 1970s and 1980s: there were campaigns for changing the Muslim names, persecution of Islam-related practices and customs and the abolition of traditional Muslim dress.[15] As a result of this policy the Muslim communities became encapsulated and restored some of their Islam-related patriarchal cultural characteristics, which had been relinquished in the process of modernization.

The specific attitude of the totalitarian State towards *all non-Eastern Orthodox confessional groups* is also evident from its approach towards the Catholic and Protestant communities in Bulgaria. Priests were persecuted and convicted in a series of court trials in the 1950s (Елдъров 2002: 666–672). In acknowledgement of these repressions Monsignor Bossilkov, one of the most prominent Catholic activists and leaders who was then executed, was canonized in 1998 by Pope John Paul II.

The inconsistent State policy towards the minorities and the periodic repressions against their cultural identity forces them to invent various survival and preservation strategies. This is reflected in their activities in the public and private space, including their clothing. Their expression at different levels is strongly influenced by their strategies for circumventing or adapting to the existing order of the day.

Religious Dress Code – Minorities and State Policy

Religious self-identification is often perceived as an ethnic or cultural identification factor. This is why in Bulgarian society specific clothing is associated not only with religious affiliation but also to a great extent with ethnos and tradition.

It can be stated that the issue of religious dress code and symbols in public places is relatively new for Bulgaria and is only beginning to emerge. There are several main reasons for this:

- The Christian Orthodox majority do not have any special dress code except for the clergy.

15 Груев, Кальонски (2008); Желязкова (1998); Иванова 2002; Кръстева-Благоева (2001); Бюксеншютц (2000); Konstantinov and Alhaug (1995).

- The local Muslim population auto-regulates the demonstrations of their difference from the majority and are cautious of open confrontation on this ground.
- Immigrants in Bulgaria are still a relatively small group. They are mostly males who strive to fit into the society, whereas women are less numerous – they mainly stay at home and are not socially active.
- The traditional Jewish,[16] Armenian,[17] Catholic and Protestant communities are relatively small and they are fully integrated in the society. They do not demonstrate publicly any special dress code. Only some of their clergy can be recognized by their specific clothes.

The above-mentioned structure of religious groups in Bulgaria corresponds directly to the attitudes of the State in regulation of the religious dress code as well as of the communities and individuals acting in public and private spheres. Both are different with regard to the costumes of the traditional Muslim (Turks, Pomaks, some Roma) groups and to the recently introduced elements of religious clothing[18] (a slow process taking place in the last 20 years). Among the traditional Muslim communities religious affiliation is also an identity marker. This identity is especially manifested through their preservation of the traditional feminine costume – shalwar pants and a headscarf.

During the course of the twentieth century there have been gradual changes in the dress of Roma women in the direction of disappearance of traditional elements, which vary between the different internal Roma groups (Decheva 2004: 84–85). Presently, only the Muslim Roma women have partially preserved the traditional feminine costume – shalwar pants, while the older ones also wear headscarves (Decheva 2004: 91–92).

Among the immigrant Muslim women in Bulgaria there are various tendencies in the change of the dress code:

1. preserving the traditional dress as in the country of origin;
2. wearing of lighter coloured clothes but still covering of the head;
3. not covering the head and wearing of modern clothes (Троева, Манчева 2011: 203–204).

Under the influence of the new environment in Bulgaria, they have exchanged the black robe and head cover (variation of the *hijab*) with a long skirt, black trousers and long jacket. The decision to keep the headscarf, which is typical for a large number of women, leads to isolation and a preference for remaining within the confined space of the home where the practising of Islam is concentrated. The women who do not wear headscarves define this as an act of their free will.

16 See Барух (2000).

17 See Мицева (2001).

18 See Троева (2012).

They often switch the dress code depending on the place visited. For example, they prefer the more conservative dress within the institutional public space and in the mosque (ibid., 203–209). As a whole, the transformation of the clothing is dependent on the insecurity of the Muslim woman as result of her different appearance and the agreement between the man and the woman with regard to the family strategy during the period of adaptation (ibid., 213–214).

However, in recent years another tendency can be observed among the traditional Muslim communities which is related to the approach towards Islam at the European level. Many young people receive an education in Islamic countries (for example Turkey, Saudi Arabia, Syria, Jordan, etc.) (Kyurkchieva et al. 2008) or have contacts with Muslim communities in Europe. From their perspective Islam in Bulgaria has been preserved at the everyday lifestyle level but it is not sufficiently canonical. Often, even at the cost of conflict with the older generation, such young people try to introduce the 'true' practices. Lately this is reflected in the feminine dress code as well – classically veiled young girls/women[19] wearing robes can be seen. It is precisely and above all these new elements that provoke social sensitivity and a negative reaction. They also attract the State's attention to the necessity for regulation of the dress code in the public sphere.

The public and media discussions are at the core of the pending revision of the School Education Act which was proposed in 2009. The proposed Article 122 (3) 6 states that students 'should not wear symbols or elements of clothing, which aggressively or imposingly demonstrate religious or ideological preferences, as well as such which incite ethnic or racial hostility or hatred'. The same regulation is envisaged for teachers in Article 134 (2) 15.[20] This proposed text has caused vigorous public discussions for over two years. It can be speculated that along with other debated issues, it is one of the reasons why the revision of the act has not been approved by the Parliament during the government of the coalition, which included the party DPS (Bulgarian acronym for Movement for Rights and Freedoms – a political party representing the interests of Muslims in Bulgaria). According to a representative of a human rights NGO in Bulgaria, this text affects mostly Muslim women and can be considered as an example of indirect multiple discrimination on the grounds of gender, religion and ethnicity.[21] Although most commentators agree that these texts concern the headscarves, some representatives of the Eastern Orthodox Church, nationalist organizations and journalists have launched the version that will effectively ban jewellery with crucifix symbols. At this stage the text is very unclear and will probably cause numerous future

19 According to the Bulgarian Muslims' tradition the headscarf does not fully cover the hair and the ears. More often it is tied in a fashion typical for the respective village thus indicating the belonging to a specific ethnic or religious group. The Chief Mufti in Bulgaria circulated an official leaflet, which explains how women's clothing should look according to the canon: Чекер (2009).

20 www.sbubg.info/files/proekt_zakon_obrazovanie.pdf (accessed 6 June 2012).

21 www.mediapool.bg/show/?storyid=121172 (accessed 6 June 2012).

debates and interpretations with regard to what might constitute 'aggressive and imposing demonstration of religious preferences'. In February 2012, a new draft law was introduced for a public discussion. It does not contain the controversial articles. There is just an article 172 (4) according to which the pupils "should visit school in clothing and appearance which corresponds to the schools' bylaws".[22] It is obvious that the state delegates the right to decide for religious symbols to the local school authorities.

It can be summarized that recently the question of religious clothing and symbols is becoming more of a hot topic in Bulgarian society and the State institutions are beginning to seek possible solutions to the issue. At the current stage there is a lack of clear positions and desire for active involvement.

Institutional Public Space and Religious Dress Code

The first cases, where the religious dress code raised issues about the relations between the State and religion, occurred in the sphere of public education,[23] i.e. in the institutional public space. Such cases will be used to illustrate the problem in Bulgaria, the public and media reaction, and the attempts of the State to regulate those issues.

Recently, there were several cases that could be noted in the above context. It is common for all these cases that the State, represented by local and central institutions, was not prepared to react. The society did not display a high level of sensitivity, either. Since the cases were mostly related to the dress code in schools, it could be concluded that there is a lack of regulation for the public display of religious symbols in the Education Act.

In all cases the issue is related to the religious clothing of Muslim women/girls. The specific examples are from occurrences in public schools. These are public spaces where the teachers perform public services and the pupils are present within this institutional space in their capacity as private individuals.

One of the first examples is from 1996. At that time public attention was suddenly drawn to the local school in Ribnovo, a village in Southwest Bulgaria populated with Bulgarian Muslims (Pomaks), where the female pupils attended school wearing traditional dress including shalwar pants and colourful headscarves. As mentioned earlier, Turks and Pomaks in Bulgaria live mainly in compact groups in rural areas and preserve their traditional dress. It is part of their everyday life and wearing it at school does not pose any problem. It was therefore strange when one of these villages became a media attraction. The ensuing debate involved the Minister of Education who was of the opinion that such practice is not coherent

22 http://www.minedu.government.bg/opencms/export/sites/mon/left_menu/documents/documentsproject/2012/proekt_zakon_obrazovanie_14-02-2012.pdf (accessed 6 June 2012).

23 About the policy of the West European countries see Taylor (2011); Scott (2007).

with the secular nature of public education. The journalists launched the version that in the region there are occurrences of Islamic fundamentalism, while the local population defended their right to wear traditional costumes, emphasizing that this is part of their tradition and identity.[24] Following aggressive media campaigns and numerous inspections by the Ministry of Education and Science (MES) it was concluded that the issue cannot be considered a case of religious propaganda and the scandal withered away.

In 2009 similar accusations were directed towards the same school and the media again activated public opinion but eventually the situation calmed down.[25] It can be stated that this was a case of clear political intrigue because various political organizations have been striving to attract the support of the Pomak population of the region. From another perspective, nationalist parties also target such regions in order to attract nationalist voter support, including the political party *Ataka* (Attack) (represented in the National Assembly since 2005) and the *RZS* Party (Bulgarian acronym for Order, Law and Justice – represented in the National Assembly since 2009). This example, however, illustrates the sporadic reactions of the politicians, the media, the public and the State institutions (represented by the MES) in debates related to the wearing of traditional dress by Muslim women.

The other example is related to the introduction of new elements in Muslim women's clothing – robes and full headscarves. In these cases the issue was raised by the representatives of the community, who felt that their rights had been violated. There were two cases involving high-school students belonging to the traditional Muslim communities in Bulgaria. The cases were reviewed by the Commission for Protection against Discrimination (CPD).

In 2006 a complaint was filed before the CPD by a local Muslim organization. The complaint was against the text of the bylaws of a high school in the city of Smolyan, which prescribed the wearing of school uniform. The plaintiff organization claimed that this was especially aimed at preventing the wearing of clothes typical for their religious affiliation, although the school principal had not restricted the access of the students to the education service. In its decision 37/27.07.2006 the CPD not only dismissed the discrimination claim but also ruled that the school principal had allowed violation of the school bylaws by the complainants, which had led to unequal treatment of the other high school students who wore the prescribed uniforms.[26] As a result the CPD imposed sanctions against all parties – the plaintiff organization, the school board and the Ministry of Education and Science for actions inciting discrimination and unequal treatment.

---

24 www.vsekiden.com/47705 (accessed 6 June 2012).

25 www.monitor.bg/article?id=192714 (accessed 6 June 2012); http://paper.standartnews.com/bg/article.php?article=270891 (accessed 6 June 2012); www.dnevnik.bg/dnevnikplus/2009/03/17/691321_ribnovo_-_partiiata_tuk_e_bashev/ (accessed 6 June 2012).

26 http://www.kzd-nondiscrimination.com/layout/images/stories/pdf/Otchet_KZD_2006.pdf (accessed 6 June 2012).

In 2008 the CPD received a complaint related to discrimination on religious grounds from female students attending school with specific Muslim clothes – robes and full headscarves (Grekova et al. 2010: 61–62, 138–139). The complaint was filed by the students who were residents of the village of Gyovren, studying in the town of Devin. The CPD could not establish discrimination, neither in the act of the school principal orally cautioning the students not to wear religious symbols at school, nor in the Regional Education Inspectorate prescriptions regarding the display of religious symbols in public schools, because there was no restriction of the access of the complainants to the education service. However, in its decision 38/22.02.2008 the CPD recommended to the Minister of Education and Science to undertake an overall analysis of the state of the Bulgarian education system in the context of complying with anti-discrimination legislation and religious rights. The decision of the CPD was appealed before the Supreme Administrative Court (SAC). The SAC ruled that the CPD decision was unsubstantial and in violation of the prescriptions of PADA, which only envisage actions for preventing or stopping discriminatory acts and not the issuing of recommendations.

A case from 2009 involved a language teacher who taught French and Turkish in a primary school in the village of Kovachevo, Pazardzhik region, and who always wore black clothes and a headscarf. According to her employers she would normally wear trousers and blouses, occasionally covering her hair with a knitted scarf or wearing a headscarf. The public interest in this case was stirred by the media, which obtained a cell phone video clip featuring the teacher in class. The parents of the pupils fully supported the teacher as a capable and skilled education professional who performed her duties. The school principal and the Head of the Regional Education Inspectorate of Pazardzhik shared the same opinion.[27] The teacher had all the required qualifications allowing her to practise her profession. There were no complaints from parents or colleagues and the School Board took no action against her. Despite the spontaneous tolerant reaction of the parents and the director, the teacher was subsequently forced to resign.[28]

A case from 2006 required a reaction from the Ministry of Education and Science. At that time 110 female students from Turkey applied to study at the Medical University in Plovdiv but with the explicit request that they be allowed to wear headscarves in class. The university management hesitantly refused. There was an interesting reaction from the Minister of Education who was an experienced lawyer with notable liberal views. At first, he considered that university students' manner of clothing is an issue of personal choice and regulatory intervention is not

27 'Neither I, nor the principal of the schools where she teaches, will force her to take off her headscarf. I think there is nothing wrong with her actions, although education is secular. And then – what is the meaning of a headscarf' – interview with Head of the Regional Education Inspectorate of Pazardzhik – www.deltanews.bg/index.php?id=13376 (accessed 6 June 2012).

28 This information was not widely publicized in the media. It was received in July 2011 from a respondent during the field research under the RELIGARE project.

desirable. A few days later his position on the issue became less liberal: 'Although the issue of religious symbols in higher education institutes is a bit different than that in high schools, we consider that higher education should be perceived as visibly secular. And it should be conducted, including from a visual perspective, according to the Bulgarian national traditions'.[29] He also suggested that regulations for dress code in the schools should be implemented for the higher education institutes as well. It is notable that different political parties supported his opinion. Those that publicly reacted were mainly human rights lawyers or activists.[30] It should be noted, though, that the Higher Education Act was not revised so as to include texts about religious clothing and symbols. However, in the Higher Education Act it is mentioned that 'the higher secular education is independent of ideology, religion and political doctrines. It is conducted in accordance with common humanitarian values and national tradition' (article 3).[31] In the context of the minister's official position and the aforementioned special treatment of the Eastern Orthodox Church as keeper of national tradition, this statement can be interpreted in the sense that specific elements of the religious dress code will not be tolerated. It is possible that in the occurrence of similar cases this text might serve as grounds for denying women the right to wear their headscarves in class.[32]

It is common to all these cases that the State, represented by local and central institutions, was not prepared to react. Society did not display a high level of sensitivity either. The examples indicate that regardless of whether a complaint was formally filed, the cases related to the religious dress code are mostly put down to interpretation and no serious sanctions are imposed. Since these are mainly occurrences in schools, it can be assumed that the problem is related to the lack of regulation with regard to religious symbols in the present School Education Act.

Another important point is that traditional clothing is not an issue at the local level – it is perceived as part of the cultural tradition. In Muslim villages children go to school dressed according to their own preferences. In this sense the case in Ribnovo was an exception, which was politically motivated. The newly introduced elements in Muslim clothing in Bulgaria meet with stricter opposition from school authorities. This in turn causes a response from the individuals wearing the disputed clothing who take their case to the authorities, thus attracting the attention of the media. It should be mentioned that even in the case of the language teacher, it was not her traditional manner of clothing – according to the local people, she adopted it after her son got married in Turkey.[33] The girls who filed a complaint with the

29 www.mediapool.bg/show/?storyid=121172 (accessed 6 June 2012).

30 www.mediapool.bg/show/?storyid=121172 (accessed 6 June 2012).

31 http://lex.bg/bg/laws/ldoc/2133647361 (accessed 6 June 2012).

32 However, in universities there are already a few women wearing headscarves but since they are Bulgarian citizens and their cases are not commented in the media, their manner of clothing is not an issue for the faculty or the other students (Archive of IMIR).

33 www.blitz.bg/news/article/41092 (accessed 6 June 2012).

CPD started veiling themselves at a more mature age due to personal reasons and not due to family tradition.[34]

In view of the above, it can be summarized that there is still a very low level of preparedness on the part of official institutions to undertake any significant restrictive or liberalizing regulatory changes. Future research and observation of the process could establish whether the institutions will be able to initiate adequate changes and implement them accordingly. The acknowledgement or denial of the dress code strategies can outline the limits of tolerance and integration in the policies of the State. The reviewed cases indicate that despite the lack of a comprehensive legal framework, the relations between religion and secularity are regulated either according to the existing legislation or in the interest of a moderate and tolerant treatment of the individual. The media seem to demonstrate a desire to push some existing practices higher up on the public agenda thus sharpening the controversies, but regardless of this, there is no significant public debate on the issue of religious dress code. The categorical statements and positions of the nationalist organizations usually attract the greatest publicity.

The reactions of the various national and local authorities towards the emerging 'new' dress codes (e.g. the case of the veiled students) show how one institution (CPD) recommends to another institution (the Ministry of Education and Science) to approach the issue starting with an overall analysis of the state of the Bulgarian education system in the context of complying with anti-discrimination legislation and religious rights, while a third institution (the Supreme Administrative Court) considers that the CPD has exceed its competences by making a recommendation, basing its ruling on the texts of that same anti-discrimination legislation (PADA), which CPD has been established to implement.

This case clearly demonstrates that there is still no coherent policy and strategy of the State for dealing with such cases, as well as possible deficiencies in the relevant legislation or the approach for its implementation.[35] This also poses a more general question about the rather chaotic approach to resolving certain legislation problems (Grekova et al. 2010).

In 2010 the problem of religious clothing emerged in another public sphere – photograph requirements for the new personal identification documents. The issue was raised by the Regional Mufti from Smolyan. Following the complaint, the problem has spread to other regions and Muslim women all over the country also insist that they be photographed with headscarves entirely covering their hair and ears. During the ensuing debate a precedent from 2002 was cited when the

---

34 www.bghelsinki.org/index.php?module=pages&lg=bg&page=obektiv13403 (accessed 6 June 2012).

35 This is further illustrated by the fact that the media periodically revive the story about students in Smolyan and Devin schools voluntarily wearing headscarves, and that the Head of the Regional Education Inspectorate in Smolyan occasionally tries to restrict the wearing of headscarves in class: www.deltanews.bg/index.php?id=13376 (accessed 6 June 2012).

Supreme Administrative Court rejected an identical request by another woman and thus the problem was considered resolved from a legal perspective.[36]

However, the State did not really have a mechanism for reacting to such requests. Finally, many of these requests have been satisfied in one of the Regional Directorates of Interior Affairs (Pazardzhik), provided that the conditions of the 'Rules on the Issuance of Bulgarian Identity Documents' were met. In appendix 3 to these rules it was stated that individuals should have their photographs taken without hats or headscarves unless they explicitly request so, in which case at least 1cm of their hair and both ears should be visible.[37] Apparently this compromise satisfied the women who had otherwise been photographed bareheaded during the previous ID issue campaigns.[38] The general public again remained moderately uninterested in the issue. Concerns were expressed mainly by some nationalist organizations that backed their statements by quoting some restrictive European practices such as the French legislation in this area. Many of the political representatives of the party which represents mainly the Muslims in Bulgaria, the Movement for Rights and Freedom, avoided expressing a firm position or commented that the rules should be followed.[39]

Religious Dress Code in the Open Public Space

The next step in examining the relations between the State and religion leads to the use of traditional Muslim clothing in Bulgaria. For the purposes of the current work it is necessary to outline how the social environment and the expectations of the people affect the dress code of Muslims in Bulgaria.

The public authorities in Bulgaria and society as a whole recognize and are accustomed to the traditional dress code of Muslims and other religious groups in the open public space because of the long-standing coexistence of the different groups.

At the same time it should be emphasized that the feminine dress code is a very important identification sign among the various ethnic and religious subgroups within the Muslim community – there are specific differences in the clothing

36 www.trud.bg/Article.asp?ArticleId=530176 (accessed 6 June 2012); www.24chasa.bg/Article.asp?ArticleId=530306 (accessed 6 June 2012); http://sites.google.com/site/pravosver/home/vas/vas-11820-2002 (accessed 6 June 2012).

37 www.dnevnik.bg/bulgaria/2010/07/12/931604_policiiata_v_pazardjik_izdava_dokumenti_sus_snimki_sus/ (accessed 6 June 2012); http://law.dir.bg/reference.php?f=pibds-99 (accessed 6 June 2012).

38 www.btv.bg/shows/tazi-sutrin/razgovori-gosti/story/79892607-Ima_li_zabrana_jenite_v_Pazardzhik_da_se_snimat_sas_zabradki_za_lichni_dokumenti.html (accessed 6 June 2012).

39 www.trud.bg/Article.asp?ArticleId=530176 (accessed 6 June 2012); www.24chasa.bg/Article.asp?ArticleId=530306 (accessed 6 June 2012).

of Turks (Sunni, Alevi), Pomaks, etc. There are also regional differences in the traditional dress. These details might not be so significant for the members of non-Muslim communities who are not interested in internal Muslim group differences and perceive women wearing shalwars as simply Turkish/Muslim. But it is important to note the persistence with which the Muslims preserved their identifying signs and kept the Quran tradition even during times of totalitarian State repression campaigns. Regardless of the restrictions they found alternative ways of visually expressing their religious difference: loose jogging pants were worn as an alternative to shalwars and protective blue work robes were worn instead of *feredje*.[40] Men wore soft caps as an identifying sign of their religious affiliation. Although these substitute clothes did not provide the opportunity to display internal community differences, they were a way of preserving and displaying identity through the dress code. It was important for them and the surrounding Christian community because it was a silent act of protest and desire to preserve their own culture.

Nowadays, having lived for quite some time in an openly – or masked – hostile social environment, Muslims have developed their own mechanisms for adaptation. Often they adapt the demonstration of their identity to the immediate social environment. The traditional feminine dress worn at home or within the village is often substituted with generic modern clothing during visits to the town and especially when contacts with representatives of official institutions – local authorities, hospitals, etc. – are expected. The purpose is to avoid negative stereotypes and a consequent reaction. There is also the reverse reason – young people studying away from their native places prefer to wear modern clothes but they put on the traditional costumes when they visit their villages in order to please the older generations. In some villages in the West Rhodope Mountains and the Central Balkan Mountains inhabited by Bulgarian Muslims (Pomaks), the women wear the typical regional variation of the traditional costume on a daily basis – colourful shalwar pants and headscarves. In these villages the majority of the younger women and girls also wear such clothes.[41] In some settlements in Southeast and Northeast Bulgaria inhabited by compact groups of Turkish people, the older women still wear dull-coloured shalwar and headscarves, whereas the younger ones rarely dress in such a fashion. Older women, especially in the mountain villages, continue to wear plain cotton shalwar pants because they are practical and comfortable for everyday wearing and work.

Among the majority of the Muslim population in the country the use or rejection of the traditional costume is perceived as a choice between tradition and modernity rather than as a demonstration of religious affiliation.

40 Garment worn mainly before 1944, which resembles a long black robe or coat covering the whole body.

41 According to some unverified media sources, the Regional Education Inspectorate of Blagoevgrad continuously receives signals that female students are actually forced to wear headscarves. www.deltanews.bg/index.php?id=13376 (accessed 6 June 2012).

The social environment affects the use of an identifying dress code by Muslim communities in Bulgaria. They choose different dress code strategies depending on their status or desired status within the community, as well as according to the expectations of the surrounding population belonging to another confessional group. Presently the religious dress code still remains in the private space, mainly among women in the home or within the settlement, i.e. within the wider boundaries of their own community. However, this dress code is visible in the open public space during the holidays and rituals of the different communities, as well as within their religious spaces.

One of the most enduring ways of demonstrating religious or ethnic affiliation by use of a dress code is the presentation of traditional costumes during folklore festivals and celebrations (regional, national, international). Such events were allowed even during the times of State-promoted atheism. After the democratic changes of 1989, the Regional Cultural Centres (*Chitalishta*) in areas with a compact Muslim population began to revive local traditions and to present them publicly as an important part of the identity of the local population.

Another way of using festive religious clothing as dress code in the open public space is related to wedding rituals. This can be illustrated by examples from two different Muslim communities – the Turkish and the Bulgarian Muslims (Pomaks).

The first example is related to the celebration of *Kına Gecesi* (Henna Night) by the Turkish community in the area of the town of Ruen (Eastern Bulgaria) (Кюркчиева 2010). The henna dyeing ritual is performed the night before the wedding when the bride-to-be and some close female relatives apply henna dye to their hands or hair. Over time in Bulgaria this custom has undergone many changes and regional transformations, to such extent that in some cases the actual henna dyeing is left out, but the event remains one of the most significant moments for the bride in the process of acquiring the status of a married woman and joining her new family. It is one of the rare examples when the women wear the traditional costume (coloured shalwars and headscarf) in its modern variation. The costume is worn only by the women participating in the ritual, which demonstrates their specific role as keepers of the tradition and the cultural identity of the local Turkish population.[42] Although somewhat modified, the traditional costumes are preserved and clearly demonstrate the Turkish identity and the related Muslim religious affiliation. At the core of the modern *Kına Gecesi* is the celebration held for the whole village population in the centre of the settlement. The idea is that the whole community is gathered in the common space and the new family is publicly recognized and accepted. Thus the original ritual is gradually transforming from a feminine family celebration into a community event. It is practised in both all-Turkish villages and in mixed villages where the Christian Bulgarians are usually invited and participate in the festivities. The custom is one

42 Some respondents consider that the requirement for the wearing of traditional clothing on Henna Night is becoming outdated (Archive of IMIR).

of the ways for the local Turkish population to express and preserve its cultural identity and to update the functions of this identity in the process. The wedding or part of the wedding rituals with their specifics within the different communities often become one of the most significant identification characteristics for the respective group.

The second example of dress code strategies in the open public space is related to the ritual of the *painted* or *disguised bride* (also called *Gelina*), which has been observed among the Bulgarian Muslims (Pomaks) from the region of Teteven (Gallata Village) (Кюркчиева 2004: 123–128) and the region of Gotze Delchev (Ribnovo Village).[43] According to this wedding custom, the bride is dressed in the typical regional traditional costume (multi-coloured shalwars and headscarf) and her face is painted and dotted with sequins of different colours forming geometric or floral shapes. For this type of decoration the eyes must remain shut and the face becomes like a mask. This custom is preserved and always practised at weddings in Ribnovo (Gotze Delchev region, Southwest Bulgaria), while in the region of Teteven (Northern Bulgaria) it has gradually become outdated and is rarely practised or demonstrated. These customs, modified but functioning in the present, are not only a preferred identity marker acknowledged by the local people but also a way for expression of the identity outside their own group. Such rituals are probably the easiest and least controversial way for the presentation of similar minority groups during their interaction with the surrounding world.

Dress code strategies in the presented examples indicate that festive clothing within the open public space (on the streets and the central square of the settlement) is a way of expressing religious affiliation. These are the places where Turks and Bulgarian Muslims (Pomaks) by use of the festive dress code can visibly express their identity at the individual and collective level. These are spaces where public and private are intertwined. The individuals present themselves and their community through the festive religious dress code. It is a way to express and demonstrate their own identity in front of others. At the same time it should be noted that most Turkish brides in the area of Ruen wear the traditional costume at the beginning of the ritual event but later in the evening they change into an official colourful long dress. This switch of dress code and preference of unified European official clothing can be interpreted as confirmation of the secular over the religious or at least as an indication of their parallel coexistence as alternative dress code strategies of the Turkish community.

43 See сп. 359-списанието за България, бр.2, ноември, 2007 г.; http://infomreja.bg/news.php?id=4685 (accessed 6 June 2012).

Conclusion

The presented cases of various dress code strategies in the institutional and the open public space indicate that in Bulgaria there can be observed a tendency for integration of the different manifestations of individual and collective identities. At the same time within public schools there is a desire to introduce and implement rules for adherence to common dress standards but the official authorities are not ready to undertake changes in the regulations, regardless of whether they are restrictive or liberalizing.

In the open public space there can be observed a certain duality – individuals use the religious dress code for their symbolic presentation and as a demonstration of their identity but they also feel an affinity towards the secular. As opposed to that tendency, the strategies for use of the religious dress code in the institutional public space are directed towards firmly expressing the religious identity.

Various forms of display of religious dress and symbols were traditionally present in Bulgarian society throughout the ages and this tendency is also preserved in the modern State. The issue of demonstrating religious affiliation through clothing is sporadically raised in public debate. However, in such cases it is related to the State policy for unification and homogenization of the nation. The displays of different religious or ethnic affiliation are usually limited to simply displaying the characteristic of being different. Religious symbols are not emphasized but are part of the cultural identity of the group. The issue of religious clothing and symbols is not perceived as an issue of the religious versus the secular but as a demonstration of difference. While in Bulgaria the society is more heterogeneous, in other parts of Europe the displays of religious difference are witnessed in a comparatively recent historical period.

From a European perspective, the Bulgarian model could provide a basis for seeking some possible solutions. On one side, the relations between the State and the Church, the religious and the secular, as well as the public display of religious symbols are traditionally not perceived as a problem in Bulgarian society and there is a long history of their acceptance and parallel coexistence. On the other side, however, the Bulgarian State and society are strongly influenced by the European processes and constantly strive to be adequate (in some cases to 'catch-up') and apply the European models – often mechanically. In many cases the application is not only unsuccessful but leads to corruption of the model. As a result, the new European processes provoke Bulgarian society and force the State to react and sometimes seek solutions to 'non-existent' issues. For the moment, the media, society, the institutions and the affected minorities try to adapt the traditionally existing mechanisms to the quickly changing realities and international political tendencies and models.

References

Барух Е. (съст.) (2000), *Евреите по българските земи: Родова памет и историческа съдба* [Barouh, E. (ed.), *Jews in the Bulgarian Lands: Ancestral Memory and Historical Destiny*] (Sofia: IMIR).

Бюксеншютц, У. (2000), *Малцинствената политика в България. Политиката на БКП към евреи, роми, помаци и турци 1944–1989* [Büchsenschütz, U., *Minority Policy in Bulgaria: The Policy of the Bulgarian Communist Party towards Jews, Roma, Pomaks and Turks 1944–1989*] (Sofia: IMIR).

Груев, М., Кальонски, А. (2008), *Възродителният процес. Мюсюлманските общности и комунистическият режим* [Gruev, M. and Kalionski, A., *The 'Revival Process'. Muslim Communities and the Communist Regime: Policies, Reactions and Consequences*] (Sofia: Ciela).

Елдъров, С. (2002), *Католиците в България (1878–1989) Историческо изследване* [Eldarov, S., *Catholics in Bulgaria (1878–1989) A Historical Study*] (Sofia: IMIR).

Желязкова, А. (1998), 'Турци' в Кръстева, А. (съст.), 371–397 [Zhelyazkova, A., 'Turks' in Krasteva, A. (ed.)] (Sofia: Petexton).

Желязкова, А., Григоров, В., Димитрова, Д. (2005) 'Имигранти от Близкия и Среден изток' в Кръстева, А. (съст.), 19–73 [Zhelyazkova, A., Grigorov, V., Dimitrova, D., 'Middle East Immigrants' in Krasteva, A. (ed.)] (Sofia: IMIR).

Иванова, Е. (2002), *Отхвърлените "приобщени"* [Ivanova, E. *Rejected by Integration*] (Sofia: Institute of East European Humanities).

Кръстева, А. (съст.) (1998), *Общности и идентичности в България* [Krasteva, A. (ed.), *Communities and Identities in Bulgaria*] (Sofia: Petexton).

Кръстева, А. (съст.) (2005), *Имиграцията в България* [Krasteva, A. (ed.), *Immigration in Bulgaria*] (Sofia: IMIR).

Кръстева-Благоева, Ев. (2001), 'За имената и преименуванията на българите мюсюлмани (1912–2000)' [Krasteva-Blagoeva, E., 'About the Names and the Renamings of the Bulgarians Muslims (1912–2000)'] – Българска етнология [in Bulgarian Ethnology], 2, 126–148 (Sofia: EIM).

Кюркчиева, И. (2004), *Светът на българите мюсюлмани от Тетевенско преход към модерност* [Kyurkchieva, I., *The World of Bulgarian Muslims from the Teteven Region – Transition to Modernity*] (Sofia: IMIR).

Кюркчиева, И. (2010), 'Аспекти на локалното културно наследство: къна геджеси в село Топчийско' [Kyurkchieva, I., 'Aspects of Local Cultural Heritage: *Kına* Gecesi in the Village of Topchijsko'] – Българска етнология [in Bulgarian Ethnology], 1–2, 123–137 (Sofia: EIM).

Мицева, Е. (2001), *Арменците в България – култура и идентичност* [Miceva, E., *Armenians in Bulgaria – Culture and Identity*] (Sofia: IMIR).

НСИ (2005), *Население и демографски процеси 2004* [NSI, *Population and Demographic Processes*] (Sofia: National Statistical Institute).

Троева, Ев. (2012) '"Традиционен" и "нов" ислям в България' [Troeva, Ev., '"Traditional" and "New" Islam in Bulgaria'] – Български фолклор [in Bulgarian Folklore], 3–4 (in print) (Sofia: IEFSEM).

Троева, Ев. Манчева, М. (2011), 'Миграция, религия и джендър: имигрантки мюсюлманки в България' в Хайдиняк, М. (съст.), 177–216 [Troeva, Ev. and Mancheva, M. 'Migration, Religion and Gender: Female Muslim Immigrants in Bulgaria', in Hajdinjak, M. (ed.)] (Sofia: IMIR).

Хайдиняк, М., (съст.) (2011), *Миграции, пол и междукултурни взаимодействия в България* [Hajdinjak M. (ed.), *Migration, Gender and Intercultural Interactions in Bulgaria*] (Sofia: IMIR).

Чекер, О. (2009), *Благоприличното облекло на жената според исляма* [Cheker, O., *Proper Female Clothing according to Islam*] (Sofia: Chief Mufti Publishing).

BHC (2004), *Survey on the Rights of Migrants in Bulgaria. Final Report of the Bulgarian Helsinki Committee* (Sofia: Bulgarian Helsinki Committee).

Butler, J., Habermas, J., Taylor, C. and West, C. (2011), *The Power of Religion in the Public Sphere* (New York: Columbia University Press).

Decheva, M. (2004), *Gypsy\Roma Dress in Bulgaria* (Sofia: EIM).

Ferrari, S. (2003), 'Conclusion: Church and State in Post-Communist Europe', in Ferrari, S. and Durham, C.W. (eds), 411–429.

Ferrari, S. and Durham, C.W. (eds) (2003), *Law and Religion in Post-Communist Europe* (Leuven: Peeters).

Grekova, M., Kyurkchieva, I., Kosseva, M. and Avramov, O. (2010), *Discrimination as a Social Practice, Bulgaria (2008 – 2010)* (Sofia: IMIR).

Konstantinov, J. and Alhaug, G. (1995), *Names, Ethnicity and Politics. Islamic Names in Bulgaria 1912–1992* (Oslo: Novus Press).

Kyurkchieva, I., Troeva-Grigorova, E., Boncheva-Lucheva, Ts., Kosseva, M. and Dimitrova, D. (2008), *Minority Rights, Inter-ethnic and Inter-religious Relations in Municipalities with Diverse Population* (Sofia: IMIR).

Peteva, J. (2003), 'Church and State in Bulgaria', in Ferrari, S. and Durham, C.W. (eds), 37–56.

Scott, J. (2007), *The Politics of the Veil* (Princeton University Press).

Taylor, C. (2011), 'Why we need a Radical Redefinition of Secularism', in Butler, J., Habermas, J., Taylor, C. and West, C., 34–59.

Zhelyazkova, A., Nielsen, J. and Kepel, G. (eds) (1995), *Relations of Compatibility and Incompatibility between Christians and Muslims in Bulgaria* (Sofia: IMIR).

Chapter 14

Comparing Burqa Debates in Europe: Sartorial Styles, Religious Prescriptions and Political Ideologies

Sara Silvestri

Introduction

This chapter examines comparatively the socio-cultural and political variables that can be identified as driving factors behind debates around the need to legislate against the wearing of the so-called 'integral veil', more commonly called *burqa*. After an examination of the religious symbolism and sociological significance of the emergence of the integral veil fashion, the chapter offers a comparative overview of different national cultures, political calculations and legal responses surrounding the emergence of the *burqa* controversy in a select number of European countries. An in-depth analysis of the French and British context is offered while the broader panorama extends from the Netherlands, to Germany, Austria, Denmark and Spain. Belgium and Italy are dealt with very concisely not because the issue is less salient there but because these two countries are covered elsewhere in this volume.[1]

Between Sartorial Styles, Religious Prescriptions and Political Ideologies

Considered to be a sign of tradition and piety by some believers and by a minority of observers, but seen as backward, oppressive and offensive by many others, the full veil has become the most popular subject around which the notion of multiculturalism has been disputed. Although the majority of the female Muslim population in Europe does not wear the *burqa* (Arabic term indicating a full head-to-toe cloak-like garment, normally colourful, with an embroidered opening for the eyes)[2] or the *niqab* (Arabic: 'face veil': typically white or black), the latter has

1 For fuller treatment of the issues covered in this chapter see Silvestri (forthcoming).

2 Although some English-language outlets use the spelling *burka*, this chapter uses *burqa* because it is more consistent with Arabic, where the letter Q, not K, is used. Moreover, several other European languages have also transliterated this common foreign word with *burqa*, not with *burka*.

spread considerably in the first decade of this century, especially among young women embracing a very conservative tradition of their religion. Both attires are different from the *hijab* (Arabic for 'headscarf', sometimes known with its Persian name *chador*) which simply covers the head and often also the neck. Although not identical to each other, the *niqab* and the *burqa* are often confused by the public and commonly referred to as 'integral' or 'full' veil.

Rarely used in some Asian cultures, the *burqa* became prominent when the Taliban came to power in Afghanistan in the 1990s and imposed it on women. The *niqab*, which always comes as an addition to the *hijab*, is usually black and is often worn in conjunction with a long (also dark/black) neck-to-toe robe; technically the robe is called *abaya* when it is more of a dress and *jilbab* (sometimes also spelt as *jellaba*) when it is more of an overcoat, but the two Arabic names are often used as synonyms. The strictest version of the *niqab* dress-code also includes black gloves. The *raison d'être* of this heavy attire is connected with Wahhabi and Salafi teachings and with the strictest of the Islamic legal schools, the Hanbali. Salafism is a conservative, puritanical and extremely prescriptive version of Islam that, together with Wahhabism and other revivalist Islamist traditions, emphasizes dogmas, gender separation (as prescribed in the *Quran*, Sura xxxiii, 53–55), and external appearances supposed to indicate religiosity.[3] Although it has come to global attention for its violent offshoots and intransigency about Sharia law, Salafism is not necessarily violent. Reinvented as a political/philosophical concept by Muslim scholars at the end of the nineteenth century, it is essentially a traditionalist and moralist movement that seeks to apply Islamic teachings literally, going back to Mohammad and to the pious ancestors (in Arabic: *salaf*) who first embraced the religion during the glorious years of the early Caliphate.

Strongly rooted in the Gulf region, the 'twin set' *niqab+jilbab* was quickly imported abroad and in Europe in the last decade. Lighter forms of *niqabs* or *litham* (another Arabic word for 'veil') were used up to the first half of the twentieth century also in the Maghreb and in Egypt, but, curiously, only by countryside women when they were visiting urban areas, as a sign of civilization (El Hamel 2002: 301). The *litham* has also been a distinctive part of Tuareg clothing, but primarily for men (Keenan 1977). The now popularized term *burqa* has been used increasingly – and inappropriately – in public debates to refer instead to the combination *niqab+jilbab+hijab*.

---

3 It should be clarified that Islamism (also called 'political Islam') is an umbrella term used to comprise a range of political positions (some more moderate, some extreme) developed the symbolism and narrative of Islamic history, theology and practices, and which ultimately aims at a social and political reform inspired by Islamic principles and ideally embodied in the notion of the Caliphate. This means that belief in Islam is a separate matter from adherence to political Islam. For more information on Islamism, and particularly Wahhabism and Salafism, see: Roy (1994); Rasheed (2002); Kepel (2004); Silvestri (2007); Meijer (2009).

From this sartorial excursus, it is clear that the integral veil is not a usual Arab, or Asian, or Balkan, or Somali way of dressing for women; this means that it is also exogenous to the religious-cultural origins of the Muslim population of Europe, who typically originate from those regions or were indeed born in Europe. In fact, the *Quran* does not prescribe specifically any of these coverings. Instead, it simply urges Muslim women (and men) to dress and act modestly (see Sura xxiv, 30–31) and in Sura xxxiii (32–33) the wives of the Prophet Mohammad are presented as the ultimate model of modesty and piety. The verses exhorting women to cover have been interpreted in different ways, so that Muslims around the world would agree, in broad terms, that the *hijab* is recommended, though not compulsory. Contemporary views on this issue held by Muslim women living in Europe and in other Western countries are variegated. Several young Muslim women consider the *hijab* as a choice more than as a tradition, and some conceive it as a form of prayer.[4] But Muslim feminist intellectuals and activists, like Haleh Afshar (2005), challenge the idea that the headscarf should be 'recommended' and argue that modesty and decency should be, above all, inner qualities that transpire from personal behaviour.

While there may be disagreement over the necessity of adopting the *hijab*, this type of veil is widely used by Muslim women (and accepted as a reasonable practice even by those who do not wear it themselves) in different regions and cultures of the world. Around the integral veil, on the other hand, there is much more disagreement among Muslims. This attire is not fully part of the cultural and religious traditions of origin of the majority of the Muslim population of the globe, let alone of Europe, where it has recently been the centre of attention. It is instead an 'imported' product of the cross-fertilization of popular culture, religious knowledge and practices in the global religious market. It is as novel and alien to the local culture in Europe as it is, for instance, in Somalia, where it is equally spreading as a new fashion. Although it is the *jilbab* plus *niqab* combination that is appearing in Europe, rather than the *burqa*, mentioning the *burqa* seems to have a more dramatic effect, because everyone has in mind the consequences of the Taliban regime and its abject treatment of women.

Fears

The mental association of veiling with the repressive regimes of the Islamic republic of Iran, of Saudi Arabia, and of the Taliban rule is one of the reasons why any form of Islamic-style head-covering is perceived with extreme anxiety in contemporary European societies. There is a fear that the fundamentalist mentality of those illiberal regimes will spill over into Europe through conservative Islamic

4 This issue came out in a conversation with a group of participants (aged 20–35) in the Women Islamic Spirituality against Extremism (WISE) conference held in Kuala Lumpur in July 2009.

practices leading to significant disruption of liberal democratic political systems. The Western apprehension with the *niqab/burqa* dressing codes goes beyond the symbolic act of hiding the female body; it has to do with the underlying Salafi/Wahhabi doctrines and their political implications. In the three decades spanning the turn of the twenty-first century, Western countries became increasingly exposed to the emergence and impact of political Islam – initially in the Middle East and North Africa, then on European soil; thus, European foreign and security policies have converged with domestic ones in the attempt to ensure stability, tackle political dissent and violence, and address the challenges emerging from the growing religious and cultural pluralism of Europe (Silvestri 2005, 2007).

Arguably, there are already sufficient measures in place in individual European countries to ban criminal acts and illegal behaviour (including hiding the face) without having to devise a new one, specifically against the integral Islamic veil. Nevertheless, two major reasons have been adduced by European policy-makers in support of *burqa* bans. One has to do with individual freedoms in democratic societies and the perceived symbolic oppression of women via the act of fully hiding their bodies from the public gaze. Those who decide to take on the full veil are often criticized for having embraced a limiting type of Islam, which impedes free communication as well as the development of independent, critical and flexible thought. Giving a prominent role to prescriptions and obedience this strict Islamic tradition can be criticized for offering a simplistic and pre-packaged vision of the world and of the relevance of religious belief. Yet the sense of clear direction offered by this tradition with rigid rules and an emphasis on authenticity is what attracts, rationally and spiritually, many young women, including native Europeans who converted to Islam.

The other reason for suspicion towards the integral veil concerns its potential instrumental use to hide terrorists and weapons. For instance, Yassin Omar, one of the bombers of 21 July 2005, fled London to Birmingham allegedly dressed in a *burqa*; the first female suicide bomber in Iraq – Belgian convert Muriel Degauque, who blew herself up in Baghdad on 9 November 2005, after having joined ultra-conservative radical groups and practices – was also fully covered; *burqa*-clad female suicide bombers carried out attacks in Afghanistan and Pakistan in 2009 and 2010. These incidents are also reminiscent of the so-called *anni di piombo* ('lead years') in the 1970s, when repeated attacks against civilians and political personalities were perpetrated by masked individuals from both right- and left-wing oriented terrorist formations; robberies have also often been carried out by burglars wearing balaclavas, and there is fear that the *burqa* could serve a similar purpose.

This combination of factors constitutes the complex – yet limiting – lens through which the Muslim population of Europe has been observed, especially as the concern with Muslim youth 'radicalization' emerged after the terrorist attacks of September 2001 (United States), October 2002 (Indonesia), May 2003 (Morocco), March 2004 (Spain), July 2005 (United Kingdom), July 2006 (India),

November 2008 (India) and December 2010 (Sweden). Such is the background against which the recent span of anti-*burqa* bans in Europe ought to be understood.

France

On 11 April 2011 France became the first European country to enforce a so-called 'anti-*burqa* law' on a national level, having adopted it the previous September, after a long and contested consultation process. At the end of April 2011 Belgium followed suit and a number of other countries consider emulating the move. Prior to reaching the crisis level, discussions of a controversial ban against hiding the face in public spaces had been making the headlines for quite some time in various European countries. Although the debate had been initiated in The Netherlands and Belgium between 2005 and 2006, it intensified when the French Parliament instructed an official commission to 'study' the grounds for such a ban in June 2009. Presided over by Communist MP André Gerin, the *Mission d'information sur la pratique du port du voile intégral sur le territoire national* ('information mission on the practice of wearing the integral veil on the national territory') produced an opinion opposed to a 'general and absolute prohibition of the integral veil'. Nevertheless, in the course of 2010, the anti-*burqa* bill was overwhelmingly approved by two chambers of the French Parliament – with 335 yes votes against one in the National Assembly (the lower chamber), and 246 to one in the Senate – and received the assent of the Constitutional Court. But whereas the headscarf ban of 2004 had caused a polarization between French political elites and secularist groups on the one hand, and the majority of the practising Muslim population on the other, the dynamics triggered this time were slightly different. The law did not prove as divisive as the two previous crises concerning the headscarf.

Following on from the *affaire du foulard* of 1989, the French debate had peaked in 1994, when the then minister for education François Bayrou issued a directive forbidding the *hijab* (but not other religious symbols) from French public schools.[5] This decision went against the 1992 ruling of the State Council, which had reasserted the right to freedom of expression and of religion in schools, as long as articulated within the respect of pluralism and of other people's freedom. Similar animosities were also stirred during 2003 and 2004, in relation to the work of the Stasi Commission and to the law of March 2004, which banned 'ostentatious' religious symbols in public institutions. De facto it outlawed the *hijab* in public institutions. A reason behind this ban is the fact that the French government – like Germany and numerous anti-veil supporters across Europe – has interpreted the headscarf (and more recently the *niqab*) as a 'political', not as a 'religious' symbol (Joppke 2009: 53). In the past headscarf affairs, Muslims and anti-discrimination and human right activists had responded condemning the

5 See El Hamel (2002); Joppke (2009). Please note that here the term 'public' is used to define state schools, not in the British sense of 'private' school. The directive excluded state-aided religious schools.

infringement of the principle of freedom of religion. But when the *burqa/niqab* crisis emerged, positions were no longer so clear-cut, and very few Muslims were ready to interpret this cloth as a 'religious symbol' or as a 'necessary' religious practice.

A similarity between past and more recent debates on different types of veiling, however, appears to lie in the ambiguous, if not schizophrenic, behaviour of the legislators in an attempt to appeal to a confused public opinion. In the course of 2009 and 2010, French left-wing parties (especially the Socialists) increasingly shifted towards sharing the centre-right anxiety regarding the practice of full veiling, but remained ambiguous or undecided in relation to the appropriate measures to address the crisis. As a result, the Socialists, the Greens and the Communists ended up abstaining from the Assembly vote of 13 July 2010. Only a few personalities had been more outspoken. Socialist politicians Martine Aubry, François Hollande and Lionel Jospin, the green Daniel Cohn-Bendit, and philosopher Bernard-Henri Lévy, for instance, signed, the previous year, the petition *Arrêtez ce debat* ('stop this debate') urging the Republic's president Nicolas Sarkozy to put a stop to the public debate on the integral veil, on the ground that it was verging on racism and proving unhealthy for French democracy. An unexpected move, on the part of the centre-right majority party Union pour le Mouvement Populaire (UMP, 'Union for a Popular Movement'), was on the eve of the National Assembly vote: the UMP head, Jean-Francois Copé, announced that the law, if confirmed by the Senate later in the summer, would be referred to the Constitutional Council (Le Roux 2010). This was, most likely, an attempt to reassure the French Council of State, which in May of the same year had expressed its 'unfavourable opinion' in regard to a 'general' measure, deemed as legally 'unfounded'. It was probably also a response to pressure coming from outside: the Council of Europe's Parliamentary Assembly had issued, in June, a unanimous resolution condemning a general such law. Simultaneously, though, the Strasbourg resolution also stated that legal restrictions may be justified 'for security purposes, or where the public or professional functions of individuals require their religious neutrality, or that their face can be seen'; it also recognized that 'no woman should be compelled to wear religious apparel by her community or family' and that European governments should educate Muslim women as to their rights and freedoms (Council of Europe 2010a, 2010b).

In the weeks leading up to the vote of July 2010, the French part of the fieldwork for the research for this publication on Muslim women (and which was initially deliberately not at all centred on any type of veiling) was being completed. The period proved particularly interesting. Paris proved to be a highly contested ground. French Muslims (both men and women) were divided among themselves though not particularly upset by the bill. Most of the female interviewees did not have strong opinions against the bill, while they were clearly against the 2004 law, and were not fond of existing government policies, whether relating to the economy or concerning state relations with Muslim communities. This finding was only partially surprising, though, given the different normative framework within which the anti-*burqa* law was discussed in French public debates (as an issue of law and order and security), if compared to the earlier anti-headscarf law (an issue of religious freedom). The attitudes detected also mirrored the outcome of a national opinion poll of April 2010, which indicated that two-thirds of the French population wanted a *burqa* ban, although half of them wished it to be restricted only to certain locations; only 10% thought that nothing should be done about the integral veil, while 22% stated that a sensitization (a concept that was not further clarified) of the concerned population was needed (TNS-Sofres-Logica 2010).

Fadela Amara, the then French minister for urban regeneration, , who is of Algerian origin and is the former president of the feminist anti-discrimination group Ni Putes Ni Soumises ('neither prostitutes nor submissive') has been an outspoken opponent both of the headscarf and of the burqa, which she defined as expressions of 'totalitarianism' and of 'the cancer of radical Islam' (BBC 2008; France24 2009). Prominent Muslim personalities and intellectuals of the French public sphere, including the head of the Grand Mosque in Paris, Dalil Boubakeur, and Bordeaux's imam Tareq Oubrou, either supported the law or did not condemn it, highlighting instead the importance for Muslims to adapt to French society and lifestyle, and contextualizing the historical and functional, not necessarily religious, origin of the *niqab*. Yet, these views were not shared uniformly by other Muslims; indeed it would be unrealistic to expect homogeneity of views among French Muslims, as with any other national, social, cultural or religious group. According to an online poll by the widely used French Muslim web portal Oumma.com (2009), 86% of French Muslims opposed the *burqa* ban in 2009. However, the representativeness of this data cannot be verified; it is possible that the most frequent users of the website – hence most likely the opinion poll participants – hold a conservative-oriented mindset that is not necessarily widespread in French society. Tensions around the bill became evident when a Parisian imam (Hassen Chalghoumi), who had openly positioned himself in favour of it, received death threats in July 2009. Another imam from Bordeaux, Mahmoud Doua, was attacked, in January 2010, by a gang of local strict traditionalist Muslims for having expressed allegedly too liberal views during a televised debate on the integral veil.

Despite these fractures within French Islam and French society, the contentious *burqa* law appears to have provoked, domestically, less animosities compared to the earlier controversies around the headscarf mentioned above. In 2009–2011 the fire came more from outside the country, as the debate on the full veil was swiftly 'imported' into Italy, Germany, Spain, Britain, Ireland, and several other countries, including Iceland. International commentators started to either praise or criticize French politics and French understandings of human rights and democracy. Some enthusiasts suggested implementing a similar law in other European countries. Although discussions around the integral veil have existed on a local/national level roughly since 2005 in several European countries, the internationalization of the debate appears to have been triggered by the widely publicized French developments of 2009 and 2010. The idea of a '*burqa* ban' thus awoke sleeping animosities and spread like a contagion, attracting supporters from parties positioned both on the right and on the left of the political spectrum.

United Kingdom

The United Kingdom is one of the few European countries whose Parliaments have not yet (as of 2012) toyed with an anti-*burqa* law. Yet, the full veil has been the object of public debate at least since 2006, when the then Leader of the House of Commons, Jack Straw (Labour) published an editorial reflecting on his meetings with fully-veiled women at his constituency office in Blackburn, an industrial city in the north-west of England with a considerably large Muslim and immigrant population. After a few visits from fully-veiled constituents, he decided not to allow the *niqab* in future meetings because he 'felt uncomfortable about talking to someone "face-to-face" who I could not see' (Straw 2006). While Mr Straw clearly did not invite an anti-*burqa* law (on the contrary he asserted: 'I defend absolutely the right of any woman to wear a headscarf. As for the full veil, wearing it breaks no laws'), he explained the problem of visually hampering the flow of communication in situations where establishing trust is important, given that most people in those meetings seek advice or help:

> the conversation would be of greater value if the lady took the covering from her face. Indeed, the value of a meeting, as opposed to a letter or phone call, is so that you can – almost literally – see what the other person means, and not just hear what they say. So many of the judgments we all make about other people come from seeing their faces.
>
> I thought it may be hard going when I made my request for face-to-face interviews in these circumstances. However, I can't recall a single occasion when the lady concerned refused to lift her veil; and most I ask seem relieved I have done so. (Straw 2006)

These words, and especially his final comment that the *niqab* is a 'visible statement of separation and of difference' (Straw 2006) provoked a storm among the British public, highlighting existing divides between conservative and liberal Muslim groups, and upsetting others simply for the patronizing tone displayed. The controversy was covered by the media to an unprecedented level, even compared to other Islam-related crises such as the Rushdie affair of 1989 (see Nickels et al. 2012). When, two years later, the French *burqa* debate emerged and began to overlap with Straw's earlier remarks, things got out of hand for the British politician. Thus, under the pressure of the general elections of 2010, he felt the need to apologize and retract, on the occasion of a public meeting with the organization Engage, which is devoted to promoting political awareness and participation among Muslims in British society (Engage 2010).

After all, the debate on the integral veil in Britain has remained more speculative and focused on its symbolic challenge of British values and British national identity – and hence on the protection of the fuzzy contours of the British state (see Meer et al. 2010; Hickman et al. 2011) – rather than centred on the need for a legal regulation to mark the secular/religious distinction. The need for such a national law only emerged as a spillover effect of the French ban, while in the previous years ad hoc bans had been discussed on a much smaller scale.

The education sector is where the discussion around the integral veil has concentrated and with a much more practical focus in mind. In the spring of 2007 the Government Department for Education and Skills (DfES) circulated a guidance document allowing schools to ban pupils from wearing full-face veils on the grounds of security, safety or effective learning, while consulting with parents and seeking to accommodate religious clothing where possible (BBC 2007). A BBC poll taken at the time revealed that only 6.37% of voters were in favour of a veil ban in schools, while 92.65% were against (BBC 2007). Since then, the controversy in this sector has had contrasting outcomes: a handful of newspapers reported on a wide range of reactions among British Muslims in relation to three independent Islamic single-sex schools (respectively in Lancaster, Leicester and London), which have incorporated the headscarf+*jilbab*+*niqab* as part of their uniforms (Barrett 2010). In contrast with the Ministerial guidelines, leaders of the University and College Union argued that banning *burqas* and other religious attires in universities would discourage diversity and inclusion in higher education (Garner 2011). At the end of June 2010, a member of the then newly elected Parliament, Conservative government minister for transport Philip Hollobone, tabled a private bill in support of measures similar to the French.[6] While stirring some debate, which often diverted onto Sharia and secularism,[7] this idea did not receive the same attention as Straw's remarks, nor the extensive support of the political elites, including fellow Conservatives: on the contrary, minister for immigration Damian Green deemed such a law proposal 'un-British', and secretary of state for the environment Caroline Spelman said that the *burqa* could actually be 'empowering' for some (quoted in Prince 2010).

As far as the attitudes of the general public are concerned, a poll conducted in July 2010 gives figures of 67% in favour of an anti-*burqa* law (YouGov and Channel 5 2010). This contrasts sharply with the figures of the earlier BBC poll mentioned above. As with all polling exercises a methodological and interpretive filter ought to be applied in order to understand the meaning of the data. Both polls were in fact skewed because the BBC's centred around the school context, and specifically inquired about the 'face-veil'. The YouGov poll for its part is inaccurate, as it does

6 'Phillip Hollobone Explains Why He Wants to Ban the Burqa', http://conservativehome.blogs.com/parliament/2010/06/phillip-hollobone explains-why-he-want-to-ban-the-burqa.html (accessed 6 July 2010).

7 Many such discussions were intertwined with arguments and remarks made by very diverse personalities: Dawkins (2006), Hitchens (2007), and Williams (2008).

not include opinions about the *niqab*. While the French law is popularly known as 'anti-*burqa*' law, this is not its technical name. It is a general law against any type of full veiling and method of hiding the face in public spaces and does not specifically mention the *burqa* intended as a particular style of clothing. Instead, the British public was asked by YouGov to respond specifically in relation to the Afghan-style *burqa*, not allowing scope for commenting on other forms of full veiling. This means that we do not know what the British public thinks of the *niqab* in general (while the BBC poll centred on schools): although worn by a tiny minority of the British Muslim population, in Britain it is nevertheless much more common than the virtually absent *burqa*.

Contemporary Britain has an almost schizophrenic relationship with the role of religion in public life. 'Schizophrenic' is an appropriate adjective because, despite having an official state religion, the country is one of the most secularized in Europe; moreover, one can clearly notice an opposition of trends, with rising practices and claims by religious minorities matched by increasing campaigns by secular voices, while government and the judiciary appear confused, thus producing contradictory laws and policies in affairs pertaining religious beliefs. With these complexities in mind, it seems that Hollobone's anti-*burqa* proposal did not gain much ground not because the *niqab* has many more supporters in Britain than in other European countries, or because Britain is a less secular society (and has a bigger Muslim population) than other countries, but because the whole issue would bring up a number of other unsolved questions about competing freedoms,[8] as well as 'British values', 'British identity', the effectiveness of social cohesion policies, and the future of constructed or imagined multicultural models. Politically, there is also the fear of upsetting minorities, namely Muslims, who in Britain make up a considerable part of the voting population: the census of 2001 gave a figure of 1.6 million Muslims in Britain but more recent estimates go as high as two million. Aware of the heavy criticism that the Labour government received for the negative impact of its counter-terrorism programme *Prevent* upon Muslim communities (see Kundnani 2009; Silvestri 2011b; HM Government 2011a, 2011b), newly-elected Liberal Democrat and Conservative politicians in July 2010 were probably very cautious and did not want to be seen as stigmatizing Muslim communities. Nevertheless the speech on multiculturalism and radicalization of Conservative Prime Minister Mr Cameron (2011) ended up having this effect.

8 For instance freedom of religion/belief vs. freedom of opinion, as it has emerged from the Mohammad cartoons controversy in Denmark; or religious freedom/belief vs. freedom of sexual orientation, as observed during the confrontation between the Catholic British adoption agency Care and the Equality Commission, whose regulations put in place in 2006 contrasted with Care's principle not to give children to homosexual couples.

Other European Countries

A striking feature of the Dutch *burqa* debate is the fact that it has developed almost disconnected from the (only apparently) similar issue of the Islamic headscarf. The *hijab* was never seen as a major problem in Holland. Apart from reservations raised in relation to very specific professional/contextual circumstances in which the headscarf was deemed inappropriate (for instance if worn by judges and in the police forces) this version of veiling was easily absorbed into the country's pillarized system of religious and cultural identities (Saharso and Lettinga 2008). Because of the non-mandatory or universal character of the face veil and because of the problematic illiberal context with which these practices have been associated (Moors 2009; Bracke 2011), the Dutch public response to the integral veil has been different and possibly harsher than in other places. Since 2005, various right-wing and also centre-right Dutch politicians have attempted to propose an anti-*burqa* law in the Netherlands, often highlighting the presumed link between *burqas* and terrorism. An informal *burqa* commission also met with experts.[9] Among the ban proponents were not only the notorious member of the right-wing Party for Freedom (PVV), Geert Wilders, but also liberal politicians, including the former minister for integration and immigration Rita Verdonk. Although the Dutch parliament concluded in 2008 that such legislation would violate the constitutional right of freedom or religion, Mr Wilders pushed repeatedly for a bill on this matter in 2010 and 2011, having acquired a strategic role in supporting a new minority coalition government between the Liberals (People's Party for Freedom and Democracy, VVD) and the Christian Democrats (CDA) (Traynor 2010).

The conservative party in Denmark also embraced the same gender equality and European versus foreign/Islamic values argument and proposed a ban on the integral veil in 2009. At around the same time, a study by the University of Copenhagen for the national '*burqa* commission' produced an estimate on the extent of the face-veil in Denmark: in the country there were, in 2010, approximately 150–200 *niqabi* women and no more than three wearing the *burqa* (Ellis 2010). While Danish authorities were not interested in an outright ban that would clash with fundamental principles of human rights and with the constitution, a pragmatic approach was adopted in the form of some guidelines, which lift the weight of the decision from government and allow individual institutions – for instance schools – to ask women wearing the full veil to remove it in specific circumstances.[10] The British government guidance for schools published in 2007 seems to hint towards a similar direction.

Although the veil debate in Spain escalated with a focus on the *burqa* in 2010, Muslim anxieties about public reactions to a simpler veiling style such as the

9 I owe this information to Titia Loenen, whom I would like to thank.

10 I would like to acknowledge Mark Sedgwick, Christel Stormhøj and Nadia Jeldtoft for clarifying some questions about Denmark.

headscarf had been latent for some time. Most of the participants in research on Muslim women in Zaragoza (Spain, spring of 2010) mentioned cases of women forced to remove their *hijab* in order to be able to take up jobs. Spanish mobilization against the integral veil has had both a regional and a national dimension. Anti-*burqa* regulations, only valid on the circumscribed territories of certain towns (including Lleida, El Vendrell and Barcelona), were put in place in the spring of 2010. However, an anti-*burqa* bill tabled by the conservatives and the centre-right nationalists in the north-eastern Spanish region of Catalonia failed to go through the regional parliament in July 2010 merely due to a technical error pointed out by the left (which in fact did not particularly dislike the idea, but did not want to let their political opponents win public support through this move). Members of the Spanish parliament in Madrid also proposed a similar ban at national level, while the minister of justice suggested tackling the issue through a new law on religious freedom.

Similar steps to those of the Spanish cities in 2010 were taken by some municipalities in northern Italy, fomented by the discourse of the federalist party Lega Nord, which in the course of the 2000s became an increasingly weighty stakeholder in the coalition government led by Mr Berlusconi (in office during 2008–2011). After some formal – though questionable – Ministerial consultations with the *Comitato per l'Islam* ('committee for Islam'), an official parliamentary discussion of an anti-*burqa* law was then tabled for September 2011.

As with the headscarf ban, which is in place only in certain *länder* (states), Germany has not legislated against the integral veil on a federal level, despite a poll of 2010 suggesting that 61% of the German population wanted a *burqa* ban (Henegan 2010). Caution in proceeding with this step has been attributed to the dynamics caused by the simultaneous publication of a controversial book by Thilo Sarrazin, a high *Bundesbank* (national bank) official, containing anti-immigration and anti-Islam comments. It seems that the public as well politicians were reluctant to be seen to criticize something associated with Islam while the book had just received widespread condemnation. While members of the CDU (Christian Democratic Union), especially in Bavaria, have lobbied for such a restriction, the minister of the interior Thomas de Maizière has been unsupportive of the *burqa* ban and has urged instead not to demonize immigrants (Spiegel 2011). Nevertheless, in early 2011, the state of Hessen entered into a dispute with a Moroccan-born employee of the city of Frankfurt, after she came back from maternity leave wearing a *niqab*. The authorities issued a decree forbidding the integral veil but only specifically for people working in public offices (Focus 2011). It is interesting to note that several Muslim personalities and leaders of German Muslim organizations supported this restriction and condemned the woman for having endangered the position of other Muslims in German society (Spiegel 2011).

The *burqa* controversy in Austria has similarities both with the Italian and with the German situation. As Gresch et al. (2008) have noted, Austrian right-wing politicians and mainstream public discourse have increasingly mobilized for placing on the policy agenda issues that are in fact of secondary importance to the country; they are either negligible phenomena with a minimal impact upon everyday life and society, or they were, previously, completely 'normal' issues, fully regulated and functioning under adequate laws.[11] But all of a sudden, the *burqa* debate proliferates everywhere, individuals are turned into exceptional threats, suspicion circulated in society and exceptionally strict prohibitive measures are invoked. The opponents to the ban have found themselves in an ambiguous situation as they seemed reluctant to completely rule out the ban: they appreciated the element of self-determination intrinsic in the choice to wear a religious symbol but also condemned the message of oppression represented by the *burqa*/*niqab*; in the end the debate was cut short though, as both the minister for women Gabriele Heinisch-Hosek and a leading Austrian Muslim organization, the Islamische Glaubensgemeinschaft ('Islamic belief community', IGGiÖ) stated that the *burqa* 'was not an issue' in Austria, although they did not support it in principle (*DiePresse* 2009).

Convergences, Specificities and Paradoxes

While national blanket anti-*burqa* laws remain disputed and require long-winded parliamentary procedures, on a regional and local level, things have progressed in a faster and irregular manner across Europe. Some points of convergence are nevertheless identifiable. Sometimes developments are ideologically-driven, on other occasions they consist of pragmatic responses, but most of the time, the dynamics of party politics and party competition appear to be the main driving force behind *burqa* bans.

Many of these reactions can be interpreted as pre-emptive emotional strikes against the fear of the unknown or based upon simple misinformation. People can be convinced of having full cognition of a situation, simply because they have heard and seen on television that Muslim women in Afghanistan were deprived of their freedoms by the Taliban and forced to wear the *burqa* and they saw the Twin Towers go down on 11 September 2001. Comments such as the following – made by a Spanish politician – are not uncommon in public debates also in other countries: 'How can our soldiers be fighting in Afghanistan for the liberty of these women while the government has no courage to defend them here?'[12] This discourse automatically frames Muslim women as objects, as victims of oppression, without taking into account key distinctions in terms of context, rationality and agency (Silvestri 2011a). The juxtaposition of issues that it operates is illogical

11 Muslims in Austria have enjoyed protections along other minorities of the former Austrian empire since the end of the nineteenth century. Its official position was consolidated in 1912, when Islam was recognized constitutionally as a religion, and in 1979, when it became recognized as a corporation of public law.

12 Soraya Saenz de Santamaria (Spain, Popular Party), quoted in Tozer (2010); for similar discourses in Holland, see Moors (2009).

and reifying. The patronizing tone about the 'subjugated women that need saving' becomes itself an expression of patriarchy, another form of oppression (see Abu-Lughod 2002).

Instead, to put things in perspective, we should appreciate that the significance of these diverse veiling styles and practices is not simply a function of the intentions and meanings attributed to them by the Muslim women who adopt them and by their cultural-religious-ethno-national communities of reference. It also changes drastically depending on the social, legal and political context of the location where these individuals live. In order to better understand the phenomenon, consideration ought to be given not to misplace questions, and not to demand that Muslim women born in Europe be accountable for what is happening in Saudi Arabia or in Afghanistan. It is also striking that many supporters of the ban, in France as in Italy, or in Spain, or in the UK, have put all their weight behind the *burqa/niqab* prohibition, while in fact their main fears are immigration and the unknowns of the economy and of the welfare state. Anti-Islam rhetoric also hides the awareness of the irreversibility of the fact of religious, cultural and ethnic diversity and a secularist suspicion that the role of religion in society might increase.

Much of the European public and citizenry will have 'seen' on television but never actually 'encountered' a Muslim. It is quite possible that if they ever see or meet a Muslim woman wearing even a simple headscarf they will not see a person in front of them, but instead the totalitarian dogmatism and machismo of the Taliban and of Al-Qaida. They will automatically consider these women as oppressed and dependent individuals lacking autonomy and will call for anti-*burqa* laws. Beside the issue of whether such an evaluation reflects reality another question emerges, that is, whether forbidding a 'symbol' of perceived oppression could actually solve the oppression problem.

Conclusions

This chapter has pointed to contradictions and idiosyncrasies inherent in public authorities' engagement with Muslim communities and with the integral veil question, and the extent to which this concern has become a cross-cutting salient issue in different European countries. It emerges that the problem with the anti-*burqa* laws that are currently enforced or discussed across Europe goes beyond the justification of laws prohibiting the disguising of faces in public institutions. It has primarily to do with the tone and categories used, with the heterogeneous – often contradictory – approaches adopted in our countries in matters pertaining freedoms and diversity, and with the effects of psychological and political processes triggered by low-cost/high symbolism slogans and actions.

While it will be interesting, in the future, to examine the personal motives of those who decide to take this step, it is crucial that legislators and policy-makers do not limit their analysis of the *burqa* trend solely by focusing on the views and psychologies of Muslim women and their communities of reference. The broader context within which this takes place needs to be addressed, taking into account complex dynamics of action and reaction to public discourses, laws and policies, as well as national narratives and imaginaries, and the impact of global transformations beyond the will of Muslim believers and the control of policy-makers.

References

Abu-Lughod, L. (2002), 'Do Muslim Women Really Need Saving?', *American Anthropologist*, 104:3, 783–790.

Afshar, H. (2005), Interview with Professor Haleh Afshar, *BBC*, 23 March, www.bbc.co.uk/religion/programmes/belief/scripts/haleh_afshah.html (accessed 1 June 2011, no longer available).

Barrett, D. (2010), 'British Schools Where Girls Must Wear the Islamic Veil', *Daily Telegraph*, 2 October, www.telegraph.co.uk/education/educationnews/8038820/British-schools-where-girls-must-wear-the-Islamic-veil.html (accessed 15 June 2011).

BBC (2007), 'Schools Allowed to Ban Face Veils', *BBC News*, 20 March, http://news.bbc.co.uk/1/hi/6466221.stm (accessed 30 May 2011).

BBC (2008), 'French Minister Denounces Burka', *BBC News*, 16 July, http://news.bbc.co.uk/go/pr/fr/-/1/hi/world/europe/7509339.stm (accessed 10 June 2011).

Bracke, S. (2011), 'Subjects of Debate: Secular and Sexual Exceptionalism, and Muslim Women in the Netherlands', *Feminist Review*, 98, 28–46.

Cameron, D. (2011), 'PM's Speech at Munich Security Conference', 5 February, http://www.number10.gov.uk/news/pms-speech-at-munich-security-conference/ (accessed July 2012).

Council of Europe, Parliamentary Assembly (2010a), *Islam, Islamism and Islamophobia in Europe*, Resolution 1743 (Strasbourg: Council of Europe).

Council of Europe, Parliamentary Assembly (2010b), *Islam, Islamism and Islamophobia in Europe*, Recommendation 1927 (Strasbourg: Council of Europe).

Dawkins, R. (2006), *The God Delusion* (London: Bantam Books).

DiePresse (2009), 'Die Burka ist in Österreich kein Thema', *DiePresse*, 23 December, http://diepresse.com/home/panorama/oesterreich/529851/Die-Burka-ist-in-Oesterreich-kein-Thema (accessed 2 July 2011).

El Hamel, C. (2002), 'Muslim Diaspora in Western Europe: The Islamic Headscarf (*Hijab*), the Media and Muslims' Integration in France', *Citizenship Studies*, 6:3, 297–299.

Ellis, L. (2010), 'Only Three Women in Denmark Wear Burqa', *University Post*, 13 January, http://universitypost.dk/article/only-three-women-denmark-wear-burqa (accessed 30 May 2011).

Engage (2010), 'Jack Straw Apologises for his Anti-Niqab Comments at ENGAGE Hustings in Blackburn', 26 April, www.iengage.org.uk/component/content/article/1-news/861-jack-straw-apologises-for-his-anti-niqab-comments-at-engage-hustings-in-blackburn (accessed 15 June 2011).

Focus (2011), 'Burka-Streit in Hessen.Vollschleier im öffentlichen Dienst verboten', *Focus online*, 1 February, www.focus.de/politik/deutschland/burka-streit-in-hessen-vollschleier-im-oeffentlichen-dienst-verboten_aid_595822.html (accessed 20 June 2011).

France24 (2009), 'Minister Says Burqa Ban would Stop "Cancer" of Radical Islam', *France24*, 15 August, http://www.france24.com/en/20090815-minister-says-burqa-ban-would-stop-cancer-radical-islam (accessed 14 June 2011).

Garner, R. (2011), 'Lecturers Back Students' Right to Wear the Burkha', *The Independent*, 29 May, www.independent.co.uk/news/education/education-news/lecturers-back-students-right-to-wear-the-burkha-2290407.html (accessed 12 June 2011).

Gresch, N., Hadj-Abdou, L., Rosenberger, S. and Sauer, B. (2008), 'Tu felix Austria? The Headscarf and the Politics of "Non-issues"', *Social Politics*, 15:4, 411–432.

Henegan, T. (2010), 'Analysis: Burqa Bans: France, then Netherlands – Who's Next?', *Reuters*, 1 October, http://www.reuters.com/article/2010/10/01/us-europe-burqa-analysis-idUSTRE6904MO20101001 (accessed 1 June 2011).

Hickman, M., Thomas, L., Silvestri, S. and Nickels, H. (2011), *Suspect Communities? Counter-terrorism Policy, the Press, and the Impact on Irish and Muslim Communities in Britain* (London: London Metropolitan University), July.

Hitchens, C. (2007), *God is not Great* (London: Atlantic Books).

HM Government (2011a), *Prevent Strategy* (London: The Stationery Office), June.

HM Government (2011b), *CONTEST. The United Kingdom's Strategy for Countering Terrorism* (London: The Stationery Office), July.

Joppke, C. (2009), *Veil: Mirror of Identity* (Cambridge: Polity).

Keenan, J.H. (1977), 'The Tuareg Veil', *Middle Eastern Studies*, 13(1): 3–13.

Kepel, G. (2004), *Jihad: The Trail of Political Islam* (London: I.B. Tauris).

Kundnani, A. (2009), *Spooked. How Not to Prevent Violent Extremism* (London: IRR).

Le Roux, G. (2010), 'Anti-Veil Law Risks Being Shot Down by Constitutional Council', *France24*, 8 July, http://www.france24.com/en/20100708-anti-veil-law-risks-being-shot-down-france-constitutional-council-burqa-ump-party-government (accessed 8 July 2010).

Meer, N., Dwyer, C. and Modood, T. (2010), 'Embodying Nationhood? Conceptions of British National Identity, Citizenship, and Gender in the "Veil Affair"', *Sociological Review*, 58:1, 84–111.

Meijer, R. (ed.) (2009), *Global Salafism* (London: Hurst).

Moors, A. (2009), 'The Dutch and the Face-Veil: The Politics of Discomfort', *Social Anthropology*, 17:4, 393–408.

Nickels, H., Thomas. L., Hickman, M. and Silvestri, S. (2012), 'Constructing "Suspect" Communities and Britishness: Mapping British Press Coverage of Irish and Muslim Communities, 1974–2007', *European Journal of Communication*, 27(2): 135–151.

Oumma.com (2009), 'Etude sur le port du voile intégral: des enseignements édifiants!', *Oumma.com*, http://oumma.com/Etude-sur-le-port-du-voile (accessed 3 June 2011).

Prince, R. (2010), 'Wearing a Burka can be "Empowering" and "Dignified" for Muslim Women, One of the Government's Most Senior Female Ministers has Said', *Daily Telegraph*, 18 July, www.telegraph.co.uk/news/7897148/Caroline-Spelman-wearing-burka-can-be-empowering.html (accessed 1 June 2012).

[*Quran*] *The Koran* (1998), translated by A.J. Arberry (Oxford: Oxford University Press).

Rasheed, M. (2002), *A History of Saudi Arabia* (Cambridge: Cambridge University Press).

Roy, O. (1994), *The Failure of Political Islam* (London: I.B. Tauris).

Saharso, S. and Lettinga, D. (2008), 'Contentious Citizenship: Policies and Debates on the Veil in the Netherlands', *Social Politics*, 16(4): 455–480.

Silvestri, S. (2005), 'EU Relations with Islam in the Context of the EMP's Cultural Dialogue', *Mediterranean Politics*, 10(3): 385–405.

Silvestri, S. (2007), 'Radical Islam: Threats and Opportunities', *Global Dialogue*, 9(3–4): 118–126.

Silvestri, S. (2011a), 'Faith Intersections and Muslim Women in the European Microcosm: Notes Towards the Study of Non-organized Islam', *Ethnic and Racial Studies*, 34(7): 1230–1247.

Silvestri, S. (2011b), 'Institutionalizing British and Italian Islam: Attitudes and Policies', in Yilmaz, H. and Aykac, C. (eds), *Perceptions of Islam in Europe: Culture, Identity and the Muslim 'Other'* (London: I.B. Tauris): 159–194.

Silvestri, S. (forthcoming), *Europe's Muslim Women: Beyond the Burqa Controversy* (London: Hurst).

Spiegel (2011), 'Vollverschleierung im Bürgeramt. "Der Anblick einer Burka erschreckt mich"', *Spiegel Online*, 2 February, www.spiegel.de/politik/deutschland/0,1518,743071,00.html (accessed 20 June 2011).

Straw, J. (2006), 'I Felt Uneasy Talking to Someone I Couldn't See', *Guardian*, 6 October, www.guardian.co.uk/commentisfree/2006/oct/06/politics.uk (accessed 10 January 2011).

TNS-Sofres-Logica (2010), *Les Français et la burqa* (Montrouge: TNS-Sofres-Logica).

Tozer, A. (2010), 'Spanish Lawmakers Reject Plan for Burqa Ban Study', *Reuters*, 20 July, http://www.reuters.com/article/2010/07/20/us-spain-burqa-idUSTRE66J5D220100720 (accessed 10 March 2011).

Traynor, I. (2010), 'Dutch Far-right Party Wins Pledge on Burqa Ban', *Guardian*, 1 October.

Yilmaz, H. and Aykac, C. (eds) (forthcoming), *Perceptions of Islam in Europe: Culture, Identity and the Muslim 'Other'* (London: I.B. Tauris).

YouGov and Channel 5 News (2010) 'Burqa Ban Survey', 14–16 July, http://today.yougov.co.uk/sites/today.yougov.co.uk/files/YG-Archives-Pol-Channel5-burkhas-160710.pdf (accessed 1 May 2011).

Williams, R. (2008) 'Civil and Religious Law in England: a religious perspective', Foundation lecture in the Temple Festival series at the Royal Courts of Justice, London, 7 February, http://www.archbishopofcanterbury.org/articles.php/1137/archbishops-lecture-civil-and-religious-law-in-england-a-religious-perspective (accessed 4 June 2012).

PART III
Religion and the Places of Worship

Chapter 15
The Right to Establish and Maintain Places of Worship: The Developments of its Normative Content under International Human Rights Law

Noel G. Villaroman

Introduction

The aim of this chapter is to track the evolution of the right to establish and maintain places of worship from its earliest appearance in human rights instruments up to its current stature as a distinct human right. This chapter will draw primarily from the work of the institutions responsible for international human rights standard-setting, particularly with respect to the right to freedom of religion or belief. This chapter concludes that the right to establish and maintain places of worship, being an integral part of the broader right to freedom of religion or belief, has its own set of constituent elements that collectively make up the right's normative content.

This chapter analyses the issues involved using the paradigm of international human rights law. The unique advantage of employing this paradigm is that it is based on international standards that are legally binding on states. Its key strength is the use of obligatory standards which can be used as a basis for assessing the compliance of states with their international commitment to safeguard religious freedom. In the words of the Universal Declaration on Human Rights (UDHR), human rights norms serve as a 'common standard of achievement for all peoples and all nations'.[1] Being obligations of governments arising from international law, these standards can be used to prod or push governments into action.

The subject matter of this chapter is limited to *built structures* that are used as 'places of worship' such as temples, mosques, synagogues, churches, *gurdwaras* and similar constructed edifices. While traditional burial grounds, sacred sites, features of the physical environment and other natural locations (where the land or the open air is regarded as sacrosanct) are also sometimes used as places of worship, they are not included in this analysis. This limitation is needed because, although equally deserving of protection, they are better dealt with under the

1 *Universal Declaration of Human Rights*, adopted 10 Dec. 1948, GA Res. 217A (III), UN GAOR, 3d Sess. (Resolutions, pt. 1), at 71, Preamble, UN Doc. A/810 (1948).

legal regime relating to the protection of the rights of Indigenous peoples and the preservation of their cultural heritage, and they involve a completely different treatment to that applied to built structures.

Places of Worship and the Right to Freedom of Religion and Belief

Three international human rights instruments are to be credited for erecting the legal architecture of the right to freedom of religion or belief: the UDHR adopted in 1948,[2] the International Covenant on Civil and Political Rights (ICCPR)[3] adopted in 1966, and the Declaration on the Elimination of All Forms of Intolerance and of Discrimination Based on Religion or Belief (Religion Declaration) adopted in 1981.[4] They have been described as 'the foundational documents' that 'constitute the basic building blocks' of the right to freedom of religion or belief (Taylor 2005: 1–2).

While these documents have delineated the general contours of the right to freedom of religion or belief, on closer analysis it becomes apparent that the constituent elements that make up this right remain imprecise and blurred. This is because the process of defining the metes and bounds of these elements is, for the most part, still ongoing and far from complete. Kevin Boyle argued that '[t]he effort to enhance religious freedom through the adoption of new standards is a continuing process' (Boyle 2007: 23, 32). The right's constituent elements are continually being refined and given precision through the process of international human rights standard-setting. One such constituent element is the right of a religious group to establish and maintain places of worship.

The right of a religious group to establish and maintain places of worship was first expressly codified in the Religion Declaration. This Declaration – the only UN instrument which deals exclusively with the right to freedom of religion or belief – can be credited with carving out, from the broader right to freedom of religion or belief, a distinct yet smaller 'freedom' to establish and maintain places of worship. Article 6 of the Religion Declaration states in part that:

> In accordance with article 1 of the present Declaration, and subject to the provisions of article 1, paragraph 3, the right to freedom of thought, conscience, religion or belief shall include, *inter alia*, the following freedoms:

2 *Universal Declaration on Human Rights* (1948) GA Res. 217A(III), UN Doc. A/3/810 (1949).

3 *International Covenant on Civil and Political Rights* (1966), 999 UNTS 171.

4 *Declaration on the Elimination of All Forms of Intolerance and of Discrimination Based on Religion or Belief (1981)*, GA Res. 36/55, UN Doc.A/36/51 (1982) ('Religion Declaration').

> To worship or assemble in connection with a religion or belief, and *to establish and maintain places for these purposes*.[5]

More than any other provision in the Religion Declaration, it is Article 6 that primarily contributed to the substantive contents of the right to freedom of religion or belief. Article 6 improved the 'condensed formula of "teaching, practice, worship and observance"' found in both the UDHR and the ICCPR by giving a 'detailed list of various forms of manifestation' (Taylor 2005: 22). Boyle described these forms of manifestation as 'the major concrete components of religious freedom that are to be recognised and guaranteed by the state' (Boyle 2007: 23, 49). Natan Lerner also praised the list of freedoms found in Article 6 as 'a detailed enunciation of rights belonging to the accepted minimum standard' (Lerner 2002: 118).

Meanwhile, the Human Rights Committee, through its General Comment No. 22 issued in 1993, is responsible for subsuming the right to establish and maintain places of worship under the broader freedom of religious manifestation in worship. Note how the Human Rights Committee characterized the construction of places of worship as being indispensable to the freedom to manifest one's religion of belief through acts of worship. The Committee stated that:

> The freedom to manifest religion or belief in worship, observance, practice and teaching encompasses a broad range of acts. The concept of worship extends to ritual and ceremonial acts giving direct expression to belief, as well as various practices integral to such acts, including the building of places of worship, the use of ritual formulae and objects, the display of symbols, and the observance of holidays and days of rest.[6]

In both the Religion Declaration and General Comment No. 22, the right to establish and maintain places of worship was explicitly recognized as emerging from the nucleus of – and thus its legal foundation anchored on – the freedom to manifest one's religion or belief. Yoram Dinstein aptly observed that 'freedom of religion, as an individual right, may be nullified unless complemented by a collective human right of the religious group *to construct the infrastructure* making possible the full enjoyment of that freedom by the individuals' (Dinstein 1992: 145, 158 [emphasis added]). The right to establish and maintain places of worship has since been unambiguously entrenched as a constituent element of the right to freedom of religion or belief and, therefore, as an important part of the broader corpus of international human rights law. Up until this point, however, the right to establish and maintain places of worship may be said to be only in its

5 Article 6, Religion Declaration.

6 Human Rights Committee, *CCPR General Comment No. 22: Article 18 (Freedom of Thought, Conscience or Religion)*, 30 July 1993, CCPR/C/21/Rev.1/Add.4, paragraph 4 ('General Comment No. 22') (emphasis added).

nascent stage of normative development because its own substantive content has not yet been elaborated.

The Importance of International Human Rights Standard-Setting

Like other human rights, the 'official' entry of the right to establish and maintain places of worship into the ranks of recognized human rights does not ensure actual compliance with such a right. Across the world, violations of the right to establish and maintain places of worship have been observed and reported. The pervasiveness of the violations is fully exemplified by a report of the Special Rapporteur on freedom of religion or belief which contained an extensive list of countries where they had been committed:

> In Brunei Darussalam and Kuwait, the authorities are said to have refused permission to build, enlarge or renovate non-Muslim places of worship … [I]n Myanmar, construction of a church was stopped by the authorities despite the fact that a construction permit had been obtained. In Greece, a Muslim religious leader was purportedly taken to court and then released after being accused of illegally building a mosque. In Azerbaijan, Christians were reportedly driven from the establishments where they were carrying out religious activities. In Georgia and Azerbaijan, Armenian Orthodox churches are said to have been closed. In Azerbaijan and the Russian Federation, religious minorities are reportedly having difficulty renting rooms to be used as places of worship. In Bulgaria, in one city, Jehovah's Witnesses are apparently banned from renting buildings. In Bosnia and Herzegovina and in Nepal, places of worship are said to have been attacked and even destroyed. In Pakistan, in Karachi, peaceful demonstrations by Christians protesting against the destruction of Christian properties including churches were allegedly suppressed by the police. In Romania and Georgia, the problem of restitution of goods and properties confiscated under the former regime has been raised.[7]

At the heart of this problem of non-compliance is the bare and austere language used in articulating the right to establish and maintain places of worship in the Religion Declaration and even in General Comment No. 22. The simple formulation 'to establish and maintain' actually masks several difficulties when the right is claimed or invoked in actual controversies. In other words, the manner in which the right was articulated did not completely fill up the 'normative gap'.[8] Hence, there arises a need for further human rights standard-setting in order to elucidate on

7 Interim Report of the Special Rapporteur on the elimination of all forms of religious intolerance, A/52/477 (16 October 1997) paragraph 34(a).

8 A 'normative gap' exists when acts or omissions that violate human rights are not adequately covered by existing human rights instruments. See, for example, International

the meaning and practical implications of the right in a manner which is consistent with the underlying rationale and purpose of the 'foundational documents' that established the legal architecture of the right to freedom of religion or belief.

Human rights instruments are usually phrased in general and broad language. Before they can be effectively implemented, there must be an elucidation of their meaning and practical consequences, which is an important aspect of the broader process of international human rights standard-setting.[9] The end-product of this process assumes different forms, including general comments, views and concluding observations of treaty-based human rights bodies as well as studies and reports prepared by the Special Procedures of the UN human rights machinery. Whatever form they take, the end-product serves the same purpose – that is, the elaboration of existing human rights norms. The UN General Assembly has recognized the importance of standard-setting and called on UN bodies charged with elaborating human rights norms to '[b]e sufficiently precise to give rise to identifiable and practicable rights and obligations'.[10]

Emphasizing the importance of formulating human rights standards, Makau Mutua argues that '[n]orms cannot be effective unless they are unpacked into clear components, spelling out obligations and rights, and identifying the path to their implementation at the national level' (Mutua 2007: 618). Because they serve as guideposts in implementing general or broad norms, human rights standards 'have transformed the nature of the relationship between governments and individuals, and made public authorities far more accountable'.[11] Mutua further argues that:

> Broad norms and standards must be unpacked, broken down, elucidated, revised, and may even need to be rejected and replaced by new and different standards. The scope, reach, and content of norms must be comprehensible to their beneficiaries, as well as to those who bear the responsibility for their implementation. Vacuous, rhetorical, and vague standards accomplish little. (Mutua 2007: 620)

Given the non-detailed manner in which the right to establish and maintain places of worship was couched, it is necessary to resort to the relevant authorities on international human rights standard-setting and, more importantly, to synthesize their pronouncements into a coherent whole with the aim of providing practical guidance to states in addressing controversies involving places of worship. In this

---

Council on Human Rights Policy, *Human Rights Standards: Learning from Experience* (2006) 7.

9 See, for example, UN General Assembly Resolution, *Setting International Standards in the Field of Human Rights,* A/RES/41/120, 4 December 1986.

10 UN General Assembly Resolution, Setting International Standards in the Field of Human Rights, A/RES/41/120, 4 December 1986, article 4(c).

11 International Council on Human Rights Policy, *Human Rights Standards: Learning from Experience* (2006) 2.

chapter, the pronouncements of two human rights authorities whose mandates are directly relevant to the right to freedom of religion or belief, namely, the Human Rights Committee and the Special Rapporteur on freedom of religion or belief, will be examined and consequently distilled for their standard-setting value in this area of international human rights law.

The Human Rights Committee established under the ICCPR is a quintessential example of a human rights standard-setter. States parties to the ICCPR submit periodic reports to the Committee about the 'measures they have adopted which give effect to the rights recognized and on the progress made in the enjoyment of those rights'.[12] The Committee then issues its 'concluding observations' on the state under review which usually includes 'recommendations for the review of legislation to bring it in compliance with the ICCPR and to ensure appropriate domestic application' (Taylor 2005: 12). The Committee also formulates general comments which are authoritative interpretations of the provisions of the ICCPR. According to an author, general comments 'represent the [Committee's] accumulated experience of years of consideration of a particular article … they have the potential to be profoundly influential … [and] perform a key function of giving some substantive content to the articles concerned' (McGoldrick 1994: 471). Furthermore, an individual whose civil or political right guaranteed in the ICCPR had been infringed can bring a complaint to the Human Rights Committee against his or her state, provided that his state has ratified the Optional Protocol to the ICCPR.[13] The Committee, in turn, issues its rulings on such complaints which significantly contribute in the understanding of the rights guaranteed in the ICCPR.[14]

Unlike the Human Rights Committee which monitors the full range of civil and political rights recognized in the ICCPR, the Special Rapporteur on freedom of religion or belief is given the specialized mandate of 'examin[ing] incidents and governmental actions in all parts of the world inconsistent with the provisions of the [Religion Declaration], and to recommend remedial measures for such situations'.[15] In the 25 years of the mandate's existence, one of the longest among the mandates in the Special Procedures of the UN human rights machinery, mandate-holders have contributed in the elaboration of the right to freedom of religion or belief through undertaking studies and preparing reports.

12 ICCPR, article 40(1).

13 Optional Protocol to the ICCPR adopted 16 December 1966, GA Res. 2200A (XXI), UN GAOR, 21st Sess., Supp. No. 16, UN Doc. A/6316 (1966), 999 U.N.T.S. 171, entered into force 23 March 1976, art 41.

14 See generally, Joseph et al. (2004).

15 Commission on Human Rights Resolution 1986/20, 42 UN ESCOR Supp. (No. 2) at 66, UN Doc. E/CN.4/1986/65 (1986). Thus far, there have been four individuals who have been appointed as Special Rapporteur on freedom of religion or belief, namely, Angelo d'Almeida Ribeiro (Portugal), 1986–1993; Abdelfattah Amor (Tunisia), 1993–2004; Asma Jahangir (Pakistan), 2004–2010; and Heiner Bielefeldt (Germany), 2010 to present.

Special Rapporteurs and other mandate-holders in the Special Procedures of the UN human rights machinery 'have played a vital role in standard-setting. They regularly identify protection gaps and initiate new standards'.[16] Human rights academics Steiner, Alston and Goodman observed that most mandate-holders use their annual reports in order to 'provide an overview of current and pressing issues ... and to develop particular interpretations of the norms in question' (Steiner et al. 2008: 769). Louise Arbour, a former UN High Commissioner for Human Rights, also recognized the contribution of mandate-holders in human rights standard-setting when she asserted that '[t]hrough the expertise they have developed over the years, the special procedures have advanced the discourse on human rights'.[17]

The Normative Content of the Right to Establish and Maintain Places of Worship

The following sections analyse and integrate the outcomes of the aforementioned human rights authorities' standard-setting activities pertaining to the right to establish and maintain places of worship. It is argued that the normative content of this right can be broken down into six distinct elements, namely:

1. the right to acquire ownership or lawful possession of real property for the purpose of building a place of worship;
2. the right to build a place of worship and to make necessary repairs, subject only to reasonable local planning regulations;
3. the right to solicit and receive voluntary financial and other contributions for the purpose of building a place of worship;
4. the right to the unhampered use and enjoyment of a place of worship;
5. the right of protection to places of worship against interference by the state and non-state actors; and
6. the right against discrimination in applications to build a place of worship.

These elements are discussed *ad seriatim*.

The Right to Acquire Ownership or Lawful Possession of Real Property for the Purpose of Building a Place of Worship

One of the first considerations by a religious group which desires to build a place of worship is whether to purchase or to lease a property. Ownership is not always

16 International Council on Human Rights Policy, *Human Rights Standards: Learning from Experience* (2006) 27.

17 UN High Commissioner for Human Rights, Strategic Management Plan 2006–2007, p. 26, at http://www.ohchr.org/Documents/AboutUs/hc_smp_2006-07.pdf (accessed July 2012).

indispensable in building a place of worship. A religious group may also be able to construct a place of worship on a rented piece of land, provided the lease agreement does not prohibit such construction. To be able to purchase or lease real property, however, a religious group must have the required legal capacity to enter into binding agreements. Therefore, by necessary implication, the right of a religious group to establish and maintain places of worship *presupposes* a prior right to own real property or otherwise to enter into contractual arrangements (such as a lease agreement) in order to obtain lawful possession of a real property for a religious use.

In some countries, this initial step may not always be easy although Article 17 of the UDHR guarantees the right of every person 'to own property alone as well as in association with others'.[18] This communal aspect of owning property assumes greater significance in the context of building a place of worship, which is owned and administered by a religious group in behalf of its members. Among the governmental actions that undermine a religious group's right to establish new places of worship, one of the most direct and immediate violations is the prohibition against owning or possessing real property for the purpose of building new places of worship other than those of the state-sponsored or dominant religion. For example, in the Kingdom of Saudi Arabia, it was reported by the Special Rapporteur that non-Muslims are not permitted to buy or lease property for the purpose of establishing a place of worship.[19] Because of this, they are forced to hold religious gatherings in private homes. But even this is not allowed by Saudi authorities. It was reported that 'individuals have been arrested and detained for non-Muslim worship, even though the worship was non-public'.[20] In March 2009, it was reported that three Christians were arrested after organizing a private religious gathering in the Eastern Province of Saudi Arabia which was raided by members of the government's Commission to Promote Virtue and Prevent Vice.[21]

The legal capacity of a religious group to own or obtain lawful possession of real property is usually made contingent on its registration status. Unregistered religious groups are oftentimes prohibited from acquiring or leasing real property. Therefore, the ability of a religious group to exercise its right to establish and maintain places of worship is directly affected by its status as a recognized legal entity within a domestic jurisdiction. In turn, its legal status depends on whether or not it has successfully satisfied a country's prescribed registration requirements. Paul Taylor observed that '[r]estrictions on the use of buildings have, for the most part, historically been imposed by means of planning regulations, although in

18 Article 17, UDHR.

19 Report of the Special Rapporteur on contemporary forms of racism, racial discrimination, xenophobia and related intolerance, A/HRC/15/53 (12 July 2010) paragraph 23.

20 Ibid.

21 Ibid.

recent years registration procedures have taken centre stage in the means by which States constrain the structural aspects of religious practice' (Taylor 2005: 242).

The Special Rapporteur on freedom of religion or belief has observed how the right to establish places of worship is being restricted, indirectly yet effectively, in many countries through the misuse of the registration process for religious groups. Without registration, religious groups are deprived of the legal capacity to own or lease real property. Enumerating the benefits of obtaining official registration, and thus a legal entity status, the Special Rapporteur stated that:

> Legal status enables religious groups to act as juridical persons in the court system; *it entitles religious communities to build places of worship*, exempts religious communities from customs duties, entitles the community to open bank accounts, secures their standing as officially registered denominations and means that such communities can be fully fledged partners with the Government.[22]

In several reports, the Special Rapporteur illustrated the adverse implications to a religious group when registration requirements included stringent or unreasonable criteria. For example, in the Slovak Republic, religious minorities have complained about a piece of legislation that prohibits religious communities with fewer than 20,000 members from obtaining legal status, which they need, *inter alia*, to enter into binding agreements such as a sale or lease of property on which to construct a place of worship.[23] In relation to Angola, the Special Rapporteur criticized the government for implementing a law that, for registration purposes, prescribes a membership of at least 100,000 persons who are domiciled in Angola and, at the same time, who are from at least two-thirds of Angola's provinces. Explaining the potential repercussions of this law, particularly to the right to build places of worship, the Special Rapporteur stated that:

> the law contains stringent requirements for registration ... It has potential practical implications for religious communities, such as a denial of permission to build places of worship, the closure of places of worship or the prohibition of religious organizations. The Special Rapporteur recommends that the law is reformed and was encouraged by the openness of the Government to review the provisions of the law.[24]

It may be concluded that guaranteeing the right to establish and maintain places of worship begins when a state grants religious communities the legal entity status which, in turn, endows them with the legal capacity to acquire ownership or lawful

22 Report of the Special Rapporteur on Angola, A/HRC/7/10/Add.4 (6 March 2008) paragraph 18 (emphasis added).

23 Report of the Special Rapporteur, E/CN.4/2004/63 (16 January 2004) paragraph 90.

24 Report of the Special Rapporteur on Angola, A/HRC/7/10/Add.4 (6 March 2008) paragraph 47.

possession of real property upon which to construct their houses of worship. However, a comprehensive and thorough protection of the right to establish and maintain places of worship requires the satisfaction or realization of the other five elements.

The Right to Build Places of Worship and Make Necessary Repairs, Subject Only to Reasonable Local Planning Regulations

The Special Rapporteur on freedom of religion or belief emphasized that places of worship have more than a 'material significance' for the religious community attached to them.[25] He attributed the importance of places of worship to 'the specific character of places of worship and their particular significance for believers'.[26] The Special Rapporteur also stressed that 'places of worship have an emotional and spiritual significance for the believers'.[27] He characterized the nature of places of worship as follows:

> [P]laces of worship are an essential element of the manifestation of the right to freedom of religion or belief to the extent that the great majority of religious communities or communities of belief need the existence of a place of worship where their members can manifest their faith.[28]

The Human Rights Committee has also recognized the centrality of places of worship in the life of religious communities. For example, concerned about the reports that 'religious practice is repressed or strongly discouraged' in North Korea, the Committee asked the Pyongyang government to provide it with up-to-date information regarding the 'number of citizens of [North Korea] belonging to religious communities and the number of places of worship'[29] in that country. This suggests that the Committee equates the existence of places of worship as a necessary companion of religious freedom. There is an underlying premise here that these places are a precondition for the full and meaningful exercise of the right to manifest one's religion or belief in worship.

25 Report of the Special Rapporteur on freedom of religion or belief, E/CN.4/2005/61 (20 December 2004) paragraphs 49–50.

26 Report of the Special Rapporteur on Tajikistan, A/HRC/7/10/Add.2 (27 November 2007) paragraph 55.

27 Report of the Special Rapporteur on Macedonia, A/HRC/13/40/Add.2 (28 December 2009) paragraph 45.

28 Report of the Special Rapporteur, Summary of cases transmitted to Governments and replies received, A/HRC/13/40/Add.1 (16 February 2010) paragraph 146.

29 Human Rights Committee, Concluding Observation on the reports submitted by the Democratic People's Republic of Korea, CCPR/CO/72/PRK, 27 August 2001, paragraph 22.

The general rule Bearing in mind the importance of places of worship to religious communities, as underscored by the Human Rights Committee and the Special Rapporteur, it may be extrapolated that states are obliged, under international human rights law, to guarantee the right to build places of worship by facilitating the entire process leading to actual construction of such places. Conversely, states have the negative duty of not imposing unreasonable legal or administrative rules that have the cumulative effect of obstructing such construction. In General Comment No. 22, the Committee stated that states parties '*should proceed* from the need to protect the rights guaranteed in the Covenant'.[30] This suggests that the default position of states must be to allow the greater exercise of religious freedom through, among other measures, the approvals of applications to build places of worship.

While religious groups have the right to build places of worship, they cannot construct them anywhere they please. Like the other aspects of the right to manifest one's religion or belief *(forum externum)*, the right is not absolute. However, it must be underscored that every rejection of an application to build a place of worship ought to be consistent with Article 18(3) of the ICCPR regarding the permissible limitations on freedom of religion or belief, which provides that:

> Freedom to manifest one's religion or beliefs may be subject only to such limitations as are prescribed by law and are necessary to protect public safety, order, health, or morals or the fundamental rights and freedoms of others.[31]

In a similar vein, law and religion scholar Cornelis de Jong argues that '[t]he right to establish places of worship and assembly is subject to the *same limitations* as the general freedom to manifest one's religion or belief' (de Jong 2000: 360 [emphasis added]). This statement is consistent with the pronouncement of the Special Rapporteur who, after analysing the incidents in Turkey involving some rejected applications to build places of worship, stated that:

> The Government should guarantee minorities the right to establish and maintain their own places of worship, and should allow them to build such facilities in places where new communities have taken root. *Any limitations in this respect, for example urban development regulations, should be consistent with international jurisprudence (see General Comment of the Human Rights Committee)*, and this means that any non-conforming regulations should be repealed or revised.[32]

Through the above pronouncement, the Special Rapporteur has made another important elaboration regarding the siting of places of worship, namely, that a

30 General Comment No. 22, paragraph 8 (emphasis added).

31 Article 18(3), ICCPR.

32 Interim Report of the Special Rapporteur, A/55/280/Add.1 (11 August 2000) paragraph.160 (d) (emphasis added).

religious group has the right to build a place of worship in a location which is most accessible to most of its members. The Special Rapporteur is elaborating on the right to establish and maintain places of worship by providing that, as far as practicable, places of worship should be allowed to be constructed 'in places where new communities have taken root'[33] or, in other words, in locations where a sufficiently numerous members are already residing. The important criterion here is the accessibility of places of worship to members of the religious community.

Aside from the right to build places of worship, there is also the accompanying right to 'maintain' them. In its ordinary acceptation, the term 'maintain' means the carrying out of ordinary and necessary repairs to keep a property in good condition or operation (*Macquarie Pocket Dictionary* 1998: 637). As a logical offshoot of its right to build places of worship, a religious group has the right to make these repairs without obstruction. Illustrating the importance of the right of a religious group to maintain its places of worship, the Human Rights Committee pressed the Egyptian government during the discussion of its periodic report to respond to the alleged obstruction experienced by the Coptic Church in Egypt 'in obtaining permits to repair and build places of worship'.[34] The underlying rationale of the right to maintain places of worship is the fact that the regular maintenance of such places ensures their prolonged use and enjoyment by members of the religious group.

Local planning regulations and places of worship The right to establish and maintain places of worship is oftentimes pitted against certain interests that underpin local planning regulations. There is no doubt that planning regulations have underlying objectives. Foremost of which is the establishment of an orderly and sound layout of residential, industrial, commercial and mixed-type structures (see generally, Rydin 2011: 1–31). Aiming to create a liveable and organized community, planning regulations aim to reduce noise, avoid traffic congestion, provide adequate parking spaces, put up effective sewerage and waste disposal, ensure the safety of different types of structures, and similar interests (ibid.).

Local planning regulations can be broadly classified into three groups. First, there are the zoning ordinances that subdivide a locality into different sectors or areas and the permissible structures allowed in each sector or area (e.g. industrial, agricultural, commercial, residential or mixed). Second, local authorities employ design or architectural guidelines that aim to regulate the structures themselves with respect to, for example, noise reduction, their allowable person-to-floor area ratio, height, parking spaces and their visual harmony with surrounding structures. Third, local authorities prescribe safety guidelines such as the requirement to put emergency exits, building materials appropriate to the locality (e.g. not fire-prone), water sprinklers and even the number, type and location of fire extinguishers to be placed within a structure.

33 Ibid.

34 E/CN.4/1990/46 paragraph 40 and E/CN.4/1992/52 paragraph 30.

Several problems may arise from the implementation of local planning regulations. First, they may be used discriminatorily to single out a minority religious group and prevent its establishment of a place of worship (to be discussed below). Second, even in the absence of discrimination, the rigid application of planning regulations may force religious groups to do any of the following:

1. a drastic reduction in the seating capacity or allowable use of a proposed place of worship, thus resulting in the group's inability to satisfy its members' increasing demand for prayer venues;
2. a substantial change or variance in the architectural design or layout of the proposed place of worship, thus adversely affecting a religious group's ceremony or liturgy as prescribed by its religious doctrines. The prohibition or restriction on the construction of Islamic minarets is a good example;
3. religious groups are sometimes forced to establish places of worship in less accessible locations or in more expensive sites, thus adversely affecting the number of worshippers; or
4. a religious group may be forced to discontinue altogether its application to build a place of worship.

Concerns about traffic congestion, insufficient parking spaces, noise, local aesthetics as well as declining property values have been used as grounds for objection against proposals to build places of worship. In most instances, applications to build places of worship are rejected on the ground that they violate one or more planning regulations. Others are approved only after making substantial changes to the original proposals. The ensuing controversy is oftentimes very passionate and confrontational that involves, on one hand, the applicant religious group and its members; and on the other hand, the local council and the local residents who usually oppose the construction of places of worship in their neighbourhood.

Local planning regulations have had the most restricting effect upon the right of religious groups to establish and maintain places of worship. The adverse impact of zoning ordinances, traffic regulations, design or architectural guidelines, parking provisions and similar local rules on the establishment and maintenance of places of worship has been observed across the world. For example, in Vietnam, a place of worship was demolished by authorities because no permission was obtained prior to its construction.[35] In Turkey, the places of worship of 23 congregations of Turkish Christians were declared to be in violation of municipal building laws and faced the possibility of being shut down.[36] In Georgia, it was reported that local authorities made it difficult for Protestant and Armenian Orthodox religious

35 Report of the Special Rapporteur, UN Doc. E/CN.4/2000/65 (15 February 2000) paragraph 99.

36 Report of the Special Rapporteur, UN Doc.A/57/274 (2002), paragraphs 52–53 (Turkey).

communities to obtain permits to build places of worship because of the pressure and influence exerted by the majority religion, the Georgian Orthodox Church.[37]

There is a restriction on the right to establish and maintain places of worship when planning regulations result in either (1) the construction of fewer places of worship that cannot sufficiently accommodate the present number of worshippers or (2) the failure to satisfy anticipated future demands for places of worship. W. Cole Durham observed that it is the 'bureaucratic roadblocks which cumulatively have the effect of significantly impairing religious liberty' (Durham 1996: 1, 12). The typical justification of the enforcers of these regulations (usually the local authorities) is that 'their task was limited to the implementation of domestic law'.[38] In response to this excuse, however, the Special Rapporteur strongly emphasized that aside from the imperatives of domestic laws and regulations 'the authorities also have to abide by human rights standards'.[39]

The Special Rapporteur has consistently advised states that they 'should ensure that religious communities do not encounter obstructions with regard to the building, opening, renting or use of places of worship'.[40] For example, the imposition of legal or policy restrictions by the authorities of Turkmenistan on places of worship did not escape scrutiny by the Special Rapporteur. According to him, these restrictions 'amount in some instances to undue limitations on freedom to manifest one's religion or belief, as well as on other rights, such as freedom of association and freedom of expression'.[41] Meanwhile, during his visit to Turkey, a secular country but where Islam is the dominant religion, the Special Rapporteur took notice of the various administrative hurdles that prevent Christian, Greek Orthodox and Armenian minorities from erecting their places of worship.[42] In another report, the Special Rapporteur characterized similar non-conforming regulations in Macedonia as 'de facto obstruction' that religious groups faced in applying for official permission to construct new places of worship. The Special Rapporteur was concerned that:

> When applying for such building permits, they allegedly underwent numerous bureaucratic procedures, which resulted in long waiting periods for the necessary documentation, and intervention from the local community which is against such projects. The relevant authorities often reject applications for building permits by religious minorities arguing that the development plan does not

37 Report of the Special Rapporteur, UN Doc. E/CN.4/2000/65 (2000) paragraph 40 (Georgia).

38 Report of the Special Rapporteur on Turkmenistan, A/HRC/10/8/Add.4 (12 January 2009), paragraph 54.

39 Ibid.

40 Ibid., summary.

41 Ibid.

42 Report of the Special Rapporteur on Turkey, A/55/280/Add.1 (10 September 2000) paragraph 160.

> foresee a religious building on this piece of land. However, the small religious communities claim that the development plans often do not provide any such designated areas at all, which obviously adversely affects their possibility to manifest their religion or belief in worship, observance, practice and teaching.[43]

In sum, these bureaucratic obstructions placed against building places of worship are an anathema to the right to freedom of religion or belief. The Human Rights Council expressed its serious concern over 'the obstacles placed in the way of construction of places of worship inconsistent with the exercise of the right to freedom of religion or belief'.[44] It may therefore be concluded that states have the positive obligation to remove these obstructions and facilitate the establishment by religious communities of their places of worship.

Another issue worth looking at when it comes to construction of places of worship is problems encountered because of unreasonable delay in the processing of applications to build such places. While these applications remain pending, members of religious groups may have to choose less accessible places of worship or set up prayer venues in locations less suitable for worshipping such as garages, function rooms in busy shopping centres or community centres. Concerned with unreasonable delays, the Special Rapporteur strongly criticized the Egyptian government because the minority Coptic Church had suffered 'building and renovating restrictions which resulted in delays of up to thirty years in the grant of permission for building or renovation work, and the closure of buildings in the interim'.[45] Similarly, the Special Rapporteur criticized the practice of delaying the grant of permits for the building of Christian places of worship in Malaysia.[46]

Another specific controversy that arises is when local planning regulations prohibit the construction of certain structures considered as religiously significant by a religious group, such as the Islamic minarets. A minaret is an elevated structure usually used by Muslims to signal their prayer times.[47] While minarets do not, strictly speaking, structurally form part of a mosque, their construction is an intrinsic part of the manifestation of the religious faith of Muslims and thus they come under the mantle of protection of international human rights law. While some non-Muslims may consider minarets as non-essential to worship itself (for instance, it has been argued that the Muslims can still pray even without the minarets), this is not how Muslims view these structures. In this regard, it is

43 Report of the Special Rapporteur on Macedonia, A/HRC/13/40/Add.2 (28 December 2009) paragraph 43.

44 Human Rights Council, Resolution 6/37: Elimination of all forms of intolerance and of discrimination based on religion or belief, 14 December 2007, p. 2.

45 Report of the Special Rapporteur, UN Doc. E/CN.4/1990/46 (1990) paragraph 40 (Egypt).

46 Report of the Special Rapporteur, UN Doc/ CN.4/1995/91 (1995) p. 59 (Malaysia).

47 Human Rights Features, 'Heightened Intolerance: Swiss Minaret Ban Should be a Wake Up Call for Europe', 31 December 2009.

the Muslims' view of minarets that should matter. This is because the religious significance of minarets forms part of the Islamic religious doctrine which *only* the Muslims themselves – and certainly not the state nor the other religions – can define. The choice to designate a place or a structure as sacred or otherwise religiously significant is part of the *forum internum* of the freedom of religion or belief which is an absolute human right.[48] That choice belongs to the religious community concerned and its truth or veracity cannot be assessed by others. An assessment made by others as to the propriety of assigning religious significance to certain structures is a direct interference – an affront – against the right to hold religious convictions of one's own choice.

Furthermore, a state's legal system should provide for an independent judicial review that allows aggrieved religious groups to challenge unreasonable delays or rejections of applications to build places of worship. In this regard, the Special Rapporteur has emphasized that 'the independence of the judiciary be fully respected and that courts be able to adjudicate upon religious matters without fear or favour'.[49]A state should ensure the availability of this judicial remedy to counter a potential abuse of discretion on the part of local authorities and other administrative agencies responsible for regulating the establishment of places of worship.

In conclusion, international human rights law does not prohibit local planning regulations per se, but it does subject them to a critical assessment if they have the effect of restricting the right to manifest one's religious belief through worship. This critical assessment is mandated by the general limitations clause found in Article 18(3) which applies to all restrictions against the freedom to manifest one's religion or belief. It involves an examination of the legal compatibility between, on one hand, local planning regulations in a given case and, on the other hand, the permissible limitations to the right to freedom of religion or belief under Article 18(3) of the ICCPR. If an application to build a place of worship is rejected on the ground of local planning regulations, the concerned state (and, depending on how international human rights norms are received and accepted into its domestic jurisdiction, its political subdivisions) carries the burden of demonstrating that such rejection is fully compatible with any of the grounds stated in Article 18(3) of the ICCPR.

48 Tahzib (1996: 88–89), citing a report by A. Krishnaswami that described the *forum internum* as 'fall[ing] primarily within the domain of the inner faith and conscience of an individual. Viewed from this angle, one would assume that any intervention from outside is not only illegitimate but impossible'. Study of Discrimination in the Matter of Religious Rights and Practices, UN Doc. E/CN.4/Sub.2/200/Rev.1, UN Sales No. 60.XIV.2 (1960) at 16.

49 Report of the Special Rapporteur on Macedonia, A/HRC/13/40/Add.2 (28 December 2009) paragraph 56.

Submitting applications to build places of worship in a referendum Related to the issue of building places of worship is the compatibility with international human rights law of allowing the voters of a locality to decide pending applications to build places of worship. The question may be framed in this manner – may an application to build a place of worship be submitted for referendum and thereby be decided by the majority of the concerned locality? It is submitted that such referendum is legally incompatible with the right to freedom of religion or belief. The rationale for this position goes into the very essence of the 'universality' principle of human rights which affirms that every human being, regardless of his station in life, where he resides, what form of government he pledges allegiance to, or whether he finds himself as part of the majority or minority population, enjoys certain fundamental freedoms and entitlements that are inherent and inalienable (Henkin 1989: 10–16). By virtue of the universality principle, the manifestation of religious freedom cannot be made contingent upon the preference of the majority population determined through referenda, plebiscites or other forms of electoral exercise. Because places of worship are integral to religious manifestation, submitting the construction of such places to a referendum is tantamount to allowing the majority to decide whether the minority may exercise its own religious freedom. Clearly, this is contrary to the universality principle of human rights.

In 2009, the construction of minarets in Switzerland was submitted to the voters in a referendum for their decision. The outcome of the electoral exercise is to prohibit the construction of minarets all over Switzerland. Switzerland's decision to hold the referendum did not sit well with the Human Rights Committee which, in its Concluding Observation on the report submitted by Switzerland for the same year, stated that:

> *The Committee is concerned about the referendum initiative aimed at prohibiting the construction of minarets* and about the discriminatory advertising campaign which accompanies it. It notes that the State party does not support this referendum initiative which, *if adopted, will bring the State party into non-compliance with its obligations under the Covenant (arts. 2, 18, 20)*. The State party should strenuously ensure respect for freedom of religion and firmly combat incitement to discrimination, hostility and violence.[50]

Although the Committee dealt with the construction of minarets and not places of worship per se, the underlying issue was the propriety of subjecting the enjoyment of the freedom of religious manifestation to a popular vote in a society which has a majority Christian population. The Committee, through the above pronouncement, attempts to guard religious freedom from any impairment as a result of measures countenanced by the majority of the population (which, in this case, was the Swiss constitutional amendment prohibiting the construction of minarets). It is

50 Concluding Observation of the Human Rights Committee, Switzerland, UN Doc. CCPR/C/CHE/CO/3 3 November 2009, paragraph 8 (emphasis added).

submitted that religious freedom, including its indispensable element of the right to establish and maintain places of worship, ought to be immune from the vagaries of popular sentiment. To guard against the so-called 'tyranny of the majority',[51] religious freedom along with all fundamental freedoms guaranteed in human rights instruments must be placed on a pedestal above and beyond the reach of the changing tides of popular opinion.

The Right to Solicit and Receive Voluntary Financial and Other Contributions for the Purpose of Building a Place of Worship

Article 6(f) of the Religion Declaration provides that the right to freedom of religion or belief includes the right '[t]o solicit and receive voluntary financial and other contributions from individuals and institutions'. An earlier phraseology of this right stated that '[r]eligious communities shall have the right to receive the funds necessary for the carrying out of their functions'.[52] The aim of the right is to ensure the continuous financing of a religious group's myriad of activities. One such activity is charity or humanitarian work; that is why Article 6(f) is oftentimes invoked in conjunction with Article 6(b) which guarantees the right '[t]o establish and maintain appropriate charitable or humanitarian institutions' (see especially, Ridge 2009: 85–109).

Aside from running charitable or humanitarian institutions, the right to solicit and receive voluntary financial and other contributions has a *direct relevance* to the right to establish and maintain places of worship. However, this particular combination of rights is rarely, if ever, invoked. Especially for newly established or small religious groups, owning or renting real property and constructing a place of worship thereon present a real financial challenge. By guaranteeing the right to solicit and receive voluntary contributions from individuals and institutions, the Religion Declaration is ensuring that religious groups have the necessary means to muster enough funds and other resources to establish and maintain their own place of worship. The right to solicit or receive contributions is, therefore, an *enabling complementary right* that ensures the realization of the right to establish and maintain places of worship. In other words, the tandem of these rights guarantees a more complete protection.

In a couple of reports, the Special Rapporteur expressed his concern over violations of the right to solicit and receive voluntary financial and other contributions, thereby acknowledging that its normative character as a distinct religious right is quite strong. For example, in relation to Tibet, the Special Rapporteur criticized the situation where certain funds donated to Buddhist

51 As propounded by John Stuart Mill, the 'tyranny of the majority' is a description of a polity where the will of the majority of the population shapes laws or policies that are designed to advance their own interest to the detriment of the interest of the minority (Mill 1859: 7).

52 E/CN.4/873, p. 68, article X (1963).

monasteries were deposited in a particular bank account only and could not be withdrawn without first securing government approval.[53] In relation to the Lao People's Democratic Republic, the Special Rapporteur voiced his concern over the arrest of Christians allegedly for, *inter alia*, receiving financial donations from overseas sources.[54] While being examples of how the right to solicit and receive voluntary financial and other contributions has been infringed, both cases are actually a validation of the existence of this right.

Regarding the permissible limitations on the right to solicit and receive voluntary financial and other contributions, the Special Rapporteur on freedom of religion or belief stated that:

> While the right to ... receive funding is not unlimited, any restrictions imposed must be prescribed by law and must be necessary to protect public safety, order, health or morals, or the fundamental rights and freedoms of others, *for example in order to prevent such institutions being misused to advance their cause through violence*.[55]

Contributions, particularly those coming from overseas, to religious groups purportedly for the purpose of building places of worship but actually intended to further acts of terrorism are therefore within a state's power to prohibit without violating the right to establish and maintain places of worship. However, it bears stressing the general rule as regards funding the construction of places of worship. When the stated purpose of a religious group's solicitation or receipt of financial contributions is the building of a place of worship, any restriction imposed against it ought to be subjected to an even greater scrutiny in order to gauge its compatibility with the general limitations clause in Article 18(3) of the ICCPR because two distinct religious human rights are in danger of being violated.

The Right to Unhampered Use and Enjoyment of a Place of Worship

Once a religious group has built a place of worship, the most important element of the right to establish and maintain places of worship is the unhampered ability of the group to use and enjoy its temple, mosque, church, synagogue, *gurdwara* or other houses of worship. There are two possible ways that the right to the unhampered use and enjoyment of a place of worship may be violated: first, outright prohibition against using an existing place of worship and, second, placing strict conditions on the use of a place of worship. With respect to the first, the Special Rapporteur has clearly stated that 'in cases where members of the community are prevented from using a place of worship that belongs to them, this thereby constituting a violation

53 Report of the Special Rapporteur, UN Doc E/CN.4/1988/45 (1988) paragraph 45.

54 Report of the Special Rapporteur, UN Doc E/CN.4/1999/58 (1999) paragraph 86.

55 Interim Report of the Special Rapporteur, A/65/207, paragraph 36 (emphasis added).

of their right to freedom of religion or belief'.[56] Meanwhile, when the use of places of worship is subjected to strict conditions (such as those relating to the number of days and allowed times when they can be used), there is a strong presumption that such conditions violate the right to religious manifestation. This is logical because the right to establish and maintain places of worship will be largely deprived of its meaning and purpose if their actual use is made dependent on the discretion or whims of state authorities.

The practical significance of the right to establish and maintain places of worship depends on whether, after such places are built, members of a religious community can freely and peacefully enjoy their benefits. Places of worship perform a critical function in the daily life of a religious community. First, they are physical locations where members of a religious group can pray in accordance with the established rituals or ceremonies of their religion. Second, churches, mosques, temples, synagogues and other places of worship cater to the educational and socio-cultural needs of members of a religious community. Lastly, places of worship serve as a religious community's proud proclamation of their existence to the general public (see generally, Sandercock 2001: 319–323; Burayidi 2001: 259–273). By building a new place of worship, a religious group affirms and proclaims its unique identity to the rest of society. Hence, places of worship amount to a religious group's symbolic public presence which it regards as an important value in itself. Here therefore lies the interface between two important human freedoms, namely, religious freedom and freedom of expression.

When a state action interrupts the use and enjoyment of a place of worship, the first issue to be analysed is whether such interruption is compatible with the general limitations clause in Article 18(3) of the ICCPR. Again, because an interruption on the use and enjoyment of a place of worship is a form of direct restriction on the right to religious manifestation, a greater onus is thereby placed upon a state to justify its action.

In addition, the state has the obligation to reduce such interruption to the minimum level possible. For example, if there is a need to close down a place of worship because there is a lawful or valid justification to do so (i.e. the situation falls under any one of the permissible limitations to freedom or religion or belief), the state has the ensuing duty of providing the affected religious community 'a suitable alternative place of worship' in the interregnum to mitigate the adverse impact to a religious group. The Special Rapporteur has confirmed the existence of this state obligation:

> The Government should ensure that religious communities are not unduly deprived of their places of worship. In cases where such deprivation is justified

56 Report of the Special Rapporteur on Romania, E/CN.4/2004/63/Add.2 (16 December 2003) paragraph 104.

> by lawful reasons and after judicial review, it should provide the community concerned with a suitable alternative place of worship.[57]

In Azerbaijan, the members of the Juma mosque community have been deprived of the use and enjoyment of their place of worship after local authorities temporarily closed it down for renovation works in 2006. The Special Rapporteur has criticized the failure of the Azerbaijan government to inform the mission on 'whether the members of the community were offered an alternative place of worship by the Government'.[58] This suggests that the interruption of the use and enjoyment of places of worship, when justified by compelling and lawful reasons, ought to be mitigated by palliative measures such as but not limited to offering a 'suitable alternative place of worship'.

The Right of Protection to Places of Worship Against Interference by the State and Non-State Actors

Because places of worship are indispensable in manifesting one's religious beliefs through worship, international human rights law affords them legal protection. The Religion Declaration envisioned the need to protect places of worship by providing that '[t]he rights and freedoms set forth in the present Declaration shall be accorded in national legislations in such a manner that everyone shall be able to avail himself of such rights and freedoms in practice'.[59] As discussed earlier, the right to establish and maintain places of worship is one such constituent freedom guaranteed in Article 6 of the Religion Declaration. The Special Rapporteur has affirmed this right of protection to be accorded to places of worship when, after his mission to Tajikistan in 2007, he denounced the government's plan to demolish the country's only synagogue which has been used for decades by the Jewish community but which was scheduled to be demolished in order to give way to the construction of a national park and a government palace. The Special Rapporteur also called the attention of the Tajikistan government to international instruments that guarantee the right of protection for places of worship. He stated that:

> [M]osques, churches and other places of worship need to be fully respected and protected by the authorities. The Special Rapporteur would like to remind the Government of article 6 (a) of the Declaration on the Elimination of All Forms of Intolerance and Discrimination Based on Religion or Belief which states that the right to freedom of thought, conscience, religion or belief includes the freedom 'to worship or assemble in connection with a religion or belief, and to establish and maintain places for these purposes'. Furthermore, in its resolution 2005/40,

---

57 Report of the Special Rapporteur on Azerbaijan, A/HRC/4/21/Add.2 (18 October 2006) paragraph 99.

58 Ibid., paragraph 70.

59 Article 7, Religion Declaration.

> the Commission on Human Rights urged States to exert the utmost efforts, in accordance with their national legislation and in conformity with international human rights law, to ensure that religious places, sites, shrines and religious expressions are fully respected and protected and to take additional measures in cases where they are vulnerable to desecration or destruction.[60]

Because the entire membership of a religious community benefits from a place of worship, conversely, any impairment, attack or restriction against such a place results in the victimization of the entire membership. The 'rights-holder' that stands to be harmed in the event of any impairment or restriction against the right to establish places of worship is not just the individual members of a religious group but the group itself as a collective rights-holder. The establishment of places of worship is, therefore, properly regarded as a collective human right. The Special Rapporteur has consistently affirmed this fact by stating that:

> unlike other forms of violations of the right to freedom of religion or belief, attacks or other forms of restriction on places of worship or other religious sites and shrines in many cases violate the right not only of a single individual, *but the rights of a group of individuals forming the community that is attached to the place in question.*[61]

Places of worship need to be protected from attacks, intrusions or other forms of interference committed by state and non-state actors that result in the impairment of the use and enjoyment of such places. A clear example of a grave violation of the right of protection to places of worship is the physical destruction of mosques, temples, churches, synagogues, *gurdwaras* or other houses of worship which takes place either in the context of an armed conflict or even during peacetime. During an international armed conflict, the legal protection of such places is expressly articulated in Article 53 of the First Additional Protocol to the Geneva Convention which provides that:

> Without prejudice to the provisions of the Hague Convention for the Protection of Cultural Property in the Event of Armed Conflict of 14 May 1954, and of other relevant international instruments, it is prohibited:

60 Report of the Special Rapporteur on Tajikistan, A/HRC/7/10/Add.2 (27 November 2007) paragraph 55.

61 Report of the Special Rapporteur, Summary of cases transmitted to Governments and replies received, A/HRC/13/40/Add.1 (16 February 2010) paragraph 146 (emphasis added).

(a) To commit any acts of hostility directed against the historic monuments, works of art or places of worship which constitute the cultural or spiritual heritage of peoples;

(b) To use such objects in support of the military effort;

(c) To make such objects the object of reprisals.[62]

The legal protection of the above provision has been extended to situations of non-international armed conflict (such as civil wars or rebellions) by Article 16 of the Second Additional Protocol to the Geneva Convention which contains a similar provision.[63] However, even in the absence of an armed conflict, places of worship also become targets of attacks in some countries. For example, in a 2009 report to the UN General Assembly, the Special Rapporteur stated that 'another general pattern [of violations of the right to freedom of religion or belief] seems to be the targeting of places of worship and other religious buildings or properties. The Special Rapporteur is concerned about reports of frequent attacks on places of worship'.[64]

Another violation of the right of protection to places of worship is the confiscation or seizure of such places and other sacred objects of religious minorities. The confiscation or seizure prevents members of religious groups from using and enjoying a place of worship; but it should be emphasized that the failure to remedy such confiscation or seizure by returning places of worship and/or by restituting sacred objects to their rightful owner constitutes another violation of the right of protection to places of worship. For example, in relation to Georgia, the Human Rights Committee 'expressed its regret that problems related to the restitution of places of worship and related properties of religious minorities, confiscated during the Communist era, have not been solved'[65] by succeeding governments. Also, in Belarus, religious communities have experienced difficulties in recovering places of worship seized during the Soviet period.[66] In both situations, the state responsible for the confiscation or seizure was no longer in existence but the obligations to return the confiscated places of worship and

62 Protocol Additional to the Geneva Conventions of 12 August 1949, and relating to the Protection of Victims of International Armed Conflicts (Protocol I), 8 June 1977, article 53.

63 Protocol Additional to the Geneva Conventions of 12 August 1949, and relating to the Protection of Victims of Non-International Armed Conflicts (Protocol II), 8 June 1977, article 16.

64 Interim Report of the Special Rapporteur, A/64/159 (17 July 2009) paragraph 11.

65 Human Rights Committee, Concluding Observations on the Report Submitted by Georgia, CCPR/C/GEO/CO/3/CRP.1 (19 October 2007) paragraph 15.

66 Report of the Special Rapporteur, E/CN.4/2004/63 (16 January 2004) paragraph 32.

to restitute the seized sacred objects to their rightful owners had devolved to the successor states, namely, Georgia and Belarus.

In addition, intrusions, attacks or other forms of interference against places of worship may also be committed by non-state actors. Strictly speaking, non-state actors are not 'duty-bearers' in regards to the right to freedom of religion or belief. It is however the obligation of the state to ensure that these actors do not hinder the free exercise of freedom of religion or belief. As regards violations committed by non-state actors, the Special Rapporteur has stated that:

> a large number of the violations of the right to freedom of religion or belief are committed by non-State actors, whether members of religious groups themselves or others. *The Special Rapporteur notes ... that there is still a tendency even today to forget about the positive human rights obligations of States. States have an obligation to ensure freedom of religion or belief to the persons finding themselves within their jurisdiction.* Where acts of violence or other acts of religious intolerance are committed against individuals, States have both an obligation to protect and an obligation to remedy the situation.[67]

A few examples illustrate how non-state actors violate the right of protection to be accorded to places of worship:

1. By another religious group – in relation to Romania where a place of worship was confiscated by a rival religious group, the Special Rapporteur criticized the government for its inaction. He stated that 'in cases where members of the community are prevented from using a place of worship that belongs to them, this thereby constituting a violation of their right to freedom of religion or belief'.[68] In India, violations of the right to freedom of religion or belief were committed by Hindu and Muslim communities against each other in relation to a dispute over the ownership of a place of worship.[69]
2. By extremist groups – in relation to Indonesia, the Special Rapporteur condemned the destruction of places of worship belonging to Christian denominations by extremist groups, the violence having been triggered by the long-running tension between Muslim and Christian communities in a locality.[70]

---

67 Report of the Special Rapporteur, E/CN.4/2005/61 (20 December 2004) paragraph 75 (emphasis added).

68 Report of the Special Rapporteur on Romania, E/CN.4/2004/63/Add.2 (16 December 2003) paragraph 104.

69 Report of the Special Rapporteur on India, E/CN.4/1997/91/Add.1, paragraph 93.

70 SR UN Doc. E/CN.4/2000/65 (2000) paragraph 49 (Indonesia).

3. By traditional rural leaders – in relation to an incident in Chiapas, Mexico, the Special Rapporteur reported the destruction of Protestant churches in the area allegedly by traditional rural leaders.[71]
4. By owners of real property – in Turkmenistan, property owners who had once allowed their properties to be rented and used as places of worship 'have however been pressured by the authorities to refrain from doing so again. As a result, it has become very difficult for these religious groups to find public meeting places'.[72]

Even though committed by non-state actors, the foregoing violations of the right to establish and maintain places of worship may cause states to incur state responsibility. The 'positive human rights obligations' of states with regard to the right to freedom of religion or belief compel them to take all necessary action to put an end to such violations and, equally important, to exact the accountability of guilty parties through civil, criminal or administrative sanctions in order to deter future violations. On the basis of their positive human rights obligations, the broader duty of states is to create the domestic conditions necessary to allow, rather than to hinder, the greater exercise of religious freedom including, *inter alia*, ensuring the protection of places of worship from attacks, intrusions or other forms of interference whether perpetrated by state or non-state agents.

The Right Against Discrimination in Applications to Build Places of Worship

Discrimination cuts across all the constituent elements of the right to freedom of religion or belief, and it may be committed by state and non-state actors. Hence, for example, a Muslim employee may be discriminated against at the workplace on the basis of his or her religious need to pray five times a day (i.e. manifestation in worship); or a Sikh student may be discriminated against at school because of his or her religious apparel (i.e. manifestation in observance); or a religious group may be discriminated against in the enforcement of local planning regulations pertinent to its application to build a place of worship. This last example deserves a special attention due to its severe restrictive effect against the right to establish and maintain places of worship. In many cases, the enforcement of local planning rules governing places of worship seems 'to be neutral (such as regulating the flow of traffic, harmony with other buildings or activities, or noise restrictions), but are selectively enforced for discriminatory purposes against disfavoured religious groups'.[73]

---

71 SR UN Doc. E/CN.4/2000/65 (2000) paragraph 66 (Mexico).

72 Report of the Special Rapporteur on Turkmenistan, A/HRC/10/8/Add.4 (12 January 2009) paragraph 38.

73 'Guidelines for Review of Legislation Pertaining to Religion or Belief' prepared by the OSCE/ODIHR Advisory Panel of Experts on Freedom of Religion or Belief in consultation with the Council of Europe's Commission for Democracy Through Law

Among religious minorities, it is the members of a migrant community that are especially 'vulnerable to discrimination based on their religion or belief and [they] face related prejudices on a societal level'.[74] Their vulnerability is largely explained by the difficulties associated with being transplanted to a foreign environment, the linguistic and cultural barrier and the economic displacement they experience as newcomers. Discrimination against migrant communities, and specifically its restricting effect upon their right to establish their own places of worship, has not escaped scrutiny by the Special Rapporteur who noted that:

> all persons within a particular country, and not just the citizens of that country, have the right to freedom of religion or belief, including the manifestation of their religion or belief in worship, observance, practice and teaching. In her reports, *the Special Rapporteur has pointed to practical limitations imposed on the freedom of migrants to manifest their religion or belief publicly, for example with regard to building places of worship*, carrying out religious rituals openly or conducting missionary activities.[75]

In response to instances of discrimination, including those being committed against minority religious groups in the context of their applications to build places of worship, the General Assembly and the Human Rights Council have stated that:

> legal procedures pertaining to … places of worship are not a prerequisite for the exercise of the right to manifest one's religion or belief, and that such procedures, when legally required at the national or local level, should be non-discriminatory in order to contribute to the effective protection of the right of all persons to practise their religion or belief, either individually or in community with others and in public or private.[76]

It is clear, therefore, that international human rights law imposes a positive obligation upon states to remain neutral and impartial in matters of religion. States have the 'primary obligation to protect individuals from acts of religious intolerance and discrimination'.[77] There are numerous situations or settings where it is legally incumbent upon a state to perform this duty of neutrality and impartiality. But in the context of applications to build places of worship, this duty assumes even

---

(Venice Commission), adopted by the Venice Commission at its fifty-ninth plenary session (Venice, 18–19 June 2004) p. 25.

74 Interim Report of the Special Rapporteur, A/64/159 (17 July 2009) paragraph 32.

75 Ibid., paragraph 33 (emphasis added).

76 General Assembly resolution 64/164, Elimination of all forms of intolerance and of discrimination based on religion or belief, A/RES/64/164 (17 March 2010), paragraph 7; Human Rights Council Res 6/37, 14 December 2007, paragraphs 4–5.

77 Report of the Special Rapporteur on Macedonia, A/HRC/13/40/Add.2 (28 December 2009) paragraph 54.

greater relevance because of the influence and pressure being exerted upon the state (specifically, upon its local authorities) by religious and secular groups that usually oppose such applications. A state should remain neutral and impartial in exercising its regulatory power over the temporal activities of religious groups including, most especially, the usually contested terrain of establishing and maintaining places of worship.

Conclusion

The right to establish and maintain places of worship is an integral component of the right to freedom of religion or belief. A denial of the former always results in the curtailment of the latter. States therefore cannot sincerely proclaim that they respect and protect religious freedom when there are violations, both direct and indirect, of the right to establish and maintain places of worship.

The separate and distinct elements of the right to establish and maintain places of worship exist simultaneously and reinforce one another, contributing to the right's legal validity and strength. Therefore, the right to establish and maintain places of worship has a composite nature. This chapter submits that these elements effectively coalesce under the general rubric of the right to establish and maintain places of worship. It is only when these elements are taken together that the normative content of the right to establish and maintain places of worship is adequately captured.

References

Boyle, K. (2007), 'Freedom of Religion in International Law', in Rehman, J. and Breau, S. (eds), 23–51.

Burayidi, M. (2001), 'The Multicultural City as Planners' Enigma', *Planning Theory and Practice*, 4:3, 259–273.

de Jong, C. (2000), *The Freedom of Thought, Conscience and Religion or Belief in the United Nations (1946–1992)* (Antwerpen, Groningen and Oxford: Intersentia-Hart).

Dinstein, Y. (1992), 'Freedom of Religion and the Protection of Religious Minorities', in Dinstein, Y. and Tabory, M. (eds), 145–169.

Dinstein, Y. and Tabory, M. (eds) (1992), *The Protection of Minorities and Human Rights* (Dordrecht: Martinus Nijhoff Publishers).

Durham, C.W., Jr. (1996), 'Perspectives on Religious Liberty: A Comparative Framework', in van der Vyver, J.D. and Witte, J. Jr. (eds), 1–44.

Henkin, L. (1989), 'The Universality of the Concept of Human Rights', *Annals of the American Academy of Political and Social Science*, 506, 10–16.

Joseph, S., Schultz, J. and Castan, M. (2004), *The International Covenant on Civil and Political Rights: Cases, Materials, and Commentary*, 2nd edition (Oxford: Oxford University Press).

Lerner, N. (2002), *Group Rights and Discrimination in International Law*, 2nd edition (The Hague, London and New York: Martinus Nijhoff Publishers).

Macquarie Pocket Dictionary (1998), 3rd edition (New York: John Wiley & Sons Australia Ltd).

McGoldrick, D. (1994), *The Human Rights Committee: Its Role in the Development of the International Covenant on Civil and Political Rights*, 2nd edition (Oxford: Clarendon Press).

Mill, J.S. (1859), *On Liberty* (London: Longman, Roberts and Green).

Mutua, M. (2007), 'Standard Setting in Human Rights: Critique and Prognosis', *Human Rights Quarterly*, 29:3, 547–630.

Rehman, J. and Breau, S. (eds) (2007), *Religion, Human Rights and International Law: A Critical Examination of Islamic State Practices* (Leiden and Boston: Martinus Nijhoff Publishers).

Ridge, P. (2009), 'The Financing of Religion: Guidelines for Legal Regulation', *Adelaide Law Review*, 30:1, 85–109.

Rydin, Y. (2011), *The Purpose of Planning: Creating Sustainable Towns and Cities* (Bristol: The Policy Press).

Sandercock, S. (2001), 'Planning in the Ethno-culturally Diverse City: A Comment', *Planning Theory and Practice*, 4:3, 319–323.

Steiner, H., Alston, P. and Goodman, R. (2008), *International Human Rights in Context: Law, Politics, Morals* (Oxford: Oxford University Press).

Tahzib, B. (1996), *Freedom of Religion or Belief: Ensuring Effective International Legal Protection* (The Hague, Boston and London: Martinus Nijhoff Publishers).

Taylor, P. (2005), *Freedom of Religion: UN and European Human Rights Law and Practice* (Cambridge: Cambridge University Press).

van der Vyver, J.D. and Witte, J. Jr. (eds) (1996), *Religious Human Rights in Global Perspective: Legal Perspectives* (The Hague: Kluwer Law International).

Chapter 16

The Places of Worship in France and the Public/Private Divide

Anne Fornerod

It would be 'of fundamental importance that the public space remains hospitable to the religious preferences of its inhabitants: the visible presence of a plurality of religions and beliefs in the streets, squares and in the schools, hospitals and so on is indispensable for the pluralism on which a democratic society is based'. In this respect, 'the place of worship issue is a privileged observatory to study how much the accessibility of the public space – even in its part that should be open to all without limitations – is questioned in a society that is not accustomed to religious plurality' (Ferrari and Pastorelli 2010). There is indeed no doubt that the effectiveness of freedom of worship depends upon the availability of sites specifically dedicated to religious celebration. The basic premise here is that access for religious groups to public space via places of worship would fully ensure this effectiveness. It remains to clarify what exactly is covered by the distinction of public and private, but also what is meant by places of worship.

In general, the public/private distinction very traditionally relates to rules of law grouped together in a regime of private or public law, 'some being classed among those that govern relations between private individuals, others among those governing the relations between public authorities themselves as well as with individuals' (Azoulai 2010: 842). But this distinction also refers to the duet public space/private space. This would stem from confusion, of a sociological nature, between public and private[1] and which it is difficult to render in legal terms. Reconciling the two senses of the public–private distinction raises a priori as many questions as it answers and today very much indicates work in progress.

Additionally, the evolution in terminology must be taken into account that has led to the use of the term 'place of worship' in preference to, or in parallel with, 'building of worship'. If there exists 'no legal definition of the building used for worship or, more broadly, the place of worship', the place of worship can nevertheless be viewed 'as any place, equipped or not, where, on a regular basis,

1 See on this idea Koubi (2003: 1055) and, in a way, Jean-Bernard Auby who highlights the development of 'situations of differentiation of public and private spaces. The shopping centre serves the same function as the public square and, indeed, sometimes we do not know if the slab on which we are walking is part of a private, commercial or residential development or if it is state-owned land' (Auby 2009).

collective religious activities are undertaken, such as common prayers, rituals and celebrations' (Messner et al. 2003: 897). If both terms 'building' and 'place' are often held to be equivalent, the latter would mean the emphasis on ritual activity as such and no longer solely on the place where it is enacted, thereby allowing us to account for the diversity of links between religious practices and space, whether public or private.[2] This 'modernized' definition of buildings of worship reflects a religious landscape characterized by pluralism. This definition also goes beyond the classic figure of the building of worship – very often associated with the Catholic Church – easily identifiable in the urban fabric but which is not sufficient anymore to account for the diversification in facilities used for worship. But despite the broader definition of a place of worship, it would be unreasonable to include within this term all the premises likely to cater for collective religious practices. Similarly to buildings of worship, a place of worship implies a long-term anchorage of the religious practices it is assigned to. Hence, the question arises of how the legal regime of places of worship, which is based on the *summa divisio* public law/private law system, can go hand-in-hand with the distinction between public space and private space.

The uncertainty surrounding the possible similarities between the traditional understanding of the public/private distinction and public space would lead us to recall that the criteria for defining the latter are 'functional, not organic: regardless of the type of entity which owns the place, what matters is that it is used collectively'.[3] Seen from this perspective, all places of worship may fall within public space from the moment when worship takes on, by definition, a collective dimension.[4] It is the issue of freedom of worship that is steering the reconciliation of places of worship with the public/private distinction in French law.

Hence, the analysis is valid only if one looks at access to public space as a guarantee of freedom of worship, both in its relevance and in its terms. A two-fold hypothesis may then be formulated. On the one hand, access to public space turns out to be a largely ineffective way of having a building of worship, as a facility for exercising freedom of worship: exercising freedom of worship in public space is not based solely on the possibility of having a building dedicated to this purpose. On the other hand, the possibility for religious groups and their

2 'If, in the late nineteenth or early twentieth centuries, it [the building of worship] could be defined as the building belonging to a public entity or institution and permanently assigned to the practice of worship, nowadays this definition is redundant. It is in fact a building in which a religion is celebrated according to the rites of each confession … Ultimately, the evolution of this concept is characterised by the change in understanding: we move from an organic understanding to a physical one' (Florès-Lonjou 2001: 15).

3 C'est ce que retient Madame Olivia Bui-Xuan à propos de la loi du 11 octobre 2010 (Bui-Xuan 2011: 551).

4 See the conclusions of the Government Commissioner Arrighi de Casanova (1998: 67).

members to have access to a place of worship has been reinforced, regardless of access to public space.

Places of Worship and Public Space, Distant Issues

By examining some legal proceedings involving the understanding of public space, we observe that the possibility of using places of worship is largely alien to the public/private issue in the sense of public space/private space.[5] However, if public space appears largely 'closed' to places of worship, it is not the case for exercising freedom of worship.

Access to Public Space for Buildings of Worship: An Ineffective Way

The Act of 11 October 2010 prohibiting the concealment of the face in public[6] is a useful starting point in that, with its inclusion in this text, the notion of public space would attain the status of a legal category,[7] possibly allowing a reconciliation of the public/private distinction in the sociological sense and in the legal sense to be observed. Article 2 of the Act of 11 October 2010 gives a tripartite definition of public space in that it would consist of public highways ('voies publiques') as well as places open to the public or assigned to a public service.[8]

Public highways may correspond to what is meant by public space open to all, within the limits of respect for public order. The Court of Cassation defined public highways as 'any accessible passage, road or path open to the public'.[9] Public highways are also associated with the idea of the visibility of activities that take place there.[10] From this viewpoint, the inclusion of public highways in public space is a priori relevant to the religiously symbolic clothing that gave rise to the Act of 11 October 2011. Even so, are they open to buildings of worship? When mentioning buildings of worship, it is buildings that come to mind and continue to embody religious practices in public space and make them visible. Is this architectural incarnation reflected in the legal framework, in the sense

5 The Act of 11 October 2010 even shows that including buildings of worship in public space can put freedom of worship at risk, which led the Constitutional Council to make them a sole exception to its decision. See the decision no. 2010-613 DC, 7 October 2010, Loi interdisant de dissimuler son visage dans l'espace public.

6 Loi no. 2010-1192 du 11 octobre 2010 interdisant la dissimulation du visage dans l'espace public, *Journal officiel*, no. 0237, 12 October 2010, 18344.

7 On this aspect mainly see Bui-Xuan (2011: 551).

8 It is specified at the beginning of Article 2 that this definition is valid for the application of Article 1, which would invite caution in not extending the definition of public space beyond the framework of the Act of 11 October 2010. Bui-Xuan (2011: 551).

9 Cour de cassation, civ. 3ème, 13 mai 2009, no. 08-14.640. Quoted by Bui-Xuan (2011: 571).

10 On this aspect, see Ferrari and Pastorelli (2010); Dubois (2005: 179).

that there will be legal provisions allowing for the construction of places of worship on public highways? In other words, can we overcome 'the organised confusion between "public" which is "visible" and "public" that responds to a legal definition'? (Koubi 2003: 1055; Bui-Xuan 2011).

In fact, the visibility of buildings of worship does not mean that they are located on public highways. One could even consider that the definition of public highways by the French Court of Cassation is enough to exclude them. In addition, their legal status does not allow it to be said that they are indiscriminately open to all. Therefore, buildings of worship built before 1905 and belonging to a public entity (usually the *communes*) and assigned for worship as guaranteed by the combination of Article 13 of the Act of 9 December 1905 and Article 5 of the Act of 2 January 1907 on worship in public, belong to the public domain. Article 13 provides that 'buildings used for public worship and the movable objects decorating them will be left for public establishments of worship to use free of charge, then for the associations called upon to replace them'. The Act of 2 January 1907, adopted following the refusal by Catholics to form religious associations, provides that these buildings 'will continue to be left available for the faithful and for ministers of religion to practise their religion'. It is clear from these texts that these places are dedicated to worship and those who practise it, in line with a legal regime that makes them incompatible with inclusion in the public highways which are open to all.

As for 'places open to the public', if they are included in law and case law (see Bui-Xuan 2011), there does not exist a precise and conclusive definition that would allow all places within public space to be identified. Like public highways, including in public space 'places open to the public' does not imply a possibility of creating a place of worship there. The list produced in the circulars on the application of the Act of 11 October 2010[11] suffices to show that the issue of places open to the public can be very far from that of places of worship, insofar as the many examples highlighted are already destined for purposes other than religious ones (cinemas, theatres, shops, banks, etc.).

However, the interest in this category of public space lies in the possibility of potentially including within it places of worship labelled 'private' under the public/private distinction in its traditional sense. Places of worship following a private property regime can mainly be divided into two categories according to whether or not they were prior to the Act of 9 December 1905.[12] Buildings of worship that were

11 Circulaire no. NOR: PRMC1106214C du 2 mars 2011 relative à la mise en œuvre de la loi no. 2010-1192 du 11 octobre 2010 interdisant la dissimulation du visage dans l'espace public, *Journal Officiel*, no. 0052 du 3 mars 2011, p. 4128, texte no. 1. Circulaire no. NOR IOCD1109134C du 31 mars 2011 d'application de la loi no. 2010-1192 du 11 octobre 2010 posant le principe de l'interdiction de la dissimulation du visage dans l'espace public.

12 It is also worth noting the State private property regime that applies to 'buildings returned to a private entity when the Act of 1905 came into force and since acquired by a

owned by public institutions within the system of recognized religions and which religious associations have inherited are indeed subject to a special assignation to religious worship under Article 13 of the 1905 Act. Buildings belonging to private entities (who may be individuals or associations, religious or not) and built after 1905 'are private constructions that fall within the law on housing and urban development' (Messner et al. 2003: 514). Premises hosting celebrations can be included in the category of buildings welcoming the public, making them subject to certain rules in terms of safety.[13] But the status of 'place of worship' does not entail in itself any specific consequence. What counts here a priori is the type of meeting held there and the distinction between public and private meetings. The first 'are open to a large and undifferentiated audience', while the second 'assemble in a specific place a group of named and personally invited individuals, having a close link to the organisers and whose identity is checked at the start' (Messner et al. 2003: 516–517). Only the first would allow 'private' buildings of worship to be considered as falling within public space. But in practice, the absence of prior notification to public authorities for public meetings and the diversity of locations of religious services outside visible buildings of worship makes the distinction between the two types of meetings fairly relative (2003: 516–517).

Moreover, this diversification – not so much of places of worship, but of the localization of worship which would be consistent with a large overlap between places of worship and public space as a functional criterion based solely on the activity – does not automatically go hand-in-hand with an extension of the protection of freedom of worship. This is illustrated by a decision of the Lyon Court of Appeal of 28 February 2005.[14] In this case, Sonacotra, the owner of a residence, made available to residents for the use of worship a multi-purpose room located in the basement. The responsibility for the proper use of the hall was entrusted to an imam, with people from outside the residence being tolerated there. Following a notice from the technical services of the town, which recalled that the room when divided into two could accommodate only 19 people in each section and a report confirming that the room did not comply with safety regulations, Sonacotra informed the imam of its decision to close the place of prayer. Some residents appealed and the Lyon Court of Appeal considered that they 'cannot rely on Article 32 of the 1905 Act on restriction of freedom of worship, as they were using a multi-purpose room for prayer and not a place of worship managed by a specific association'. In addition, the court decided that 'they cannot seriously claim their use of the room to oppose the closure of the premises which was being rented to them' under a ruling dating from 1993.

Finally, in relation to premises assigned to a public service, 'the issue of buildings of worship calls for a single remark: the idea of erecting a building for the sole purpose of assigning it for religious use deserves to be immediately

---

public entity through donation, bequest, sale or expropriation', Florès-Lonjou (2011: 244).

13 See articles R 123-1 to 123-55 of the Building Construction Code.

14 Cour d'appel de Lyon, 28 février 2005, no. 05/01953.

discarded, as religion no longer corresponds to a public service, ever since the Act of 9 December 1905, which ended the public service of worship'.

In contrast, places of public service in no way exclude religious practices, but independently of buildings of worship. In those portions of public space devoted to public service, the practice of worship by definition implies the absence of a religious building.

Freedom of Worship in Public Space, without a Building of Worship

Seen from the viewpoint that is of interest here, it can be observed that what is protected is the possibility to practise worship, regardless of having a building specifically dedicated to it. The expression of freedom of worship in public space, regardless of the existence of a building of worship, encompasses two main forms: processions and spiritual assistance in public services. But it also depends on the temporary availability of places of worship.[15] Under Article 27 of the Act of 9 December 1905, 'ceremonies, processions and other external manifestations of worship are regulated in accordance with Article 97 of the Code of Communal Administration'. In the sometimes troubled historical context of the separation of Church and State, the administrative judge has repeatedly had the opportunity to clarify the legal regime of processions. As a result, 'traditional ceremonies and processions are exempted, because of their regular nature, of the need for prior notification', in view of the fact that 'the traditional nature of a procession or ceremony which is evaluated locally, results from its age and its proper and peaceful running' (Prélot 2011: 549). In a decision of 21 December 2010, the Administrative Court of Appeal in Bordeaux gave a recent example of this issue in a dispute concerning the Limousin processions known as *ostensions limousines*.[16] According to the Court, 'the septennial processions are intended to celebrate the saints of the region; these processions consist in a solemn presentation by the clergy of the relics of saints from, or having lived in, Limousin, with veneration of these relics by the faithful and this takes place during Christian religious ceremonies such as processions and the Eucharist; they therefore constitute the practice of worship'. The court also emphasizes 'the traditional and popular character of these ceremonies'. However, 'ceremonies not of a traditional nature are subject to prior notification to the municipal authorities at least three days before the date of the event' (Prélot 2011: 549). Whether one or other regime applies to religious ceremonies outdoors on public highways depends on their age and traditional character, which is a source of mismatch between the Catholic religion and more recent religious communities, foremost among which are Muslim communities (Messner et al. 2003: 520).

Secondly, if a building of worship cannot belong to public space on the grounds that it has been assigned to a public service, as discussed above, the

15 In this way, see Le Carpentier (2003: 1062) and Koubi (2003: 1055).

16 Cour administrative d'appel de Bordeaux, 21 décembre 2010, no. 10BX00541.

very fact of being in a place of public service does not constitute for the user a definitive obstacle to practising worship. Drawing on the implications of Article 1 of the 1905 Act, which guarantees free practice of worship, the lawmaker has provided for chaplaincy services in public services that fall outside the ban on funding religions from public funds. Therefore, spiritual assistance is available for users who are required to spend a length of time in a place of public service and who cannot then access a place of worship, such as school, hospital, military or prison establishments. For some institutions, where premises are specifically made available for such use, the definition of place of worship selected above could well apply, i.e. a 'place, equipped or not, where collective religious activities such as prayers, rituals, celebrations are practised regularly' (Messner et al. 2003: 897).

Finally, the guarantee of freedom of worship in public space without the facility of a building of worship can involve the temporary provision of places of worship. This simplified access to public space for religious practices requires that they be limited in time. This is illustrated by the Order of the Council of State of 26 August 2011, *Commune of Saint-Gratien.*[17] In this case, the mayor in the *commune* of Saint-Gratien had refused to make available a community hall to the Franco-Muslim Association for a few days during the month of Ramadan, as the mosques located in the surrounding municipalities were saturated during that period. It was decided that 'the rejection of the application by the Franco-Muslim Association of Saint-Gratien was a serious and manifestly illegal breach of freedom of assembly and worship'. But the Council of State clearly states that 'local authorities may not, without disregarding the provisions of the Act of 9 December 1905 on the separation of Church and State, decide that a premise they own will be made available exclusively and permanently to an association for the exercise of worship and thus constitute a building of worship'. It is the aim of promoting freedom of worship that is protected here and again the idea that the reconciliation of places of worship and public space would depend on a functional criterion and that it is freeing itself, as in this case, from the notion of the building of worship as a building specifically devoted to worship can be seen. In addition – and this contribution could be important – the Council of State provides a definition of a building of worship. It can indeed be inferred from this ruling that 'no building is in itself architecturally, so to speak, a place of worship: only a permanent and exclusive assignation for worship turns it into a building of worship' (Domino and Bretonneau 2011: 1667). Although it is usual to be able

17 Conseil d'État, ordonnance, 26 August 2011, *Commune de Saint-Gratien*, no. 352106. For another example, see Conseil d'État, ordonnance du 30 mars 2007, *Ville de Lyon*, no. 304053: in this case, the Council of State ruled that the refusal by the city of Lyon to grant a religious association the hire of a municipal hall for a religious celebration violates the freedoms of association and assembly, particularly since the *commune* did not make any mention of a threat to public order and the price of hiring the municipal hall was 'more favourable than the rates for private rooms which would apply to the association and this cannot be regarded as subsidising worship, as is prohibited by the Law of 9 December 1905'.

to identify a place of worship by its distinctive architecture, it is the functional criterion that prevails here, breaking the link between the building of worship, public space and visibility. The Council of State does in fact confirm the essence of a ruling given a month before, although it is the financial aspect of the operation that was at issue there, not directly freedom of worship. The applicants challenged the legality of the provision of a multi-purpose hall built by the town for the benefit of any association wishing to use it as a place of prayer. The Council of State considered that, in view of, *inter alia*, the provisions of Article L. 2144-3 of the General Code for Local Government, a *commune* may 'authorise, in accordance with the principle of neutrality of religion and the principle of equality, the use of premises belonging to it for the practice of worship by an association, when the financial terms of this authorisation exclude donations and, consequently, any aid for a faith'.[18]

If a broader understanding of worship is retained, the decision by the Council of State of 19 July 2011, *Urban Community of Le Mans, Le Mans metropolis*,[19] forms part of this trend in that it concerns financing by the Urban Community of Le Mans of works to fit out a temporary slaughterhouse for sheep during the three days of the feast of the Eid-el-Kébir. It is apparent that the provisions of the Act of 1905 do not prevent a local community from 'constructing or acquiring equipment or authorising the use of existing equipment, so as to allow the exercise of practices of a ritual nature related to the free exercise of worship, provided that a local public interest – particularly related to the necessity that worship should be exercised in conditions which comply with the requirements of public order, in particular, public health and safety – justifies such intervention and, in addition, that the right to use the equipment is conceded in conditions, including cost-related, consistent with the principle of religious neutrality and the principle of equality and which exclude any donation and, consequently, any aid for a faith'.[20] Certainly, the legality of the intervention of the public authority has to be evaluated in the light of considerations of public order and does not amount to a sort of philanthropy towards the faith concerned (Domino and Bretonneau 2011: 1667). But the fact remains that the interests of all parties unite so as to enable, in concrete terms, ritual practices.

That said, it is necessary to understand the terms of access not to public space, but to the possibility of using a place of worship, which has recently evolved in a manner favourable to the collective expression of religious convictions.

18 Conseil d'État, 19 juillet 2011, *Commune de Montpellier*, no. 313518.

19 Conseil d'État, 19 juillet 2011, *Communauté urbaine du Mans, Le Mans métropole*, no. 309161.

20 Conseil d'État, 19 juillet 2011, *Communauté urbaine du Mans, Le Mans métropole*, no. 309161.

A Regime of Buildings of Worship More Favourable to Freedom of Worship, Outside Public Space

It is by referring to the public/private distinction in its 'traditional' sense that a change affecting buildings of worship can be observed, which is proving favourable to freedom of worship, without the need to consider access to public space, whereas the way the system works in France is based on a traditionally narrow approach to the practice of worship.

A Traditionally Narrow Approach to Worship

Under the influence of the European Convention on Human Rights, and specifically its Article 9, today it goes undisputed that access to a place of celebration is an essential means of guaranteeing freedom of worship. At first glance, the situation in France might appear unsatisfactory in this area. It is characterized by sustained uncertainty as to a true recognition of freedom of worship. Certainly, the principle is contained in Article 1 of the Act of 9 December 1905, according to which the Republic 'guarantees free religious practice'. What is missing is in fact a clear, official statement on the constitutionality of this freedom.[21] Without being recognized by the Constitutional Council, freedom of worship has been enshrined as a fundamental freedom by the Council of State in several pieces of litigation.[22] One might read into this reluctance a sign of the French understanding of worship – an inheritance from the revolution (Messner et al. 2003: 45), which tends to limit the practice of worship to buildings devoted to it. Here, the issue of buildings of worship has the greatest resonance with issues around the consistency of public space, when the latter is understood as consisting of 'physical or symbolic places where public debate, democratic exchange, the confrontation of people and ideas all take place'.[23] As such, the underlying issue in the debate on places of worship in public space consists in exploring the role that governments are willing to grant to freedom of worship, of which places of worship are at first sight only the physical and visible manifestation. It is clear that here a classic debate is entered, on the place assigned to religion, outside the very intimate sphere of religious convictions as such, regardless of their outward manifestations. The myth that religion belongs

21 On this point, see Prélot (2006: 135).

22 Conseil d'État, ordonnance, 16 février 2004, *Benaissa*, no. 264314; Conseil d'État, ordonnance, 25 août 2005, *Commune de Massat*, no. 284307; Conseil d'État, ordonnance, 7 avril 2004, *Époux Kilicikesen*, no. 266085: in this *ordonnance* 'la possibilité d'exprimer dans des formes appropriées ses convictions religieuses constitue une liberté fondamentale'.

23 Auby (2009): 'The idea has basically both a physical and a socio-political sense. In the former, it refers to the physical locations of social exchange, communication, movement of people and things. In the latter, it refers to the places, physical or symbolic, of public debate, democratic exchange and confrontation of people and ideas'.

to the private sphere and excludes any outward manifestation is never far away, leading to the question of the legitimacy of 'cultural ceremonies in public [that] are in fact readily perceived in France as a violation of the neutrality of public space and freedom of conscience' (Messner et al. 2003: 519).

Specifically concerning places of worship and the insufficient numbers of them to meet the needs of freedom of worship, to the 'inheritance from the revolution' should be added the combination of historical circumstances and a legal framework seeking to adapt to religious pluralism.[24] Under the influence of religious pluralism, the concept of place of worship has evolved, breaking down the somewhat monolithic conception of the building of worship (developed along the Catholic model of the church where Mass is celebrated), including different activities and thereby bringing into question the boundaries of what is meant by worship. Attention should also be paid to recent developments in litigation about places of worship which are contributing to an improved implementation of freedom of worship.

Developments in Case Law in Favour of Freedom of Worship

In respect of public authority support for places of worship, whether for their maintenance or construction, French law has long been guided by the provisions of Article 2 of the 1905 Act which prohibits public subsidies for religions. In recent case law, a balance appears to have been struck with Article 1, which guarantees freedom of worship. The administrative judge has acted as a 'regulator of parish life',[25] in that he has, since 1905, found in the Acts of Separation the appropriate responses to disputes he presided over. These developments in case law can be understood in terms of the traditional public/private distinction and they include improvements to the category of buildings of worship that follow a regime of private law, in terms of greater support, directly or indirectly, for the practice of worship.

The first, relatively minor, development concerns existing buildings. It is first necessary to clarify that it is still impossible today for a public entity owning a building to assign it to worship and thereby include it in the public domain. The public domain of worship cannot be extended beyond what was decided in 1905 and 1907 and, even used for religious purposes, the building that fulfils both conditions of belonging to the public domain[26] cannot be considered a place of

---

24 See Fornerod (2010: 161–176).

25 According to the famous expression of Le Bras (1950: 67).

26 According to Article L.2111-1 of the General Code of Ownership of Public Entities (CGPPP), 'unless subject to special legislation, the public domain of a public entity referred to in Article L.1 consists of property it owns that is assigned to direct use by the public or assigned to a public service, provided that in this case the property undergoes development essential to the execution of the tasks of this public service'.

worship under the Acts of Separation,[27] if it was not public property and used for worship in 1905. So, an agreement in which a *commune*, owner of a building, makes it available to an association with a view of allowing worship there 'cannot be regarded as having assigned this building for the direct use of the public and consequently did not enter it as such into communal public ownership'.[28] This solution, which results from the constraints imposed by the protective regime of the public domain for public entities which are also owners, was recently upheld by the Council of State.[29]

A fortiori, public property used for worship cannot be extended beyond the limits set earlier in the century by the Acts of Separation through the public entities acquiring new buildings. More specifically, the ability of a *commune* to become an owner of a place of worship clashes with Article 2 of the 1905 Act prohibiting State subsidies to faiths and a strict interpretation of the Act of 13 April 1908.[30] The Council of State ruled out the possibility for a *commune* to purchase a building with the aim of assigning it to worship and thus inserting it into the public domain.[31] A 2005 ruling, which seemed to pave the way for this, was never followed up. In this case, the government commissioner considered in his conclusions that 'here it is not the act of 2 January 1905 (Art. 5) [*sic*] that assigns it to the faithful and to the Ministry [*sic*] of Religious Affairs, but the will of the *commune*. However, without prejudicing the legality of this assignation, it is not clear how it should be seen as assigned less for public use than the churches built before 1905'.[32]

On the other hand – and the difference comes from the nuance – a *commune* can acquire a building *already* assigned to worship.[33] In the *Commune of*

---

27 By 'Laws of Separation' are meant the Law of 9 December 1905 and the two laws that supplemented it: the Law of 2 January 1907 on the practice of worship in public and that of 13 April 1908 on the assignment of properties, in particular buildings of worship, in the absence of religious associations.

28 Conseil d'État, Section, 19 octobre 1990, *Association Saint-Pie V et Saint-Pie X de l'Orléanais, Actualité Juridique. Droit Administratif*, 1991, p. 46 et s.

29 Conseil d'État, 19 juillet 2011, *Commune de Montpellier*, no. 309161.

30 The Law of 13 April 1908 amended Article 13 of the 1905 Law by giving public entities who were owners of the buildings of worship under the Act of Separation the possibility 'to undertake the necessary expenditure to maintain and conserve buildings of worship whose ownership is recognised by the current law'.

31 See Conseil d'État, 19 octobre 1990, *Association Saint Pie V et Saint Pie X de l'Orléanais*, *AJDA*, 1991, 46.

32 Tribunal administratif de Grenoble 26 octobre 2005, *Fédération de l'Isère de la fédération nationale de la libre pensée française*, Conclusions Sorel, *AJDA*, 2006, 202.

33 Cour administrative d'appel de Lyon, 19 février 2008, *Commune de Moirans*, no. 05LY02064. Ultimately, the decision by the City Council was overturned anyway on the grounds that the agreement between the *commune* and the diocesan association contained a clause whereby the *commune* committed itself to the reconstruction of the building in case of its destruction, whereas the costs of reconstruction are not allowed within the category of authorized repairs.

Moirans ruling of 19 February 2008, the Administrative Court of Appeal in Lyon considered that 'neither the aforementioned provisions of Articles 2 and 13 of the Act of 9 December 1905, nor any other legislative or regulatory provision, nor any general principle of law shall preclude the possibility for a *commune* to acquire, even for free, a building assigned to public worship and belonging to an association referred to in Article 18, and the expenditure required for its repair may be legally borne by said *commune* under the provisions of Article 19 of this Act'. This solution is based in reality on an equivalence between expenses incurred in respect of Articles 13 and 19 of the Act of 1905, as indicated by the findings of the rapporteur public in this case that 'the notion of repair in the sense of Article 19 [of the Act of 1905] cannot be different from the concept of maintenance and conservation referred to by Article 13 concerning buildings of worship originally devolved to the *communes*'.

This progress in case law also deals with the construction of places of worship.[34] Since 1905, the implementation of various mechanisms has enabled public authorities to make up for – in part – the impossibility of providing financial remedies for the shortage of places of worship affecting certain religious groups. Therefore, resorting to emphyteutic leases consists for a local authority in 'making land available to an association using a long-term lease (18 to 99 years) to erect a building of worship' on its private domain (Conseil d'État 2004: 286). This possibility was extended to the public domain of local authorities by the Order of 21 April 2006 relating to the legislative part of the General Code of Ownership by Public Entities that allows for resorting to administrative emphyteutic leases 'with a view to assigning to a religious association a building for worship open to the public'.[35] Administrative courts have repeatedly quashed decisions by municipal councils to provide land to facilitate the construction of mosques on the grounds that the rent being charged at a nominal amount was akin to a public subsidy, which is forbidden.[36] However, the Administrative Court of Appeal of Versailles has upheld that a symbolic rent of one Euro was not a 'hidden subsidy' to the extent that the cost of construction and maintenance of the mosque were paid for by the religious association.[37] The intervention of the Council of State in this case

34 Although the lack of places of worship affects mainly faiths from recent history, it would be wrong to say they are the only ones concerned. Thus, the Catholic faith, as a result of rural migration and the development of new towns or suburbs after the Second World War, was faced with a shortage of places of worship in those areas.

35 These measures have been integrated in the article L. 1311-2 of the General Code for Local Government.

36 Tribunal administratif de Lille, 9 janvier 2007, *Mme Stéphanie R.*, no. 0401078 (mosque project in Roubaix); Tribunal administratif de Marseille, 17 avril 2007, *M. Hubert Savon et autres*, no. 0605998 (mosque project in Marseille); Tribunal administratif de Cergy-Pontoise, 12 juin 2007, *Mme Patricia Vayssière*, no. 0306171 (mosque project in Montreuil).

37 Cour administrative d'appel de Versailles, 3 juillet 2008, *Commune de Montreuil-sous-Bois*, no. 07VE01824.

has clarified applicable law and opened up new perspectives.[38] In its decision of 19 July 2011, it was specified that the lawmaker of 2006 intended to depart from the provisions of the 1905 Act. Also, in respect of low rents, which was at the heart of the disputes, the Council of State gives the impression of making a specific feature of this type of emphyteutic lease by doubly justifying it: by the 'fact that its titleholder engages in non-profit activities' and by including in the heritage of the local communities concerned 'the building, whose design, construction, maintenance and conservation costs they will not have borne'.

This analysis of places of worship, as seen through the lens of the public/private distinction, emphasizes that it is futile to seek a homogeneous category of buildings of worship. It enables us to focus on the flaws that are still preventing a more satisfactory protection of freedom of worship, but to be fair, progress has recently been made in this area. More generally, reconciling places of worship, public space and freedom of religion, it can be observed that protecting freedom of worship does not as much involve buildings that are visible in public space, as ensuring that the activity may be practised. In addition, it is not sure that belonging to public space will be translated into a greater protection of religious freedom. On all these points, places of worship differ from religiously symbolic clothing, the visibility of which has recently given rise to difficulties and has justified resorting to the use of this still legally vague notion of public space.

References

Arrighi de Casanova, J. (1998), 'Conclusions', *Revue Française de Droit Administratif*, janvier–février, 61–69.

Auby, J.-B. (2009), 'Espace public, espaces publics', *Droit administratif*, 7, 1–2.

Azoulai, L. (2010), 'Sur un sens de la distinction public/privé dans le droit de l'Union européenne', *Revue trimestrielle de droit européen*, 4, 842–860.

Bui-Xuan, O. (2011), 'L'espace public: l'émergence d'une nouvelle catégorie juridique? Réflexions sur la loi interdisant la dissimulation du visage dans l'espace public', *Revue Française de Droit Administratif*, 551–560.

Conseil d'État (2004), *La laïcité* (Paris: La Documentation Française).

Domino, X. and Bretonneau, A. (2011), 'Le sacré et le local', *Actualité Juridique droit administratif*, 1667–1681.

Dubois, J.-P. (2005), 'Pluralisme, laïcité, sphères publiques et sphère privée', *Archives de philosophie du droit*, 49, 171–184.

Ferrari, S. and Pastorelli, S. (2010), 'The Public Space: The Formal and Substantive Neutrality of the Public Sphere', *RELIGARE Working Paper*, No. 4, September 2010.

Florès-Lonjou, M. (2001), *Les lieux de culte en France* (Paris: Cerf).

38 Conseil d'État, 19 juillet 2011, *Madame V.*, no. 320796.

Florès-Lonjou, M. (2010), 'Édifice cultuel-Droit français', in Messner, F. (ed.), 243–246.

Fornerod, A. (2010), 'Entre cultuel et culturel: la construction de lieux de culte en France', *Quaderni di diritto e politica ecclesiastica*, 1, 161–176.

Gonzalez, G. (ed.) (2006), *Laïcité, liberté de religion et Convention européenne des droits de l'homme* (Bruxelles: Nemesis Bruylant).

Koubi, G. (2003), 'Le juge administratif et la liberté de religion', *Revue Française de Droit Administratif*, 1055–1061.

Le Bras, G. (1950), 'Le Conseil d'État, régulateur de la vie paroissiale', *Études et Documents du Conseil d'État*, 4, 63–76.

Le Carpentier, P. (2003), 'Le juge administratif, régulateur de l'expression religieuse dans la vie sociale: des sonneries de cloches aux interdits rituels', *Revue Française de Droit Administratif*, 1062–1065.

Messner, F. (ed.) (2010), *Dictionnaire de droit des religions* (Paris: Éditions du CNRS).

Messner, F., Prélot, P.H. and Woehrling, J.-M. (2003), *Traité de droit français des religions* (Paris: Litec).

Prélot, P.-H. (2006), 'Définir juridiquement la laïcité', in Gonzalez, G. (ed.), 115–149.

Prélot, P.-H. (2010), 'Police des cultes', in Messner, F. (ed.), 546–550.

Chapter 17
'*Stopp Minarett*'? The Controversy over the Building of Minarets in Switzerland: Religious Freedom versus Collective Identity

Vincenzo Pacillo

The Question of Minarets in the Perspective of a 'Multiculturalism of Foreigners'

It is well known that the dawn of the twenty-first century has led to profound re-thinking of the term 'pluralism', above all thanks to the work of Giovanni Sartori. Whether he is loved or fiercely criticized, his pamphlet *Pluralism, Multiculturalism and Foreigners* (Sartori 2000) has forced intellectuals to tackle a concept which in the second half of the twentieth century had enjoyed quite a solid framework of reference, at least for Italian legal experts.

From the political science point of view the main reference was Norberto Bobbio's famous entry in the *Dizionario di Politica* where Bobbio defined pluralism as:

> that idea which puts forward as a model a society composed of diverse groups or centres of power, which may be in conflict with one another, which are entrusted with the function of limiting, controlling, countering, even to the extent of eliminating, the dominant centre of power historically identified with the State. As such, Pluralism is one of those currents of political theory that resists the typical tendency of the formation of modern States to concentrate and unify power.[1]

It is well known that this view of pluralism tended to exalt the role of intermediate social formations in which an individual was considered free to fully develop his own personality (De Luca 1970; Vitali 1980: 24–66). Rather than a 'Montesquieian'

1 Bobbio (1990: 789). Here, and elsewhere in this chapter, unless otherwise indicated, the quotations have been translated into English by Susan Phillips.

division of powers, Bobbio's view advocated a distinction between powers whereby the State should guarantee the right for groups to exist and regulate themselves whenever they were provided with a chance to achieve the dignity of the individual (Casuscelli 1978: 235–313; Bellini 1972: 188–189).

This view was not new to the panorama of political science, culture and law in Switzerland. Indeed the idea of the Swiss Confederation as a model of a State founded on linguistic and religious pluralism seemed perfectly to endorse the exaltation of diversity in the spirit of constructing a common identity.

Thus pluralism could not in any way be considered a danger for the Swiss Federal State: its pluralist essence, formulated along the axes of the three Christian religions traditionally rooted in the territory and of the four national languages, became an identifying feature of Switzerland, as it was an element that had been present from the myth of its foundation until the present day.

In his *Mythos Schweiz*, Ulrich Im Hof includes 'plurilingualism' among the elements characterizing Swiss identity over the centuries, along with federalism and Christian values: from this point of view the valorization of diversity is evidently a means to create unity thanks to the decentralization of public powers and a profoundly shared axiological foundation which goes beyond theological differences.

According to Im Hof, the Christian Churches present in Switzerland were intermediate organizations which had to be fully guaranteed in their spiritual, ethical and social actions, as their potential to deconstruct the State progressively diminished (also thanks to a theological policy which increasingly favoured cooperation and acceptance of the State's secular character). This led to policies aimed at loyal cooperation and an increasingly close partnership between the Churches and the State (Im Hof 1991: *passim*). This approach was – on the whole – well received in Italy too when discussion on revising the concordat with the Catholic Church intensified in the 1970s, also in the light of the proposals aiming to lead the system of Church–State relations back into the fold of *jus commune*. The difference was that Italian religious law succeeded in opening up the partnership to include non-Christian religious experiences, both in virtue of the very open spirit of article 8 of the Constitution, and thanks to the instrument of agreements which – initially – seemed to be a great opportunity for fully achieving religious pluralism.

In reality these considerations were inserted into a social reality in which religious diversity was a much less complex phenomenon than it is now. The social panorama – both in Switzerland and in Italy – was characterized by the presence of strong religious ethics, firmly present in the territory, in which traditional minorities operated that were perfectly integrated in the community's background. It is true that the wave of secularization had already largely eroded the bond between traditional religions and private ethics: however, there was still a very solid link between the values of traditional religions and those of public ethics, to the extent that episodes of rupture were always experienced as exceptions to two stable equivalences:

1. the values recognized by the political community as basic elements for the development of legal principles involved in the orientation of legislators systematically encounter a reference in the dominant religion's theology, and, at the same time;
2. the ethical framework of reference for individuals, regardless of how far the latter adhered to the dogma of a Church, raised no systematic problems of compatibility with the aforesaid principles as both were influenced (more or less directly) by a widely accepted cultural and historical legacy that also fed on the dominant religion's ethical values. Obviously, individuals often did not belong to or did not identify with the dominant religious tradition, whether from an ideological or from a religious point of view. Nevertheless, the laws in force did not give rise to many 'improper conflicts of duties' of an absolute character with the ethical provisions of reference within the various ideological orientations.

The Swiss and Italian (and more generally European) social panorama has changed considerably since the 1980s and 1990s. Migration flows have brought in Europe people belonging to religions not traditionally present in the territory, with their axiological baggage which does not coincide – and often conflicts – with some of the values recognized by the political community as founding elements of the system's structure. This has led Sartori to speak of a 'new pluralism', or in his own words, of a 'multiculturalism of strangers' basically incapable of working as a means of development of human personality or as a cornerstone of democratic society: a kind of multiculturalism which opposes pluralism, since it 'demands cultural secession, and … ends up with a tribalization of culture'.

This problem is particularly evident for immigration from Islamic countries. Indeed, according to Sartori:

> the Islamic view of the world is theocratic and does not admit the separation of Church and State, religion and politics, upon which contemporary western civilization is constitutionally founded. Likewise, Islamic law does not recognise human rights (of the person) as universal and unassailable individual rights; another cornerstone of liberal civilization. This is the real heart of the matter. Westerners do not see Muslims as 'infidels', while for Muslims Westerners are just that. (Sartori 2000: 48–49)

Countercultures would thus be produced that would systematically reject the basic rules of living together as a community (Sartori 2000: 45). They would be founded on a religious practice structured around binding rules of conduct capable of undermining democratic society.

One may agree or disagree with Sartori. But, broadly speaking, the fact that natural law does not exist in Islam, together with the observation that traditionalist Islamic leadership has a basically holistic view of relations between politics and religion (Guolo 2007), would seem to prove Sartori's point.

However, for the legal expert the issue of the transformation of pluralism into a 'multiculturalism of strangers' cannot be limited to the findings of political science. First of all, also 'strangers', as human beings, have some fundamental and inviolable rights that are a series of faculties tightly connected to the right to religious freedom (which is explicitly guaranteed in the Constitution). Secondly, because the secular nature of the State – a fundamental principle expressed in the jurisprudence by the Federal Court – imposes the respect of a regime of religious pluralism which, though based upon the principles of political and ideological pluralism, is a partly different concept to those just mentioned.

Freedom of religion, secularism and religious pluralism are in effect three profoundly interconnected principles which generate legal effects even though the social panorama is complex. Likewise, freedom of religion, secularism and religious pluralism affect religious majorities and minorities regardless of their extraneousness or distance from the basic values on which Western democracies are founded. The problem – if anything – is to understand what the followers of 'foreign' religions have the right to do, what they have the right to ask the State, and what kind of behaviour may be precluded to them for reasons internal to the system, i.e. of pure and simple respect of those principles which a court system is based upon regardless of the religion followed (or not) by individuals. The idea of a law founded on religious equality and which is capable of intervening on facts and not on internal attitudes, is after all the result of secularization and of the complete separation between law and morals. Thus, in open democracies loyalty to the Republic cannot be interpreted as loyalty to a particular ideology, but rather as a 'loyalty to dialogue', the obligation not to impose one's own ideas with violence (Toso 1990: 426). In other words, what counts in law is behaviour, not internal attitudes, and intolerance towards constitutional values has to be 'tolerated', unless it leads to instigation to crime, to acts *contra legem* or even to subversive behaviour. Moreover, the idea of a law 'blind' to cultural identity does not mean that it should take no interest in religions. Secularism and freedom of religion, in both Switzerland and Italy, have the task of guiding law-making towards an 'open' religious pluralism, which regards religion as a positive factor, and not as a dangerous enemy to be destroyed. So although 'foreigners' have the right to remain so, it is the duty of the public powers to promote and monitor integration to make sure that fundamental rights are respected also within religious communities.

The Minarets Question in the Swiss Legal System: Step by Step

These assertions are nevertheless very far from being a 'take-all' argument, a 'killer argument' capable of solving all the legal issues emerging from such a complex form of multiculturalism as Switzerland is having to deal with today. Indeed it is evident that the three-in-one concept of freedom–integration–protection of fundamental rights is constantly put to the test by calls for intervention by minority religious groups that aim at obtaining concrete enjoyment of religious freedom through the aid of the public powers, above all when such intervention clashes with values deeply rooted in the population.

One of these requests concerned the possibility of building minarets on the territory of some Swiss towns. Western European countries have strong ties to a solid architectural tradition and they have always been committed to preserving a natural landscape that is perceived as an existential dimension. To build a minaret in such a context creates considerable axiological tension between the demands of minority religious groups and the identity values of the majority of the population. It therefore requires the local authorities to perform a complex balancing act, at least in Switzerland, though this situation does not appear to be different in other European legal systems. In Switzerland building permits are issued by the municipal authorities: they can be denied if the town planning department has set aside the chosen plot of land for some other purpose, or because the type and size of the building can give rise to problems of law and order or of landscape conservation.

The question of building minarets in Switzerland arose in 2005 when the Olten Türk Kültür Ocağı association, based in the town of Wangen bei Olten (Canton of Solothurn), requested authorization to erect a six-metre-high minaret on the roof of the building housing their headquarters.

The local population immediately opposed the project to build the minaret in Wangen and it was subsequently turned down by the local Baukommission. The latter claimed that the new building would not comply with the area's town-planning standards as it would be too tall and not in keeping with the commercial purposes of the neighbourhood where the association was based. This despite the fact that there was no law forbidding the building of minarets or any other buildings related to religions not traditionally widespread in Switzerland, and in spite of the broad protection provided by the Federal Constitution to the right to freedom of belief and conscience.[2]

2 Art. 15 of the Federal Constitution of 18 April 1999 expressly guarantees 'the freedom of conscience and belief', which is not different to what was established by the first paragraph of art. 49 of the 1874 Constitution. This is a guarantee which has comprehensive scope: it ensures the full externalization of the religious and philosophical convictions of the individual against any interference from the State power and at the same time it forbids all public and private subjects from forcing the individual to embrace any kind of *Bekenntnis* (religious confession) or from carrying out any religious act. Every physical person has the right to freedom of belief and of conscience, whatever his/her citizenship; in virtue of the combined provisions of art. 11 paragraph 2 of the Constitution and of art. 303 paragraph 1 Civil Code parents can decide about the religious education of their children who, once they are 16 years old, can freely decide about their religious affiliation. The guarantee expressed in the first paragraph of art. 15 is reinforced by the provisions of the second paragraph, which establishes that 'everyone has the right to choose freely his own religion and his own philosophical convictions, and to profess them individually or in the community'. This is the so-called 'sens positif' of religious freedom, which entails, in the opinion of the federal

The Baukommission of Olten's decision was challenged by the Türk Kültür Ocağı before the Bau- und Justizdepartement of Canton of Solothurn which gave its verdict on 12 July 2006. In its decision the Bau- und Justizdepartement accepted the appeal, upholding the possibility of building places of worship also in areas generally set aside for commercial activities. Nevertheless, the verdict pointed out that the function of the minaret could only be symbolic, and it could not be used to broadcast the call to prayer, not even via reproduction of a previously recorded voice.[3] The Bau- und Justizdepartement's decision was confirmed by the administrative Court of Canton of Solothurn and subsequently by the Federal Court.[4]

This initial step reveals how the legal question concerning the building of minarets is extremely technical in nature and it essentially regards the possibility to use areas bound by zoning laws as areas of mixed-use buildings. However, the judges did not tackle various other issues raised by associations contrary to Türk Kültür Ocağı's request, such as the need to preserve the traditional *Heimat* in spite of the freedom of worship of religious minorities, and the concern that the right to build minarets in Switzerland could open the way to the progressive 'Islamization' of the Swiss Confederation.

---

jurisprudence, the freedom to believe or not to believe, to participate in acts of worship, to freely communicate one's religion or view of the world. In this context, the scope of the expressions contained in the first paragraph has been interpreted very broadly by the doctrine and jurisprudence. Indeed the constitutional laws guarantee any intellectual or spiritual conviction regarding the relationship between man and the divinity or the transcendent. All religions and all *Weltanschauungen* are thus protected, independently from their numerical importance or their bonds with national traditions, as long as they have a certain essential and philosophical meaning and correspond to a comprehensive worldview. According to the provision, the public powers have a dual obligation:

(1) The State cannot prevent those acts that are directly referred to manifesting and expressing one's own belief; indeed, in virtue of paragraph 2 of art. 15, the State can be obliged to act to preserve the freedom of each person to manifest his own religion or his own convictions. All individual and community acts of worship cannot therefore be prevented, but instead they can be the subject of protection against undue interference, as can all the 'regles cultuelles impératives ou … règles de comportement' which are the direct expression of a religious prescript; this guarantee can however be limited according to art. 36 Const. 1999.

(2) The same provision can also establish the right to positive action by the State. Wherever there are concrete obstacles that prejudice the free exercise of acts that are directly related to one's own religious or philosophical convictions, it is the task of the public powers to act to remove such impediments. On this subject see Pacillo (2009: 32ff.).

3 www.so.ch/staatskanzlei/medienmitteilungen/archiv/2006/juli/wangen-bei-olten-minarett-bewilligt.html (accessed 15 December 2011, no longer available).

4 Decision 4 July 2007, I. öffentlich-rechtliche Abteilung, 1P.26/2007 /ggs, http://jumpcgi.bger.ch/cgi-bin/JumpCGI?id=04.07.2007_1P.26/2007 (accessed 15 December 2011).

As a consequence politicians embraced the cause of those social groups that were against the building of minarets in Switzerland. The first to do so was city councilwoman Helena Morgenthaler, a member of the SVP (Swiss People's Party) in Langenthal, Canton of Bern, who stood out against the project to build a mosque proposed by the Islamic association Xhami. Defining a minaret as an 'aggressive missile-shaped symbol',[5] her words earned her the approval of 3,500 people who signed the petition titled: 'Stop the Minarets'.[6] Next was a member of parliament from the Canton of St. Gallen, Lukas Reiman (also SVP), who proposed a motion calling for a minaret construction ban on cantonal territory, following a proposal by the Islamic community of the town of Wil to build a new mosque with a minaret. Reimann's motion explicitly originated with the aim of preserving the local *Heimat*.[7] A few months later in Canton of Ticino a generic parliamentary initiative was presented to introduce into cantonal construction laws a regulation forbidding the building of minarets. This initiative was presented by the Member of Parliament Lorenzo Quadri (a member of the Ticino League, the second-largest party in Ticino) and was rejected by the Commission for Legislation on 19 November 2008.

The initiatives promoted by local politicians regarding *Heimatsschutz* and *Bauverbot für Minarette* deserve to be examined in greater depth, as some of them are crucial to understanding the debate on a national level.

First of all, it is worth pointing out that the political struggle against the building of minarets concentrated almost exclusively around one political party: the SVP. This party was founded in 1971 and with 26.6% of votes and 54 seats in the National Council is the largest party in Switzerland[8] It is strong above all in the countryside of the German-speaking cantons, and in the last 20 years it has more than doubled its voters for various reasons, such as popular discontent arising from the economic situation; the party's total opposition to Switzerland's joining the European Union (seen as a threat to 'national identity', independence, neutrality and direct democracy); its calls for a reduction in immigration – above all from non-European countries; a stricter asylum policy; its defence of the Christian tradition and its rejection of demands of a religious nature by non-Christian minorities.[9]

The '*Stopp Minarett*' movements and the SVP have never explicitly declared that they are against the building of mosques, but they have campaigned – and continue to campaign – exclusively against the erection of minarets. Although

5 *Langenthaler Tagblatt*, 17 August 2006.

6 *Neue Zuercher Zeitung*, 6 November 2006. The petition then became an appeal against the building of minarets which is still pending before the Administrative Court of Canton Bern.

7 *Wiler Zeitung*, 11 November 2006; 30 November 2006.

8 One should bear in mind the considerable support given to the initiative by two other political parties present above all at the local level: the EDU (Eidgenössisch-Demokratische Union), a party of the Christian religious right, and the 'Lega dei Ticinesi'.

9 SVP (2007), election platform 2007– 2011. My house – our Switzerland (Bern).

this position would (at least in part) appear to diminish the importance of the religious element in the debate, it is nevertheless always accompanied by very strong declarations about the 'Islamization of society' (seen as the possibility that Swiss Muslims might impose the *Shari'a* on the whole population),[10] 'the need for minorities to express their own culture within the limits established by the benevolence of the majority of the population' and 'the need to preserve religious peace from fundamentalism' (Freudiger 2009: 1).

The impression is that behind the question of minarets there lies a xenophobic and Islamophobic religious policy, whereby the Muslim presence is portrayed as potentially capable of 'perforating' the national flag and thus destroying the fundamental values upon which the Confederation is based, like in the posters conceived by the Committee behind the initiative 'Against the construction of minarets'.

In any case, on 1 May 2007 various local initiatives aimed at introducing a ban on building minarets on Swiss territory united at the national level, giving birth to a popular movement (promoted and coordinated by the committee 'Gegen den Bau von Minaretten'). Their goal was to change the Swiss Federal Constitution (in force since 1999) by adding a third paragraph to article 72 of the document with an amendment stating that 'the building of minarets is prohibited'.[11]

On 8 July 2008, the 'Gegen den Bau von Minaretten' committee collected 113,540 signatures to support the initiative, and it was therefore scheduled to be put to a vote on 29 November 2009. Towards the end of July 2008 the government sent a message to parliament recommending the electorate to reject the initiative as it was incompatible with the fundamental principles of safeguarding equal

10 Initiative Committee 'Against the building of minarets' (2009), Argumentarium JA zur Minarettverbots-Initiative, pp. 8–11.

11 In this context it should be remembered that art. 194 of the Federal Constitution of 1999 sanctions the right of the People to request the partial revision of the Fundamental Charter (paragraph 1): this right is exercised by means of a popular initiative, which has to focus on a single subject and be signed by at least 100,000 citizens with the right to vote. The people proposing the initiative have 18 months to collect voters' signatures. Once the signatures have been collected and certified, the initiative is presented as a referendum. The Constitution will be modified only if the initiative receives a favourable vote from the majority of those voting and if it is approved in the majority of the cantons. As shall be seen later on, once accepted by the people and by the cantons, the 'Gegen den Bau von Minaretten' initiative entailed the absolute and binding/mandatory prohibition to build minarets anywhere in Switzerland. However, according to art. 139.2 of the Federal Constitution, no popular initiative can violate cogent provisions of international law. This provision is confirmed by the principle according to which total or partial revisions of the Constitution must not violate cogent international law: this rule is expressed by art. 193 cpv. 4 and by art. 194 cpv. 2 of the Federal Constitution. Art. 72 – in the provisions of the first and second paragraph – attributes to the cantons the power to regulate the relations with the religious denominations, leaving, however, the possibility of enacting general laws – valid throughout Switzerland – up to the Confederation to protect peace among the religions.

rights and freedom of religion and conscience. Doubts were also raised by authoritative doctrine about this initiative being contrary to cogent international law.[12] However, these doubts were not taken into consideration by the Federal Council. In the latter's opinion, 'a ban on building minarets would not prevent Muslims from freely developing and living a religious belief nor from practising and spreading their religion. The ban on minarets would not therefore compromise the real essence of the fundamental right to freedom of religion'.[13]

The Federal Council's opinion is debatable. It cleared the way for an electoral campaign in which the question of the relationship between *Heimatsschutz* and *Glaubensfreiheit* progressively faded into the background.

According to a pamphlet edited by the committee 'Gegen den Bau von Minaretten' in 2009, article 72, paragraph 3 of the Federal Constitution had to include a ban on the building of minarets for the following reasons:

- 'Islam does not separate religion from State. Islam incorporates all of the legal system. Minarets as symbols of Islamic power therefore express a totally anti-democratic claim to hegemony'.[14]

As a consequence of this lack of separation: 'Minarets represent a symbol of the religious and political power of Islam'; it 'is a demonstration of how Muslims are no longer content just to practise their own religion, but *will make more and more demands on society*'.[15] According to the committee, this is a part of a larger process as:

- 'In Europe we are undoubtedly witnessing a tendency towards Islamization'.[16]

From this perspective the new article 72, paragraph 3, would become a sort of law-cum-manifesto: its value would lie not so much in what it provides as because 'it clearly establishes that we expect the foreigners who live here to make an effort to integrate' (Freudiger 2009: 1).

The committee's evident aversion to minarets is not so much because of their characteristic of modifying the Swiss traditional landscape, as because they would represent an excessive visibility of the Islamic minority within the Confederation.

12 Message from the Federal Council concerning the popular initiative 'Against the building of minarets' of 27 August 2008, www.admin.ch (website consulted on 15 December 2011).

13 Message from the Federal Council concerning the popular initiative 'Against the building of minarets' of 27 August 2008, www.admin.ch (website consulted on 15 December 2011).

14 Freudiger (2009: 1).

15 Freudiger (2009: 1).

16 Freudiger (2009: 1).

Islam, which is the subject of an 'a priori' theological and political judgment lacking in any scientific examination or foundation, thus becomes a *Weltanschauung* to be fought, as it is (too dogmatically) seen as contrary to the values upon which Switzerland is based, besides being an expression of a 'foreign culture' forced to integrate into society without staking too many claims. The objection could be made that the equation 'Muslim = foreigner' is basically wrong (how many Muslim Swiss citizens are there?) and that what these 'foreigners expect' (at least as regards minarets) is only for their rights to be recognized. And these rights, as already explained, would have a solid basis in international law.

As for 'Islamization', it is clear that the noun does not refer to a sociological scenario like the mass conversion of Swiss citizens to Islamic precepts. Instead it regards a process which would see Muslims entering the political scene through the creation of an organized political party whose aim would be to establish a legal system founded on the *Shari'a* or a system that could at least legitimize the regime of personal statutes. This process, based on the 'Eurabia' theory (or at least the version of it whose main exponents are Bat Ye'or and Oriana Fallaci)[17] – would in the medium term entail the loss of the Christian values at the base of the constitutional principles of Western Europe and progression towards *dhimmitude*, i.e. the submission of Christianity to political Islam. According to this theory, minarets represent the first (and symbolic) moment of Islamization, since they would be the image of the beginning of the conquest of the territory and of the consequent *dhimmitude* of Christians.

Contrary to all predictions, the cantons and the Swiss people welcomed the initiative aimed at banning the building of minarets, with 57% of votes in favour: it was only rejected in the cantons of Basel, Vaud, Neuchâtel and Geneva. The new article 72, paragraph 3 of the Federal Constitution thus came into force, which provides for an absolute and legally-binding ban on the building of minarets throughout Switzerland. The ban axiologically prevails over the right to freedom of religion, following the principle '*lex specialis derogat legi generali*' with no exception.

Suggestions and Prospects after the Vote of 29 November 2009

How should the outcome of the vote of 29 November 2009 be interpreted? Should its importance be downplayed (as the Minister of Justice and Police Eveline Widmer-Schlumpf did, who emphasized how freedom of religion is widely guaranteed in the Confederation despite the results of the referendum[18])? Or is the

17 Ye'or (2005); O. Fallaci, 'Il nemico che trattiamo da amico', *Il Corriere della Sera*, 16 July 2005.

18 Interview on Radio DRS of 30 November 2009, www.drs.ch/lib/player/radio.php?audiourl=rtsp%3A%2F%2Fa1533.v23910e.c23910.g.vr.akamaistream.net%2Fondemand%2F7%2F1533%2F23910%2F4b13bb3a%2Faudio.drs.ch%2Fdrs1%2Ftagesgespra

President of the Commission against Racism, Georg Kreis, correct, who raised the slippery-slope argument when he stated that the referendum of 29 November could be just the first of a long series of initiatives aimed at impeding freedom of worship for Muslims?[19]

Of course the new article 72, paragraph 3 of the Federal Constitution does not totally limit the religious freedom of Muslims in Switzerland who, as Sami Aldeeb points out, can 'pray anywhere, provided it is a clean [*sic*] place. This initiative does not forbid prayer, nor even the building of mosques'.[20] At the same time it could be asserted, as Fiamma Nierenstein does, that the 29 November vote simply represents a rejection of Islamic fundamentalism and the political implications that – from the Islamist point of view – accompany the building of minarets.[21]

There is no doubt that Aldeeb's and Nierenstein's considerations are broadly based on truth: nevertheless, a lawyer cannot help noticing how the enacting of a law which provides for a specific ban directed at the worshippers of only one religion generates a difference in treatment which it is hard to consider reasonable. It also has to be considered that the new article 72, paragraph 3 of the Fundamental Charter risks becoming the first step of a series of polls aimed at increasingly limiting the freedom of worship of Muslims, thus creating a strongly discriminatory sort of 'personal statute'.

Moreover, it is suspected that behind article 72, paragraph 3 there might be a religious policy scheme aimed at protecting a *religiöse Heimat* hostile to the requests of religious minorities rather than the Swiss *Heimat* in general: however, this stratagem does not appear able to fully safeguard that 'religious peace' which, according to article 72, paragraph 2 of the Federal Constitution, should constitute one of the fundamental principles of action of the powers of the State.

As a result of such hermeneutics, two initiatives began in 2010. Their aim was to repeal article 72, paragraph 3 of the Federal Constitution.

The first was announced by the central Islamic Council of Switzerland. Its purpose was to create a committee which undertakes to collect 100,000 signatures to propose a popular initiative aimed at repealing the constitutional ban on the building of minarets.[22] However, it was likely to become a boomerang. If it would have failed, , it would have played into the xenophobes' hands.

The second initiative regards the applications brought before the European Court for Human Rights by four associations ('Ligue des musulmans de Suisse',

---

ech%2F2009%2F091130_tagesgespraech.MP3&sg=10000031&sh=10110440 (accessed 15 December 2011).

19 G. Kreis, 'Die Einheit einer Wolke', *Basler Zeitung*, 9 December 2009.

20 S.A. Salieh (2009), *Sì all'iniziativa contro i minareti*, http://blog.sami-aldeeb.com (website consulted on 15 December 2011).

21 F. Nirenstein, 'Ma la religione non c'entra: i minareti sono simboli politici', *Il Giornale*, 3 December 2009.

22 www.voceevangelica.ch/news/news.cfm?id=13687 (accessed 15 December 2011).

'Fondation communauté musulmane-Genève', 'Association culturelle des musulmans de Neuchâtel' and 'Association genevoise des musulmans') which believe that the new article 72, paragraph 3 of the Federal Constitution runs counter to article 9 of the 1950 Rome Convention (applications no. 65840/09 and 66274/09).

In my opinion, this initiative raised questions as to whether the Court of Strasbourg can assess the conformity of a constitutional norm regarding a provision of international conventional law. In terms of general source theory, and taking into account the role of the Constitution as a formal and procedural *Grundnorm* directed at the production of ordinary law, and as a crystallization of a *Grundordnung* which is adopted as a guide for all positive law (Rhinow 2003; Oeter 1997: 29–75), it is extremely debatable as to whether the superiority of the provisions of the 1950 European Convention can be asserted over those of the European Council Member States' constitutions. It is even more debatable if one examines the explicit self-limitation of the Swiss constitutional system with regard to international law as provided by article 194, paragraph 2, of the Federal Constitution, which expressly refers to *jus cogens* as the only set of norms of international law which cannot be changed by popular will (while leaving the task of verifying eventual conflicts between the *jus cogens* in question and the initiative to change the Constitution to another national body, the Federal Council).

However, the European Court of Human Rights declared the applications inadmissible, on the ground that the applicants could not claim to be the victims of a violation of the Convention (decision of 28 June 2011).

In my opinion, the complexity of the 'minarets question' can only be fully understood when considering how the expression 'multicultural Switzerland' – apparently a consequence of globalization and modernity – contains the fundamental ontological dimension of the Confederation. The latter was founded as a *Willensnation* – 'a nation created by its own will' – which is a model of civil cohabitation among confederates, in the respect of the autonomy of each political body. Sure enough, if one observes Switzerland close up one discovers a set of small areas which differ in climate and territory, and especially in language and culture: what keeps citizens together is only their will to form one sole nation. What has been happening recently is simply yet another change in the cultural panorama of reference of the *Willensnation.*

The first change in Switzerland's cultural panorama was the proclamation of freedom of residence in article 41 of the 1848 Constitution. This freedom, which was extended to Jews in 1866, marked the end of religious boundaries deriving from the Kappel wars.[23] In reality article 41 of the 1848 Federal Charter did not shift the religious balance excessively. Instead it marked the end of that hostile denominationalism which had characterized the three centuries following the

23 The wars of Kappel (1529–1531), fought between Protestant and Roman Catholic cantons during the Reformation, defined the Swiss Confederation as a State with two religions, in which every canton decided freely its own official confession(s).

second Kappel war and at the same time the beginning of the ecumenical opening between Roman Catholics and Protestants that would yield so many benefits in the course of the twentieth century. The second change was represented by the migratory flows which brought many immigrants from Southern Europe into Switzerland between 1945 and 1970. As they were Christians – above all Catholics – they based their lives on principles and values that were generally shared by the social fabric which was receiving them. In this context xenophobes stirred up fears of 'foreignerization' (a Swiss expression indicating a percentage of foreign residents considered excessive by the local populace). However, in this case it was sufficient for the CFS (the Federal Commission for Foreigners) to start formulating a series of proposals aimed at promoting integration, so that foreigners could progressively approach and adjust to Swiss culture through the adoption of local habits, customs and traditions, as well as of local values and mentality.

This communitarian policy of integration seemed to work until the beginning of the 1990s, when new migrations arrived to upset the Swiss social panorama. The new *Gastarbeiter*s, who from 1990 onwards radically transformed Swiss society, came from ex-Yugoslavia, Africa and the Middle East. They brought with them a cultural background which was very different from that of the *Südländer*s': most of the newcomers were not Christian, and the majority were unable to speak any of the four national languages.

These new migrations have increased cultural diversity through an increase in religious diversity. The percentage of the Swiss population belonging to one of the three official national Churches in Switzerland fell from 96% (1970) to 75% (2000), while Muslim and Christian Orthodox communities became more numerous (from 0.3% to 4.3% in the case of Muslims and from 0.3% to 1.8% for the Orthodox). The influx of new immigrants brought religious issues to the centre of the debate on multiculturalism. The cultural rules followed by the most recent arrivals were also expressions of their own culture and were an irreplaceable tool for the development of their personality but, as has been discussed, they are not always considered compatible with federal law, which is strongly influenced by the Swiss Confederation's Christian roots.

At this point a question arises. Can Switzerland absorb this third big multicultural change without suffering an excessive trauma? There can be no doubt that recently Swiss society has adopted positions that have not always been favourable to requests coming from religious groups not traditionally rooted in its territory. Beside the building of minarets on public land, such requests have concerned issues such as the possibility for Muslim teachers of religious education to wear a veil, or to slaughter livestock according to religious rules.

These requests for intervention have been addressed to the public subjects in charge of governance over religious affairs. They have sometimes involved a conflict with the cultural background in which the historically consolidated laws of the Swiss legal system are rooted, such as laws requiring cattle to be stunned before they are slaughtered, or the requirement for teachers to respect the religious neutrality of State schools. From this point of view legislators and the Federal

Court are proceeding very cautiously. On the one hand, they are opening up to the recognition of new faculties deriving from the right to freedom of religion (decision 134 I 114 of the Federal Court), but on the other they confirm the possibility to limit the exercise of behaviour that is abstractly guaranteed by article 15 of the Federal Constitution in the name of the need to preserve values pertaining to the material public order of the Confederation. In this light, religious freedom can never be exercised in contrast with other fundamental rights – considered pre-eminent – and human dignity.

Basically, the expression 'Masters in our own house' which is vividly used by some political parties (as the Italian Northern League) as an electoral slogan, cannot help summarizing – albeit very roughly – the idea that the blindness of law towards religious affiliation has to work just in one direction. Such blindness simply has to prevent the cultural markers of principles and norms of the Swiss legal system (which is inevitably of a Christian – but also liberal and democratic – nature) from being erased in the name of the need to build an intercultural law founded on an axiological 'koine' (common language).

Unlike others (Consorti 2009), in my opinion there is no scandal in keeping steady the cultural matrix of a legal system according to the constants that can be found in common popular consciousness at a given historical moment.

In Switzerland, as well as in Italy, there are collective cultural identities which can oppose the claims of groups that have arrived more recently. So, it can be argued, Government must use a certain degree of caution when it comes to forcing dynamic processes of transformation of identity: caution, which obviously does not mean the suspension of freedom of religion, worship and propaganda for members of non-Christian religions, but simply the impossibility of forcedly redefining the moral frame of reference of the system by means of an imposed hybridization (Ferrari, S. 2007). However, the impossibility of pressuring the legal dictates in force in the intercultural direction does not mean that the legal system must be immutable and hostile towards religious diversity. First of all, there is the position of European bodies on the subject of intercultural and inter-religious dialogue. The latter is considered fundamental to 'give a significant contribution to the development of a free, cohesive and orderly society', capable of 'overcoming philosophical and religious extremism, stereotypes and prejudices, ignorance and indifference, intolerance and hostility, which also in the recent past have been the cause of tragic conflicts and bloodshed in Europe'.[24] Second, if the perspective according to which the theory of the *clash of civilizations* is the result of ideas not supported by rational knowledge and by a critical awareness of the diversity existing in the plural society (Consorti 2009) is firmly adopted, it will be certainly possible, in the next few years, to find reasonable solutions to petitions put forward

24 Statement on inter-faith dialogue and social cohesion, adopted by the ministers of the interior at the Rome Conference of October 2003 and by the European Council, Annex of doc. n. 15983/03 of the Council of the European Union, www.consilium.europa.eu (accessed 15 December 2011).

by minority religious communities (such as the issues of ritual slaughter and the burial of Muslim believers) that do not involve forcing the moral framework of reference of the Swiss people. Moreover, it is evident that the best legal instrument for such 'reformist' (and not 'maximalist') implementation of religious freedom should be made up of general laws, enacted (in virtue of article 72 of the Federal Constitution) at a cantonal level, which enforce article 15 of the Federal Constitution.

Indeed nowadays the majority of cantons limit themselves to the regulation of the legal status of religions endowed with public legal personality by means of specific laws, without detailed provisions on the exercise of freedom of religion of all residents. A series of provisions could be inserted into such general laws in order to balance the requests put forward by the followers of religions that have recently settled in Switzerland with the constitutional principles and traditional values of the Swiss people. This would make utterly superfluous the rather 'odious' provision of the new third paragraph of article 72 of the Federal Constitution.

References

Bellini, P. (1972), *Principi di Diritto ecclesiastico* (Bresso: Cetim).

Bobbio, N. (1990), 'Pluralismo', in Bobbio, N. et al. (eds), 789–794.

Bobbio, N., Matteucci, N. and Pasquino, G. (eds) (1990), *Dizionario di Politica* (Milano: Tea).

Casuscelli, G. (1978), 'Pluralismo confessionale e organizzazione dei culti acattolici. Contributo all'interpretazione sistematica del primo e secondo comma dell'art. 8 della Costituzione', in *Scritti in onore di Salvatore Pugliatti* (Milano: Giuffrè), 235–313.

Consorti, P. (2009), 'Nuovi razzismi e diritto interculturale. Dei principi generali e dei regolamenti condominiali nella società multiculturale', *Stato, Chiese e pluralismo confessionale*, www.statoechiese.it (accessed 15 December 2011).

De Luca, L. (1970), *Diritto ecclesiastico ed esperienza giuridica* (Milano: Giuffrè).

Epiney, A. and Siegwart, K. (eds) (1997), *Direkte Demokratie* (Freiburg i. Ue: Editions universitaires).

Ferrari, S. (2007), 'Tra geo-diritti e teo-diritti. Riflessioni sulle religioni come centri di identità', *Quaderni di diritto e politica ecclesiastica*, 1.

Freudiger, P. (2009), *Argomentario breve sull'iniziativa contro i minareti* (Comitato d'iniziativa contro l'edificazione di minareti).

Guolo, R. (2007), *L'Islam è compatibile con la democrazia?* (Roma-Bari: Laterza).

Im Hof, U. (1991), *Mythos Schweiz. Identität – Nation – Geschichte* (Zürich: NZZ).

Oeter, S. (1997), 'Souveränität und Legitimität staatlicher Herrschaft im europäischen Mehrebenensystem', in Epiney, A. and Siegwart, K. (eds), 29–75.

Pacillo, V. (2009), *Stato e Chiesa cattolica nella Repubblica e Cantone Ticino. Profili giuridici comparati* (Lugano: Eupress).

Rhinow, R. (2003), *Grundzüge des Schweizerischen Verfassungsrechts* (Basel: Helbing & Lichtenhahn).

Sartori, G. (2000), *Pluralismo, multiculturalismo ed estranei* (Milano: Rizzoli).

Toso, P. (1990), 'Dovere di fedeltà e diritto di resistenza. L'obiezione di coscienza del pubblico funzionario', *Rivista Trimestrale di Diritto Pubblico*, 2, 426–445.

Vitali, E. (1980), 'Legislatio libertatis e prospettazioni sociologiche nella recente dottrina ecclesiasticistica', *Il Diritto ecclesiastico*, 1, 24–66.

Ye'or, B. (2005), *Eurabia: The Euro-Arab Axis* (Fairleigh: Dickinson University Press).

Chapter 18
Places of Worship: Between Public and Private: A Comparison between Bulgaria, Italy and the Netherlands

Tymen J. van der Ploeg

Introduction: Places of Worship and the Neutrality of Public Space

This chapter deals with the regulation of places of worship and other symbols of worship usually connected with such places. Worshipping in a building or another place is an important way in which religious individuals manifest their faith. Places of worship are clear symbols of religious communities and the protection of these places is included in the principle of the freedom of religion.[1] As all countries in the EU are party to the European Convention on Human Rights (ECHR), they all adhere to the principle of the freedom of religion. Article 9 of the ECHR, in combination with article 14 (principle of equal treatment) and the twelfth protocol of the ECHR, provides a strong guarantee of this freedom.

At a basic level the member states must approach religions in the same way, insofar as there must be a separation between Church and State. Nevertheless, the adoption of the principles mentioned above does not necessarily lead to the same practice, with various models of the relationship between the State and religion in force in Europe.[2] This chapter will not elaborate on this, focusing instead on a comparison of the approaches to places of worship in three EU member states which have different characteristics regarding religion and use different models of

1 The scope of what can fall under 'religion' was set rather narrowly by the European Court on Human Rights (ECtHR); see de Jong (2000: 699ff.). It only applies to what is a necessary expression of religion, neglecting the subjective side. Cf. also McCrea (2010: 125ff.). An outspoken plea for the use of the subjective approach can be found in Sullivan (2005: 9).

2 See Vermeulen and Kanne (2004) and van der Burg (2009). The last author is a strong defender of the model of pluralistic cooperation between the State and religious communities, which is practised in the Netherlands.

the relationship between the State and religion. They are Bulgaria,[3] Italy[4] and the Netherlands. They are briefly characterized below.

During the communist era (before 1990), the State of Bulgaria was anti-religious but it is now open to religion. The Orthodox Church is predominant, while there is also an important Islamic minority. The Bulgarian Constitution (arts. 13 and 37) suggests more government involvement with respect to the exercise of the freedom of religion than article 9 of the ECHR. Article 37 instructs the government to assist in the maintenance of tolerance and respect (non-violence) between adherents of different denominations and between believers and non-believers (Krussteff 2011). As such, this peacekeeping task seems quite acceptable; however, it may come into conflict with the principle of equal treatment of religious groups. It is understood that the European Court of Human Rights (ECtHR) is not very strict on equal treatment with regard to religious groups as long as this is in conformity with efforts to maintain harmonious relationships within society (McCrea 2010: 104).

In Italy, apart from the constitutionally founded freedom of religion, the State has a concordat with the Roman Catholic Church (the Holy See), which is the dominant religious group in Italy. It appears that the Italian courts, including the constitutional court, generally rely on the relevant parts of the Italian Constitution of 1947, which encompasses international law, rather than refer to the ECHR and the ECtHR. Nevertheless, the ECtHR has condemned Italy several times because its law and the application of it was not in accord with the ECHR (Ventura 2011: 223ff.).

In the Netherlands, the freedom of religion has a long history: there are two major Christian Churches, the Protestant Church and the Roman Catholic Church, as well as many smaller Churches of Protestant or Catholic character. Over the past 40 years, the Muslim population has also grown steadily due to immigration. Article 6 of the Dutch Constitution theoretically provides more room for restrictions on the freedom of religion than article 9 of the ECHR.[5]

It is remarkable that the constitutions of these States have a slightly different approach to the principle of the freedom of religion than article 9 of the ECHR and that national courts deal differently with the principles of the ECHR.

While the histories of the relationship between the State and religion may differ between these countries, they have in common that new foreign religious groups have entered each country: in Bulgaria new Christian groups, in Italy and the Netherlands Islamic communities and Christian groups of foreign origin. At the same time, the traditional religions have lost quite a few members. In this

3 I would like to thank Maya Kosseva and her team for their information regarding law and practice in Bulgaria and for their clear translation of the Bulgarian Law on Religions.

4 I would like to thank Daniela Milani, Cristiana Cianitto, Mariagrazia Tirabassi and Silvio Ferrari for their information regarding law and practice in Italy.

5 Vermeulen and Aarass (2009: 72–78). For an alternative point of view see Bos (2007: 727–736).

somewhat fluid time each religious community wants their own place of worship. Thus, it is important that the legal and administrative system and practices adapt to the new circumstances.

This chapter is organized as follows: the next section discusses places of worship and legal personality; the third section, the administrative rules and practice concerning the construction, rent or use of places of worship; the fourth section, places of worship as monuments; the fifth section, the private and/or public character of the place of worship; and the sixth section, the rules regarding the abandoning and selling of a place of worship. The chapter will then turn to a number of subjects related to places of worship, with the seventh section discussing calls to worship, the eighth section looking at processions as manifestations of worship and the ninth section examining rituals and worship concerning death and funerals. The final section will offer some conclusions.

Places of Worship and Legal Personality

There is a clear connection between places of worship and a religious community being recognized as a legal entity. Without legal personality, a religious community cannot own or rent a permanent place where it can worship. As a general rule, the right to legal personality follows from the freedom of religion.[6] The establishment and maintenance of a place of worship is also generally accepted as part of the freedom of religion in Europe (de Jong 2000: 359ff.). In the three countries discussed here, the State's recognition of religion as a socially beneficial phenomenon can also be observed in the tax treatment of religious organizations and places of worship.[7]

Legal personality is not only a legal-technical instrument allowing an entity to act in the legal sphere, as such a status also allows a religious community to act like every other legal person in society. Thus, it obtains a place in public space, and within the framework of the organized body (legal person) it can make its own rules, which are norms for its members. When a religious community has legal personality it also grants a certain societal recognition to its members.

6 See OSCE/ODIHR, *Guidelines for Review of Legislation Pertaining to Religion or Belief*, 2004, 17, points 3–8, available at: www.osce.org/odihr/13993?download=false.

7 In Bulgaria, the State may give tax benefits and other preferential treatment to registered religious denominations (see article 25 LoR). In this case, they are obliged to send their annual financial statements to the tax authorities together with an independent financial audit. In Italy, places of worship enjoy fiscal benefits (exemption from municipal tax on immovable property) if effectively used for worship. This is not dependent on the status of the religious community. In the Netherlands, in general, places of worship are exempted from local tax. This fiscal benefit is not dependent on the form of the religious community that owns (uses, leases) the building.

Nevertheless, the positions of various religious communities not only differ across the three countries being discussed here but also within each country. In Bulgaria, according to the LoR,[8] people are free to establish religious communities (article 6 LoR). Before this law was established in 2002, the freedom to found religious communities in Bulgaria was rather limited.[9] At present, a religious community may obtain legal personality by registration at the Sofia city court (article 14ff. LoR). When applying for registration the religious denomination needs to hand in its by-laws (article 17 LoR). There are no requirements regarding the internal structure of the religious community. At least partly the court decisions about registration are based on the nature of the religious belief and practices. This may also require an expert opinion from the Directorate of Religious Denominations (arts. 16 and 17). Local branches can have their own legal personality when the by-laws of the religious denomination provide for this and the central administration of this entity has decided to establish a local branch.[10] To become a legal entity, the branch has to be registered as such at the district court of the headquarter of the denomination (article 20).[11] Religious communities may choose any legal form they think appropriate to their beliefs, according to article 6 (1) LoR. However, it is not clear from the law how this relates to the obtainment of legal personality by religious communities in article 14 and with the establishment of non-profit entities in article 27 LoR.

In Italy, the government recognizes religious communities as legal persons on certain grounds.

Public recognition not only results in legal personality but also in preferential treatment in other areas such as taxation. The Roman Catholic Church has a special position that is laid down in a concordat between the Holy See and the State. There are also some other religious groups that have an 'entente' with the State. In addition to the recognized religious communities, there may also be religious communities that take the form of an association.[12]

In the Netherlands, there is a special form of private legal person that religious communities can take according to article 2:2 Dutch Civil Code: *kerkgenootschap*. The law declares a *kerkgenootschap* to be a legal person. There is no involvement

8 Prom. SG. 120/29 Dec 2002, amend. SG. 33/21 Apr 2006, amend. SG. 59/20 Jul 2007, amend. SG. 74/15 Sep 2009.

9 See ECtHR 26 October 2000 (2002) 34 EHRR 1339 (*Hasan and Chaush* v. *Bulgaria*).

10 The establishment must be recorded in a register of the county mayor, who must notify the Directorate on Religious Denominations. See article 19 LoR.

11 According to an answer of the Chief Mufti of the Muslims in Bulgaria office (R-IMIR-6, Sofia, 21 June 2011, interviewer Iva Kyurkchieva, field research 2010–2011 conducted under RELIGARE project), local branches rarely choose to use this option.

12 Religious communities may choose the form of an unrecognized association (article 36-38 CC) or a recognized association (article 14-35 CC). On the basis of article 8 (2) of the Constitution, religious denominations enjoy self-determination in their internal organization, within the limits of the Italian legal system.

by government and no formality at the establishment.[13] In principle, this form of legal person is available to all religious communities. In practice, it is mostly used by traditional Christian and Jewish religious communities. Islamic groups do not want to use this form, because of its Christian connotation, while small, more recent Christian or other groups are hesitant as there is no formal requirement for the establishment of a *kerkgenootschap* and they cannot show any legal document of their existence as a legal person. Many religious communities have chosen an association or foundation as their form of legal person. Generally the form of legal person does not make a difference in the relationship between the government and the religious community.

How important the legal personality of a religious community is and how it is connected to the place of worship can be observed in the conflicts that have arisen in the Netherlands around Church property in the case of a Church splitting into separate entities (van Kooten and van der Ploeg 2004: 145ff.), or in such cases as the merger of three Protestant Churches, which certain communities resisted. When a local community belongs to a Church federation, it has independent legal personality. When it is organized as a part of a national Church, its legal personality is dependent on the national Church. In case a local parish with dependent legal personality did not want to be part of the merger of its (national) Church with two other (national) Churches the local Church council cannot decide to leave the national Church. Local parishioners can eventually establish a new religious community (legal person) next to the existing local parish. The church building and other properties continue to belong to the parish that as legal person was dependent on the national Church.[14] This rather formal systematic solution can be expected in a civil law approach, while a common law/equity approach would be more likely to find a more pragmatic solution.[15]

13 Since the new Act on the Trade Register of 2008, Churches must register themselves, albeit in a limited way.

14 See HR (Supreme Court) 19 December 2003, NJ 2004, 559, in which the Supreme Court confirmed that the merged Church was the legal continuation of, amongst others, the Nederlandse hervormde kerk (Dutch Reformed Church).

15 The merged Church has however established committees for special care to help to come to reasonable solutions about the use or even the property of the building of the local parish with the parish that has been formed by the members who opposed the merger of the national Church and left that Church.

Administrative Rules and Practice Concerning Building, Renting or Using a Place of Worship

In general, the construction or use of places of worship is not a problem for the established religions. Mostly they already have their places of worship, or when wanting to build or use a new church, the local authorities will facilitate this. Most minority religions (Islamic groups, but also other new religious groups) initially make use of unused warehouses, garages and shops as places of worship and thus the external manifestation of the religion is not obvious. While this may not cause public division (Dassetto 2000: 31ff., esp. 37), the government may oppose this use. However, its intervention should be motivated by arguments based on public health and safety.[16] When the religion becomes more prominent, displaying symbols such as mosques and minarets, the tension with the surrounding population becomes greater. This may have influence on the policy of local governments because they have responsibility for local law and order (Dassetto 2000: 38).

In Bulgaria, religious communities which have acquired legal personality according to article 14ff. of the LoR have the right to establish a place of worship.[17] The religious communities have to respect laws concerning land use. The State and municipalities have the right to lease real estate to religious communities and to subsidize their costs (article 21 [3] LoR). In article 25 LoR, the State is permitted to support and encourage registered religious communities in many ways.[18] In Bulgaria, in practice, the preferential treatment that the State and municipalities might provide regarding the building of houses of worship is not offered to Islamic communities and non-traditional religions.[19] However, local authorities hire out libraries and other buildings to new and non-traditional religious communities. This difference in treatment is clearly not in line with the freedom of religious worship and the equal treatment of religions. Only in smaller towns and villages where Muslims and Christians live together in greater harmony do the local authorities treat both religious communities equally.

16 For example, the ECtHR decided that the condemnation of the use of a building for religious purposes without the approval of the Greek authorities (which after 12 years had not responded to the request) was an illegitimate restriction of the freedom of religion, ECtHR 26 September 1996, no 8748/91 (*Manoussakis* v. *Greece*).

17 See explicitly article 12 s.1 LoR.

18 Usually the available funds are insufficient to cover the needs of all the denominations.

19 In Sofia and some other big cities (Burgas, for example) local authorities have found various technical reasons to prevent Muslims from building mosques. In Sofia, the Chief Mufti owns some land but the Muslim community still cannot obtain an official licence to start the construction (see Chief Mufti of the Muslims in Bulgaria office R-IMIR-6, Sofia, 21 June 2011, interviewer Iva Kyurkchieva; Higher Islamic Institute R-IMIR-11, 21 June 2011, interviewer Maya Kosseva, field research 2010–2011 conducted under RELIGARE project).

In Italy, religious groups have the right to a place of worship. Until the 1950s, this was only applicable to 'admitted cults', but since a judgment by the Constitutional Court of 18 November 1958 (decision no. 59), it has been extended to all religious groups. This collective dimension of the freedom of religion (the right to build a place of worship) is protected by the Italian Constitution and must be equally granted to all religious denominations (article 19 and 8). This right is also implied in the exercise of the freedom of association (article 17).[20] Regulation of places of worship is a matter of regional law, and while there are national laws, they only determine general principles. These laws require municipalities to reserve land for the construction of religious buildings[21] and to finance the construction with contributions drawn from the taxes levied on the construction of new buildings.[22] These areas are assigned to the religious communities that have requested them according to criteria based on the religious needs of the population. The national laws give regional laws the power to define the criteria for the identification of areas and to establish financial support. In practice, municipalities do not always respect the obligation to support the building of a new place of worship. Some regions only grant financial support to 'recognized religious groups' without specifying what 'recognized' means; other regions simply give financial support to the religious groups that have signed an agreement with the State according to article 8.3 of the Italian Constitution. This last requirement was declared illegal by the Italian Constitutional Court.[23] According to this Court, religious communities should only comply with the following requirements: some form of recognition by public authorities and/or the existence of a statute (Church regulations) and/or a form of acknowledgement by the local community. The Court has also established a standard for the municipalities when more than one religious community legitimately appeals for financial support: such support should be given to the community which is socially more important. In practice, the public authorities only serve the Catholic Church in this.

Religious groups (legal persons) must respect the laws on urban planning, health requirements and security, and the application of these laws is sometimes used by municipalities to make it difficult for controversial religious groups to build or open a place of worship.

In the Netherlands, the right to exercise public worship in a building has been constitutionally recognized since 1848 (article 164ff., now article 6). Religious communities must normally finance their own places of worship. From 1962

---

20 Formally, it does not matter whether the religious community is recognized or not, but in practice local authorities could use their powers to discriminate against some religious groups and this is possible because of the discretionary nature of the prescribed requirements in question.

21 L. n. 167/1962 and l. n. 765/1967.

22 L. n. 10/1977 as amended by D.P.R. n. 380/2001.

23 Sentences no. 195/1993 and 346/2002.

to 1975 there was a law on the financing of churches.[24] From 1976 to 1984, a global regulation with regard to subsidizing prayer halls (Islamic) was in force.[25] The regulation was repealed when the separation of Church and State was constitutionally enshrined in 1983 (Vermeulen 2011: 53 ff.). Local authorities may support the building of a new house of worship.[26] It is often easier to obtain a subsidy when the place of worship is part of a building with other functions (social, educational, cultural), as local communities are sometimes hesitant to subsidize purely religious activities.[27] In fact, there is a new trend to replace purely religious buildings (churches) with places of worship that are part of a building that includes shops and/or apartments. The additional spaces around the place of worship can also be used for small meetings by other organizations, and in this way the religious community develops a closer relationship with the broader society.

When a religious community wants to construct a place of worship its planning should involve consultation with the broader community. The capacity to build a place of worship is not dependent on the legal form of the religious community, but on its financial capability. Rules concerning security and health in relation to the use of any building will generally be applied to places of worship as well (Vermeulen 2011: 57ff.), but it is possible that some dispensation may be given if the conditions are too burdensome.

Places of Worship as Monuments

Monumental status usually gives some right to a subsidy as well as obligations regarding maintenance. The differences between the three countries discussed here are noteworthy.

In Bulgaria, the law on cultural monuments[28] had as a rule that a place of worship recognized as a monument must be put at the disposal of the State as a cultural object. The revised law now provides for the possibility that, following

24 Wet premie kerkenbouw, Stb 538.1.

25 From 1976 to 1981 one requirement was that the religious community had at least 1,000 members; between 1981 and 1984 this requirement was not in force. Of the building costs, 30% were subsidized, to a maximum of NLG 30,000. Between 1976 and 1981, 31 mosques were built using these subsidies and between 1981 and 1984, 69 mosques. See Shadid and Van Koningsveld (1995: 28–29).

26 This applies to different religious groups. See for example, Shadid and Van Koningsveld (1995: 30). In 2009, the Union of Dutch Communities published a rather supportive report about the way communities could cooperate with, support or otherwise have connections with religious communities and what the limits were for this: 'VNG: Tweeluik religie en publiek domein, handvatten voor gemeenten' (Diptych of Religion and the Public Domain: Guidelines for Municipalities), 2009.

27 For the development of prayer halls and mosques in the Netherlands, see Shadid and Van Koningsveld (1995: 23–35).

28 Law of 11 April 1969, prom. S.G. 29.

the request of a religious community, the council of ministers or the municipal council will allow the use of a monument for worship. The religious community has a right to use the structure for worship if it is the only place of worship in the settlement, until the authorities provide another place of worship. In addition, many former places of worship have been converted from cultural buildings back into places of worship during the last 20 years, that is from public property to the property of religious communities.

In Italy, if a place of worship is a monument, there are limitations to the right to refuse visitors, particularly when restoration has been subsidized by the government. When the place of worship is a historical monument, State authorization is required for any changes to the place of worship (for example, the removal of an altar). In the agreements between the State and six religious communities there are specific provisions for these types of places of worship. Apparently, in Italy the monumental churches are generally owned by the Church and not by the government.

In the Netherlands, monumental places of worship (churches) may receive certain subsidies from the government, but these are usually not enough for the maintenance of the building (see de Wit 2009: 145ff.). Often these places are brought under the management of a monument foundation which is responsible for administering subsidies and is involved in revenue-generating activities such as hiring out the building for various occasions.

The Private and/or Public Character of the Place of Worship

Although religion is accepted as a phenomenon that is beneficial to society, it does not follow that worship should be a public activity. It is an exercise of the collective freedom of religion for a community of individual believers (and for the religious organization as a whole), and the question of whether worship is public or private depends on the approach of the particular religious organization concerned.

In most religions the place of worship is where believers seek communion with God or gods through a service in which the explanation of the Word of God and/or an offering (for example, the Eucharist) are central.[29] From a theological perspective, the sacred place or place of worship is central for believers.[30] In Roman Catholic canonical terms, a place of worship is a place of God which is

29 See Bakker (2009: 105–116), which describes the approach of Judaism, Islam and Hinduism to places of worship. On Islam and Judaism see Turner (1979: 260ff. and 278ff.).

30 See Turner (1979: 13–31). However, in Protestant or Evangelical circles the place of worship is no more than an arbitrary meeting place for the congregation (Turner 1979: 222ff.). Turner also argues that the place of worship should be taken seriously in a theological sense (see 323ff.).

open to all believers in Christ and in this way it is public.[31] However, the word 'public' in this context does not mean open to the public in general. The religious community, as the legal owner, user or lessee of the premises, may claim privacy for the premises on the basis of this legal position. A proper way of protecting the proceedings within the place of worship is a regulation that restricts noise levels in the vicinity of the place of worship during the proceedings by local laws and regulations.[32] Religious communities also receive the normal protection as owners or lessee of the place of worship: in the case of vandalism, the police provide security and the prosecution starts an investigation to track down those responsible.

Many religious services are open to the public. Has the place of worship thus become a public place? It appears that within Europe there are different approaches determining the character of places of worship.

In Bulgaria it appears that the place of worship is considered the private space of the religious community. The Law on Religions states that freedom of religion may be restricted on such grounds as public safety or morality and when used for political objectives (see article 7 [3]). It is clear that these restrictions encompass possible conflicts (hidden or otherwise) between 'the State and the freedom of speech and the freedom of religion'.[33] The State has a commitment to protect the freedom of religion and to avoid tensions around places of worship. Intruders are not acceptable, but a peaceful person cannot be forbidden to worship.

In Italy, the place of worship is seen as both private and public. On the one hand, property rules apply: the owner of a place of worship can exclude unwanted visitors. However, there are limitations to this right in the case of places of worship that are also places of cultural or historical importance, particularly if they also receive financial support from the State as part of the nation's cultural heritage. In any case, a religious community can prevent visitors from entering a place of worship during services or if dressed in an inappropriate manner. According to the general rules and the free exercise of religious freedom, the municipality cannot restrict this right to exclude visitors.

On the other hand, sermons are considered public speeches in the sense that they have to respect criminal law provisions (a preacher is not allowed to incite violence, hatred, etc.), although there is a good degree of tolerance in this matter. Friday afternoon sermons in mosques raise security concerns and parts of the public and certain political parties would like to oblige preachers to give their sermons in Italian (they are frequently given in Arabic). At present, however, no specific provision has been enacted.[34] The police can enter a place of worship

31 Preferably, admission should also be free; cf. Meijers (2009: 59ff.).

32 See in the Netherlands the Zondagswet (Act regarding Sunday), article 2, section 1, in which it is forbidden to make unnecessary noise in the vicinity of places of worship. See Vermeulen (2011: 67ff.).

33 There have been no preachers accused of insult or inciting hatred in Bulgaria.

34 There have been no condemnations on the grounds of insult or inciting hatred.

during a service if it is suspected that a crime is occurring. In other situations, the authorities need the authorization of the ecclesiastical authority.[35]

In the Netherlands, the place of worship is considered a private place with a public element. The religious group may allow non-members of the community to enter the place of worship or may refuse them entrance. There is no rule that urges a religious community to allow entrance to non-members during worship. The owner (or lessee) of the place of worship may ask the court to prohibit unwanted persons from entering the premises, but there must be reasonable grounds.[36] A priest or imam with religious convictions other than that which prevails in a religious community may be refused entrance by this community and may be refused the right to participate in the religious activities of the community.[37] The religious organization may call the police for assistance when unwanted visitors refuse to leave the building.[38] However, the police or judicial authorities have no right to raid the premises during services.[39]

The fact that worship has occurred – ultimately open to the public – does not mean that a service has been delivered to the public.[40] The act of worship, however, is not seen as a fully private matter. When preachers (Muslim) trespass the limits of the freedom of speech, they can face prohibition and a fine.

A very specific use of the place of worship is as a place of asylum. This is an old tradition in the Roman Catholic Church – which has roots in the Old Testament – which allows people to seek refuge in a church, providing them protection from the authorities (or from the family of a supposed victim of the asylum seeker) (see Hoeksma 1982). In some countries the law has respected this church asylum, in other countries it has never had any official status. Moreover, since it is not officially recognized in many countries, it is now no longer regulated in the *codex iuris canonici* (see Boelens and Meijers 2009: 63–64). In the three countries discussed here, church asylum does not officially exist. Nevertheless, the fact that

35 Article 5(2) Concordat between the Italian State and the Roman Catholic Church, L. 121/1985.

36 District court, Rotterdam, 25 June 2008, LJN BD5420 foundation *Mosque Essalam* v. *Visitor*. The board of the foundation may on specific grounds refuse entrance and may establish conditions. The court of appeal judged that the refusal was not legitimate: Court of Appeal, The Hague, 6 June 2009, LJN BK 4987.

37 See District court 's-Hertogenbosch, 25 February 2009, LJN BH4029. The Court of Appeal, The Hague, 16 June 2009 LJN BK4987 annulled this decision stating that the decision was not sufficiently argued. With Vermeulen (2011: 70), the decision of the Court of Appeal appears to be too strict.

38 A famous case in 2010 involved the removal of gay protesters from the basilica in 's-Hertogenbosch on request of the Church Board.

39 See article 12 Algemene Wet op het binnentreden (General law on entering private premises). A famous case in which it was claimed in vain that the building was a church and a church service was occurring is HR 31 October 1986, NJ 1987, 173 and HR 22 March 1989, BNB 1990, 161 (Satanskerk; Satanic Church).

40 See article 7 Algemene Wet gelijke behandeling (General law on equal treatment).

authorities may not enter a place of worship during a service may be regarded as a form of asylum. In addition, in the Netherlands, church asylum is sometimes used symbolically to attract attention to people with no official recognition by society. The police authorities generally respect such church asylum, not on legal but on ethical grounds (see Raad van kerken in Nederland 1999; Schulz-Süchting 2000).

The Rules and Practices Regarding the Abandoning and/or Selling of a Place of Worship

Many countries must deal with the problem of what to do with places of worship that are no longer used for religious purposes. The religious organization may cease to use the building for religious purposes and may also want to dispense with the building. If it is a monument, there will be many barriers to the sale of the building as it has a public cultural value and as such the buyer will be obliged to respect all sorts of rules, thus making it difficult to sell.

The question does not seem to be an issue in Bulgaria as the number of religious groups is growing and they are attempting to acquire more places of worship rather than abandoning them. The general rule – article 22 of the Law on Religions – is that a religious organization may dispose of its properties according to its own by-laws, which should encompass methods of dissolution and liquidation (article 17 [8] LoR). This means that it is the responsibility of the religious community, as the government has no specific rules on the issue.

In Italy, there are no State rules about the disposal of buildings that are abandoned as places of worship, unless the building is of historical, cultural or artistic value. In that case, State authorization is required. The Catholic Church has enacted internal rules governing the transformation and selling of places of worship. Its policy is that a church that is not being used by the church may be used as a place of worship by another Christian Church but not by the members of another religion. In addition, other uses should be as respectful as possible to the original consecration. If this is not possible, then the building should be demolished.[41]

In the Netherlands, many churches have closed due to the process of secularization. Each religious group has its own rules about what can be done with places of worship that are no longer used as such. These abandoned buildings have been given various new roles, including supermarkets, office buildings, bookstores and apartment buildings.[42] It is very important that a religious community has the opportunity to sell the building – or at least the land – at a market price as it may be obliged to pay subsidies back to the relevant governmental authority. However,

41 Boelens and Meijers (2009: 75ff.). See also Frankort and Schoenmaker (2009: 169ff.).

42 For the policy of the Roman Catholic Church on this matter see the paragraph above.

if it is a monument it can be very hard to sell. One solution in such instances is to sell the building to the local government for the nominal price of one euro and then hire it back. The often burdensome maintenance costs are then no longer the responsibility of the religious community. Another barrier to the disposal of a place of worship may be the designation of the area in the local government plan. Generally, places of worship are given a 'spiritual' or 'cultural' designation. To have this designation removed requires a cooperative attitude from the local government and thus ultimately the political will.

Calls to Worship

A question that is closely related to places of worship is whether the religious community may literally call believers to worship or prayer.

In Bulgaria this is regulated on the local level on the basis of the volume of the noise; however, it is possible that neighbours and others may be irritated even when the noise stays within the limits. On 21 May 2011, there was a demonstration against the call of the muezzin from the Sofia mosque. The authorities have promised to control the volume, but if it is too loud they can only ask the muezzin to sing more quietly.

In Italy there are several rules that may apply to bell-ringing;[43] however, the question is whether or not the general rules contained in these sources of law actually apply to the ringing of bells. The main judgments in this regard distinguish between the ringing of bells not directly connected with worship and that directly connected with worship. The 'non-worship' use of bells is subject to the same rules of any other noise emission. The ringing of bells connected to a Roman Catholic service is considered to be an expression of the free exercise of the Catholic religion and explicitly protected by article 7 of the Constitution and article 2 of the Concordat between the Catholic Church and the Italian State (1984). There are many cases where the court argued that the sound of bells, as long as it is for liturgical use, is something that should not be regulated in terms of noise pollution and public health.[44] The regulation of the ringing of bells, in this case, is the responsibility of the ecclesiastical authority. However, this does not mean that there are no limits.[45] Exceeding 'normal tolerability' may constitute an offence,

43 Law of 26 October 1995 n. 447, Framework law on noise pollution, Gazzetta Ufficiale 30 October 1995, N. 254; Decree of the President of the Council of Ministers, 1 March 1991, Maximum limits of exposure to noise in homes and in the external environment, Gazzetta Ufficiale, n. 57, as amended by D.P.C.M. 14 November 1997; Determination of limit values of sound sources, Gazzetta Ufficiale 12 December 1997, n. 280. Moreover, there are regional laws implementing the national framework and municipal regulations.

44 Lombardy Administrative Court, 1st section, ordinance 25 January 2000, n. 229.

45 See article 844 Civil Code. The limit of what a neighbour may expect is that it does not exceed normal tolerability.

as established in article 659.1 Criminal Code (disturbance to the occupations of others). In identifying the notion of 'normal tolerability', the State must take into account the specific provisions enacted by the ecclesiastical authority 'designed to incorporate traditions and customs that allow better identification of the limit of normal tolerance in relation to the non-continuity of sound and its connection with special moments in the life of the Church'.[46] It is presumed that calls for worship by religious communities other than the Roman Catholic are subject to the general rules regarding noise pollution and public health.

In the Netherlands, article 10 of the (general) law on public manifestations provides the regulation concerning bell-ringing.[47] The article states that bell-ringing on occasion of religious ceremonies and burial or cremation ceremonies is allowed, but that the local council may regulate the length and the level of the sound. There have been cases brought against unwanted bell-ringing and other noise in the Netherlands.[48]

Processions as Manifestations of Worship

A procession is a form of worship. As a public manifestation of religion, it may be limited for reasons of public health and public order. In international treaties the right to a procession is not explicitly included in the freedom of religion. This matter is apparently left to the States to regulate according to their own traditions or wishes (see de Jong 2000: 273). In Bulgaria, according to the Law on Religions, there is a general permission to organize a procession (see article 12 [2]). However, the permission of the local authorities is also necessary.[49]

46 On that ground a parish priest was acquitted by the Court of Appeal in Milan (1st section, 27 April–9 June 1994, n. 2097).

47 For more extensive details about this, see Vermeulen (2011: 60ff.).

48 See, for example, State Council 1 April 2010 (Sound amplification Leger des Heils [Salvation Army] Zutphen), where the State council judged that sound amplification is not in itself protected under the principle of the freedom of religion. See also District court Breda, 20 October 2010 (Bell-ringing in Tilburg), www.rechtspraak.nl LJN BO 1112 (Roman Catholic parish – municipality Tilburg): the General Police Ordinance of Tilburg that restricts bell-ringing is not against the constitution because the bell-ringing surpassed the allowable noise levels. On 26 November 2007, LJN BB 8689, the same court decided that the Municipal Police Regulation did not adequately regulate bell-ringing, and because the freedom of religion included this right to ringing, it could not be enforced.

49 This is also true for other public expressions of religion. An example of this is that the Chief Mufti now asks and receives special permission from the mayor of Sofia to use the space in front of the mosque when there is not space inside for all the believers. This happens every Friday and on other special occasions. According to an interview to the Chief Mufti of the Muslims in Bulgaria office: R-IMIR-6, Sofia, 21 June 2011, interviewer Iva Kyurkchieva, field research 2010–2011 conducted under RELIGARE project.

In Italy, part II of a Decree of 1931[50] on public security had as a general rule that in relation to processions and ceremonies outside religious buildings the police commissioner must be notified three days beforehand. Moreover, the police were able to restrict or prohibit the ceremony or procession if it was considered to endanger public order or in relation to public health requirements.[51] In a ruling of the Constitutional Court of 8 March 1957, no. 45, the Decree was declared invalid on some points related to the freedom of religion and assembly as stated by the Constitution (1948). A general limit established for all gatherings was that they could be restricted if this was in the best interests of social harmony. As a result, in relation to sensitive areas, consent from the police commissioner may be a prerequisite. Prefects are stimulated by a Law of 1 April 1981, n. 121, to establish rules about this.[52]

Until 1983 processions in the Netherlands were only allowed in parts of the country where they were traditionally held, these being the Roman Catholic southern parts of the country. However, they can now also be held in other parts. The local councils may make their own rules concerning religious manifestation occurring in the open but may only limit the freedom of religion and assembly on the grounds of public health, traffic,[53] or to combat or prevent riots. Usually there is a regulation requiring the organizers to provide local authorities with notice of any procession.

Rituals and Worship Concerning Death and Funerals

As religion is concerned with questions of life and death, many religions have special rituals and traditions concerning death, funerals, graves and cemeteries: 'If religion is anything, it could be said to be about what human beings do in relation to their mortality'.[54] Respect for the rituals and ceremonies with regard to burying or cremating the dead can be considered as an important element of the right to express one's religion (see de Jong 2000: 111).

In Bulgaria, religious groups have their own cemeteries, in which they can follow their own rituals and rules in accordance with article 24 LoR. In villages

50 Royal Decree of 18 June 1931, n. 773, Gazzetta Ufficiale 26/06/1931. n. 146.

51 See articles 25 and 26. In article 27 the funeral processions are exempted from this rule.

52 Lombardy Administrative Court Ruling 15 January 2010, n. 19, declared such a regulation by the Mayor of Trenzano to be unlawful, as restrictions to this freedom should be exceptional.

53 de Jong (2000: 272), states that disruption to traffic is not a legitimate reason to forbid a procession. This seems dubious.

54 Sullivan (2005: 9). In this book, Sullivan describes and analyses a case about the removal of private grave monuments, observing that in fact serious individual freedom of religion does not exist. She asks 'How can a court decide which religion is authentic?'.

with a Muslim population, the local trustees of the mosque are responsible for the ceremony and the cemetery. In larger towns, the cemeteries are controlled by the municipalities; however, those concerned are permitted to follow their own religious ceremonies.

In Italy, general rules are established in a Decree of 1990 (National Mortuary Police Regulation).[55] Each municipality must have a cemetery,[56] in which, according to the cemetery planning regulations, provision may be made for separate sections for non-Catholics.[57] For health reasons, the use of a coffin is obligatory; however, corpses are exhumed after a certain number of years, which is a problem for some religions, especially Judaism. There is an agreement between the State and the Jewish communities that they may lease specific sections of a cemetery for a period of 99 years.[58] There are also specific laws on cremation.[59] The possibility of Islamic cemeteries or the allocation of sections of public cemeteries for the burial of Muslims is approached in the same way as the building of places of worship (see above, pp. 358 ff.) (Ferrari 2002).

In the Netherlands, the Wet op de lijkbezorging (Law on burial and cremation) lays down the relevant rules. Cemeteries are owned either by municipalities or by religious communities. Religious groups may also reserve a specific section of a public cemetery.[60] It appears that the Law and the Decree on burial and cremation[61] take the differences between religions into account. Grave-rights can last up to 30 years and there is some room for particular rules, for example, related to Jewish cemeteries. Generally, religious rituals concerning the burying of the dead are respected (see Shadid and van Koningsveld 1995: 98), with the law providing for the possibility of burial within 24 hours after death,[62] and also for burying without a coffin,[63] both Islamic practices (see van Bijsterveld 2000: 125ff., esp. 129–130). The freedom of worship guaranteed by the constitutional rule concerning worshiping in buildings and closed areas related to buildings also applies to worshipping in cemeteries as they conform to the definition of closed areas: while they are not covered, they are surrounded by walls, hedges, etc. and separated from the public road (Vermeulen 2011: 4).

55 Decree of the President of the Republic, 10 September 1990, n. 285, Gazzetta Ufficiale 12 October 1990, n. 239.

56 Small municipalities may form a consortium to establish one collective cemetery.

57 Article 100.1 Decree 1990.

58 Law of 8 March 1989, n. 101, Gazzetta Ufficiale 23 March 1989, n. 69.

59 Law of 30 March 2001, n. 30, Provisions concerning cremation and scattering of ashes, Gazzetta Ufficiale 19 April 2001, n. 91.

60 This seems to be done by Islamic groups. See van Bijsterveld (2000: 130).

61 Law of 7 March 1991 and Decree of 4 December 1997.

62 According to article 16 of the Law on burial and cremation, burial is not allowed until 36 hours after the death of the person. Article 17 states that, after consulting with a doctor, the mayor of the community may allow burial earlier, with the agreement of the public prosecutor.

63 See article 3 Law on burial and cremation.

Conclusions

First, in principle, freedom of religion implies the right to a place of worship. In order to be able to build or lease a place of worship, it is necessary to be a legal person. In the countries considered here it seems theoretically possible for all religious communities to obtain legal personality in one way or another. Legal personality is not the central subject of this chapter but it is clear that the ability to acquire a place of worship is connected with the possibility of obtaining legal personality.

Second, regarding the establishment of places of worship, the administrative rules on planning, health and security are generally applicable. This includes acquiring a licence from the government.

A specific point concerns the possibility to obtain financial support from the government. In Bulgaria and Italy, the law provides for the financial support of the State and/or lower authorities for the construction of places of worship. It seems, however, that the equal treatment of different religious communities is not always practised. In the Netherlands, financial support is no longer allowed at the State level because of the strict separation of Church and State written into the Constitution of 1983. However, on a local level, financial support is sometimes given. The practice of governmental approval for the construction of places of worship is – in all three countries – somewhat dependent on local politics. Freedom of religion is not the only priority.

Third, in all three countries, the place of worship is seen principally as a private place where the religious community can worship according to its own rules. In Bulgaria, the freedom to refuse access to visitors is more limited than in the other two countries; however, the right of public authorities to enter places of worship is limited in all cases. Nevertheless, the circumstances in which government authorities can enter the place of worship vary across the countries considered. In Bulgaria, the threat of a sermon that is against morality or is used for political objectives may provide a reason for access, while in Italy the suspicion that a crime is occurring during a service seems to be the only valid reason for disturbing the privacy of a Roman Catholic church. In the Netherlands, government authorities cannot enter during a service; however, a sermon is considered to be a public speech and is thus subject to other regulations. The exercise of the freedom of religion would certainly be served by clear rules on these points.

Fourth, the abandonment of places of worship is predominantly ruled by regulations of the religious community itself. The Roman Catholic Church especially has detailed regulations, while for the others it depends on the administrative bodies concerned to find solutions that are beneficial for the religious community and for society at large. Rules regarding monuments may be burdensome in this respect.

Fifth, the public call to worship is a phenomenon that may cause annoyance in a multicultural society. However, the historical traditions of religious communities in calling the believers to worship that date from times when there was a homogeneous population have still their value also in a pluralistic society. When exercised in a moderate way it seems an appropriate way to draw attention to the spiritual aspect of life. In this regard, it does not seem legitimate to treat religious groups differently. It would be a sign of intolerance to abolish this right.

Sixth, processions associated with public worship are allowed in all three countries, provided permission is granted by an appropriate authority. This is regulated by law and the authority must evaluate the likelihood of the procession leading to social conflict. The exact formulation of criteria used to refuse permission differs in each country and the administrative practice in relation to permissions also differs. It is probably not possible to formulate stricter limitations.

Finally, rituals and worship concerning death and funerals are important elements of religion. The freedom of religion clearly includes these practices and in all of the three countries discussed here religious communities are permitted to have their own cemeteries or a designated section of a public cemetery. The ways in which specific religious wishes regarding the dead are taken into account differ between the three countries. It is remarkable that, in one country, bodies can now be buried without a coffin, while in other countries this is forbidden for health reasons.

References

Bakker, F.L. (2009), 'De heilige ruimte buiten de christelijke wereld: de ontmoeting met de/het heilige' (The Holy Space outside the Christian World: The Encounter with the Holy), in Boelens, O. and Meijers, T. (eds), 105–116.

Boelens, O. and Meijers, T. (eds) (2009), *Het kerkgebouw als religieus erfgoed* (The Church Building as Religious Inheritance) (Bergambacht: TVM).

Bos, J. (2007), 'Geeft Nederland juiste toepassing aan de beste beschermingsclausule bij het waarborgen van de vrijheid van godsdienst?' (Does the Netherlands Correctly Apply the Best Protection Clause in Guaranteeing the Freedom of Religion?), *Ars Aequi*, 727–736.

Broeksteeg, H. and Terlouw, A. (eds) (2011), *Overheid, recht en religie* (Deventer: Kluwer).

Dassetto, F. (2000), 'The New European Islam', in Ferrari, S. and Bradney, A. (eds), 31ff.

de Jong, C.D. (2000), *The Freedom of Thought, Conscience and Religion or Belief in the United Nations (1946–1992)* (Antwerp: Intersentia).

de Wit, Leonard (2009), 'Het religieus erfgoed in de Monumentenwet 1988', in Boelens, O. and Meijers, T. (eds), 145ff.

Emilianides, A. (ed.) (2011), *Religious Freedom in the European Union* (Leuven: Peeters).

Ferrari, S. (2002), 'Islam and the Western European Model of Church and State Relations', in Shadid, W.A.R. and Van Koningsveld, P.S. (eds).

Ferrari, S. and Bradney, A. (eds) (2000), *Islam and European Legal Systems* (Aldershot: Ashgate).
Frankort, M. and Schoenmaker, V. (2009), 'Herbestemming van het kerkgebouw' (Reallocation of Church Buildings), in Boelens, O. and Meijers, T. (eds), 169ff.
Hoeksma, J.A. (1982), *Tussen vrees en vervolging* (Between Fear and Prosecution) (Assen: Van Gorcum).
Krussteff, A. (2011) 'The Application of the Freedom of Religion Principles of the European Convention on Human Rights in Bulgaria', in Emilianides, A. (ed.), 73ff.
McCrea, R. (2010), *Religion and the Public Order of the European Union* (Oxford: Oxford University Press).
Meijers, T. (2009), 'Sacrum sacre tractandum', in Boelens, O. and Meijers, T. (eds), 59ff.
Nieuwenhuis, A.J. and Zoethout, C.M. (eds) (2009), *Rechtsstaat en religie* (State of Law and Religion) (Nijmegen: Ars Aequi).
Raad van kerken in Nederland (Council of Churches in the Netherlands) (1999), *Overwegingen rond kerkasiel* (Considerations on Church Asylum) (Amersfoort).
Schulz-Süchting, N. (2000), *Kirchenasyl* (Frankfurt am Main: Peter Lang).
Shadid, W.A.R. and Van Koningsveld, P.S. (eds) (1995), *Religious Freedom and the Position of Islam in Western Europe* (Kampen: Kok Pharos).
Sullivan, F.W. (2005), *The Impossibility of Religious Freedom* (Princeton: Princeton University Press).
Turner, H.W. (1979), *From Temple to Meeting House: The Phenomenology and Theology of Places of Worship* (Mouton: The Hague).
van Bijsterveld, S. (2000), 'The Legal Status of Islam in The Kingdom of The Netherlands', in Ferrari, S. and Bradney, A. (eds), 125ff.
van der Burg, W. (2009), 'Het ideaal van de neutrale staat' (The Ideal of the Neutral State), inaugural lecture (Erasmus University, Rotterdam).
van Drimmelen, L.C. and van der Ploeg, T.J. (eds) (2004), *Kerk en recht* (Church and Law) (Utrecht: Lemma).
van Kooten, T. and van der Ploeg, T.J. (2004), 'Fusie en splitsing van kerkgenootschappen, civielrechtelijke aspecten' (Merger and Splitting of Church Organizations), in van Drimmelen, L.C. and van der Ploeg, T.J. (eds), 145ff.
Ventura, M. (2011), 'The Application of the Freedom of Religion Principles of the European Convention on Human Rights in Italy', in Emilianides, A. (ed.), 223ff.
Vermeulen, B.P. (2011), 'Over kerk en minaretten' (On Churches and Minarets), in Broeksteeg, H. and Terlouw, A. (eds), 53ff.
Vermeulen, B.P. and Aarass, B. (2009), 'De reikwijdte van de vrijheid van godsdienst in een pluriforme samenleving' (The Scope of the Freedom of Religion in a Pluralist Society), in Nieuwenhuis, A.J. and Zoethout, C.M. (eds), 72–78.

Vermeulen, B.P. and Kanne, M.J. (2004), 'Kerk en staat en mensenrechten' (Church and State and Human Rights), in van Drimmelen, L.C. and van der Ploeg, T.J. (eds), 69–92.

Index

Figures and Tables indexed in **bold**.

www.ingramcontent.com/pod-product-compliance
Ingram Content Group UK Ltd.
Pitfield, Milton Keynes, MK11 3LW, UK
UKHW022007180926
475701UK00003B/240
9781138279377